CHINA

DOING BUSINESS AND INVESTING IN CHINA GUIDE

VOLUME 1

STRATEGIC, PRACTICAL INFORMATION, REGULATIONS, CONTACTS

International Business Publications, USA
Washington DC, USA - China

CHINA

DOING BUSINESS AND INVESTING IN CHINA GUIDE

VOLUME 1 STRATEGIC, PRACTICAL INFORMATION, REGULATIONS, CONTACTS

UPDATED ANNUALLY

Cover Design: International Business Publications, USA

We express our sincere appreciation to all government agencies and international organizations which provided information and other materials for this guide

2019 Edition Updated Reprint International Business Publications, USA
ISBN 1-4330-1052-6

This guide provides basic information for starting or/and conducting business in the country. The extraordinary volume of materials covering the topic, prevents us from placing all these materials in this guide. For more detailed information on issues related to any specific investment and business activity in the country, please contact Global Investment Center, USA
Please acquire the list of our business intelligence and marketing reports and other business publications. We constantly update and expand our business intelligence and marketing materials. Please contact the center for the updated list of reports on over 250 countries.

For additional analytical, business and investment opportunities information, please contact Global Investment & Business Center, USA at (703) 370-8082. Fax: (703) 370-8083. E-mail: ibpusa3@gmail.com
Global Business and Investment Info Databank - www.ibpus.com

Printed in the USA

CHINA

DOING BUSINESS AND INVESTING IN CHINA GUIDE

VOLUME 1
STRATEGIC, PRACTICAL INFORMATION, REGULATIONS, CONTACTS

TABLE OF CONTENTS

STRATEGIC AND DEVELOPMENT PROFILES

STRATEGIC PROFILE

Capital	Beijing 39°55′N 116°23′E39.917°N 116.383°E
Largest city	Shanghai
Official languages	Standard Chinese
Recognised regional languages	Mongolian Tibetan Uyghur Zhuang various others
Official written language	Vernacular Chinese
Official script	Simplified Chinese
Ethnic groups	91.51% Han 55 minorities
Demonym	Chinese
Government	Single-party socialist state
- President	Xi Jinping
- Premier	Li Keqiang
- Congress Chairman	Zhang Dejiang
- Conference Chairman	Yu Zhengsheng
Legislature	National People's Congress
Formation	
- Unification of China under the Qin Dynasty	221 BCE
- Republic established	1 January 1912
- People's Republic proclaimed	1 October 1949
Area	
- Total	9,596,961 km^2 (3rd/4th) 3,705,407 sq mi
- Water (%)	0.28%
Population	
- 2013 estimate	1,357,380,000 (1st)
- 2010 census	1,339,724,852 (1st)
- Density	2013 estimate: 145/km^2 (83rd) 373/sq mi
GDP (PPP)	2013 estimate
- Total	$16.149 trillion (2nd)
- Per capita	$11,868 (85th)
GDP (nominal)	2013 estimate
- Total	$9.469 trillion (2nd)
- Per capita	$6,959 (80th)
Gini (2014)	55.0 high
HDI (2013)	0.719

	high · 91st
Currency	Renminbi (yuan)(¥) (CNY)
Time zone	China Standard Time (UTC+8)
Date format	yyyy-mm-dd or yyyy年m月d日 (CE; CE-1949)
Drives on the	right
Calling code	+86
ISO 3166 code	CN
Internet TLD	.cn .中國 .中国

China officially the **People's Republic of China** (**PRC**), is a sovereign state located in East Asia. It is the world's most populous country, with a population of over 1.35 billion. The PRC is a single-party state governed by the Communist Party, with its seat of government in the capital city of Beijing. It exercises jurisdiction over 22 provinces, five autonomous regions, four direct-controlled municipalities (Beijing, Tianjin, Shanghai, and Chongqing), and two mostly self-governing special administrative regions (Hong Kong and Macau). The PRC also claims the territories governed by the Republic of China (ROC), a separate political entity commonly known as Taiwan today, as a part of its territory, which includes the island of Taiwan as Taiwan Province, Kinmen and Matsu as a part of Fujian Province and islands the ROC controls in the South China Sea as a part of Hainan Province, a claim which is controversial due to the complex political status of Taiwan.

Covering approximately 9.6 million square kilometers, China is the world's second-largest country by land area, and either the third or fourth-largest by total area, depending on the method of measurement.

China's landscape is vast and diverse, ranging from forest steppes and the Gobi and Taklamakan deserts in the arid north to subtropical forests in the wetter south. The Himalaya, Karakoram, Pamir and Tian Shan mountain ranges separate China from South and Central Asia. The Yangtze and Yellow Rivers, the third- and sixth-longest in the world, run from the Tibetan Plateau to the densely populated eastern seaboard. China's coastline along the Pacific Ocean is 14,500 kilometres (9,000 mi) long, and is bounded by the Bohai, Yellow, East and South China Seas.

The history of China goes back to the ancient civilization – one of the world's earliest – that flourished in the fertile basin of the Yellow River in the North China Plain. For millennia, China's political system was based on hereditary monarchies, known as dynasties, beginning with the semi-mythological Xia of the Yellow River basin (c. 2000 BCE).

Since 221 BCE, when the Qin Dynasty first conquered several states to form a Chinese empire, the country has expanded, fractured and been reformed numerous times. The Republic of China (ROC) overthrew the last dynasty in 1911, and ruled the Chinese mainland until 1949. After the defeat of the Empire of Japan in World War II, the Communist Party defeated the nationalist Kuomintang in mainland China and established the People's Republic of China in Beijing on 1 October 1949, while the Kuomintang relocated the ROC government to its present capital of Taipei.

Base 802714AI (R00152) 3-01

China had the largest and most complex economy in the world for most of the past two thousand years, during which it has seen cycles of prosperity and decline. Since the introduction of economic reforms in 1978, China has become one of the world's fastest-growing major economies. As of 2013, it is the world's second-largest economy by both nominal total GDP and purchasing power parity (PPP), and is also the world's largest exporter and importer of goods.

China is a recognized nuclear weapons state and has the world's largest standing army, with the second-largest defence budget. The PRC has been a United Nations member since 1971, when it replaced the ROC as a permanent member of the U.N. Security Council. China is also a member of numerous formal and informal multilateral organizations, including the WTO, APEC, BRICS, the Shanghai Cooperation Organization, the BCIM and the G-20. China is a regional power within Asia and has been characterized as a potential superpower by a number of commentators

GEOGRAPHY

Location: Eastern Asia, bordering the East China Sea, Korea Bay, Yellow Sea, and South China Sea, between North Korea and Vietnam

Geographic coordinates: 35 00 N, 105 00 E

Map references: Asia

Area:
total: 9,596,960 sq km *land:* 9,326,410 sq km *water:* 270,550 sq km

Area—comparative: slightly smaller than the US

Land boundaries:
total: 22,143.34 km

border countries: Afghanistan 76 km, Bhutan 470 km, Burma 2,185 km, Hong Kong 30 km, India 3,380 km, Kazakhstan 1,533 km, North Korea 1,416 km, Kyrgyzstan 858 km, Laos 423 km, Macau 0.34 km, Mongolia 4,673 km, Nepal 1,236 km, Pakistan 523 km, Russia (northeast) 3,605 km, Russia (northwest) 40 km, Tajikistan 414 km, Vietnam 1,281 km

Coastline: 14,500 km

Maritime claims:
contiguous zone: 24 nm
continental shelf: claim to shallow areas of East China Sea and Yellow Sea
territorial sea: 12 nm

Climate: extremely diverse; tropical in south to subarctic in north

Terrain: mostly mountains, high plateaus, deserts in west; plains, deltas, and hills in east

Elevation extremes:
lowest point: Turpan Pendi -154 m
highest point: Mount Everest 8,848 m

Natural resources: coal, iron ore, petroleum, mercury, tin, tungsten, antimony, manganese, molybdenum, vanadium, magnetite, aluminum, lead, zinc, uranium, hydropower potential (world's largest)

Land use: *arable land:* 10%
permanent crops: 0% *permanent pastures:* 43%
forests and woodland: 14% *other:* 33%

Base 802714AI (R00152) 3-01

Irrigated land: 498,720 sq km

Natural hazards: frequent typhoons (about five per year along southern and eastern coasts); damaging floods; tsunamis; earthquakes; droughts

Environment—current issues: air pollution (greenhouse gases, particulates) from the overwhelming use of high-sulfur coal as a fuel, produces acid rain which is damaging forests; water shortages experienced throughout the country, particularly in urban areas and in the north; future growth in water usage threatens to outpace supplies; water pollution from industrial effluents; much of the population does not have access to potable water; less than 10% of sewage receives treatment; deforestation; estimated loss of one-fifth of agricultural land since 1949 to soil erosion and economic development; desertification; trade in endangered species

Environment—international agreements:
party to: Antarctic-Environmental Protocol, Antarctic Treaty, Biodiversity, Climate Change, Desertification, Endangered Species, Hazardous Wastes, Law of the Sea, Marine Dumping,

Nuclear Test Ban, Ozone Layer Protection, Ship Pollution, Tropical Timber 83, Tropical Timber 94, Wetlands
signed, but not ratified: none of the selected agreements

Geography—note: world's fourth-largest country (after Russia, Canada, and US)

PEOPLE

Population: 1,236,914,658

Age structure:
0-14 years: 26% (male 169,347,516; female 149,897,253)
15-64 years: 68% (male 431,164,591; female 404,513,208)
65 years and over: 6% (male 38,398,920; female 43,593,170) (July 1998 est.)

Population growth rate: 0.83%

Birth rate: 15.73 births/1,000 population

Death rate: 6.99 deaths/1,000 population

Net migration rate: -0.41 migrant(s)/1,000 population

Sex ratio:
at birth: 1.15 male(s)/female
under 15 years: 1.13 male(s)/female
15-64 years: 1.07 male(s)/female
65 years and over: 0.88 male(s)/female

Infant mortality rate: 45.46 deaths/1,000 live births

Life expectancy at birth:
total population: 69.59 years
male: 68.32 years
female: 71.06 years

Total fertility rate: 1.8 children born/woman

Nationality:
noun: Chinese (singular and plural)
adjective: Chinese

Ethnic groups: Han Chinese 91.9%, Zhuang, Uygur, Hui, Yi, Tibetan, Miao, Manchu, Mongol, Buyi, Korean, and other nationalities 8.1%

Religions: Daoism (Taoism), Buddhism, Muslim 2%-3%, Christian 1% (est.)
note: officially atheist, but traditionally pragmatic and eclectic

Languages: Standard Chinese or Mandarin (Putonghua, based on the Beijing dialect), Yue (Cantonese), Wu (Shanghaiese), Minbei (Fuzhou), Minnan (Hokkien-Taiwanese), Xiang, Gan, Hakka dialects, minority languages (see Ethnic divisions entry)

Literacy:
definition: age 15 and over can read and write
total population: 81.5%
male: 89.9%
female: 72.7%

GOVERNMENT

Country name:
conventional long form: People's Republic of China

conventional short form: China

local long form: Zhonghua Renmin Gongheguo

local short form: Zhongguo

abbreviation: PRC

Government type:
Communist state

Capital:
name: Beijing

geographic coordinates: 39 55 N, 116 23 E

time difference: UTC+8 (13 hours ahead of Washington, DC, during Standard Time)

note: despite its size, all of China falls within one time zone; many people in Xinjiang Province observe an unofficial "Xinjiang time zone" of UTC+6, two hours behind Beijing

Administrative divisions:
23 provinces (sheng, singular and plural), 5 autonomous regions (zizhiqu, singular and plural), and 4 municipalities (shi, singular and plural)

provinces: Anhui, Fujian, Gansu, Guangdong, Guizhou, Hainan, Hebei, Heilongjiang, Henan, Hubei, Hunan, Jiangsu, Jiangxi, Jilin, Liaoning, Qinghai, Shaanxi, Shandong, Shanxi, Sichuan, Yunnan, Zhejiang; (see note on Taiwan)

autonomous regions: Guangxi, Nei Mongol (Inner Mongolia), Ningxia, Xinjiang Uygur, Xizang (Tibet)

municipalities: Beijing, Chongqing, Shanghai, Tianjin

note: China considers Taiwan its 23rd province; see separate entries for the special administrative regions of Hong Kong and Macau

Independence:
1 October 1949 (People's Republic of China established); notable earlier dates: 221 B.C.

(unification under the Qin Dynasty); 1 January 1912 (Qing Dynasty replaced by the Republic of China)

National holiday:

anniversary of the founding of the People's Republic of China, 1 October (1949)

Constitution:
several previous; latest promulgated 4 December 1982; amended several times, last in 2005 (2005)

Legal system:
civil law influenced by Soviet and continental European civil law systems; legislature retains power to interpret statutes; note - criminal procedure law revised in early 2012

International law organization participation:
has not submitted an ICJ jurisdiction declaration; non-party state to the ICCt

Suffrage:
18 years of age; universal

Executive branch:

head of government: Premier LI Keqiang (since 16 March 2013); Executive Vice Premiers HAN Zheng (since 19 March 2018), SUN Chunlan (since 19 March 2018), LIU He (since 19 March 2018), HU Chunhua (since 19 March 2018)
cabinet: State Council appointed by National People's Congress
elections/appointments: president and vice president indirectly elected by National People's Congress for a 5-year term (unlimited terms); election last held on 17 March 2018 (next to be held in March 2023); premier nominated by president, confirmed by National People's Congress

election results: XI Jinping reelected president; National People's Congress vote - 2,970 (unanimously); WANG Qishan elected vice president with 2,969 votes
President XI Jinping (since 14 March 2013); Vice President WANG Qishan (since 17 March 2018)

Legislative branch:
description: unicameral National People's Congress or Quanguo Renmin Daibiao Dahui (maximum of 3,000 seats; members indirectly elected by municipal, regional, and provincial people's congresses, and the People's Liberation Army; members serve 5-year terms); note - in practice, only members of the Chinese Communist Party (CCP), its 8 allied independent parties, and CCP-approved independent candidates are elected
elections: last held in December 2017-February 2018 (next to be held in late 2022 to early 2023)
election results: percent of vote - NA; seats by party - NA; composition - men 2,238, women 742, percent of women 24.9%

Judicial branch:
highest courts: Supreme People's Court (consists of over 340 judges including the chief justice, 13 grand justices organized into a civil committee and tribunals for civil, economic, administrative, complaint and appeal, and communication and transportation cases)

judge selection and term of office: chief justice appointed by the People's National Congress (NPC); limited to 2 consecutive 5-year-terms; other justices and judges nominated by the chief justice and appointed by the Standing Committee of the NPC; term of other justices and judges determined by the NPC
subordinate courts: Higher People's Courts; Intermediate People's Courts; District and County People's Courts; Autonomous Region People's Courts; International Commercial Courts; Special People's Courts for military, maritime, transportation, and forestry issues

Political parties and leaders:
Chinese Communist Party or CCP [XI Jinping]
note: China has 8 nominally independent small parties controlled by the CCP

International organization participation:
ADB, AfDB (nonregional member), APEC, Arctic Council (observer), ARF, ASEAN (dialogue partner), BIS, BRICS, CDB, CICA, EAS, FAO, FATF, G-20, G-24 (observer), G-5, G-77, IADB, IAEA, IBRD, ICAO, ICC (national committees), ICRM, IDA, IFAD, IFC, IFRCS, IHO, ILO, IMF, IMO, IMSO, Interpol, IOC, IOM (observer), IPU, ISO, ITSO, ITU, LAIA (observer), MIGA, MINURSO, MINUSMA, MONUSCO, NAM (observer), NSG, OAS (observer), OPCW, Pacific Alliance (observer), PCA, PIF (partner), SAARC (observer), SCO, SICA (observer), UN, UNAMID, UNCTAD, UNESCO, UNFICYP, UNHCR, UNIDO, UNIFIL, UNMIL, UNMISS, UNOCI, UN Security Council (permanent), UNTSO, UNWTO, UPU, WCO, WHO, WIPO, WMO, WTO, ZC

Diplomatic representation in the US:
chief of mission: Ambassador CUI Tiankai (since 3 April 2013)
chancery: 3505 International Place NW, Washington, DC 20008
telephone: [1] (202) 495-2266
FAX: [1] (202) 495-2138
consulate(s) general: Chicago, Houston, Los Angeles, New York, San Francisco

Diplomatic representation from the US:
chief of mission: Ambassador Terry BRANSTAD (since 12 July 2017)
embassy: 55 An Jia Lou Lu, 100600 Beijing
mailing address: PSC 461, Box 50, FPO AP 96521-0002
telephone: [86] (10) 8531-3000
FAX: [86] (10) 8531-3300
consulate(s) general: Chengdu, Guangzhou, Shanghai, Shenyang, Wuhan

Flag description:
red with a large yellow five-pointed star and four smaller yellow five-pointed stars (arranged in a vertical arc toward the middle of the flag) in the upper hoist-side corner; the color red represents revolution, while the stars symbolize the four social classes - the working class, the peasantry, the urban petty bourgeoisie, and the national bourgeoisie (capitalists) - united under the Communist Party of China

National symbol(s):
dragon

National anthem:
name: "Yiyongjun Jinxingqu" (The March of the Volunteers)

ECONOMY

Since the late 1970s, China has moved from a closed, centrally planned system to a more market-oriented one that plays a major global role. China has implemented reforms in a gradualist fashion, resulting in efficiency gains that have contributed to a more than tenfold increase in GDP since 1978. Reforms began with the phaseout of collectivized agriculture, and expanded to include the gradual liberalization of prices, fiscal decentralization, increased autonomy for state enterprises, growth of the private sector, development of stock markets and a modern banking system, and opening to foreign trade and investment. China continues to pursue an industrial policy, state support of key sectors, and a restrictive investment regime. Measured on a purchasing power parity (PPP) basis that adjusts for price differences, China in 2016 stood as the largest economy in the world, surpassing the US in 2014 for the first time in modern history. China became the world's largest exporter in 2010, and the largest trading nation in 2013. Still, China's per capita income is below the world average.

After keeping its currency tightly linked to the US dollar for years, China in July 2005 moved to an exchange rate system that references a basket of currencies. From mid-2005 to late 2008, the renminbi appreciated more than 20% against the US dollar, but the exchange rate remained virtually pegged to the dollar from the onset of the global financial crisis until June 2010, when Beijing announced it would allow a resumption of gradual liberalization. From 2013 until early 2015, the renminbi (RMB) appreciated roughly 2% against the dollar, but the exchange rate fell 13% from mid-2015 until end-2016 amid strong capital outflows in part stemming from the August 2015 official devaluation; in 2017 the RMB resumed appreciating against the dollar – roughly 7% from end-of-2016 to end-of-2017. From 2013 to 2017, China had one of the fastest growing economies in the world, averaging slightly more than 7% real growth per year. In 2015, the People's Bank of China announced it would continue to carefully push for full convertibility of the renminbi, after the currency was accepted as part of the IMF's special drawing rights basket. However, since late 2015 the Chinese Government has strengthened capital controls and oversight of overseas investments to better manage the exchange rate and maintain financial stability.

The Chinese Government faces numerous economic challenges including: (a) reducing its high domestic savings rate and correspondingly low domestic household consumption; (b) managing its high corporate debt burden to maintain financial stability; (c) controlling off-balance sheet local government debt used to finance infrastructure stimulus; (d) facilitating higher-wage job opportunities for the aspiring middle class, including rural migrants and college graduates, while maintaining competitiveness; (e) dampening speculative investment in the real estate sector without sharply slowing the economy; (f) reducing industrial overcapacity; and (g) raising productivity growth rates through the more efficient allocation of capital and state-support for innovation. Economic development has progressed further in coastal provinces than in the interior, and by 2016 more than 169.3 million migrant workers and their dependents had relocated to urban areas to find work. One consequence of China's population control policy known as the "one-child policy" - which was relaxed in 2016 to permit all families to have two children - is that China is now one of the most rapidly aging countries in the world. Deterioration in the environment - notably air pollution, soil erosion, and the steady fall of the water table, especially in the North - is another long-term problem. China continues to lose arable land because of erosion and urbanization. The Chinese Government is seeking to add energy production capacity from sources other than coal and oil, focusing on natural gas, nuclear, and clean energy development. In 2016, China ratified the Paris Agreement, a multilateral agreement to combat climate change, and committed to peak its carbon dioxide emissions between 2025 and 2030.

The government's 13th Five-Year Plan, unveiled in March 2016, emphasizes the need to increase innovation and boost domestic consumption to make the economy less dependent on government investment, exports, and heavy industry. However, China has made more progress on subsidizing innovation than rebalancing the economy. Beijing has committed to giving the market a more decisive role in allocating resources, but the Chinese Government's policies continue to favor state-owned enterprises and emphasize stability. Chinese leaders in 2010 pledged to double China's GDP by 2020, and the 13th Five Year Plan includes annual economic growth targets of at least 6.5% through 2020 to achieve that goal. In recent years, China has renewed its support for state-owned enterprises in sectors considered important to "economic security," explicitly looking to foster globally competitive industries. Chinese leaders also have undermined some market-oriented reforms by reaffirming the "dominant" role of the state in the economy, a stance that threatens to discourage private initiative and make the economy less efficient over time. The slight acceleration in economic growth in 2017—the first such uptick since 2010—gives Beijing more latitude to pursue its economic reforms, focusing on financial sector deleveraging and its Supply-Side Structural Reform agenda, first announced in late 2015.

GDP (purchasing power parity):
$23.12 trillion (2017 est.)
$21.66 trillion (2016 est.)
$20.3 trillion (2015 est.)
note: data are in 2017 dollars
country comparison to the world: 1

GDP (official exchange rate):
$11.94 trillion (2017 est.)
note: because China's exchange rate is determined by fiat rather than by market forces, the official exchange rate measure of GDP is not an accurate measure of China's output; GDP at the official exchange rate substantially understates the actual level of China's output vis-a-vis the rest of the world; in China's situation, GDP at purchasing power parity provides the best measure for comparing output across countries

GDP - real growth rate:
6.8% (2017 est.)
6.7% (2016 est.)
6.9% (2015 est.)
country comparison to the world: 13

GDP - per capita (PPP):
$16,600 (2017 est.)
$15,700 (2016 est.)
$14,800 (2015 est.)
note: data are in 2017 dollars
country comparison to the world: 106

Gross national saving:
45.4% of GDP (2017 est.)
45.9% of GDP (2016 est.)
47.5% of GDP (2015 est.)
country comparison to the world: 4

GDP - composition, by end use:
household consumption: 39.1%
government consumption: 14.6%

investment in fixed capital: 43.3%
investment in inventories: 1.1%
exports of goods and services: 19.6%
imports of goods and services: -17.7% (2017 est.)

GDP - composition, by sector of origin:
agriculture: 8.2%
industry: 39.5%
services: 52.2%
(2017 est.)

Agriculture - products:
world leader in gross value of agricultural output; rice, wheat, potatoes, corn, tobacco, peanuts, tea, apples, cotton, pork, mutton, eggs; fish, shrimp

Industries:
world leader in gross value of industrial output; mining and ore processing, iron, steel, aluminum, and other metals, coal; machine building; armaments; textiles and apparel; petroleum; cement; chemicals; fertilizer; consumer products (including footwear, toys, and electronics); food processing; transportation equipment, including automobiles, railcars and locomotives, ships, aircraft; telecommunications equipment, commercial space launch vehicles, satellites

Industrial production growth rate:
6.2% (2017 est.)
country comparison to the world: 32

Labor force:
806.7 million
note: by the end of 2012, China's population at working age (15-64 years) was 1.004 billion (2017 est.)
country comparison to the world: 1

Labor force - by occupation:
agriculture: 28.3%
industry: 29.3%
services: 42.4% (2016 est.)

Unemployment rate:
4% (2017 est.)
4% (2016 est.)
note: data are for registered urban unemployment, which excludes private enterprises and migrants
country comparison to the world: 48

Population below poverty line:
3.3%
note: in 2011, China set a new poverty line at RMB 2300 (approximately US $400)

Household income or consumption by percentage share:
lowest 10%: 2.1%
highest 10%: 31.4%
note: data are for urban households only (2012 est.)

Distribution of family income - Gini index:

46.5 (2016 est.)
46.2 (2015 est.)
country comparison to the world: 31

Budget:
revenues: $2.672 trillion
expenditures: $3.146 trillion (2017 est.)

Taxes and other revenues:
22.4% of GDP (2017 est.)
country comparison to the world: 134

Budget surplus (+) or deficit (-):
-4% of GDP (2017 est.)
country comparison to the world: 143

Public debt:
18.6% of GDP (2017 est.)
16.1% of GDP (2016 est.)
note: official data; data cover both central government debt and local government debt, including debt officially recognized by China's National Audit Office report in 2011; data exclude policy bank bonds, Ministry of Railway debt, and China Asset Management Company debt
country comparison to the world: 190

Fiscal year:
calendar year

Inflation rate (consumer prices):
1.8% (2017 est.)
2% (2016 est.)
country comparison to the world: 82

Central bank discount rate:
2.25% (5 December 2017 est.)
2.25% (31 December 2016 est.)
country comparison to the world: 115

Commercial bank prime lending rate:
4.4% (5 December 2017 est.)
4.35% (30 December 2016 est.)
country comparison to the world: 154

Stock of narrow money:
$8.16 trillion (31 October 2017 est.)
$7.001 trillion (31 December 2016 est.)
country comparison to the world: 1

Stock of broad money:
$25.24 trillion (October 2017 est.)
$22.3 trillion (December 2016 est.)
country comparison to the world: 1

Stock of domestic credit:
$26.87 trillion (31 December 2017 est.)

$23.02 trillion (31 December 2016 est.)
country comparison to the world: 1

Market value of publicly traded shares:
$7.321 trillion (31 November 2017 est.)
$8.188 trillion (December 2016 est.)
$6.005 trillion (December 2015 est.)
country comparison to the world: 2

Current account balance:
$162.5 billion (2017 est.)
$196.4 billion (2016 est.)
country comparison to the world: 4

Exports:
$2.157 trillion (2017 est.)
$1.99 trillion (2016 est.)
country comparison to the world: 1

Exports - commodities:
electrical and other machinery, including computers and telecommunications equipment, apparel, furniture, textiles

Exports - partners:
US 18.2%, Hong Kong 13.8%, Japan 6.1%, South Korea 4.5% (2016)
Imports:
$1.731 trillion (2017 est.)
$1.495 trillion (2016 est.)
country comparison to the world: 2

Imports - commodities:
electrical and other machinery, including integrated circuits and other computer components, oil and mineral fuels; optical and medical equipment, metal ores, motor vehicles; soybeans

Imports - partners:
South Korea 10%, Japan 9.2%, US 8.5%, Germany 5.4%, Australia 4.4%

Reserves of foreign exchange and gold:
$3.194 trillion (31 December 2017 est.)
$3.098 trillion (31 December 2016 est.)
country comparison to the world: 1

Debt - external:
$1.649 trillion (31 December 2017 est.)
$1.467 trillion (31 December 2016 est.)
country comparison to the world: 14

Stock of direct foreign investment - at home:
$1.514 trillion (31 December 2017 est.)
$1.391 trillion (31 December 2016 est.)
country comparison to the world: 6

Stock of direct foreign investment - abroad:
$1.342 trillion (31 December 2017 est.)

$1.227 trillion (31 December 2016 est.)
country comparison to the world: 12

Exchange rates:
Renminbi yuan (RMB) per US dollar -
6.7588 (2017 est.)
6.6445 (2016 est.)
6.2275 (2015 est.)
6.1434 (2014 est.)
6.1958 (2013 est.)

ENERGY

Electricity - production:
5.398 trillion kWh (2013)
country comparison to the world: 1

Electricity - consumption:
5.322 trillion kWh (2013)
country comparison to the world: 1

Electricity - exports:
18.67 billion kWh (2013)
country comparison to the world: 12

Electricity - imports:
7.438 billion kWh (2013)
country comparison to the world: 31

Electricity - installed generating capacity:
1.247 billion kW (2013 est.)
country comparison to the world: 1

Electricity - from fossil fuels:
69.1% of total installed capacity (2013 est.)
country comparison to the world: 109

Electricity - from nuclear fuels:
1.2% of total installed capacity (2013 est.)
country comparison to the world: 30

Electricity - from hydroelectric plants:
22.5% of total installed capacity (2013 est.)
country comparison to the world: 85

Electricity - from other renewable sources:
7.2% of total installed capacity (2013 est.)
country comparison to the world: 34

Crude oil - production:
4.197 million bbl/day (2013 est.)
country comparison to the world: 4

Crude oil - exports:
33,000 bbl/day (2013 est.)
country comparison to the world: 49

Crude oil - imports:
5.664 million bbl/day (2013 est.)
country comparison to the world: 2

Crude oil - proved reserves:
17.3 billion bbl (1 January 2013 est.)
country comparison to the world: 14

Refined petroleum products - production:
9.371 million bbl/day (2012 est.)
country comparison to the world: 3

Refined petroleum products - consumption:
9.79 million bbl/day (2011 est.)
country comparison to the world: 3

Refined petroleum products - exports:
664,000 bbl/day (2013 est.)
country comparison to the world: 9

Refined petroleum products - imports:
922,000 bbl/day (2013 est.)
country comparison to the world: 6

Natural gas - production:
117.1 billion cu m (2013 est.)
country comparison to the world: 7

Natural gas - consumption:
150 billion cu m (2013 est.)
country comparison to the world: 4

Natural gas - exports:
2.4 billion cu m (2013 est.)
country comparison to the world: 42

Natural gas - imports:
53 billion cu m (2013 est.)
country comparison to the world: 6

Natural gas - proved reserves:
3.1 trillion cu m (1 January 2013 est.)
country comparison to the world: 12

Carbon dioxide emissions from consumption of energy:
10 billion Mt (2013 est.)

COMMUNICATIONS

Telephones - fixed lines:
total subscriptions: 206.624 million
subscriptions per 100 inhabitants: 15
country comparison to the world: 2

Telephones - mobile cellular:
total: 1,364.934 million
subscriptions per 100 inhabitants: 99 (July 2016 est.)
country comparison to the world: 1

Telephone system:

general assessment: domestic and international services are available for private use; unevenly distributed domestic system serves principal cities, industrial centers, and many towns; China continues to develop its telecommunications infrastructure; China in the summer of 2008 began a major restructuring of its telecommunications industry, resulting in the consolidation of its six telecom service operators to three, China Telecom, China Mobile, and China Unicom, each providing both fixed-line and mobile services (2016)

domestic: interprovincial fiber-optic trunk lines and cellular telephone systems have been installed; mobile-cellular subscribership is increasing rapidly; the number of Internet users now over 50% of the population; a domestic satellite system with several earth stations is in place

international: country code - 86; a number of submarine cables provide connectivity to Asia, the Middle East, Europe, and the US; satellite earth stations - 7 (5 Intelsat - 4 Pacific Ocean and 1 Indian Ocean; 1 Intersputnik - Indian Ocean region; and 1 Inmarsat - Pacific and Indian Ocean regions)

Broadcast media:

all broadcast media are owned by, or affiliated with, the Communist Party of China or a government agency; no privately owned TV or radio stations; state-run Chinese Central TV, provincial, and municipal stations offer more than 2,000 channels; the Central Propaganda Department lists subjects that are off limits to domestic broadcast media with the government maintaining authority to approve all programming; foreign-made TV programs must be approved prior to broadcast; increasingly, Chinese turn to online television to access Chinese and international films and television shows (2017)

Internet country code:
.cn

Internet users:
total: 730,723,960
percent of population: 53.2%
country comparison to the world: 1

TRANSPORTATION

Airports:
507
country comparison to the world: 14

Airports - with paved runways:
total: 463
over 3,047 m: 71
2,438 to 3,047 m: 158
1,524 to 2,437 m: 123
914 to 1,523 m: 25
under 914 m: 86

Airports - with unpaved runways:
total: 44
over 3,047 m: 4
2,438 to 3,047 m: 7
1,524 to 2,437 m: 6
914 to 1,523 m: 9
under 914 m:
18

Heliports:
47

Pipelines:
condensate 9 km; gas 48,502 km; oil 23,072 km; oil/gas/water 31 km; refined products 15,298 km; water 9 km

Railways:
total: 86,000 km
country comparison to the world: 3
standard gauge: 86,000 km 1.435-m gauge (36,000 km electrified)

Roadways:
total: 4,106,387 km
country comparison to the world: 3
paved: 3,453,890 km (includes 84,946 km of expressways)
unpaved: 652,497 km

Waterways:
110,000 km (navigable waterways)
country comparison to the world: 1

Merchant marine:
total: 2,030
country comparison to the world: 3
by type: barge carrier 7, bulk carrier 621, cargo 566, carrier 10, chemical tanker 140, container 206, liquefied gas 60, passenger 9, passenger/cargo 81, petroleum tanker 264, refrigerated cargo 33, roll on/roll off 8, specialized tanker 2, vehicle carrier 23
foreign-owned: 22 (Hong Kong 18, Indonesia 2, Japan 2)
registered in other countries: 1,559 (Bangladesh 1, Belize 61, Cambodia 177, Comoros 1, Cyprus 6, Georgia 10, Honduras 2, Hong Kong 500, India 1, Indonesia 1, Kiribati 26, Liberia 4, Malta 6, Marshall Islands 14, North Korea 3, Panama 534, Philippines 4, Saint Kitts and Nevis 1, Saint Vincent and the Grenadines 65, Sao Tome and Principe 1, Sierra Leone 19, Singapore 29, South Korea 6, Thailand 1, Togo 1, Tuvalu 4, UK 7, Vanuatu 1, unknown 73)

Ports and terminals:
major seaport(s): Dalian, Ningbo, Qingdao, Qinhuangdao, Shanghai, Shenzhen, Tianjin
river port(s): Guangzhou (Pearl)
container port(s) (TEUs): Dalian (6,400,300), Guangzhou (14,260,400), Ningbo (14,719,200), Qingdao (13,020,100), Shanghai (31,739,000), Shenzhen (22,570,800), Tianjin (11,587,600)

MILITARY

Military branches:
People's Liberation Army (PLA): Ground Forces, Navy (PLAN; includes marines and naval aviation), Air Force (Zhongguo Renmin Jiefangjun Kongjun, PLAAF; includes Airborne Forces), and Second Artillery Corps (strategic missile force); People's Armed Police (Renmin Wuzhuang Jingcha Budui, PAP); PLA Reserve Force

Military service age and obligation:
18-24 years of age for selective compulsory military service, with a 2-year service obligation; no minimum age for voluntary service (all officers are volunteers); 18-19 years of age for women high school graduates who meet requirements for specific military jobs; a recent military decision allows women in combat roles; the first class of women warship commanders was in 2011

Manpower available for military service:
males age 16-49: 385,821,101
females age 16-49: 363,789,674

Manpower fit for military service:
males age 16-49: 318,265,016
females age 16-49: 300,323,611

Manpower reaching militarily significant age annually:
male: 10,406,544
female: 9,131,990

Military expenditures:
1.99% of GDP
country comparison to the world: 40
2% of GDP (2011)
1.99% of GDP

TRANSNATIONAL ISSUES

Disputes - international:
continuing talks and confidence-building measures work toward reducing tensions over Kashmir that nonetheless remains militarized with portions under the de facto administration of China (Aksai Chin), India (Jammu and Kashmir), and Pakistan (Azad Kashmir and Northern Areas);

India does not recognize Pakistan's ceding historic Kashmir lands to China in 1964; China and India continue their security and foreign policy dialogue started in 2005 related to the dispute over most of their rugged, militarized boundary, regional nuclear proliferation, and other matters; China claims most of India's Arunachal Pradesh to the base of the Himalayas; lacking any treaty describing the boundary, Bhutan and China continue negotiations to establish a common boundary alignment to resolve territorial disputes arising from substantial cartographic discrepancies, the largest of which lie in Bhutan's northwest and along the Chumbi salient; Burmese forces attempting to dig in to the largely autonomous Shan State to rout local militias tied to the drug trade, prompts local residents to periodically flee into neighboring Yunnan Province in China; Chinese maps show an international boundary symbol off the coasts of the littoral states of the South China Seas, where China has interrupted Vietnamese hydrocarbon exploration;

China asserts sovereignty over Scarborough Reef along with the Philippines and Taiwan, and over the Spratly Islands together with Malaysia, the Philippines, Taiwan, Vietnam, and Brunei; the 2002 Declaration on the Conduct of Parties in the South China Sea eased tensions in the Spratlys but is not the legally binding code of conduct sought by some parties; Vietnam and China continue to expand construction of facilities in the Spratlys and in March 2005, the national oil companies of China, the Philippines, and Vietnam signed a joint accord on marine seismic activities in the Spratly Islands; China occupies some of the Paracel Islands also claimed by Vietnam and Taiwan;

China and Taiwan continue to reject both Japan's claims to the uninhabited islands of Senkaku-shoto (Diaoyu Tai) and Japan's unilaterally declared equidistance line in the East China Sea, the site of intensive hydrocarbon exploration and exploitation; certain islands in the Yalu and Tumen rivers are in dispute with North Korea; North Korea and China seek to stem illegal migration to China by North Koreans, fleeing privations and oppression, by building a fence along portions of the border and imprisoning North Koreans deported by China; China and Russia have demarcated the once disputed islands at the Amur and Ussuri confluence and in the Argun River in accordance with their 2004 Agreement;

China and Tajikistan have begun demarcating the revised boundary agreed to in the delimitation of 2002; the decade-long demarcation of the China-Vietnam land boundary was completed in 2009; citing environmental, cultural, and social concerns, China has reconsidered construction of 13 dams on the Salween River, but energy-starved Burma, with backing from Thailand, remains intent on building five hydro-electric dams downstream despite regional and international protests;

Chinese and Hong Kong authorities met in March 2008 to resolve ownership and use of lands recovered in Shenzhen River channelization, including 96-hectare Lok Ma Chau Loop;

Refugees and internally displaced persons:
refugees (country of origin): estimated 30,000-50,000 (North Korea) (2012); 300,896 (Vietnam)

IDPs: 90,000

Trafficking in persons:
current situation: China is a source, transit, and destination country for men, women, and children trafficked for the purposes of sexual exploitation and forced labor; the majority of trafficking in China occurs within the country's borders, there are many reports that Chinese men, women, and children may be subjected to conditions of sex trafficking and forced labor in numerous countries and territories worldwide; women and children are trafficked to China from Burma, Vietnam, Laos, Mongolia, Russia, North Korea, and even as far away as Europe and Africa for forced labor and prostitution; some Chinese adults and children are forced into prostitution and various forms of forced labor, including begging, stealing, and working in brick kilns, coal mines, and factories

tier rating: Tier 3 - China does not fully comply with the minimum standards for the elimination of trafficking and was downgraded to Tier 3 after the maximum of two consecutive annual waivers; the government has not demonstrated significant efforts to comprehensively prohibit and punish all forms of trafficking and to prosecute traffickers; the government also has not reported providing comprehensive victim protection services to domestic or foreign, male or female victims of trafficking; in 2013, the government released an eight-year national action plan, which includes measures to improve interagency and other internal coordination among anti-trafficking stakeholders and victim protection (2013)

Illicit drugs:
major transshipment point for heroin produced in the Golden Triangle region of Southeast Asia; growing domestic consumption of synthetic drugs, and heroin from Southeast and Southwest Asia; source country for methamphetamine and heroin chemical precursors, despite new regulations on its large chemical industry (2008)

IMPORTANT INFORMATION FOR UNDERSTANDING CHINA[1]

PROFILE

OFFICIAL NAME **People's Republic of China**

Total area: 9,596,960 sq. km. (about 3.7 million sq. mi.).
Cities: *Capital*--Beijing. *Other major cities*--Shanghai, Tianjin, Shenyang, Wuhan, Guangzhou, Chongqing, Harbin, Chengdu.
Terrain: Plains, deltas, and hills in east; mountains, high plateaus, deserts in west.
Climate: Tropical in south to subarctic in north.

PEOPLE

Nationality: *Noun and adjective*--Chinese (singular and plural). Population (2001 est.): 1.3 billion.
Population growth rate: About 1%.
Health : *Infant mortality rate*--28.92/1,000. *Life expectancy*--71.38 years (overall); 69.6 years for males, 73.33 years for females.
Ethnic groups: Han Chinese--91.9%; Zhuang, Manchu, Hui, Miao, Uygur, Yi, Mongolian, Tibetan, Buyi, Korean, and other nationalities--8.1%.
Religions: Officially atheist; Taoism, Buddhism, Islam, Christianity.
Language: Mandarin (Putonghua), plus many local dialects.
Education: *Years compulsory*--9. *Literacy*--81.5%.
Work force (2001 est., 711 million): *Agriculture and forestry*--50%; *industry and commerce*--23%; *other*--27%.

GOVERNMENT

Type: Communist party-led state.
Constitution: December 4, 1982.
Independence: Unification under the Qin (Ch'in) Dynasty 221 BC; Qing (Ch'ing or Manchu) Dynasty replaced by a republic on February 12, 1912; People's Republic established October 1, 1949.
Branches: *Executive*--president, vice president, State Council, premier. *Legislative*--unicameral National People's Congress.
Judicial--Supreme People's Court.
Administrative divisions: 23 provinces (the P.R.C .considers Taiwan to be its 23rd province); 5

[1] US State Department Profile

autonomous regions, including Tibet; 4 municipalities directly under the State Council.
Political parties: Chinese Communist Party, 63 million members; 8 minor parties under communist supervision.
Suffrage: Universal at 18.

PEOPLE

Ethnic Groups

The largest ethnic group is the Han Chinese, who constitute about 91.9% of the total population. The remaining 8.1% are Zhuang (16 million), Manchu (10 million), Hui (9 million), Miao (8 million), Uygur (7 million), Yi (7 million), Mongolian (5 million), Tibetan (5 million), Buyi (3 million), Korean (2 million), and other ethnic minorities.

Language

There are seven major Chinese dialects and many sub dialects. Mandarin (or Putonghua), the predominant dialect, is spoken by over 70% of the population. It is taught in all schools and is the medium of government. About two-thirds of the Han ethnic group are native speakers of Mandarin; the rest, concentrated in southwest and southeast China, speak one of the six other major Chinese dialects. Non-Chinese languages spoken widely by ethnic minorities include Mongolian, Tibetan, Uygur and other Turkic languages (in Xinjiang), and Korean (in the northeast).

The Pinyin System of Romanization

On January 1, 1979, the Chinese Government officially adopted the pinyin system for spelling Chinese names and places in Roman letters. A system of Romanization invented by the Chinese, pinyin has long been widely used in China on street and commercial signs as well as in elementary Chinese textbooks as an aid in learning Chinese characters. Variations of pinyin also are used as the written forms of several minority languages.

Pinyin has now replaced other conventional spellings in China's English-language publications. The U.S. Government also has adopted the pinyin system for all names and places in China. For example, the capital of China is now spelled "Beijing" rather than "Peking."

Religion

Religion plays a significant part in the life of many Chinese. Buddhism is most widely practiced, with an estimated 100 million adherents. Traditional Taoism also is practiced. Official figures indicate there are 18 million Muslims, 4 million Catholics, and 10 million Protestants; unofficial estimates are much higher.

While the Chinese constitution affirms religious toleration, the Chinese Government places restrictions on religious practice outside officially recognized organizations. Only two Christian organizations--a Catholic church without official ties to Rome and the "Three-Self-Patriotic" Protestant church--are sanctioned by the Chinese Government. Unauthorized churches have sprung up in many parts of the country and unofficial religious practice is flourishing. In some regions authorities have tried to control activities of these unregistered churches. In other regions, registered and unregistered groups are treated similarly by authorities and congregations worship in both types of churches. Most Chinese Catholic bishops are recognized by the Pope, and official priests have Vatican approval to administer all the sacraments.

Population Policy

With a population officially just under 1.3 billion and an estimated growth rate of about 1%, China is very concerned about its population growth and has attempted with mixed results to implement a strict family planning policy. The government's goal is one child per urban family, and two children per rural family, with handbooklines looser for ethnic minorities with small populations. Enforcement varies widely, and relies upon "social compensation fees" for extra children as a means of keeping families small. Official government policy opposes forced abortion or sterilization, but occasional allegations of coercion persist in localities that take their population growth targets most seriously. Recent international efforts, including those funded by the UN Population Fund (UNFPA), are demonstrating to government officials that a voluntary, non-coercive approach to family planning can be effective in promoting sustainable population growth. The government's goal is to stabilize the population in the first half of the 21st century, and current projections are that the population will peak at around 1.6 billion by 2050.

GOVERNMENT

Chinese Communist Party

The more than 63 million member CCP, authoritarian in structure and ideology, continues to dominate government. Nevertheless, China's population, geographical vastness, and social diversity frustrate attempts to rule by fiat from Beijing. Central leaders must increasingly build consensus for new policies among party members, local and regional leaders, influential non-party members, and the population at large.

In periods of relative liberalization, the influence of people and organizations outside the formal party structure has tended to increase, particularly in the economic realm. This phenomenon is most apparent today in the rapidly developing coastal region. Nevertheless, in all important government, economic, and cultural institutions in China, party committees work to see that party and state policy guidance is followed and that non-party members do not create autonomous organizations that could challenge party rule. Party control is tightest in government offices and in urban economic, industrial, and cultural settings; it is considerably looser in the rural areas, where the majority of the people live.

Theoretically, the party's highest body is the Party Congress, which is supposed to meet at least once every 5 years. The primary organs of power in the Communist Party include:

- The Politburo Standing Committee, which currently consists of seven members;
- The Politburo, consisting of 22 full members, including the members of the Politburo Standing Committee (one seat vacant due to a death);
- The Secretariat, the principal administrative mechanism of the CCP, headed by the General Secretary;
- The Central Military Commission;
- The Discipline Inspection Commission, which is charged with rooting out corruption and malfeasance among party cadres.

State Structure

The Chinese Government has always been subordinate to the Chinese Communist Party (CCP); its role is to implement party policies. The primary organs of state power are the National People's Congress (NPC), the President (the head of state), and the State Council. Members of the State Council include Premier Zhu Rongji (the head of government), a variable number of vice premiers (now four), five state councilors (protocol equivalents of vice premiers but with narrower portfolios), and 29 ministers and heads of State Council commissions.

Under the Chinese constitution, the NPC is the highest organ of state power in China. It meets annually for about 2 weeks to review and approve major new policy directions, laws, the budget, and major personnel changes. These initiatives are presented to the NPC for consideration by the State Council after previous endorsement by the Communist Party's Central Committee. Although the NPC generally approves State Council policy and personnel recommendations, various NPC committees hold active debate in closed sessions, and changes may be made to accommodate alternate views.

When the NPC is not in session, its permanent organ, the Standing Committee, exercises state power.

PRINCIPAL GOVERNMENT AND PARTY OFFICIALS

Principal Government and Party Officials

PRESIDENT

Xi Jinping (习近平/ 習近平) 15 June 1953 (age 61)	15 November 2012	Present

STATE COUNCIL

Office		Officeholder(s)	Tenure
Premier		Li Keqiang	2013-
Vice Premier(s)	(1st)	Zhang Gaoli	2013-
	(2nd)	Liu Yandong	2013-
	(3rd)	Wang Yang	2013-
	(4th)	Ma Kai	2013-
State Councilor(s)	(1st)	Yang Jing*	2013-
	(2nd)	Chang Wanquan*	2013-
	(3rd)	Yang Jiechi	2013-
	(4th)	Guo Shengkun*	2013-
	(5th)	Wang Yong	2013-
Secretary General		Yang Jing	2013-
Foreign Minister		Wang Yi	2013-
Defense Minister		Chang Wanquan	2013-
Development Commissioner		Xu Shaoshi	2013-
Education Minister		Yuan Guiren	2013-
Science and Technology Minister		Wan Gang	2013-
Industry and Information Minister		Miao Wei	2013-
State Ethnic Affairs Commissioner		Wang Zhengwei	2013-
Public Security Minister		Guo Shengkun	2013-
State Security Minister		Geng Huichang	2013-
Supervision Minister		Huang Shuxian	2013-
Civil Affairs Minister		Li Liguo	2013-

Justice Minister	Wu Aiying	2013-
Finance Minister	Lou Jiwei	2013-
Labor Minister	Yin Weimin	2013-
Resources Minister	Jiang Daming	2013-
Environment Minister	Zhou Shengxian	2013-
Construction Minister	Jiang Weixin	2013-
Transport Minister	Yang Chuantang	2013-
Water Minister	Chen Lei	2013-
Agriculture Minister	Han Changfu	2013-
Commerce Minister	Gao Hucheng	2013-
Culture Minister	Cai Wu	2013-
Health Commissioner	Li Bin	2013-
Central Bank Governor	Zhou Xiaochuan	2013-
Auditor General	Liu Jiayi	2013-

POLITICAL CONDITIONS

Legal System

The government's efforts to promote rule of law are significant and ongoing. After the Cultural Revolution, China's leaders aimed to develop a legal system to restrain abuses of official authority and revolutionary excesses. In 1982, the National People's Congress adopted a new state constitution that emphasized the rule of law under which even party leaders are theoretically held accountable.

Since 1979, when the drive to establish a functioning legal system began, more than 300 laws and regulations, most of them in the economic area, have been promulgated. The use of mediation committees--informed groups of citizens who resolve about 90% of China's civil disputes and some minor criminal cases at no cost to the parties--is one innovative device. There are more than 800,000 such committees in both rural and urban areas.

Legal reform became a government priority in the 1990s. Legislation designed to modernize and professionalize the nation's lawyers, judges, and prisons was enacted. The 1994 Administrative Procedure Law allows citizens to sue officials for abuse of authority or malfeasance. In addition, the criminal law and the criminal procedures laws were amended to introduce significant reforms. The criminal law amendments abolished the crime of "counter- revolutionary" activity, although many persons are still incarcerated for that crime. Criminal procedures reforms also encouraged establishment of a more transparent, adversarial trial process. The Chinese constitution and laws provide for fundamental human rights, including due process, but theses are often ignored in practice.

Human Rights

China has acknowledged in principle the importance of protection of human rights and has taken steps to bring its human rights practices into conformity with international norms. Among these steps are signature in October 1997 of the International Covenant on Economic, Social, and Cultural Rights (ratified in March 2001) and signature in October 1998 of the International Covenant on Civil and Political Rights (not yet ratified). China also has expanded dialogue with foreign governments. Most average Chinese go about their daily lives with significantly less interference from the government than in years past. However, authorities are quick to suppress any person or group, whether religious, political or social, they perceive to be a threat to government power.

In 1999, China banned the Falun Gong spiritual movement and has since implemented a crackdown on the movement. Reliable reports indicate that thousands of Falun Gong practitioners are in re-education through labor camps; hundreds are in prisons or psychiatric facilities. More than 200 practitioners reportedly have died in prison as a result of mistreatment and torture.

ECONOMY

Rank	2nd (nominal) 1st (PPP)
Currency	Renminbi (RMB); Unit: Yuan (CNY)
Fiscal year	Calendar year (1 January to 31 December)
Trade organisations	WTO, APEC, G-20 and others
	Statistics
GDP	$10.355 trillion (nominal; 2014 est.) $17.632 trillion (PPP; 2014 est.)
GDP growth	9.5% (nominal; 2013) 7.5% (real)
GDP per capita	$6,959 (nominal; 82nd;) $11,868 (PPP; 89th;)
GDP by sector	agriculture: 10.0%, industry: 43.9%, services: 46.1%
Inflation (CPI)	2.0%
Population below poverty line	6.1%
Gini coefficient	0.48
Labour force	787.6 million
Labour force by occupation	agriculture: 36.7%, industry: 28.7%, services: 34.6%
Unemployment	4.1%
Average gross salary	$657 monthly
Main industries	mining and ore processing, iron, steel, aluminum, and other metals, coal; machine building; armaments; textiles and apparel; petroleum; cement; chemicals; fertilizers; consumer products, including footwear, toys, and electronics; food processing; transportation equipment, including automobiles, rail cars and locomotives, ships, and aircraft; telecommunications equipment, commercial space launch vehicles, satellites
Ease-of-doing-business rank	96th
	External
Exports	$2.21 trillion
Export goods	Electrical and other machinery, including data processing equipment, apparel, textiles, iron and steel, optical and medical equipment. As well as almost every single category of industrial products.
Main export partners	Hong Kong 17.4% United States 16.7% Japan 6.8%

	South Korea 4.1% (2013 est.)
Imports	$1.95 trillion
Import goods	Electrical and other machinery, oil and mineral fuels, optical and medical equipment, metal ores, plastics, organic chemicals
Main import partners	South Korea 9.4% Japan 8.3% Taiwan 8.0% United States 7.8% Australia 5.0% Germany 4.8%
FDI stock	$1.344 trillion
Gross external debt	$863.2 billion
	Public finances
Public debt	22.15% of GDP
Revenues	$2.118 trillion
Expenses	$2.292 trillion
Credit rating	AA- (Domestic) AA- (Foreign) AA- (T&C Assessment) (Standard & Poor's)
Foreign reserves	$3.99 trillion

The socialist market economy of the People's Republic of China is the world's second largest economy by nominal GDP and the world's largest economy by purchasing power parity. Until 2015, China was the world's fastest-growing major economy, with growth rates averaging 10% over 30 years. Due to historical and political facts of China's developing economy, China's public sector accounts for a bigger share of the national economy than the burgeoning private sector. According to the IMF, on a per capita income basis China ranked 71st by GDP (nominal) and 78th by GDP (PPP) per capita in 2016.

The country has an estimated $23 trillion worth of natural resources, 90% of which are coal and rare earth metals. China also has the world's largest total banking sector assets of $39.9 trillion (252 trillion CNY) with $26.54 trillion in total deposits.

China is the world's largest manufacturing economy and exporter of goods. It is also the world's fastest-growing consumer market and second-largest importer of goods. China is a net importer of services products. It is the largest trading nation in the world and plays a prominent role in international trade and has increasingly engaged in trade organizations and treaties in recent years. China became a member of the World Trade Organization in 2001. It also has free trade agreements with several nations, including ASEAN, Australia, New Zealand, Pakistan, South Korea and Switzerland. The provinces in the coastal regions of China tend to be more industrialized while regions in the hinterland are less developed. As China's economic importance has grown, so has attention to the structure and health of the economy.

To avoid the long-term socioeconomic cost of environmental pollution in China, it has been suggested by Nicholas Stern and Fergus Green of the Grantham Research Institute on Climate Change and the Environment that the economy of China be shifted to more advanced industrial development with high-tech, low carbon emissions with better allocation of national resources to innovation and R&D for sustainable economic growth in order to reduce the impact of China's heavy industry. This is in accord with the planning goals of the central government. Xi Jinping's Chinese Dream is described as achieving the "Two 100s", namely the material goal of China becoming a "moderately well-off society" by 2021, the 100th anniversary of the founding of the Communist Party and the modernization goal of China becoming a fully developed nation by

2049, the 100th anniversary of the founding of the People's Republic. The internationalization of the Chinese economy continues to affect the standardized economic forecast officially launched in China by the Purchasing Managers Index in 2005. As China's economy grows, so does China's Renminbi, which undergoes the process needed for its internationalization. China initiated the founding of the Asian Infrastructure Investment Bank in 2015. The economic development of Shenzhen is dubbed as the next Silicon Valley in the world.

In recent years, government claimed growth numbers have come under increased scrutiny, with both non-chinese financial and economic observes as well as chinese government officials claiming the government has been inflating it's economic output. Examples include the provincial government in Liaoning publicly admitting that the government had been overstating GDP by 20% when publishing its economic data from 2011 to 2014. Tianjin's trillion yuan GDP claim for 2016 was in fact a third lower, at 665 billion yuan ($103 billion). In 2015, one United States-focused financial commentator suggested China's official figures for GDP growth might be double the actual rate.

A *Wall Street Journal* survey of 64 select economists found that 96% of respondents think China's GDP estimates do not "accurately reflect the state of the Chinese economy". However, a paper by the National Bureau of Economic Research in 2017 argued in the opposite direction. Regarding the credibility of official data, China's premier has been quoted as saying the GDP numbers are "man-made" and unreliable and should be used "for reference only"

Agriculture

Most of China's labor force is engaged in agriculture, even though only under 10% of the land is suitable for cultivation. There are 329 million Chinese farmers--roughly half the work force--mostly laboring on tiny plots of land relative to U.S. farmers. Virtually all arable land is used for food crops, and China is among the world's largest producers of rice, potatoes, sorghum, millet, barley, peanuts, tea, and pork. Major non-food crops, including cotton, other fibers, and oil seeds, furnish China with a large proportion of its foreign trade revenue. Agricultural exports, such as vegetables and fruits, fish and shellfish, grain and grain products, and meat and meat products, are exported to Hong Kong. Yields are high because of intensive cultivation, but China hopes to further increase agricultural production through improved plant stocks, fertilizers, and technology. Incomes for Chinese farmers are stagnating, leading to an increasing wealth gap between the cities and countryside. Government policies that continue to emphasize grain self-sufficiency and the fact that farmers do not own--and cannot buy or sell--the land they work have contributed to this situation.

Industry

Major state industries are iron, steel, coal, machine building, light industrial products, armaments, and textiles. These industries completed a decade of reform (1979-89) with little substantial management change. The 1999 industrial census revealed that there were 7,930,000 industrial enterprises at the end of 1999 (including small-scale town and village enterprises); total employment in state-owned industrial enterprises was approximately 24 million. High-tech industries are well positioned to take advantage of opportunities created by WTO; the response of moribund industries--such as autos--is less clear. Machinery and electronic products have become China's main exports.

Energy and Mineral Resources

According to Chinese statistics, China has managed to keep its energy growth rate at just half the rate of GDP growth over the past decade. Though these numbers are not reliable, there is agreement that China has improved its energy efficiency significantly over this period. China's total energy consumption may double by 2020 according to some projections. China is expected to add approximately 15,000 megawatts of generating capacity a year, with 20% of that coming from foreign suppliers.

Beijing, due in large part to environmental concerns, would like to shift China's current energy mix from a heavy reliance on coal, which accounts for 75% of China's energy, toward greater reliance on oil, natural gas, renewable energy, and nuclear power.

China has closed thousands of coal mines over the past 5 years to cut overproduction. According to Chinese statistics, this has reduced coal production by over 25%. Since 1993, China has been a net importer of oil. Net imports are expected to rise to 3.5 million barrels per day by 2010. China is interested in developing oil imports from Central Asia and has invested in Kazhakstan oil fields. Beijing is particularly interested in increasing China's natural gas production--currently just 10% of oil production--and is incorporating a natural gas strategy in its tenth 5-year plan (2001-05) with the goal of expanding gas use from its current 2% share of China's energy production to 4% by 2005 (gas accounts for 25% of U.S. energy production).

Beijing also intends to continue to improve energy efficiency and promote the use of clean coal technology. Only one-fifth of the new coal power plant capacity installed from 1995 to 2000 included desulphurization equipment. Interest in renewable sources of energy is growing, but except for hydropower, their contribution to the overall energy mix is unlikely to rise above 1%-2% in the near future.

China's energy sector continues to be hampered by difficulties in obtaining funding, including long-term financing, and by market balkanization due to local protectionism that prevents more efficient large plants from achieving economies of scale.

ENVIRONMENT

One of the serious negative consequences of China's rapid industrial development has been increased pollution and degradation of natural resources. A 1998 World Health Organization report on air quality in 272 cities worldwide concluded that seven of the world's 10 most polluted cities were in China. According to China's own evaluation, two-thirds of the 338 cities for which air-quality data are available are considered polluted--two-thirds of them moderately or severely so. Respiratory and heart diseases related to air pollution are the leading cause of death in China. Almost all of the nation's rivers are considered polluted to some degree, and half of the population lacks access to clean water. Ninety percent of urban water bodies are severely polluted. Water scarcity also is an issue; for example, severe water scarcity in Northern China is a serious threat to sustained economic growth and has forced the government to plan a largescale diversion of water from the Yangtze River to northern cities, including Beijing and Tianjin. Acid rain falls on 30% of the country. Various studies estimate pollution costs the Chinese economy about 7% of GDP each year.

China's leaders are increasingly paying attention to the country's severe environmental problems. In March 1998, the State Environmental Protection Administration (SEPA) was officially upgraded to a ministry-level agency, reflecting the growing importance the Chinese Government places on environmental protection. In recent years, China has strengthened its environmental legislation and made some progress in stemming environmental deterioration. In 1999, China invested more than one percent of GDP in environmental protection, a proportion that will likely increase in coming years. During the 10th 5-Year Plan, China plans to reduce total emissions by 10%. Beijing in particular will invest heavily in pollution control as part of its campaign to host a successful Olympiad in 2008. Some cities have seen improvement in air quality in recent years.

China is an active participant in the climate change talks and other multilateral environmental negotiations, taking environmental challenges seriously but pushing for the developed world to help developing countries to a greater extent. It is a signatory to the Basel Convention governing the transport and disposal of hazardous waste and the Montreal Protocol for the Protection of the Ozone Layer, as well as the Convention on International Trade in Endangered Species and other major environmental agreements.

The question of environmental impacts associated with the Three Gorges Dam project has generated controversy among environmentalists inside and outside China. Critics claim that erosion and silting of the Yangtze Rîver threaten several endangered species, while Chinese officials say the dam will help prevent devastating floods and generate clean hydroelectric power that will enable the region to lower its dependence on coal, thus lessening air pollution.

The United States and China have been engaged in an active program of bilateral environmental cooperation since the mid-1990s, with an emphasis on clean energy technology and the design of effective environmental policy. While both governments view this cooperation positively, China has often compared the U.S. program, which lacks a foreign assistance component, with those of Japan and several European Union (EU) countries that include generous levels of aid.

SCIENCE AND TECHNOLOGY

Science and technology have always preoccupied Chinas leaders; indeed, China's leading technocrats--both Jiang and Zhu were trained as electric power engineers--have a great reverence for science. Deng called it "the first productive force." Distortions in the economy and society created by party rule have severely hurt Chinese science, according to some Chinese science policy experts. The Chinese Academy of Sciences, modeled on the Soviet system, puts much of China's greatest scientific talent in a large, under-funded apparatus that remains largely isolated from industry, although the reforms of the past decade have begun to address this problem.

Chinese science strategists see China's greatest opportunities in newly emerging fields such as biotechnology and computers where there is still a chance for China to become a significant player. Most Chinese students who went abroad have not returned, but they have built a dense network of transpacific contacts that will greatly facilitate U.S.-China scientific cooperation in coming years. The United States is often held up as the standard of modernity in China. Indeed, photos of the Space Shuttle often appear in Chinese advertisements as a symbol of advanced technology. China's small but growing space program, which may put a man in space within a few years, is a focus of national pride.

The U.S.-China Science and Technology Agreement remains the framework for bilateral cooperation in this field. A 5-year agreement to extend the S&T Agreement was signed in April 2001. There are currently over 30 active protocols under the Agreement, covering cooperation in areas such as marine conservation, renewable energy, and health. Japan and the European Union also have high profile science and technology cooperative relationships with China.

TRADE AND INVESTMENT

According to IMF statistics, China's global trade totaled $454 billion in 2000; the trade surplus stood at $20 billion. China's primary trading partners include Japan, the EU, the United States, South Korea, Hong Kong, and Taiwan. According to U.S. statistics, China had a trade surplus with the U.S. of $83 billion in 2000.

China is taking steps to decentralize its foreign trading system and integrate itself into the world trading system. In November 1991, China joined the Asia Pacific Economic Cooperation (APEC) group, which promotes free trade and cooperation in the economic, trade, investment, and technology spheres. China served as APEC chair in 2001, and Shanghai hosted the annual APEC leaders meeting in October.

China formally joined the WTO in December 2001. Accession marks the end of a 16 year long cycle of negotiations. As part of this far-reaching trade liberalization agreement, China agreed to lower tariffs and abolish market impediments after it joins the WTO. Chinese and foreign businessmen, for example, will gain the right to import and export on their own, and to sell their products without going through a government middleman. Average tariff rates on key U.S. agricultural exports will drop from 31% to 14% in 2004 and on industrial products from 25% to 9% by 2005. The agreement also opens up new opportunities for U.S. providers of services like banking, insurance, and telecommunications.

Export growth continues to be a major component supporting China's rapid economic growth. To increase exports, China has pursued policies such as fostering the rapid development of foreign-invested factories, which assemble imported components into consumer goods for export and liberalizing trading rights.

The United States is one of China's primary suppliers of power generating equipment, aircraft and parts, computers and industrial machinery, raw materials, and chemical and agricultural products. However, U.S. exporters continue to have concerns about fair market access due to strict testing and standards requirements for some imported products. In addition, nontransparency in the regulatory process makes it difficult for businesses to plan for changes in the domestic market structure.

FOREIGN INVESTMENT

Foreign investment stalled in late 1989 in the aftermath of Tiananmen. In response, the government introduced legislation and regulations designed to encourage foreigners to invest in high-priority sectors and regions.

In 1990, the government eliminated time restrictions on the establishment of joint ventures, provided some assurances against nationalization, and allowed foreign partners to become chairs of joint venture boards. In 1991, China granted more preferential tax treatment for wholly foreign-owned businesses and contractual ventures and for foreign companies which invest in selected economic zones or in projects encouraged by the state, such as energy, communications, and transportation. China also authorized some foreign banks to open branches in Shanghai and allowed foreign investors to purchase special "B" shares of stock in selected companies listed on the Shanghai and Shenzhen Securities Exchanges. These "B" shares are sold to foreigners but carry no ownership rights in a company. China revised significantly its laws on Wholly Foreign-Owned Enterprises and China Foreign Equity Joint Ventures in 2000 and 2001, easing export performance and domestic content requirements. In 2000, China received nearly $41 billion in foreign direct investment.

Opening to the outside remains central to China's development. Foreign-invested enterprises produce about 45% of China's exports, and China continues to attract large investment inflows. For the past 8 years, China has been the world's second-largest recipient of foreign direct investment after the United States. Foreign exchange reserves totaled about $165 billion in 2000.

FOREIGN RELATIONS

Since its establishment, the People's Republic has worked vigorously to win international support for its position that it is the sole legitimate government of all China, including Hong Kong, Macao, and Taiwan. In the early 1970s, Beijing was recognized diplomatically by most world powers. Beijing assumed the China seat in the United Nations in 1971 and became increasingly active in multilateral organizations. Japan established diplomatic relations with China in 1972, and the U.S. did so in 1979. The number of countries that have established diplomatic relations with Beijing has risen to 156, while 28 have diplomatic relations with Taiwan.

After the founding of the P.R.C., China's foreign policy initially focused on solidarity with the Soviet Union and other communist countries. In 1950, China sent the People's Liberation Army into North Korea as "volunteers" to help North Korea halt the UN offensive that was approaching the Yalu River. After the conclusion of the Korean conflict, China sought to balance its identification as a member of the Soviet bloc by establishing friendly relations with Pakistan and other Third World countries, particularly in Southeast Asia.

In the 1960s, Beijing competed with Moscow for political influence among communist parties and in the developing world generally. Following the 1968 Soviet invasion of Czechoslovakia and clashes in 1969 on the Sino-Soviet border, Chinese competition with the Soviet Union increasingly reflected concern over China's own strategic position.

In late 1978, the Chinese also became concerned over Vietnam's efforts to establish open control over Laos and Cambodia. In response to the Soviet-backed Vietnamese invasion of Cambodia, China fought a brief border war with Vietnam (February-March 1979) with the stated purpose of "teaching Vietnam a lesson."

Chinese anxiety about Soviet strategic advances was heightened following the Soviet Union's December 1979 invasion of Afghanistan. Sharp differences between China and the Soviet Union persisted over Soviet support for Vietnam's continued occupation of Cambodia, the Soviet invasion of Afghanistan, and Soviet troops along the Sino-Soviet border and in Mongolia--the so-called "three obstacles" to improved Sino-Soviet relations.

In the 1970s and 1980s China sought to create a secure regional and global environment for itself and to foster good relations with countries that could aid its economic development. To this end, China looked to the West for assistance with its modernization drive and for help in countering Soviet expansionism, which it characterized as the greatest threat to its national security and to world peace.

China maintained its consistent opposition to "superpower hegemonism," focusing almost exclusively on the expansionist actions of the Soviet Union and Soviet proxies such as Vietnam and Cuba, but it also placed growing emphasis on a foreign policy independent of both the U.S. and the Soviet Union. While improving ties with the West, China continued to follow closely economic and other positions of the Third World nonaligned movement, although China was not a formal member.

In the immediate aftermath of Tiananmen crackdown in June 1989, many countries reduced their diplomatic contacts with China as well as their economic assistance programs. In response, China worked vigorously to expand its relations with foreign countries, and by late 1990, had reestablished normal relations with almost all nations. Following the collapse of the Soviet Union in late 1991, China also opened diplomatic relations with the republics of the former Soviet Union.

In recent years, Chinese leaders have been regular travelers to all parts of the globe, and China has sought a higher profile in the UN through its permanent seat on the United Nations Security Council and other multilateral organizations. Closer to home, China has made efforts to reduce tensions in Asia; it has contributed to stability on the Korean Peninsula, cultivated a more cooperative relationship with members of the Association of Southeast Asian Nations (Brunei, Burma, Indonesia, Laos, Malaysia, Philippines, Singapore, Thailand, Vietnam), and participated in the ASEAN Regional Forum. China has improved ties with Russia. President Putin and President Jiang signed a Treaty of Friendship and Cooperation in July 2001. The two also joined with the Central Asian nations of Kazakhstan, Kyrgyzstan, Tajikistan, and Uzbekistan to establish the Shanghai Cooperation Organization (SCO) in June 2001. The SCO is designed to promote regional stability and cooperate to combat terrorism in the region. China has a number of border and maritime disputes, including with Vietnam in the Gulf of Tonkin, with a number of countries in the South China Sea, as well as with Japan and India. Beijing has resolved many of these disputes, notably including a November 1997 agreement with Russia that resolved almost all outstanding border issues and a 2000 agreement with Vietnam to resolve some differences over their maritime border, though disagreements remain over islands in the South China Sea. Working with India, China has also stepped up efforts to define a line of control on the Sino-Indian border.

DEFENSE

Establishment of a professional military force equipped with modern weapons and doctrine was the last of the "Four Modernizations" announced by Zhou Enlai and supported by Deng Xiaoping. In keeping with Deng's mandate to reform, the People's Liberation Army (PLA), which includes the strategic nuclear forces, army, navy, and air force, has demobilized millions of men and women since 1978 and introduced modern methods in such areas as recruitment and manpower, strategy, and education and training.

Following the June 1989 Tiananmen crackdown, ideological correctness was temporarily revived as the dominant theme in Chinese military affairs. Reform and modernization appear to have since resumed their position as the PLA's priority objectives, although the armed forces' political loyalty to the CCP remains a leading concern.

The Chinese military is trying to transform itself from a land-based power, centered on a vast ground force, to a smaller, mobile, high-tech military capable of mounting defensive operations beyond its coastal borders.

China's power-projection capability is limited but has grown over recent years. China has acquired some advanced weapons systems, including Sovremmeny destroyers, SU-27 and SU-30 aircraft, and Kilo-class diesel submarines from Russia. However, the mainstay of the air force continues to be the 1960s-vintage F-7, and naval forces still consist primarily of 1960s-era technology.

NUCLEAR WEAPONS AND ARMS CONTROL POLICY

Nuclear Weapons. In 1955, Mao Zedong's Chinese Communist Party decided to proceed with a nuclear weapons program; it was developed with Soviet assistance until 1960. After its first nuclear test in October 1964, Beijing deployed a modest but potent ballistic missile force, including land and sea-based intermediate-range and intercontinental ballistic missiles.

China became a major international arms exporter during the 1980s. Beijing joined the Middle East arms control talks, which began in July 1991 to establish global handbooklines for conventional arms transfers, but announced in September 1992 that it would no longer participate because of the U.S. decision to sell F-16A/B aircraft to Taiwan.

China was the first state to pledge "no first use" of nuclear weapons. It joined the International Atomic Energy Agency (IAEA) in 1984 and pledged to abstain from further atmospheric testing of nuclear weapons in 1986. China acceded to the nuclear Non-Proliferation Treaty (NPT) in 1992 and supported its indefinite and unconditional extension in 1995. In 1996, it signed the Comprehensive Test Ban Treaty (CTBT) and agreed to seek an international ban on the production of fissile nuclear weapons material. However, as of September 2001, China had not ratified the CTBT.

In 1996, China committed not to provide assistance to unsafeguarded nuclear facilities. China attended the May 1997 meeting of the NPT Exporters (Zangger) Committee as an observer and became a full member in October 1997. The Zangger Committee is a group that meets to list items that should be subject to IAEA inspections if exported by countries that have, as China has, signed the Non-Proliferation Treaty. In September 1997, China issued detailed nuclear export control regulations. China began implementing regulations establishing controls over nuclear-related dual-use items in 1998. China also has decided not to engage in new nuclear cooperation with Iran (even under safeguards), and will complete existing cooperation, which is not of proliferation concern, within a relatively short period.

Based on significant, tangible progress with China on nuclear nonproliferation, President Clinton in 1998 took steps to bring into force the 1985 U.S.-China Agreement on Peaceful Nuclear Cooperation.

Chemical Weapons. China is not a member of the Australia Group, an informal and voluntary arrangement made in 1985 to monitor developments in the proliferation of dual-use chemicals and to coordinate export controls on key dual-use chemicals and equipment with weapons applications. In April 1997, however, China ratified the Chemical Weapons Convention (CWC) and, in September 1997, promulgated a new chemical weapons export control directive.

Missiles. While not formally joining the regime, in March 1992 China undertook to abide by the handbooklines and parameters of the Missile Technology Control Regime (MTCR), the multinational effort to restrict the proliferation of missiles capable of delivering weapons of mass destruction. China reaffirmed this commitment in 1994, and pledged not to transfer MTCR-class ground to ground missiles. In November 2000, China committed not to assist in any way the development by other countries of MTCR-class missiles. The U.S. Government imposed trade sanctions on the China Metallurgical Equipment Corporation on September 1, 2001. The sanctions were imposed because CMEC transferred items controlled under Category II of the Missile Technology Control Regime (MTCR) Annex to a Pakistani entity. This transfer contributed to Pakistan's MTCR Category I missile program. The penalties imposed are:

- A 2-year ban on all new individual export licenses for Commerce Department- or State Department-controlled MTCR Annex items, and on all new U.S. government contracts related to MTCR Annex items;
- In addition, because a Chinese entity engaged in sanctionable activity, U.S. law also requires a 2-year ban on new licenses for State Department-controlled MTCR exports and on new U.S.Government contracts for MTCR items associated with all activities of the Chinese Government involved in the development or production of MTCR Annex items, electronics, space systems or equipment, and military aircraft.

U.S.-CHINA RELATIONS

FROM LIBERATION TO THE SHANGHAI COMMUNIQUÉ

As the PLA armies moved south to complete the communist conquest of China in 1949, the American embassy followed the Nationalist government headed by Chiang Kai-shek, finally moving to Taipei later that year. U.S. consular officials remained in mainland China. The new P.R.C. Government was hostile to this official American presence, and all U.S. personnel were withdrawn from the mainland in early 1950. Any remaining hope of normalizing relations ended when U.S. and Chinese communist forces fought on opposing sides in the Korean conflict.

Beginning in 1954 and continuing until 1970, the United States and China held 136 meetings at the ambassadorial level, first at Geneva and later at Warsaw. In the late 1960s, U.S. and Chinese political leaders decided that improved bilateral relations were in their common interest. In 1969, the United States initiated measures to relax trade restrictions and other impediments to bilateral contact. On July 15, 1971, President Nixon announced that his Assistant for National Security Affairs, Dr. Henry Kissinger, had made a secret trip to Beijing to initiate direct contact with the Chinese leadership and that he, the President, had been invited to visit China.

In February 1972, President Nixon traveled to Beijing, Hangzhou, and Shanghai. At the conclusion of his trip, the U.S. and Chinese Governments issued the "Shanghai Communiqué," a statement of their foreign policy views. (For the complete text of the Shanghai Communiqué, see the *Department of State Bulletin*, March 20, 1972).

In the Communiqué, both nations pledged to work toward the full normalization of diplomatic relations. The U.S. acknowledged the Chinese position that all Chinese on both sides of the Taiwan Strait maintain that there is only one China and that Taiwan is part of China. The statement enabled the U.S. and China to temporarily set aside the "crucial question obstructing the normalization of relations"--Taiwan--and to open trade and other contacts.

LIAISON OFFICE, 1973-78

In May 1973, in an effort to build toward the establishment of formal diplomatic relations, the U.S. and China established the United States Liaison Office (USLO) in Beijing and a counterpart Chinese office in Washington, DC. In the years between 1973 and 1978, such distinguished Americans as David Bruce, George Bush, Thomas Gates, and Leonard Woodcock served as chiefs of the USLO with the personal rank of Ambassador.

President Ford visited China in 1975 and reaffirmed the U.S. interest in normalizing relations with Beijing. Shortly after taking office in 1977, President Carter again reaffirmed the interest expressed in the Shanghai Communiqué. The United States and China announced on December 15, 1978, that the two governments would establish diplomatic relations on January 1, 1979.

NORMALIZATION

In the Joint Communiqué on the Establishment of Diplomatic Relations dated January 1, 1979, the United States transferred diplomatic recognition from Taipei to Beijing. The U.S. reiterated the Shanghai Communiqué's acknowledgment of the Chinese position that there is only one China and that Taiwan is a part of China; Beijing acknowledged that the American people would continue to carry on commercial, cultural, and other unofficial contacts with the people of Taiwan. The Taiwan Relations Act made the necessary changes in U.S. domestic law to permit such unofficial relations with Taiwan to flourish.

U.S.-China Relations Since Normalization

Vice Premier Deng Xiaoping's January 1979 visit to Washington, DC, initiated a series of important, high-level exchanges, which continued until the spring of 1989. This resulted in many bilateral agreements--especially in the fields of scientific, technological, and cultural interchange and trade relations. Since early 1979, the United States and China have initiated hundreds of joint research projects and cooperative programs under the Agreement on Cooperation in Science and Technology, the largest bilateral program.

On March 1, 1979, the United States and China formally established embassies in Beijing and Washington, DC. During 1979, outstanding private claims were resolved, and a bilateral trade agreement was concluded. Vice President Walter Mondale reciprocated Vice Premier Deng's visit with an August 1979 trip to China. This visit led to agreements in September 1980 on maritime affairs, civil aviation links, and textile matters, as well as a bilateral consular convention.

As a consequence of high-level and working-level contacts initiated in 1980, U.S. dialogue with China broadened to cover a wide range of issues, including global and regional strategic problems, political-military questions, including arms control, UN and other multilateral organization affairs, and international narcotics matters.

The expanding relationship that followed normalization was threatened in 1981 by Chinese objections to the level of U.S. arms sales to Taiwan. Secretary of State Alexander Haig visited China in June 1981 in an effort to resolve Chinese questions about America's unofficial relations with Taiwan. Eight months of negotiations produced the U.S.-China joint communiqué of August 17, 1982. In this third communiqué, the U.S. stated its intention to reduce gradually the level of arms sales to Taiwan, and the Chinese described as a fundamental policy their effort to strive for a peaceful resolution to the Taiwan question. Meanwhile, Vice President Bush visited China in May 1982.

High-level exchanges continued to be a significant means for developing U.S.-China relations in the 1980s. President Reagan and Premier Zhao Ziyang made reciprocal visits in 1984. In July 1985, President Li Xiannian traveled to the United States, the first such visit by a Chinese head of state. Vice President Bush visited China in October 1985 and opened the U.S. Consulate General in Chengdu, the U.S.'s fourth consular post in China. Further exchanges of cabinet-level officials occurred between 1985-89, capped by President Bush's visit to Beijing in February 1989.

In the period before the June 3-4, 1989 crackdown, a large and growing number of cultural exchange activities undertaken at all levels gave the American and Chinese peoples broad exposure to each other's cultural, artistic, and educational achievements. Numerous Chinese professional and official delegations visited the United States each month. Many of these exchanges continued after Tiananmen .

Bilateral Relations After Tiananmen

Following the Chinese authorities' brutal suppression of demonstrators in June 1989, the U.S. and other governments enacted a number of measures to express their condemnation of China's blatant violation of the basic human rights of its citizens. The U.S. suspended high-level official exchanges with China and weapons exports from the U.S. to China. The U.S. also imposed a number of economic sanctions. In the summer of 1990, at the G-7 Houston summit, Western nations called for renewed political and economic reforms in China, particularly in the field of human rights.

Tiananmen disrupted the U.S.-China trade relationship, and U.S. investors' interest in China dropped dramatically. The U.S. Government also responded to the political repression by suspending certain trade and investment programs on June 5 and 20, 1989. Some sanctions were legislated; others were executive actions. Examples include:

- The U.S. Trade and Development Agency (TDA)--new activities in China were suspended from June 1989 until January 2001, when then-President Clinton lifted this suspension.
- Overseas Private Insurance Corporation (OPIC)--new activities suspended since June 1989.
- Development Bank Lending/IMF Credits--the United States does not support development bank lending and will not support IMF credits to China except for projects, that address basic human needs.
- Munitions List Exports--subject to certain exceptions, no licenses may be issued for the export of any defense article on the U.S. Munitions List. This restriction may be waived upon a presidential national interest determination.
- Arms Imports--import of defense articles from China was banned after the imposition of the ban on arms exports to China. The import ban was subsequently waived by the Administration and reimposed on May 26, 1994. It covers all items on the Bureau of Alcohol, Tobacco, and Firearms' Munitions Import List.

In 1996, the P.R.C. conducted military exercises in waters close to Taiwan in an apparent effort at intimidation. The United States dispatched two aircraft carrier battle groups to the region. Subsequently, tensions in the Taiwan Strait diminished, and relations between the U.S. and China have improved, with increased high-level exchanges and progress on numerous bilateral issues, including human rights, nonproliferation, and trade. Chinese President Jiang Zemin visited the United States in the fall of 1997, the first state visit to the U.S. by a Chinese president since 1985. In connection with that visit, the two sides reached agreement on implementation of their 1985 agreement on Peaceful Nuclear Cooperation, as well as a number of other issues. President Clinton visited China in June 1998. He traveled extensively in China, and direct interaction with the Chinese people included live speeches and a radio show, allowing the President to convey first hand to the Chinese people a sense of American ideals and values.

Relations between the U.S. and China were severely strained by the tragic accidental bombing of the Chinese Embassy in Belgrade in May 1999. By the end of 1999, relations began to gradually improve. In October 1999, the two sides reached agreement on humanitarian payments for families of those who died and those who were injured as well as payments for damages to respective diplomatic properties in Belgrade and China.

In April 2001, a Chinese F-8 fighter collided with a U.S. EP-3 reconnaissance aircraft flying over international waters south of China. The EP-3 was able to make an emergency landing on China's Hainan Island despite extensive damage; the P.R.C. aircraft crashed with the loss of its pilot. Following extensive negotiations, the crew of the EP-3 was allowed to leave China 11 days later, but the U.S. aircraft was not permitted to depart for another 3 months. Subsequently, the relationship, which had cooled following the incident, gradually improved. Following the September 11 terrorist attacks in New York City and Washington, D.C., China offered strong public support for the war on terrorism and has been an important partner in U.S. counterterrorism efforts.

U.S.-China Economic Relations

U.S. direct investment in China covers a wide range of manufacturing sectors, several large hotel projects, restaurant chains, and petrochemicals. U.S. companies have entered agreements establishing more than 20,000 equity joint ventures, contractual joint ventures, and wholly foreign-owned enterprises in China. More than 100 U.S.-based multinationals have projects in China, some with multiple investments. The U.S. trade deficit with China, $84 billion in 2000, was the United States' largest bilateral trade deficit. Some of the factors that influence the U.S. trade deficit with China include:

- The strength of the U.S. economy.
- A shift of low-end assembly industries to China from the newly industrialized economies (NIEs) in Asia. China has increasingly become the last link in a long chain of value-added production. Because U.S. trade data attributes the full value of a product to the final assembler, Chinese value added gets overcounted.
- U.S. demand for labor intensive goods exceeds domestic output.
- China's restrictive trade practices, which include a wide array of barriers to foreign goods and services, often aimed at protecting state-owned enterprises. These practices include high tariffs, lack of transparency, requiring firms to obtain special permission to import goods, unevenness of application of laws and regulations, and leveraging technology from foreign firms in return for market access. China's accession to WTO should help address these barriers.

In economics and trade, there are two main elements to the U.S. approach:

- First, the United States seeks to fully integrate China into the global, rules-based economic and trading system. China's participation in the global economy will nurture the process of economic reform and increase China's stake in the stability and prosperity of East Asia.
- Second, the United States seeks to expand U.S. exporters' and investors' access to the Chinese market. As China grows and develops, its needs for imported goods and services will grow even more rapidly.

The United States and China maintain a very active dialogue on bilateral trade issues. The two countries have implemented or are considering agreements on IPR, textiles, and aviation, among others.

At the September 2001 Joint Economic Committee meeting in Washington, the United States continued dialogue with the Chinese on macroeconomic and finance issues. The meetings discussed two main themes: global integration and structural reforms in China and the challenge of combating financial crime. The prospect of closer Chinese integration with the world economy will continue to spur state-owned enterprise and banking reform but may also lead to an increase in illegitimate economic activities.

ECONOMIC RELATIONS WITH HONG KONG

Under the 1984 Sino-British Joint Declaration, Hong Kong became a Special Administrative Region (SAR) of the P.R.C. on July 1, 1997. Hong Kong has autonomy in its international trade and economic relations. The United States has substantial economic and social ties with Hong Kong, with an estimated $16 billion invested there. There are 1,100 U.S. firms and 50,000 American residents in Hong Kong. The United States was Hong Kong's second-largest market in 1997--the U.S. imported $10.2 billion. Hong Kong took $15.1 billion in U.S. exports in that year. (See separate Background Notes on Hong Kong for additional information.)

CHINA'S NORMAL TRADE STATUS

China gained Permanent Normal Trade Relations with the United States when it acceded to the WTO, ending the yearly debate regarding the extension of China's normal trade status. The reciprocal granting of normal trade treatment was the main pillar of the U.S.-China Trade Agreement signed in 1979, which marked the beginning of normal commercial relations between the two countries. As a nonmarket-economy country, China's normal trade status had to be renewed annually by a U.S. presidential waiver stipulating that China meets the freedom of emigration requirements set forth in the Jackson-Vanik amendment to the Trade Act of 1974. China had received the waiver routinely prior to 1989, but after Tiananmen, although the presidential waiver continued, Congress began to exert strong pressure opposing normal trade status renewal. In 1991 and 1992, Congress voted to place conditions on normal trade status renewal for China, but those conditions were vetoed by the Bush Administration, which stressed the importance of the U.S. relationship with China and the belief that normal trade status was not the correct tool to exert pressure on China and would only result in isolating it.

In 1994, the annual normal trade status process was delinked from China's human rights record. At the same time, the United States decided to adopt a new human rights strategy, maintaining human rights concerns as an essential part of the U.S. engagement with China but in a broader context.

In May 2000, the U.S. House of Representatives, followed by the Senate, voted to approve Permanent Normal Trade Relations (PNTR) for China. PNTR went into effect on January 1, 2002, after China formally joined the WTO.

Chinese Diplomatic Representation in the United States

Ambassador-- Terry Branstad

Ambassador Terry Branstad was born, raised and educated in Iowa. A native of Leland, Branstad was elected to the Iowa House in 1972, '74 and '76, and elected as Iowa's lieutenant governor in 1978.

On December 7, 2016, Governor Branstad announced that he had accepted the nomination from President-elect Donald Trump to serve as Ambassador of the United States to the People's Republic of China. He was confirmed by the Senate on May 22, 2017, and was sworn in on May 24, 2017.

Deputy Chief of Mission Daniel J. Kritenbrink

In addition to China's Embassy in Washington, DC, there are Chinese Consulates General in Chicago, Houston, Los Angeles, New York, and San Francisco.

Embassy of the People's Republic of China
2300 Connecticut Avenue, NW
Washington, DC 20008
Tel.: (202) 328-2500

Consulate General of the People's Republic of China-New York
520 12th Avenue
New York, NY 10036
Tel.: (212) 868-7752

Consulate General of the People's Republic of China-San Francisco
1450 Laguna Street
San Francisco, California 94115
Tel.: (415) 563-4885

Consulate General of the People's Republic of China-Houston
3417 Montrose Blvd.
Houston, Texas 77006
Tel.: (713) 524-4311

Consulate General of the People's Republic of China-Chicago
100 West Erie St.
Chicago, Illinois 60610
Tel.: (312) 803-0098

Consulate General of the People's Republic of China-Los Angeles
502 Shatto Place, Suite 300
Los Angeles, California 90020
Tel.: (213) 807-8088

U.S. Diplomatic Representation in China
Ambassador--Clark Randt

In addition to the U.S. Embassy in Beijing, there are U.S. Consulates General in Chengdu, Guangzhou, Shanghai, Shenyang, and Wuhan.

American Embassy Beijing
Xiu Shui Bei Jie 3
Beijing 100600
People's Republic of China
Tel.: (86) (10) 6532-3831, FAX: (86) (10) 6532-3178

IMPORTANT DEVELOPMENTS

Following the founding of the People's Republic of China, China and the United States had a long period of estrangement. In February 1972, U.S. President Richard Nixon visited China at the invitation of Premier Zhou Enlai, starting the process of normalization of China-U.S. relations. In May 1973, China and the United States opened liaison offices in each other's capital. On January 1, 1979, the two counties officially established diplomatic relations at the ambassadorial level. The United States announced that it would sever its "diplomatic relations" with Taiwan, withdraw U.S. military forces from Taiwan, and terminate the Mutual Defense Treaty.

Based on the Five Principles of Peaceful Coexistence, China and the U.S. issued the Joint Communiqué of the People's Republic of China and the United States of America (Shanghai Communiqué) on February 29, 1972, the Joint Communiqué on the Establishment of Diplomatic Relations between the People's Republic of China and the United States of America on December 16, 1978, and the August 17 Joint Communiqué of 1982. The three joint communiqués are the foundation for China and the U.S. to develop stable, sound and normal bilateral relations.

Since the establishment of diplomatic ties, China-U.S. relationship has been moving forward steadily despite some twists and turns. The two sides have conducted extensive exchanges and cooperation in political, economic, military, cultural, people-to-people and sub-national areas as well as on international affairs. China-U.S. relationship is assuming greater global implications and strategic dimensions. It has become one of the most important bilateral relationships in the world.

1. POLITICAL RELATIONS

Since China and the U.S. resumed contact, the two sides have seen frequent high-level visits and improving dialogue mechanisms. In January 1979, Vice Premier Deng Xiaoping visited the U.S., opening a new page in China-U.S. relations. In 1985, President Li Xiannian visited the U.S., the first state visit to the U.S. by China's head of state since the founding of the PRC. President Jiang Zemin visited the U.S. in 1997 and 2002 respectively. During his visit in 1997, the two sides issued the China-U.S. Joint Statement. Presidents Richard Nixon (1972), Gerald Ford (1975), Ronald Reagan (1984), George H.W. Bush (1989), Bill Clinton (1998) and George W. Bush (2001, 2002, 2005, and 2008) paid a total of nine visits to China when in office.

In recent years, high-level exchanges of visits have been frequent between the two countries. President Hu Jintao visited the U.S. in 2006. In November 2009, President Barrack Obama paid a state visit to China. The two sides issued a Joint Statement during the visit. President Hu made a state visit to the U.S. in January 2011, and the two sides issued another Joint Statement during the visit. And they also jointly made the strategic decision to work together to build a China-U.S. cooperative partnership based on mutual respect and mutual benefit, which charted the direction of China-U.S. relations. In the past three-plus years, the two presidents have had 12 face-to-face meetings during bilateral visits and on multilateral occasions. Vice President Joe Biden visited China in 2011, and Vice President Xi Jinping paid a return visit in 2012.

Since the 1980's, China and the U.S. have established more than 60 dialogue mechanisms, including the Strategic and Economic Dialogues (S&ED), the Joint Commission on Commerce and Trade (JCCT), the High-Level Consultation on People-to-People Exchanges (CPE), and the Joint Commission on Science and Technology Cooperation. These mechanisms cover political, economic, military, educational, scientific and technological, cultural, counterterrorism, nonproliferation, and regional and international affairs, as well as exchanges between the two legislatures.

Given the differences in their political systems, historical and cultural traditions and levels of economic development, it is natural that China and the U.S. have different views on certain issues. China stands ready to work with the U.S. to steer bilateral relationship toward a cooperative partnership, deepen mutual trust and cooperation, properly handle Taiwan, Tibet, human rights and other sensitive issues, and ensure that China-U.S. relations will continue to grow in a stable and sound way.

2. ECONOMIC AND TRADE RELATIONS

China-U.S. economic and trade relations is mutually beneficial in nature. It is a critical pillar for China-U.S. relations. As the biggest developing country and the biggest developed country, China and the U.S. enjoy great complementarity in terms of natural and human resources, market, capital and technology. Since the establishment of diplomatic ties, bilateral economic and trade relations have been growing rapidly, with broadening areas of cooperation, increasing substance and greater interdependence. Compared with the early days of diplomatic relations, China-U.S. business ties have moved from a predominantly trade relationship to one that covers almost all aspects of economic life.

In the area of trade, according to statistics from the Chinese Customs, bilateral trade in 2011 reached US$446.7 billion, an increase of over 180 times from the beginning of diplomatic relations. China and the U.S. are the second largest trading partner for each other. The U.S. is China's second largest export market and sixth largest source of import. China is the third largest export market and the largest source of import for the U.S. It has been the fastest growing export market of the U.S. for 10 consecutive years. Based on U.S. statistics, U.S. exports to China grew by 468% between 2000 and 2010 while its exports to its other trading partners only grew by 55% during the same period.

In the area of investment, the U.S. is one of the largest sources of foreign investment. In 2011 alone, China approved 1,426 new U.S. businesses in China. By the end of 2011, the U.S. had invested in 61,000 projects in China with a total paid-in value of US$67.59 billion. Since 2005, Chinese investment in the U.S. has been growing at a rapid pace. Currently, non-financial Chinese direct investment in the U.S. has exceeded US$6 billion, covering industry, science & technology, clothing, food processing and other areas. Chinese companies have opened 1,600 businesses in the U.S., hiring 15,500 local employees.

China and the U.S. have put in place a number of dialogue mechanisms to oversee their economic and trade relations, including the Sino-U.S. Joint Economic Committee in 1979, the JCCT since 1983, the Strategic Economic Dialogue (SED) launched in 2006, and the S&ED as of 2009. Since 2009, Chinese Vice Premier Wang Qishan and U.S. Treasury Secretary Timothy Geithner have co-chaired four rounds of Economic Dialogues under the framework of S&ED, which have produced concrete results on 218 items covering wide ranging areas such as macroeconomic policy, finance, trade, investment, international rules and global economic governance. These dialogue mechanisms have played a significant role in building a sound and stable economic and trade relationship.

China is ready to work with the U.S. to properly handle the issues and disputes in their economic and trade relations, expand collaboration in trade, investment, new energy and infrastructure, and promote bilateral business ties to greater depth, breadth and scope. It is hoped that the U.S. would accommodate China's concerns when reforming the U.S. export control regime, promote the export of civilian high-tech products to China, and take concrete steps to provide a fair and hospitable environment for Chinese investment in the U.S.

3. MILITARY-TO-MILITARY RELATIONS

Military-to-military relations is an important component of China-U.S. relations. Since 1979, China and the U.S. have had exchanges and cooperation in the military field. The two militaries have established a number of dialogue and consultation mechanisms, such as the Military Maritime Consultative Agreement, the Defense Consultative Talks, and the Defense Policy Coordination Talks.

In recent years, the two militaries continue to have high-level exchanges and institutionalized dialogues, and have worked together in military archives, humanitarian disaster relief and other areas. In May 2012, General Liang Guanglie, Chinese State Councilor and Minister of Defense, visited the U.S. and exchanged views with the U.S. side on mil-to-mil relations as well as regional and international hotspot issues. The visit was a positive step in the development of China-U.S. military ties.

The mil-to-mil relations still faces some difficulties and obstacles, the major ones being U.S. arms sale to Taiwan, U.S. reconnaissance activities and relevant U.S. legislations that have negative implications on bilateral military exchanges. China is willing to work with the U.S. to move forward mil-to-mil ties on the basis of mutual respect, mutual trust, equality and reciprocity.

4. PEOPLE-TO-PEOPLE EXCHANGES AND SUB-NATIONAL COOPERATION

Since 1979, bilateral exchanges in culture, science and technology and education have become increasingly robust. The two sides have signed the Agreement on Cultural Cooperation, Agreement on Educational Cooperation and China-U.S. Agreement on Cooperation in Science and Technology, and set up a number of dialogue forums including the Joint Commission on Science and Technology Cooperation, and China-U.S. Cultural Forum. Chinese State Councilor Liu Yandong and U.S. Secretary of State Hillary Rodham Clinton co-chaired three rounds of the CPE. This mechanism has provided strong guidance and impetus for bilateral cultural and people-to-people exchanges. The two sides also launched a series of initiatives in the fields of education, science and technology, culture, sports, women and youth. China has pledged to provide scholarships for 10,000 U.S. students to study in Chinese universities, sponsor 10,000 scholarships under the "Chinese Bridge" program, and send 10,000 Chinese to pursue doctorate degrees in the U.S. The U.S. has launched the "100,000 Strong" initiative, i.e., sending 100,000 U.S. students to study in China within four years. Today, over three million visits are made between China and the U.S. each year, with more than 9,000 Chinese and Americans traveling across the Pacific each day. There are over 157,000 Chinese students in the U.S., and about 20,000 American students in China.

Sub-national exchanges and cooperation have served as an important foundation and driving force in the development of China-U.S. relations since the establishment of diplomatic relations. To date, the two countries have established 39 pairs of sister province/state relationships and 180 pairs of sister city relationships. Since 2000, business ties at the sub-national level has been expanding with a strong momentum. Forty-eight U.S. states have enjoyed a three-digit growth rate in their exports to China, which is far higher than that with other countries and regions. Exchanges and mutually beneficial collaboration in education, culture, tourism and other areas are also growing rapidly. In July 2011, the China-U.S. Governors Forum was established, which aims to provide a platform for engagement between local leaders and expand cooperation in trade, investment, energy, the environment, culture and people-to-people exchanges. Two rounds of dialogues have been held in Salt Lake City, Utah and Beijing respectively. To facilitate economic cooperation between Chinese and U.S. cities, the China Association of Mayors and the U.S. Conference of Mayors have held two conferences in Seattle, Washington in April 2011 and Nanjing, China in June 2012.

5. CHINA-U.S. COOPERATION IN INTERNATIONAL ARENA

China and the U.S. maintain close and effective communication and coordination on major regional and international as well as global issues. Areas of cooperation include regional hotspots such as the situation on the Korean Peninsula, Iranian nuclear issue and South Asia, non-traditional security issues such as counterterrorism, nonproliferation, energy security, public health, disaster prevention and reduction, and global challenges such as global financial crisis and climate change. The two sides have also put in place a series of region-specific consultation mechanisms that cover Africa, Latin America, South Asia and Central Asia, and have agreed to launch the mechanism on Middle East. Through close coordination, China and the U.S. are contributing to regional and global peace, stability and prosperity.

In recent years, China and the U.S. have conducted constructive dialogues and productive cooperation on Asia-Pacific affairs. The two sides initiated the China-U.S. Asia-Pacific Consultation in 2011, and have held three rounds of dialogues. This mechanism has played an important role in enabling China and the U.S. to work together to promote stability and prosperity in the Asia-Pacific region, facilitate open and inclusive regional cooperation and build a pattern of positive interactions and mutually beneficial cooperation between the two countries in the Asia-Pacific region.

TRAVEL AND BUSINESS INFORMATION

The U.S. Department of State's Consular Information Program provides Consular Information Sheets, Travel Warnings, and Public Announcements.

Consular Information Sheets exist for all countries and include information on entry requirements, currency regulations, health conditions, areas of instability, crime and security, political disturbances, and the addresses of the U.S. posts in the country.

Travel Warnings are issued when the State Department recommends that Americans avoid travel to a certain country.

Public Announcements are issued as a means to disseminate information quickly about terrorist threats and other relatively short-term conditions overseas which pose significant risks to the security of American travelers. Free copies of this information are available by calling the Bureau of Consular Affairs at 202-647-5225 or via the fax-on-demand system: 202-647-3000. Consular Information Sheets and Travel Warnings also are available on the Consular Affairs Internet home page: http://travel.state.gov. Consular Affairs Tips for Travelers publication series, which contain information on obtaining passports and planning a safe trip abroad are on the internet and hard copies can be purchased from the Superintendent of Documents, U.S. Government Printing Office, telephone: 202-512-1800; fax 202-512-2250.

Emergency information concerning Americans traveling abroad may be obtained from the Office of Overseas Citizens Services at (202) 647-5225. For after-hours emergencies, Sundays and holidays, call 202-647-4000.

Passport information can be obtained by calling the National Passport Information Center's automated system ($.35 per minute) or live operators 8 a.m. to 8 p.m. (EST) Monday-Friday ($1.05 per minute). The number is 1-900-225-5674 (TDD: 1-900-225-7778). Major credit card users (for a flat rate of $4.95) may call 1-888-362-8668 (TDD: 1-888-498-3648). It also is available on the internet.

Travelers can check the latest health information with the U.S. Centers for Disease Control and Prevention in Atlanta, Georgia. A hotline at 877-FYI-TRIP (877-394-8747) and a web site at http://www.cdc.gov/travel/index.htm give the most recent health advisories, immunization recommendations or requirements, and advice on food and drinking water safety for regions and countries. A booklet entitled Health Information for International Travel (HHS publication number CDC-95-8280) is available from the U.S. Government Printing Office, Washington, DC 20402, tel. (202) 512-1800.

Information on travel conditions, visa requirements, currency and customs regulations, legal holidays, and other items of interest to travelers also may be obtained before your departure from a country's embassy and/or consulates in the U.S. (for this country, see "Principal Government Officials" listing in this publication).

U.S. citizens who are long-term visitors or traveling in dangerous areas are encouraged to register at the U.S. embassy upon arrival in a country (see "Principal U.S. Embassy Officials" listing in this publication). This may help family members contact you in case of an emergency.

STRATEGIC INFORMATION FOR INVESTMENT AND BUSINESS ACTIVITY

HONG KONG ECONOMIC AND TRADE POLICY

1.GENERAL POLICY FRAMEWORK

Since becoming a Special Administrative Region of the People's Republic of China on July 1, 1997, Hong Kong has continued to manage its own financial and economic affairs, its own currency, and its independent role in international economic organizations and agreements.

The Hong Kong Government generally pursues policies of noninterference in commercial decisions, low and predictable taxation, government spending increases within the bounds of real economic growth, competition subject to transparent laws (albeit without antitrust legislation) and consistent application of the rule of law. With few exceptions, the government allows market forces to set wages and prices, and does not restrict foreign capital flows or investment. It does not impose export performance or local content requirements, and allows free repatriation of profits. Hong Kong is a duty-free port, with few barriers to trade in goods and services.

Until 1998, the government regularly ran budget surpluses and thus has amassed large fiscal reserves. The corporate profit tax is 16 percent and personal income is taxed at a maximum of 15 percent. Property is taxed; interest, royalties, dividends, capital gains and sales are not.

Because monetary policy is tied to maintaining the nominal exchange rate linked to the U.S. Dollar, Hong Kong's monetary aggregates have effectively been demand-determined. The Hong Kong Monetary Authority, responding to market pressures, occasionally adjusts liquidity through interest rate changes and intervention in the foreign exchange and money markets.

Financial contagion spreading throughout Asia caused major downturns in Hong Kong in 1997 and 1998. The government made modest accommodations in its 1998 budget and halted government property sales from mid-1998 to mid-1999 to arrest a steady decline in property prices (which had sparked fears for the banking sector). In August 1998, the government made a "one-time" intervention in the stock, futures, and currency markets (spending about $15 billion) to defend itself from market manipulators. In October 1999, the government began to divest itself of the shares it acquired in this intervention through sales to the public. By late 1999, the Hong Kong economy had begun a modest recovery, but unemployment remained high and Hong Kong's services-dependent market lagged behind some of its neighbors in shaking off the regional crisis.

2.EXCHANGE RATE POLICIES

The Hong Kong Dollar is linked to the U.S. Dollar at an exchange rate of HK$7.8 = US$1.00. The link was established in 1983 to encourage stability and investor confidence in the run-up to Hong Kong's reversion to Chinese sovereignty in 1997. PRC officials have supported Hong Kong's policy of maintaining the link.

There are no foreign exchange controls of any sort. Under the linked exchange rate, the overall exchange value of the Hong Kong Dollar is influenced predominantly by the movement of the U.S. Dollar against other major currencies. The price competitiveness of Hong Kong exports is therefore affected the value of the U.S. Dollar in relation to third country currencies.

3.STRUCTURAL POLICIES

The government does not have pricing policies, except in a few sectors such as telecommunications which remain partially regulated. Even in those areas, the government continues to pursue sector-by-sector liberalization. Hong Kong's personal and corporate tax rates remain low and it does not impose import or export taxes. Since 1996, Hong Kong has deregulated most interest rates, removing the rate cap for deposits of seven days or more. In July 1999, the Hong Kong Monetary Authority announced that remaining interest rate caps would be removed in two stages: the interest rate restrictions on time deposits with a maturity of less than 7 days in July 2000 and interest rate cap on savings and current accounts in July 2005. Consumption taxes on tobacco, alcoholic beverages, and some fuels probably restrict demand for some U.S. exports. Hong Kong generally adheres to international product standards.

Hong Kong's lack of antitrust laws has allowed monopolies or cartels -- some of which are government-regulated -- to dominate certain sectors of the economy. These monopolies/cartels can use their market position to block effective competition indiscriminately but do not discriminate against U.S. goods or services in particular.

4.DEBT MANAGEMENT POLICIES

The Hong Kong Government has minuscule public debt. Repeated budget surpluses have meant the government has not had to borrow. To promote the development of Hong Kong's debt market, the government launched an exchange fund bills program with the issuance of 91-day bills in 1990. Since then, maturities have gradually been extended. Five-year notes were issued in October 1993, followed by 7-year notes in late 1995 and 10-year notes in 1996. In March 1997, the Hong Kong Mortgage Corporation was set up to promote the development of the secondary mortgage market. The Corporation is 100 percent owned by the government through the Exchange Fund. The Corporation purchases residential mortgage loans for its retained portfolio in the first phase, followed by packaging mortgages into mortgage-backed securities for sale in the second phase.

Hong Kong does not receive bilateral or multilateral assistance.

5.SIGNIFICANT BARRIERS TO U.S. EXPORTS

Hong Kong is a member of the World Trade Organization, but does not belong to the WTO's plurilateral agreement on civil aircraft. As noted above, Hong Kong is a duty-free port with no quotas or dumping laws, and few barriers to the import of U.S. goods.

Hong Kong requires import licenses for textiles, rice, meats, plants, and livestock. The stated rationale for most license requirements is to ensure that health standards are met. The requirements do not have a major impact on U.S. exports.

There are several barriers to entry in the services sector:

-- In 1998, the Hong Kong Government announced it would open the international voice telecommunications sector to full competition. The Government decided in May 1999 not to issue any additional licenses for the local fixed network market, now contested by four companies, until the end of 2002. Hong Kong is currently adjudicating license applications for local fixed wireless and external fixed network services (undersea cable and satellite-based). Hong Kong has eliminated a regulation that required foreign broadcasters to use the Hong Kong Telecom satellite uplink and has also promised comprehensive liberalization of the broadcasting regime.

-- Our bilateral civil aviation agreement does not permit code sharing or allow U.S. carriers new fifth freedom passenger rights to carry passengers beyond Hong Kong. These factors limit expansion of U.S. passenger carriers in the Hong Kong market.

-- Foreign law firms are barred from hiring local lawyers to advise clients on Hong Kong law, even though Hong Kong firms can hire foreign lawyers to advise clients on foreign law. Foreign law firms can become "local law firms" and hire Hong Kong attorneys, but they must do so on a 1:1 ratio with foreign lawyers.

-- Foreign banks established after 1978 are permitted to maintain only three branches (automated teller machines meet the definition of a branch). The Hong Kong Monetary Authority has promised to consider further relaxation of this limit in the first quarter of 2005. Foreign banks, however, can acquire local banks that have unlimited branching rights.

6.EXPORT SUBSIDIES POLICIES

The Hong Kong Government neither protects nor directly subsidizes manufacturers who export. It does not offer exporters preferential financing, special tax or duty exemptions on imported inputs, resource discounts, or discounted exchange rates. The Trade Development Council, a quasi-governmental statutory organization, engages in export promotion activities and promotes Hong Kong as a hub for trade services. The Hong Kong Export Credit and Insurance Corporation sells insurance protection to exporters.

7.PROTECTION OF U.S. INTELLECTUAL PROPERTY

Hong Kong is a member of the WTO. In addition, the Berne Convention for the Protection of Literary and Artistic Works, the Paris Convention on Industrial Property, and the Universal Copyright Convention (Geneva, Paris) apply to Hong Kong by virtue of China's membership. Hong Kong passed a new Copyright Law in June 1997. Enforcement of copyright and trademarks has improved measurably in recent months, but eliminating optical disc piracy will require sustained effort.

Copyrights: Sale of pirated discs at retail shopping arcades is less widespread than it used to be but remains a problem. The United States has urged the government at senior levels to crack down on this retail trade, and on the distributors and wholesalers behind them. Hong Kong has responded by doubling Customs' enforcement manpower and conducting more aggressive raids at the retail level. Recent raids have closed down some of the most notorious retail arcades and dispersed this illicit trade. Hong Kong Customs intelligence operations and raids on underground production facilities have forced pirate retailers to rely more on smuggled products. Nevertheless, pirated goods remain available throughout the territory. The judiciary has begun to increase sentences and fines for copyright piracy and recently handed down Hong Kong's first conviction for unauthorized dealer hard-disk loading. Computer end-user piracy remains a significant problem for the business software industry. In 1999 the government introduced legislation to reclassify piracy under Hong Kong's Organized and Serious Crimes Ordinance, which would facilitate interrogations and allow the seizure of assets. As of November, approval by the Legislative Council is still pending.

Trademarks: Sale of counterfeit items, particularly handbags and apparel, is widespread in Hong Kong's outdoor markets. Customs officials have conducted numerous raids, but these actions have had little impact on the overall availability of counterfeit goods.

New Technologies: U.S. industry reports that Hong Kong-based web sites are being used to sell and transmit pirate software and music. The Government asserts that Hong Kong's 1997

Copyright Ordinance established civil liability for internet service providers to who host such pirate web sites, but concedes that this theory has yet to be tested in court.

The International Intellectual Property Alliance estimated total losses due to piracy against American copyright holders at $243.5 million in 1998 - slightly less than half of which was entertainment software. The Business Software Alliance reported in early 1999 that software piracy in Hong Kong had dropped from 67 to 59 percent.

8.WORKERS RIGHTS

a. The Right of Association: Local law provides for right of association and the right of workers to establish and join organizations of their own choosing. Trade unions must be registered under the Trade Unions Ordinance. The basic precondition for registration is a minimum of seven persons who serve in the same occupation. The government does not discourage or impede the formation of unions

Workers who allege antiunion discrimination have the right to have their cases heard by the Labor Relations Tribunal. Violation of antiunion discrimination provisions is a criminal offense. Although there is no legislative prohibition of strikes, in practice, most workers must sign employment contracts that state that walking off the job is a breach of contract and can lead to summary dismissal.

b. The Right to Organize and Bargain Collectively: In June 1997, the Legislative Council passed three laws that greatly expanded the collective bargaining powers of Hong Kong workers, protected them from summary dismissal for union activity, and permitted union activity on company premises and time. However, the Provisional Legislature repealed these ordinances, removing workers' new statutory protection against summary dismissal for union activity. New legislation passed in October 1997 permits the cross-industry affiliation of labor union federations and confederations, and allows free association with overseas trade unions (although notification of the Labor Department within one month of affiliation is required), but removes the legal stipulation of trade unions' right to engage employers in collective bargaining and bans the use of union funds for political purposes. Collective bargaining is not widely practiced.

c. Prohibition of Forced or Compulsory Labor: Compulsory labor is prohibited under the Bill of Rights Ordinance. While this legislation does not specifically prohibit forced or bonded labor by children, there are no reports of such practices in Hong Kong.

d. Minimum Age for Employment of Children: The "Employment of Children" Regulations prohibit employment of children under age 15 in any industrial establishment. Children ages 13 and 14 may be employed in certain non-industrial establishments, subject to conditions aimed at ensuring a minimum of 9 years of education and protecting their safety, health, and welfare. In 1998, there were ten convictions for violations of the Employment of Children Regulations.

e. Acceptable Conditions of Work: Aside from a small number of trades and industries in which a uniform wage structure exists, wage levels are customarily fixed by individual agreement between employer and employee and are determined by supply and demand. Some employers provide workers with various kinds of allowances, free medical treatment and free subsidized transport. There is no statutory minimum wage except for foreign domestic workers (US$ 500 per month). To comply with the Sex Discrimination Ordinance, provisions in the Women and Young Persons (Industry) Regulations that had prohibited women from joining dangerous industrial trades and limited their working hours were dropped. Work hours for people aged 15 to 17 in the manufacturing sector remain limited to 8 per day and 48 per week between 6 a.m. and 11 p.m.

Overtime is prohibited for all persons under the age of 18 in industrial establishments. Employment in dangerous trades is prohibited for youths, except 16 and 17 year old males.

The Labor Inspectorate conducts workplace inspections to enforce compliance with these and health and safety regulations. Worker safety and health has improved, but serious problems remain, particularly in the construction industry. In 1998, a total of 63,526 occupational accidents (43,034 of which are classified as industrial accidents) were reported, of which 68 were fatal. Employers are required under the Employee's Compensation Ordinance to report any injuries sustained by their employees in work-related accidents.

f. Rights in Sectors with U.S. Investment: U.S. direct investment in manufacturing is concentrated in the electronics and electrical products industries. Aside from hazards common to such operations, working conditions do not differ materially from those in other sectors of the economy. Relative labor market tightness and high job turnover have spurred continuing improvements in working conditions as employers compete for available workers.

U.S. INVESTMENT IN SELECTED INDUSTRIES

-- U.S. Direct Investment Position Abroad on an Historical Cost Basis -- 1998

(Millions of U.S. Dollars)

Category	Amount
Petroleum	600
Total Manufacturing	3,122
Food & Kindred Products	4
Chemicals & Allied Products	348
Primary & Fabricated Metals	282
Industrial Machinery and Equipment	167
Electric & Electronic Equipment	1,230
Transportation Equipment	29
Other Manufacturing	1,062
Wholesale Trade	5,054
Banking	1,637
Finance/Insurance/Real Estate	5,007
Services	1,009
Other Industries	4,373
TOTAL ALL INDUSTRIES	20,802

TRADE AND BUSINESS RELATIONS WITH SELECTED COUNTRIES

TRADE RELATIONSHIP WITH HONG KONG

PROFILE OF HONG KONG

[Formation] Hong Kong comprises four parts of the island of Hong Kong, Kowloon, the New Territories and 235 adjacent islands covering 1097 square km (as end of 1998).

[Location] Hong Kong locates itself south to the Shenzhen River, north to 22°09' of northern latitude, between 113°52' and 114°30' east longitudes. It lies to the south Pearl River delta, to the east of mouth of Pearl River and is situated the north coast of the South China Sea and is separated by the sea with Macao. It is connected with Shenzhen Special Economy District to the north and is away from Guangzhou City for about 140 km.

[Population] There are 6.97 million people in Hong Kong as end of 1999 and it is one of the densest areas in the world. Among the people, 95% are Chinese descendents, and 485800 people hold pass ports of other nations mainly of Philippine, Indonesia, USA, Canada, Thailand and the Great Britain.

[Climate] Spring: 18°C-27°C,dampness 70%;Summer:º26°C-33°C ,dampness 80%; Autumn:18°C-28°C,dampness 72%; winter:14°C-20°C,dampness 72%.

[Administrative Executive] Mr. Dong Jianhua

[Law system] The current laws in Hong Kong Special Administrative Region consists of the Basic Law and its appendix or appended national laws, the applied Hong Kong's original laws before July 1, 1997 approved by the Standing Committee of National People's Conference and the laws legislated by the Hong Kong SAR legislatures.

[Main Industries] The four underpinning industries in Hong Kong are finance, real estate, tourism and manufacturing, which can be concretely divided into wholesale, retail, import/export trade, food and hotel (accounting for 31% of the total working population); finance, insurance, tenement and commercial service (accounting for 14% of the total working population); community, society and individual service (accounting for 23% of the total working population); and shipment, storage and communication (accounting for 12% of the total working population).

[GDP] The local annual GDP of Hong Kong in 1999 was 166 billion USD and the per capita GDP was 26.4 thousand USD only inferior to Japan in Asia. During 1999 Hong Kong had undergone a process from recession to resuscitation and its GDP has increased in the year 1999 by 2.9%.

[Other data]
Hong Kong is a free port charging no tax except tobacco and alcohol;
The total foreign trade volume in 1999 was 354.3 billion USD and posts the eighth trade entity in the world.
The port loading and unloading volume of container in 1999 was 16.211 million containers and ranks the first in the world.
There are 157 foreign capital bank institutions in Hong Kong and ranks the third in the world as end of 1999;
The market value of share capital of Hong Kong attained 606.1 billion USD in 1999 and ranks the tenth capital market in the world.
The foreign exchange reserves of Hong Kong as end of 1999 was 96.3 billion USD and ranks the fourth in the world.

At present, Hong Kong is the second largest ready-made clothes source in the world only inferior to Italy, if its entrepot trade is taken into account, it is the largest in the world.
Fund from Hong Kong accounts for about 50% of the total amount invested to mainland China, and Hong Kong is the greatest source of foreign investment for mainland China.
2. The trade communication between mainland China and Hong Kong/Macao

Import/export Trade

According to statistics by China Custom, in 1999, the import/export trade volume between mainland and Hong Kong was 43.783 billion USD, Among it export from mainland to Hong Kong was 36.891 billion USD (accounting for 19% of the total export volume from mainland) and import from Hong Kong was 6.892 billion USD and the similitude increments against 1998 were -3.6%, 4.8% and 3.5% respectively.
In the first six months of 2000, the import/export trade volume between mainland and Hong Kong was 24.916 billion USD, Among it export from mainland to Hong Kong was 20.679 billion USD and import from Hong Kong was 4.237 billion USD and the increments against 1999 were 36.4%, 37.7% and 30.6% respectively. Hong Kong has become the third largest trade partner and the second export market for mainland China.

(2) Absorbed capital from Hong Kong
According to statistics by China Foreign Trade Ministry, in 1999, the mainland had absorbed 5876 direct investment projects from Hong Kong (accounting for 34.36% of the total investment projects absorbed by the mainland in the year); the contract investment amount was 13.048 billion USD (accounting for 31.64% of the total investment fund absorbed by the mainland in the year) and the actual applied fund was 15.843 billion (accounting for 39.22% of the total investment fund absorbed by the mainland in the year), and the decrements against 1998 were 24.96%, 21% and 15.69% respectively.

In the first six months of 2000, the mainland had absorbed 3391 direct investment projects from Hong Kong (accounting for 33.57% of the total investment projects absorbed by the mainland in the year); the contract investment amount was 7.712 billion USD (accounting for 31.9% of the total investment fund absorbed by the mainland in the year) and the actual applied fund was 6.736 billion (accounting for 39.24% of the total investment fund absorbed by the mainland in the year), and the increments against 1999 were 25.73%, 19.91% and -8.54% respectively, but the decrement range has been lessened. As end of June 2000, the mainland had absorbed 188214 direct investment projects from Hong Kong, the contract investment amount was 317.312 billion USD and the actual applied fund was 161.294 billion, they respectively accounted for 53.6%, 49.8% and 49.7% of the total investment fund absorbed in the year. In nowadays, Hong Kong still acts as the largest foreign fund source for the mainland.

(3) Contract Engineer & Labor Cooperation

In the first six months of 2000 there were 460 contract projects of contract engineer, labor cooperation and design consultation in Hong Kong that were carried out by the mainland. The currency amount of the contracts was 1.526 billion USD and the completed turnover was 1.05 billion USD, as end of the June, there were 17831 staffs serving Hong Kong from the mainland.
3. Introduction to Hong Kong-based Commercial Institutions
Address of the Trade Office of the Dept. Economy of the Hong Kong-based Central Government Liaison Office: Room 4007, Huarun Mansion, and 26 Bay Avi. Wanchai, Hong Kong
Tel: 852 25190199 Fax: 852 28244395
Principal Industrial & Commercial Institutions in Hong Kong SAR
(1) The Chinese General Chamber of Commerce
This chamber was originated in 1900 with 6000 members from sino-capital companies, Chinese merchants and other Chinese Professionals. It provides services of e-trade files and commercial inquiries, issuing certificates of origin, holding symposiums, and arranging trade visit and other trade promotion activities with its advantage of close touch with worldwide trade organizations.
Chairman: Mr. Chen Youqing
Tel: 00852-25256385 Fax: 00852-28452610

Website: www.cgcc.org.hk
Address: 4/F., 24-25 Connaught Road, Central, Hong Kong

(2) The Chinese Manufactures' Association of Hong Kong
This association was originated in 1934 and is a member of the China Chamber of International Commerce with 4000 members. It provides services of issuing certificates of origin, handling trade inquiries, arranging activities of industrial and trade promotion, holding symposium and training courses.
Chairman: Mr. Chen Yongqi
Tel: 00852-25456166 Fax: 00852-25414541
Website: www.cma.org.hk
Address: 5th Floor, CMA Building, and 64 Connaught Road Central, Hong Kong :

(3) The Hong Kong General Chamber of Commerce
This chamber was originated in 1861 with 4000 members. It is a trade institution of the longest history in Hong Kong. Its principles are arranging trade visit group going abroad, accommodating guest trade groups from both overseas and mainland China, sponsoring information activities and handling trade inquiries.
Chairman: Mr. Dong Jiancheng
Tel: 00852-28231203 Fax: 00852-25279843
Website: www.chamber.org.hk
Address: 22/F, Unite Center, No. 95, Gold Bell Avi, Hong Kong

(4) The Federation of Hong Kong Industries
This federation was originated in 1960 with 2700 members with a purpose of promoting and maintaining the profit of Hong Kong industrial and trade society. It provides services of issuing certificates of origin, promoting the best Hong Kong goods symbol plan, ISO 9000 QC management inquiries and intellectual property matters.
Chairman: Mr. Tang Yingnian
Tel: 00852-27323188 Fax: 00852-27213494
Website: www.fhki.org.hk
Address: Room 407, Hankou Center, 5-15, Hankou Avi. Jianshazui, Hong Kong

(5) The Hong Kong Chinese Enterprises Association
This association was originated in 1991 with 1100 members from companies independently invested by mainland investors or their joint ventures with Hong Kong or overseas investors. Its purpose is to promote the industrial, commercial, financial, trade and technical cooperation and development for both mainland-Hong Kong and other nations or districts.
Chairman: Mr. Liu Jinbao
Tel: 00852-28272831 Fax: 00852-28272606
Address: Room 3203, 32/F, Huarun Mansion, and No. 26 Bay Avi. Hong Kong

(6) Hong Kong Trade & Development Council
This council was originated in 1966 and it is a semi-official organization taking charge of Hong Kong overseas trade. Its mission and purpose are to extending market for Hong Kong companies, promoting Hong Kong's overall credit in the worldwide market including products and services, fortifying Hong Kong's head position as the capital of commercial expo of Asia and promoting Hong Kong's international profile as an opened market and fair trade. This council distributes its offices over 34 nations and districts besides 10 in mainland China, with this commercial network, the council actively serves the manufacturers, merchants and service enterprises of Hong Kong with international promotion activities.

The annually promotion activities hold by the council are: 1) Sponsoring over 300 trade promotion subjects worldwide besides more than half undertaken in the new emerging markets. 2) Actively partaking overseas large-scale expos by setting up Hong Kong part, holding Hong Kong product

expos in the main export destination markets and holding consumption product expos with the local renown departments or retail groups. 3) Annually sponsoring 20 large-scale international expos in Hong Kong attracting 8300 companies and 1.2 million visitors. 4) Providing computerized trade consultation service. In the council's commercial and trade databank, information of 624000 companies from Hong Kong, overseas or mainland China is available, with which the databank can assist the commercial users in seeking supplier merchants, purchasers and agents as well as providing various goods information. 5) Collecting latest information of the local markets by its worldwide office network and presenting it to the commercial and trade society to grasp the latest status of the intended markets in the forms of research report, issues, short message and market profile, etc. 6) Publishing 19 flacks on Hong Kong products and services with an annual circulation of 2.3 million copies worldwide. 7) Routinely arranging the high-rank representative visits between Hong Kong and other places in the world to strengthen the economic and trade liaison of Hong Kong-world. For many years, the council has accomplished wonderful work and has taken a large part in developing Hong Kong's overseas trade.
Tel: 00852-25844333 Fax: 00852-28240249
Website: www.tdc.org.hk
Address: 38/F, Expo Center, No. 1, Bay Avi, Wanchai, Hong Kong
5. Hong Kong Trade & Development Council www.tdctrade.com
6. Hong Kong economic and trade statistics and other related sites www.info.gov.hk

TRADE RELATIONSHIP WITH MACAO

PROFILE OF MACAO

[Formation] Macao consists three parts of the Macao Peninsula (9.1 square km) and islands of Taipa (6.33) and Coloane (8.07) covering a total area of 23.5 square km. Although a peninsula and two islands form Macao, its transportation is convenient. The south-north distance of all Macao is 11.9 km and the east-west equivalent is 7 km.

[Population] As end of Dec. 31, 1999, 438 thousand people reside in Macao.

[Geographic Feature] Macao lies in the East Asia monsoon climate area. The northeast monsoon wind from the northern continent in winter dries and chills it while the southeast and southwest monsoon winds from southern ocean in summer warms and damps it. The cross and alternate control of the winds formed Macao's natural season changes. Its average annual temperature is 22.3¡æ. July is its hottest month with an average lunar temperature of 28.6¡æ while January is its coldest month with an average lunar temperature of 14.5¡æ. The rainfall in Macao is affluent with an average of 2030 mm annually, with which Macao is listed in the rainy areas in South China.

[Economy] Macao adopts policies of free port and free economy characterized by an extraordinarily outwardly oriented economy. Before Hong Kong initiated its port trade, Macao once acted as one of the largest place of entrepot trade in the orient and as a must-pass venue for the Europeans to trade with China and Japan. However, Macao's leading role faded after Hong Kong opened its port. At present, Macao has formed four kinds of underpinning industries of tourism/lottery, processing for export (mainly textiles and clothes), finance/insurance and real estate/construction.

During the years of 1971-1981, Macao speeded its economy with an increasing rate of 16.7£¥; of 1982-1990, Macao increased its gross product with an increasing rate of 18.7%. During the above periods, Macao posted as one of the highest speed of economy increasing rate in the world and the periods therefore are called the Gold Times for Macao economic development. However, suffering the 1990s' worldwide economic stagnation and inner structure adjustment, Macao slackened its pace of economic increase, despite this, per capital general local product of Macao in 1996 was still on a level of 17.6 thousand USD and was listed the 21st in 159

nations/districts by the World Bank statistics and it still kept its position in the high income nation/district series. After its returning to China, Macao's economy is coming through and its lottery industry becomes prosperous and the processing for export increases on a stable basis, construction/real estate and finance are all improved.
Macao also takes an important part in regional economic cooperation. For instance, in 1992, Macao and EU established Europe Consultation Center taking advantage of its special relationship with the EU in the fields of trade, culture and history. Meanwhile, Macao spreads its name as orient Monte Carlo and attracts millions ourists worldwide especially from the Asia-Pacific region, the annual tourists to Macao is about 8 million.

Macao takes the opportunity of returning to China, along with maintaining and developing its relationship with the nations of EU and Portuguese-spoken, to emphasize its regional cooperation on with mainland China and Hong Kong with a purpose of advantages benefiting each other and co-development.
[Administrative Executive] Mr. He Houhua

2. The trade communication between mainland China and Hong Kong/Macao

(1) Import/export Trade
Since the year 1999 the import/export trade between mainland and Macao has been in stagnation and the situation was improved in the second half-year. According to statistics by China Custom, in 1999, the import/export trade volume between mainland and Macao was 734 million USD with a similitude decrement of 15.6%, Among it export from mainland to Macao was 638 million USD with a similitude decrement of 14.7% and import from Macao was 97 million USD with a similitude decrement of 21.2%. However, from this year the export from the mainland to Macao increases some, according to statistics by China Custom, in the first six months of 2000, the import/export trade volume between mainland and Macao was 394 million USD with a similitude increment of 19.1%, among it export from mainland to Macao was 349.6 million USD with a similitude increment of 23.9% and import from Macao was 44.4 million USD with a similitude decrement of 8.7%.

(2) Absorbed capital from Macao
In 1999, the mainland had absorbed 255 investment projects from Macao with a simillitude decrement of 3.41% and the contract investment amount was 435 million USD with a similitude increment of 31.82%, the actual applied fund was 330 million with a similitude decrement of 24.63%.
In the first six months of 2000, the mainland had absorbed 152 direct investment projects from Macao, the contract investment amount was 177 million USD and the actual applied fund was 126 million and the increments against the counterpart in 1999 were 50.5%, -19.77% and -4.76% respectively. As end of June 2000, the mainland had absorbed 6570 investment projects from Macao, the contract investment amount was 9.627 billion USD and the actual applied fund was 3.762 billion.

(3) Contract Engineer & Labor Cooperation
In the first six months of 2000 there were 463 contract projects of contract engineer, labor cooperation and design consultation in Macao that was carried out by the mainland. The currency amount of the contracts was 89 million USD and the completed turnover was 103 million USD, as end of the June, there were 29415 staffs serving Macao from the mainland.

3. Principal Industrial & Commercial institutions in Macao

(1) Macao Chamber of Commerce
This chamber was originated in 1913 with 3000 members and the incumbent Chairman is Mr. Ma Wanqi. This chamber devotes itself to protect the legal right of the industrial and trade society, to promote social stability and economic prosperity and to promote the friendship between Chinese

and Portuguese.
Tel 00853-576833 Fax: 00853-594513
Address: Rua de Xangai 175, Ed.ACM.5, Macao

(2) Macao Exporters & Importers Association
This association was originated in 1965. It devotes itself to promoting export/import trade of Macao, developing Macao economy, rallying peers and coordinating relationships. The incumbent Chairman is Mr. Wu Rongge who is also a committee of the Chinese People's Political Consultative Conference, a legislator and selectman of Macao SAR.
Tel: 00853-375859 Fax: 00853-512174
Address: AVENIDA DO INFANTE D. HENRIQUE 60-62,
CENTRO COMERCIAL CENTRAL, 3 ANDAR, MACAO

(3) The Small and Medium Enterprises Association of Macao
This association was originated in 1998 with a purpose of rallying the small and medium enterprises in Macao to foster their competitive ability, and striving to change the current economic stagnation. It provides services of trade consultation, training and arranging expos worldwide.
Tel: 00853-750507 Fax: 00853-750508
AVENIDA DR. MARIO SOARES
CENTRO COMERCIAL YANG CHENG
9 ANDAR - 'F', MACAO
4. Li Webster in Macao www.infomac.gov.mo
Trade Relationship with Taiwan
Profile of Taiwan
Taiwan is the largest island in China locating in the continental shelf of southeast sea coast covering Taiwan island itself (covering 35873 square km), the 21 affiliated islets of the Orchid islet, the Green island and the Fishing island, etc. , and the Pescadores of 64 islands. The currently so-called Taiwan District also comprises the Taiwan local government controlled islands of Jinmen and Mazu belonging to Fujian Province, all in all the total area of Taiwan is 36006 square km.
The population of Taiwan is 23 million, 98% are Han nationality, 2% (038 million) are minorities.
2. Economic Profile of Taiwan
(1) 1999' economic profile of Taiwan
Trade: Powered by continuously dynamic American economy and the economic resuscitation of Japan and other southeast Asian nations as well as the stable, fast and healthy economy of mainland China, Taiwan's export obviously rebounded, in May its export hit a record high of the past 25 months. Its total import/export volume attained 232.34 billion USD with an increment of 7.9%, among it export volume was 121.64 billion USD with an increment of 10% and the import volume was 110.7 billion USD with an increment of 5.8%. its favorable balance of trade was 10.94 USD with an increment of 84.9%.
Foreign exchange reserves: its foreign exchange reserves kept rebounding for 16 months and attained 106.2 billion USD as end of 1999.
Investment: in 1999, the civilian investment from Taiwan only increased 0.19% ranking the lowest for the past 9 years, but the investment to Taiwan by the foreign capital attained a very high of 4.18 billion of the entire year with an increment of 26% and hit a second highest for the past years. The industries that absorbing the foreign capital are mainly communication electronics, finance/insurance, services, wholesale and retail and trade.
Share market: Although Taiwan share market has suffered twice heavy frustration, it finally obviously rebounded and attained 8448.84 point with an increment of 31.63% at the end of the year.
Foreign exchange market: Caused by favoring export and increased favorable balance, the NT enjoys an appreciation trend therefore at the end of the year the closing rate was one USD exchanges for 31.395 NT with an appreciation of 2.62% (0.82 NT.) and hit a new high of the past

two years.
Economic growth rate: it attained 5.6% in 1999.
(2) Taiwan suffered an unfavorable balance in the first half year of 2000
According to the statistics from "the Finance Ministry", the export amount of Taiwan was 70.67 billion USD and the import equivalent was 67.98 billion USD with increments of 23.2% and 32.8% respectively against the same period of 1999. Its accumulative favorable was 2.69 billion USD with a decrement of 3.5 billion USD against the same period of 1999. In June, its export volume was 12.41 billion USD and the import volume was 11.56 billion USD with increments of 26% and 27.6% respectively against the same period of 1999 and has extended with a two-digital speed for 9 months since last October. The " Finance Ministry Statistics Executive" Xu Guozhong pointed out that the rising trend of import/export of the current year was optimistic and the annual export increasing rate can be estimated over 20% and the import can be estimated to 23.5%. The yearly favorable balance was estimated in the range of 7-9 billion USD.
3. Brief Introduction to the economy and trade relationships across the straits
With co-endearment of the Chinese across the straits after 20 years' development, the economy and trade communication across the straits was initiated from zero and boomed to a situation of cross-straits economical remedial and mutual benefit. As end of 1999, the accumulative total import/export trade volume across the straits was 160.4 billion USD, Among it export from mainland to Taiwan was 26 billion USD and import from Taiwan was 134.4 billion USD. Taiwan has become the fifth trade partner of the mainland and the second import market and the mainland has served Taiwan as the second export destination and the largest favorable balance source. In the year of 1999 the yearly total trade amount was 23.48 billion USD and again hit a new high following the last year's 20 billion USD break through.
Taiwan still serves the mainland as the fifth trade partner only inferior to Japan, USA, Hong Kong and Korea. Among it, export from mainland to Taiwan was 3.95 billion USD with only an increment of 2.1% and import from Taiwan was 19.53 billion USD with an increment of 17.43% and the mainland suffered a unfavorable balance of 15.58 USD and therefore Taiwan still is the mainland's largest source of unfavorable balance. From a view of goods structure, the exported goods from the mainland are mechanics and electronics, clothes and textiles, coals, steels and containers and the imported goods from Taiwan are raw materials of plastics, raw materials of textile, machine equipment and parts and steels, etc.
The large import increment from Taiwan is mainly caused by the mainland's policy of enlarging inner demand and its effect of enlarged market. The increments against 1999 were 36.4%, 37.7% and 30.6% respectively. Hong Kong has become the third largest trade partner and the second export market for mainland China.

Along with the mainland's reform and open, the Taiwan traders by and by invest their money into the mainland. According to the statistics by China Foreign Trade Ministry, as end of 1999, the mainland totally has approved 43945 enterprises of Taiwan capital, and the contract investment amount was 44.67 billion USD accounting for 7.8% of the total investment fund absorbed by the mainland and ranks the fourth only inferior to Hong Kong, USA and Japan.
In 1999 there were 2523 investment projects that had been approved with a decrement of 14.1% and the actual applied fund was 2.62 billion with a decrement of 13.8% and for the first time the fund was lower than 3 billion USD in the past five years. However the newly approved contract currency from Taiwan capital still attained 3.42 USD with an increment of 10.2% and was much better than the mainland's overall level of foreign capital application. The traders from Taiwan still were very optimistic to the expectance of investment in mainland. In 1999, the characteristics of Taiwan trader's investment were: 1) Electronics and information industry became the newest investment hotspot. 2) The traders from Taiwan continuously scurried to occupy the mainland-oriented market. 3) In 1999, the mainland additionally approved the cross-straits agricultural cooperation trial area in the provinces of Shandong, Hainan and Heilongjiang, thus the cross-straits economic and trade cooperation was placed on a new stage.

From this year, the cross-straits economy and trade communication runs at a high speed. According to the statistics by the Custom, in the first six months, the total import/export trade volume across straits was 14.037 billion USD with a similitude increment of 31.7%. Among it export from the mainland to Taiwan was 2.414 billion USD with a similitude increment of 36.4% and import from Taiwan was 11.624 billion USD with a similitude increment of 30.8%. According to the statistics by China Foreign Trade Ministry, in the first six months, the mainland had newly approved 1399 investment projects from Taiwan with a similitude increment of 13.65% and the contract investment amount was 1.991 billion USD with a similitude increment of 31.29%. The actual applied fund was 1.028 billion with a decrement of 16.95%.

4. The favorable laws/regulations legislated by the mainland to absorb investment from Taiwan compatriots.

The specification on encouraging investment from Taiwan compatriots legislated by the State Department

P. R. China's Law to protect investment from Taiwan compatriots

Execution details for P. R. China's Law to protect investment from Taiwan compatriots

5. Brief introduction to principal industrial and commercial institutions in Taiwan

(1) The General Industrial Association
This association was originated in 1942 with 139 industrial entity members.
Chief Director: Li Qunzhong
Address: 12/F 390 1st section, south Fuxing Rd. Taipei
Tel: 00886£2£27033500
Fax: 27033982
Website: http://www.industry.net.tw
Email: cnfi@mail.cnfi.org.tw

(2) The general chamber of commerce
This chamber was originated in Nov. 11, 1946 with 2120 commercial entity members and 1263744 companies/shops.
Chief Director: Wang Youzeng
Address: 6/F 390, 1st section of south Fuxing Rd. Taipei
Tel: 00886£2£27012671
Fax: 27555493
Website: http://www.rocchamber.org.tw
Email: manager@roccoc.org.tw

(3) Industrial And Trade Enterprises Association
This association was originated in Dec. 10, 1993.
Members:
Chief Director: Xu Shengfa
Address: 17/F No. 39, 2nd section of south Dunhua Rd, Taipei
Tel: 00886£2£27010810
Fax: 27010804

(4)Straits Commercial Coordination Association
This association was originated in Sept. 1993.
Members:
Chief Director: Zhang Pingzhao
Address: 1 of the 7/F Dragon door, No. 38, the 2nd section of south Dunhua Rd. Taipei
Tel: 00886£2£27050888
Fax: 27050822

(5) International Trade Association of R.O.C.
This association was originated in July 1962 with 10 thousand entity members besides 13 thousand foreign members and 110 thousand individual members.
Chairman: Tao Hongjie
Address: 8f, 148, ChungHsiao E Rd., Sec 4, and Taipei, Taiwan
Tel: 00886£2£27516730
Fax: 27772767

(6)The Association Union of Import/Export Business of Taiwan Province
This union was originated in 1953.

Members: 20 sub-associations of county or city level.
Chief Director: Zhang Qingfeng
Address: 14/F, No. 2, north Fuxing Rd. Taipei
Tel: 00886£2£27731155

(7) The Association Union of Import/Export Business of Gaoxiong City
This union was originated in 1948.
Members: 530 memebers.
Chief Director: Wang Jinbiao
Address: 4/F No. 472, the 2nd Zhongshan Rd. Gaoxiong City
Tel: 00886£7£2411191
Fax: 2016193

(8) Taipei World Trade Center
President: Lin Zhenguo
Address: No. 5, 5th Section, Xinyi Rd. Taipei
Tel: 00886£2£27251111
Fax: 27251314
Website: http://www.twtc.cetra.org.tw
6. Directory of import/export traders in Taiwan
Trade companies: http://tw.yahoo.com/Business_and_Economy/Trade/
Enterprises: http://tw.yahoo.com/Business_and_Economy/Companies/
Union: http://tw.yahoo.com/Business_and_Economy/Organizations/Trade_Associations/

IMPORTANT FOREIGN INVESTMENT AND BUSINESS REGULATIONS

THE NOTIFICATION OF SOME ISSUES ON THE INTRODUCTION OF ADVANCED TECHNOLOGY OF FOREIGN-INVESTED ENTERPRISES[2]

With reference to the purchase and payment of hard currency for introducing advanced technology of foreign-invested enterprises the Ministry of Foreign Trade and Economic Cooperation (MOFTEC) consulted with the State Administration of Foreign Exchange. After consultation the State Administration of Foreign Exchange gave a notice of simplifying the Procedure of handling the purchase and payment of hard currency for introducing advanced technology of foreign-invested enterprises on Sep.28, 1999. In order to make the cooperation well the following is issued by the Ministry of Foreign Trade and Economic Cooperation:

A. in compliance with the government's laws and regulations of absorbing foreign investments and the rules from the notice issued by the State .administration of Foreign Exchange on Sep.28,1999the competent authorities of foreign trade and economic affairs in different regions and provinces must have well-handling of the examination and approval of the contracts of introducing advanced technology of foreign-invested enterprises.

B. During the procedure of newly-approval of registration (or set-up) of foreign invested enterprises(their joint-venture contracts and reles)the relevant authorities must clarify the approved joint-venture contracts including the appendix to the technology introduced contracts

[2] (Issued by the Ministry of Foreign Trade and Economic Cooperation of the People's Republic of China on September28, 1999)

(showing the name of the contract of introducing advanced technology) while the enterprises taking the technology introduced contracts as the appendix to the joint-venture contracts.

C. Refer to the approved technology-introduced contracts, which were taken as the appendix to the joint-venture contracts of foreign-invested enterprises the foreign investment dept. Of the previous approval organs should produce the letters of confirmation, which show the names of technology-introduced contracts.

D. The competent authorities of foreign trade and economic affairs in different regions and provinces must strengthen the examination and verification of the reality of technology-introduced contracts. Foreign investors taking their advanced technology as a part of their investments is beyond the scope of confirmation.

INTERIM PROCEDURES OF EXAMINATION AND APPROVAL OF WHOLLY FOREIGN-OWNED SHIPPING COMPANY

Article 1
In accordance with the "Law of the People's Republic of China on Wholly Foreign-owned Enterprise" and other relative rules & regulations on shipping, the Interim Procedures hereby is formulated in order to normalize the investment and operation of foreign shipping companies in the People's Republic of China and protect the investors' legal rights.

Article 2
The Interim Procedures applies to foreign shipping companies that are going to set up wholly foreign-owned shipping companies in China.

The foreign shipping companies mentioned in Article 1 are shipping companies that have been established in foreign countries under foreign laws (herein after referred to as the Foreign Shippers).

Article 3
The Ministry of Foreign Trade and Economic Cooperation (hereinafter referred to as MOFTEC) and the Ministry of Communications shall be responsible for examination and approval of the establishment of the wholly foreign-owned shipping companies in China by the Foreign Shippers.

Article 4
The establishment of wholly foreign-owned shipping company in China by the Foreign Shipper shall be examined and approved in accordance with the agreement on shipping between China Government and the foreign country of the Foreign Shipper, and relative laws and rules as well.

Article 5
As for the Foreign Shipper that plans to set up a wholly foreign-owned shipping company in China, it should meet the following qualifications:

1. The Foreign Shipper shall have over 15 years experience in shipping;

2. The Foreign Shipper shall have set up a resident representative office approved by the Ministry of Communications for three years in the port city where the wholly foreign-owned shipping company is going to be set up;

3. The Foreign Shipper's liners shall berth at least once every month at the port of the city where the wholly foreign-owned shipping company is going to be set up (The enterprise, which is engaged in management of shipping lines with cooperative ways such as joint dispatching of shipping, exchange of accommodations and joint operation, and has been issued the right of management on shipping lines against approval, is regarded as meeting the qualifications);

The Foreign Shipper, who is engaged in shipping with trampers, should have fixed sources of goods in China;

4. The Foreign Shipper shall have operated in China without violating the Chinese laws, administrative rules and regulations continuously for two years.

Article 6
The Foreign Shipper shall submit the following documents for application of setting up a wholly foreign-owned shipping company:

1. Application;

2. Feasibility Study Report;

3. Articles of Association;

4. Legal documentation and credit certification of the applicant;

5. Letter of Appointment for the legal representative, the list on members of the board of directors and their resumes of the wholly foreign-owned shipping company;

6. Sample of B/L of the applicant;

7. Copies of approval documents on management of shipping lines and resident representative office;

8. Other documents required by MOFTEC and the Ministry of Communications.

Article 7
The procedures for establishing wholly foreign-own shipping company is as follows:

1. The applicant shall submit all the documents mentioned in Article 6 to the department in charge of foreign trade and economic cooperation of the province, autonomous region or municipality directly under the Central Government where the wholly foreign-owned shipping company is going to be set up. The department in chare of foreign trade and economic cooperation shall

preliminarily examine the documents submitted by the applicant. After approved, they shall be submitted to MOFTEC for approval and reported to the Ministry of Communication.

2. MOFTEC shall examine the application documents and take counsels with the Ministry of Communications. After MOFTEC and the Ministry of Communications have agreed unanimously, MOFTEC shall issue an approval. With the approval, the applicant shall get the "Certificate of Approval for Foreign-investment Enterprise" (or the "Certificate of Approval for Hong Kong/Macao/Taiwang-Investment Enterprise) from MOFTEC.

3. After approval of application, the applicant shall, within set time limit, go through registration formalities at the industrial and commercial administration and get the Business License according to stipulations on registration. Besides, the "Business License for Wholly Foreign-owned Shipping Company" shall be obtained from the Ministry of Communications before business starts.

Article 8
The approved wholly foreign-owned shipping company or its branch can contract for goods shipment, issue B/L, collect freight and sign service contract for the shipping owned or managed by its parent company.

Article 9
The registered capital of the wholly foreign-owned shipping company shall not be less than US$1 million.

Article 10
The wholly foreign-owned shipping company can apply to set up branches in other port cities as business demands. To set up branches, the wholly foreign-owned shipping company shall meet the following qualifications:

1. The registered capital of the wholly foreign-owned shipping company shall have been paid completely, and it has been one year since the Company went into operation;

2. Its parent company shall already have had liners (including cooperative ways as joint dispatching of shipping, exchange of accommodations and joint operation) berth at the ports of the city where the wholly foreign-owed shipping company is going set up a branch.

3. Its parent company shall have established a resident representative office approved the Ministry of Communications for one year in the city where the wholly foreign-owned shipping company is going to set a branch.

4. The wholly foreign-owned shipping company and its parent company shall have operated in China without any activities violating Chinese laws, administrative rules and regulations continuously for one year.

Article 11
In case the wholly foreign-owned shipping company sets up a branch, its registered capital shall correspondingly increase US$ 120,000 or more.

Article 12
The Chinese employees of the wholly foreign-owned shipping company shall cover more than 85% of the total employees.

Article 13
The wholly foreign-owned shipping company shall submit a report on state of operation of the previous year to MOFTEC and the Ministry of Communications at the end of April every year. Report on state of operation shall including the following contents:

1. Shipping lines of the liners berthing at the China ports;

2. Total employees and number of Chinese employees;

3. Freight volume (ten thousand ton) shipped from and to China ports, total volume of containers (TEU) and freight income;

4. Total amounts of business, profit and tax payment of that year.

Article 14
The establishment of shipping companies exclusively invested by shipping companies of Hong Kong Special Administrative Region, Macao Special Administrative and Taiwang in other provinces, autonomous regions and municipalities directly under the Central Government of china shall refer to the Provisions.

Article 15
The article shall come into force on the day of issuance.

PROVISIONS ON PILOT OF COMMERCIAL FOREIGN-INVESTMENT ENTERPRISES

Article1
In accordance with the "Law of the People's Republic of China on Equity Joint Ventures Using Chinese Foreign Investment", the "Law of the People's Republic of China on Contractual Joint Ventures Using Chinese Foreign Investment" and other relative Chinese laws, rules and regulations, the Provisions is hereby formulated in order to further expand opening to the outside, promote the reform and development of commercial enterprises, accelerate the construction of domestic market and make the pilot use of foreign investment in commercial field healthy and orderly.

Article 2
The Provisions applies to commercial Chinese-foreign equity joint venture companies and

commercial Chinese-foreign contractual joint venture companies (hereinafter referred to as Commercial Joint Venture Companies) jointly established by foreign companies/enterprises and Chinese companies/ enterprises in China. Exclusively foreign-owned commercial enterprises are prohibited to be established in China for the moment.

Article 3
The Commercial Joint Venture Company must accord with the commercial development plan of the city where it is located and be able to introduce advanced world marketing art and management experience, promote modernization of domestic enterprises, bring along export of homemade products and create perfect economic and social benefits.

Article 4
The regions where the Commercial Joint Venture Companies can be set up shall be stipulated by the State Department. At present, it is limited to provincial capitals, capitals of autonomous regions, municipalities directly under the Central Government, cities directly under State planning and special economic regions (hereinafter referred to as the Pilot Regions).

Article 5
The investor of Commercial Joint Venture Company shall have the following qualifications:

1. The foreign partners or main partner of the foreign partners (hereinafter referred to as the Foreign Partners) shall be an enterprise that has powerful economic strength, advanced business management experiences and marketing art, wide international sales network, perfect reputation and performance. And it shall be able to bring along the export of Chinese products through the planned Commercial Joint Venture Company.

For the Foreign Partner who applies for establishing Commercial Joint Venture Company engaged in retail, its average annual sales income within three years before application shall be more than US$2 billion, and its assets one year before application shall be over US$200 million.

For the Foreign Partner who applies for establishing Commercial Joint Venture Company engaged in wholesale, its average annual sales income within three years before application shall be more than US$2.5 billion, and its assets one year before application shall be over US$300 million.

2. The Chinese partners or main partner of the Chinese partners (hereinafter referred to as the Chinese Partners) should be a circulation enterprise that has powerful economic strength and business capacity. Its assets one year before application should be more than RMB 50 million (for enterprise in the middle and west part of China, its assets shall be RMB 30 million). In case the Chinese Partner is a commercial enterprise, its average annual sales income within three years before application shall be RMB 300 million (for enterprise in middle and west part of China, its sales income shall be over RMB 200 million). Incase the Chinese Partner is a foreign trade enterprise, its average annual value of self-managed import and export within three years before the application shall be over US$50 million, of which, the export value shall not be less than US$30 million.

Article 6
The enterprise that applies for establishing Commercial Joint Venture Company shall has following qualifications:

1. Conforming to relative Chinese laws, rules and regulations;

2. Conforming to commercial development plan of the city where the enterprise is located;

3. The Commercial Joint Venture Company undertaking retail shall have a registered capital of no less than RMB 50 million; as for the enterprise in middle and west China, its registered capital shall not be less than RMB 30 million. The Commercial Joint Venture Company undertaking wholesale shall have a registered capital of no less than RMB 80 million; as for the enterprise in middle and west China, its registered capital shall not less than RMB 60 million;

4. As for chain Commercial Joint Venture Company with over three branch stores (except convenient stores, specialized stores and monopoly stores), the contribution proportion of the Chinese Partner of shall be no less than 51%. As for the chain Commercial Joint Venture Company, who enjoys quite good operation; whose Foreign Partner has purchased a large quantity of products in China and who should be able further to expand the export of home products through the Foreign Partner's international sales network, the Foreign Partner is permitted to hold majority of shares after approval of the State Department;

As for the Commercial Joint Venture Company with three (or less) sub stores or convenient chain-stores, specialized chain-stores and monopoly chain-stores, the contribution proportion of the Chinese Partner shall not be less than 35%;

As for the Commercial Joint Venture Company undertaking wholesale (including retail enterprise that concurrently manages wholesale), the contribution proportion of the Chinese Partner shall not be less than 51%;

5. The Commercial Joint Venture Company can only set up chain branch stores that are directly invested and managed by the Chinese Partner and Foreign Partner jointly. Other chain stores like free chain and franchise chain are prohibited at the moment;

6. The operation duration shall not exceed 30 years. As for the Commercial Joint Venture Company in middle and west China, its duration shall not exceed 40 years.

Article 7
As for the Foreign Partner that has signed trademark & brand name license contract and technical transfer contract, the total of relevant charges drawn by the Foreign Partner shall not exceed 30% of the sales income (excluding VAD) of the Commercial Joint Venture Company of that year. The drawing period shall not be more than 10 years.

Article 8
Procedures for setting up Commercial Joint Venture Company shall be handled as follows:

- The Chinese Partner submits feasibility study report (as project proposal) and relative documents to local economic and trade commission (Economy Commission and Planning Commission). The local economic and trade commission, jointly with department in charge of internal trade, shall submit all the documents to the state Economic & Trade Committee in according to stipulated process. After having taken counsels with the Ministry of Foreign Trade and Economic Cooperation (MOFTEC), the State Economic & Trade Committee shall examine and approve the project.

- Against the approval of the feasibility study report (as project proposal), the local Foreign Economic Relations & Trade Department shall submit the joint venture contract and articles of association to MOFTEC according to stipulated process. MOFTEC shall be responsible for examination and approval of the contract and articles of association.

- After approval of establishment, the Commercial Joint Venture Company shall, within one month since the day that it is issued the Certificate of Approval, handle formalities for registration at the state industrial and commercial administration with the "Certificate of Approval for Foreign-Investment Enterprise" issued by MOFTEC.

Article 9
Following documents shall be submitted for establishment of Commercial Joint Venture Company

1. Application documents of feasibility Study

a. Feasibility study report (as project proposal) jointly prepared by each party to the joint venture;

b. Credit Certification of bank, Registration Certificate (copy) and Certificate of legal representative (copy);

c. Each party's annual statement of assets & liabilities and statement of gains & losses within the latest three years audited by accounting firms;

d. Assessment report on state-owned assets issued by administration of state-owned assets in case the Chinese Partner invests with state-owned assets;

e. Commodity lines managed by the Commercial Joint Venture Company;

f. Other relevant documents.

2. Application documents of contract and article of association

a. Application document s of feasibility study and its certificate of approval;

b. Joint venture contract and articles of association signed by authorized representative of each party;

c. Import and export commodities lists;

d. List of board of directors of the Commercial Joint Venture Company and letters of appointment for director by each party;

e. Notice of preliminary ratification on company name issued by the State Administration for Industry and Commerce;

f. Other relevant documents.

Except the documents specified as copies, all the above-mentioned documents shall be formal and original files. In case the documents are not signed by legal representative, the letters of authorization shall be presented.

Article 10
As for the Commercial Joint Venture Company with investment contributed by state-owned circulation enterprise, the evaluation agency authorized by administration of state-owned assets shall carry out scientific and just assessment on tangible and intangible assets contributed by state-owned circulation enterprise in accordance with the "Provisions of Assessment on State-owned Assets". The result of the assessment shall become basis for evaluation of the state-owned assets invested after it is approved by the administration of state-owned assets above provincial level.

Article 11
In case the established Commercial Joint Venture Company applies for managing wholesale concurrently, setting up branch stores or altering partners, MOFTEC shall be responsible for examination and approval after having taken counsels with the State Economic & Trade Committee. Any other alteration of the established Commercial Joint Venture shall be submitted to the original examination and approval authority for approval in accordance with current relative stipulations on foreign-investment enterprises. The Commercial Joint Venture Company shall present the following documents:

1. Application Report;

2. Report on State of Operation of the Company;

3. Report on Verification of Capital of the Company;

4. Report on State of Export and documentation of the Company;

5. Relative resolution of the board of directors;

6. Agreement on amending contract and articles of association;

7. Other relative documents.

The Commercial Joint Venture Company shall go through registration formalities for alteration at the state industrial and commercial administration within one month since approval of the amended contract and articles of association.

Article 12
Business scope of the Commercial Joint Venture Company

1. Business scope of the Commercial Joint Venture Company engaged in retail:

a. Retail business (including sale by proxy and consignment sale);

b. Organizing export of home products;

c. Self-management of import and export;

d. Management of relative services.

2. Business scope of the Commercial Joint Venture Company engaged in wholesale:

Wholesale of home commodities and import commodities with self-management; organizing export of home products.

Article 13
The Commercial Joint Venture Company engaged in retail may concurrently undertake whole against approval.

Article 14
The Commercial Joint Venture Company is prohibited to undertake agency business of export and import.

Article 15
In case the Commercial Joint Venture Company manages commodities with special regulations by the state or import & export commodities requiring quota and license, the Company shall go through approval formalities according to relative stipulations of the state.

The annual value of import commodities of the Commercial Joint Venture Company shall not be more than 30% of its sales income of commodities of that year.

Article 16
The Commercial Joint Venture Company shall be governed by Chinese laws, rules and regulations. Its legitimate operation and legal rights shall be protected by Chinese laws, rules and regulations.

In case the Commercial Joint Venture Company violates Chinese laws, rules and regulations, it shall be dealt with according to Chinese laws, rules and regulations.

Article 17
The governments of the Pilot Regions shall strictly establish the Commercial Joint Venture Companies according to the Provisions. Any activities violating the Provisions shall be dealt with

by the State Economic & Trade Committee, MOFTEC and the State Administration for Industry and Commerce. Local Economic & Trade Commissions and Foreign Economic Relations & Trade Departments shall trace and learn from the Pilot Commercial Joint Venture Companies in time jointly with relative departments. Any questions emerging in pilots shall be reasonably resolved.

Article 18
The State Economic & Trade Committee, MOFTEC, the State Administration for Industry and Commerce or its authorized agencies shall supervise and administrate the Commercial Joint Venture Companies according to laws.

Article 19
Investors from Hong Kong Special Administrative Region, Macao Special Administrative Region and Taiwan, who plan to set up Commercial Joint Venture Companies in China Mainland, shall refer to the Provisions.

Article 20
The Provision shall be construed by the State Economic & Trade Committee and MOFTEC.

Article 21
The Provisions shall come into force on day of issuance.

CHINA'S ATTRACTING FOREIGN INVESTMENT POLICY

I.FRAME OF FOREIGN INVESTMENT LAWS

Laws and regulations for foreign investment enterprises mean the total of legal norms formulated by China to readjust the economic relations of foreign investment in the Process of establishment,alteration,termination and management control.

Laws and regulations for foreign investment enterprises mainly in dude The three basic laws: Chinese-foreign Joint Ventures Law The Chinese-foreign Co-operative Enterprise Law The Foreign-funded Enterprise Law and their implementing regulations. For foreign investment limited liability companies, adapting to The Company Law; but if there are any other regulations in the above-mentioned three, adapts to them. The contracts of Chinese and foreign investors in establishing foreign investment enterprises are foreign economic contracts, bound by The Company Law of our Country.

Besides, aiming at the establishment,management,termination and dearing of foreign investment enterprises, our country have correspondingly formulated a series of laws,regulations,rules and measures, formed a whole set of more complete system of laws and regulations, and effectively protected the legal rights of domestic and foreign investors.
In order to heighten the investment security sense of foreign investors and protect the legal rights of enterprises, Chinese government, with relevant countries, has signed a treaty to encourage and mutually protect investment and a treaty to avoid double taxation,

II.BASIC FORMS OF FOREIGN DIRECT INVESTMENT

Our country attract foreign investment, direct investment generally in ways of and other ways. Mostly adopted direct investment ways are China-foreign joint ventures China-foreign co-operative enterprises, wholly foreign-owned enterprises and cooperative development Other investment includes compensation trade, processing and assembling, etc.

(I) China-foreign joint ventures.

China-foreign joint ventures may also be called equity joint ventures. It is established by foreign companies, enterprises and other economic organizations or individuals and Chinese counterparts to invest to invest together in China (Rights and duties of each Bide are stipulated in the contracts signed by different sides. China-foreign).

Its characteristics are as follows :all joint side invest together,manage together,share risks according to the investment proportion and share losses and benefits,Investment of every side should be converted to investment proportion and the proportion of foreign investment can't shill ranks a considerable proportion in attracting foreign investment.

(II)China-foreign co-operative enterprises

2t can also be called contractual joint ventures.

In establishing this kind of enterprises, usually foreigners provide all or most of funds, Chinese enterprises or individuals provide land,factory buildings,available device and facilities, some of which also provide some fund.

(III)Wholly foreign-owned enterprises

It means enterprises established in china by foreign companies,enterprises,other economic organist or individuals, according to china's Laws, in which all the funds are invested by foreign investors.

According to the stipulation of the foreign Investment Enterprise Law, establishing this kind of enterprises should favor the development of our national economy, and at least meets with one of the following: adopting advanced international technology and device, most or au products exported. The form of it is commonly Limited Liability Company.

(IV)COOPERATIVE DEVELOPMENT.

It is the short form of offshore and Land co-operative oil prosecution and development 2t is now a way of economic co-operation widely adopted in international natural resource field. 2t5 characteristics are high risk,high investment and high benefits. The process is usually divided in to three stages: prosecution-development and manufacture. 2t only rank s a small rate compared with the former three kinds.

(V)New investment means

When we gradually broaden investment fields and further open domestic markets, we also positively explore and broaden new means to utilize foreign funds.

1.BOT: The BT Items in the field of projects for basic facilities have been tried For example, the BOT Item in Guangxi Laibin Electric Power Plant has been approved.

2. Investment Company: In April 1995, the Foreign Trade and Economic Administration published Temporary Provisions On Foreign Investment Running Investment Companies, so as to encourage Large overseas companies to develop their serial investment plans. Up to now, more than 160 investment companies have been set up, whose investment activities have been constantly broadened.

3.Foreign Investment stock Company: Stock companies may be set up in ways of initiation or collection. The present foreign investment limited liability companies may apply for alteration in to joint stock companies limited.

4. Incorporative purchase: Trans-international inoperative purchase has come to one of the main ways of direct international investment. At present, our country is researching and formulating relevant policies.

III.MANAGEMENT PROCEDURES FOR FOREIGN INVESTMENT ENTERPRISES

Establishment Procedure:

According to the current rational laws and regulations, in establishing foreign investment enterprises, a term wise government approval and registration system is being carried out, In applying for establishment of China-faeigu joint ventures and co-operative enterprises, four steps are generally needed:

1. Submit item propositions for establishing enterprises; after the approval from relevant Departments C Project admin is triton or technical transformation administration, investors may embark on work with item feasibility study as center;

2. Submit reports on item feasibility study. After approval, investors may negotiate and sign Laws and documents such as contracts and statutes of establishing enterprises;

3. Submit contracts and statutes of establishing enterprises; after approval from foreign trade administrations, the Approving authorities may issue approval license to foreign investment enterprises.

4. Investors may go through formalities in industrial and commercial administrations with the approval license issued by approving authorities.

The procedure of establishing foreign funded enterprises is easy, After initial item application is approved in a written form by the governmental approving authorities, relevant documents such as formal application and company statutes may be submitted. After approval, investors may go through formalities of registration with approval license.

(II) Time limit for operation and enterprise termination:

1.Time limit for operation: The time limit of foreign investment enterprises, usually 10-30years, 20years at longest, may be stipulated by investors through negotiation under national regulations in terms of specific conditions of different industries and items. If particularly approved by the State Council, time limit needs no stipulation. For foreign investment enterprises with appointed time limit for operation, when the expiration comes, their termination comes, If investors want to prolong the time of operation, they may apply to approving authorities for approval at least 180 days before the former time limit.
During the Period of enterprise operation, enterprises have self-operation power, and the government can't implement nationalization and collection about foreign investment enterprises, under special conditions, any collection in line with the need of social public interests should be done in accord with law procedures, and some relevant Compensation should be given to the enterprises.

2. Termination:

If any terminal conditions appear in foreign investment enterprises, the enterprises should submit termination application to approving authorities, with the approval date as that of enterprise termination.

(III) Limits of approval powers

Our country implements Level-to-Level administration for foreign in vestment, the provinces, municipalities directly under the Central Government autonomous regions and singly-planned cities have powers to approve the investment value not more than US & 30 million. The items of restricted-class and above the limited level should be approved by the Foreign Trade and Economic Cooperation Administration.

IV.BASIC CHINA POLICIES FOR ATTRACTING FOREIGN INVESTMENT

(I).Industrial policies

1. Temporary Provisions and Master List

In order to make foreign investment further meet the national industrial development direction and avoid blind investment, in sune1995, our country formulated and published Temporary Provisions for Direction of Foreign In vestment and M aster List for Foreign Investment Industries, announcing the industrial policies of attracting foreign investment in the form of regulations, and lightened the transparency of policies. The provisions and list divide in dustrial items into four kinds including the encouraged-the permitted the restricted and the forbidden, making investors clear at first sight.

According to the development of our economy, in DECEMBER 1997, the State planning Commission the State Economy and Trade Commission and the Administration of Foreign Trade and Economic Co-operation jointly revised the Master list for Foreign Investment Industries. The revised list has broaden the scope of foreign investment encouraged by the state, Laying stress in key industrial points, further meeting the demands of industrial structure adjustment and the principle of favoring absorbing advanced technologies, and fully embodied the policies of encouraging foreign investors to invest in the middle-and-lvestern regions. The revised list encourages foreign investors to set up export enterprises and has put the permitted items 100 per cent of whose products are for export into the encouraged items.

2. Items in which foreign investment is encouraged

Current items of this kind mainly include: items in new agricultural technology,,comprehensive agricultural development,energy,transportation and important taw and semifinished materials industry; items with high technology; export-oriented items; items in comprehensive utilization of resources and renewable resources, environmental pollution protection; items which can exploit the advantages of the middle-and-western regions to the full, etc. Positively guide foreign investment to the technical transformation of traditional industries and old industrial bases, and further develop labor-intensive items in accord with industrial policies.

3. For the foreign investment utilization in the field of service trade, experiments should be made first. On the base of experiments, we sum up the experience, formulate laws and regulations, normalize the development and expand gradually.

At present,the fields such as Business,foreigntrade,finance,insurance,transportation,international transportation agency,legal service,tourism,advertisement,medical health,accountancy,property valuation,education,leasing,engineering design,consultation,real estate and so on hoe been opened to foreign investors in varying degrees; the opening of service has formed an entire structure initially.

(II) Regional Policies

When further giving full scope to eastern regions in opening to the world and utilizing foreign

investment and supporting eastern regions to develop fund-intensive and tech-intensive in dustries and export industries, we'll take powerful measures to guide and encourage foreign investment to the middle-and western regions.
The current policies encouraging foreign investors to invest in the middle-and-western region mainly are as follows.

1. The middle-and-western regions may choose really advantageous industries and items, enjoy the policy for the encouraged items stipulated in the Master List with the government approval; establishment conditions and market opencig degree for the restricted items and items in which foreign stock proportion is restricted may be wider to some degree than in eastern regions.

2. Properly increase domestic supporting fund loan for the middle-and-western regions to draw foreign investment, loans from foreign government and preferential loan from in serration financial administrations and mainly pa put into items of great basic facilities and environmental protection construction;

3. For the state-encouraging foreign investment enterprises in the middle-and-western regions, during the three years after the expiration of current preferential tax policy, their business income tax may be collected at the lower rate of 15 percent;

4. Encourage the foreign investment enterprises in the eastern regions to reinvest to the middle-and-western regions; the items in which foreign funds amount to over 25 per cent may enjoy relevant treatment to foreign investment enterprises;

5. Permit the foreign investment enterprises in the coastal regions to go to the middle-and-lvestern regions to contract and operate foreign investment enterprises and national-funded enterprises;

6. Permit the middle-and-eastern provinces,autonomous regions,municipalities directly under the Central Government may choose a built development zone,in their capital cities to apply for a national-grade economic and technical development zone;

7. The state will priory allow a batch of items in agriculture,water conservancy,transportation,energy,raw and semi finished materials and environment protection to draw foreign investment in the middle-and-western regions, and tighten the support for item supporting funds and relevant measures.

(III)Tax Policy

china implements a low-lax policy for foreign investment enterprises and implements preferential tax policies in the industries and regions where investment is encouraged by the state. At present, taxes for foreign investment enterprises and foreign individuals (including compatriots in Hong Kong, Macao and Taiwan): business income tax,Personal income tax, turnover tax (value-added tax,Consumption tax and business tax included) ,tariff, land increment tax,,resource tax,urban real estate tax. etc.

1. Income tax

(1) Income tax rate: The government collect business in come tax from foreign investment enterprises at the rate of 33 per cent, but only 15 percent from enterprises in special economic zones, the national hi-tech industrial zones and national-grade economic and technical development zones: 24 percent from enterprises in open coastal regions and capital cities of local provinces.

(2) Reducing-tax policy: Foreign investment enterprises may enjoy the treat meat of which

business income tax may not be collected during the first two years after their beneficial year and half collected during the next three years; for foreign investment enterprises encouraged by the state in the middle-and-western regions, after the expiration of 5 years' tax collection reduction or exemption, the government con prolong for another 3 years to collect half income tax. For advanced technology enterprises established by foreign funds, their income tax may be exempted For two yens and half collected for later six years; for export enterprises, apart from the preferential treatment of two years' exemption and three-year half reduction, if their yearly export value amounts to over to per cent of gross enterprise sales, they may enjoy the preferential treat meat that half of business in come tax is reduced; if foreign investment purchase domestic device in the range of investment sum, and if this kind of import device belongs to the list of device whose tax is exempted, their business income tax may be of credit.

2. Turnover tax

(1)Since January 1, 1994, we have implemented value-added tax, consumption tax and business tax for foreign in vestment enterprises in accordance with domestic enterprises, exempted business tax for the technical transformation of foreign enterprises and foreign investment enterprises, If foreign investment enterprises purchase domestic device in the range of total investment and the device belongs to the list among which import tax of goods can be exempts the value-added tax of dogmatic device can be completely given back.

3. Import tax

(1) Tariff rate: Chinese government has reduced import tariff rate for eight times since 1991, The current tariff rate is down to 16.5 per cent.

(2) Duty exemption of import device: At present, if device needs importing for foreign investment and domestic investment items encouraged and supported by the state, the tariff and import value-added tax can be exempted.

Current policies to encourage foreign investment

In order to further attract foreign funds, encourage the import of advanced device and technology, promote the adjustment of industrial structure and technical advance, maintain the fast constant healthy development of national economy, in August 1999, the Foreign Economic and Trade Administration, the State Planning Commission, the State Economic and Trade Commission, the National Ministry of Finance, the People's Bank of China, the Custom Bureau, the General State Tax Bureau, the State Exchange Authority and the State Entry and Exit Test Bureau formulated some relevant policies to further encourage foreign investment.

(I) Encourage foreign investment in technical development and innovation

1. For the technical transformation of the established encouraged, Class B foreign invest mont. Enterprises, foreign investment research and development centers and foreign investment enterprises with advanced technology and whose products are for export, if the enterprises need to import device which can't be made internally or whose functions can't satisfy their need and the supporting technology, attachments and accessories with in the former manufacture scope, the import tariff and import tax may be exempted according to the Information for Adjusting Import Device Tariff by the State Council.

2. If the foreign investment enterprises belonging to the encouraged or the restricted class B want to purchase domestic device within the total investment value, and if the device belongs to the scope in which import tax can be exempted, their domestic-device value0added tax can be filled returned. If foreign investment enterprises perform technical transformation in accord with national industrial policies and produce hi-tech products, the business income tax of the device purchased may be exempted according to relevant regulations.

3. If the research and development centers established by foreign investors import self-use device which can't be made domestically or whose functions can satisfy their needs, as well as the supporting technology, accessories and attachments within the total investment value, their import tariff and import tax can be exempted according to the Information for Adjusting Import Device Tariff by the state Council.

4. Exempt business tax of foreign enterprises transferring technology to China; if their technology is advanced and conditions are preferential, their business income tax can be exempted approved by the State Council Taxation Authority, The business tax for the technical transformation income of foreign investment enterprises (including research and development Centers) can be exempted.

5. If the technical development cost of foreign investment enterprises rises by 10 per cent than last year, with the approval of taxation authorities, 50 per cent of the real technical development cost may balance the income tax of current year, just according to the Administrate Measures for Before-tax Deduction of Enterprise Technical Development Cost by the State Tax Burma.

6. In order to broaden the export of foreign investment enterprises, with the approval of the tax authorities, the old foreign investment enterprises established before 1993 can be permitted to export commodities and before the year 2000, adapt to the policy"No collection, No return or" "No balance"(one policy only)

(II) Lighten the financial support for foreign investment enterprises

1. when foreign investment enterprises circulate funds domestically, Chinese-funded banks may be allowed to accept the guarantee from foreign stockholders. Foreign investment enterprises may apply to domestic specified-exchange Chinese-funded banks for Renminbi Loan in the way of exchange pledge. All the exchange funds of foreign in vestment enterprises may be used for pledge; overseas financial authorities or domestic foreign-funded financial authorities may provide credit guarantee for Renminbi loan under the guarantee in exchange. Abolish the registration step under exchange pledge and exchange guarantee as well as the special control for credit grade of foreign-funded banks offering exchange guarantee.

The foreign Renminbi loan with exchange guarantee or with stockholders guarantee should meet the industrial policies, which may be used to satisfy the needs of fixed investments and fund circulation but not to buy exchange.

2. Special industrial investment funds are established to relieve the shortage of Chinese stock at the tame of capital increase of current foreign investment enterprises, and mean while, allow domestic Chinese-founded Comerica banks give Chinese stockholders a certain stock loan with the prerequisite of the synchronous arrival of the stocks which should be increased by foreign stockholders of Chinese-foreign joint ventures and co-operative enterprises.

3.permit domestic foreign investment enterprises to provide mortgage for overseas branch of domestic Chinese-funded banks with their overseas estate, and loan is delivered by overseas or domestic branch of Chinese-funded commercial banks.

4.the foreign investment enterprises fitting the conditions may of ask to issue stock A or B
5.according to the principle "positive and safe", insurance's such as political risk insurance, performance insurance guarantee insurance should be provided for foreign investors who invest in energy and transportation greatly encouraged by the state.

(III) encourage foreign investors to invest in the middle-and -western regions

1. the list of advantageous foreign-investment-used industries and items formulated by the provinces, autonomous regions and municipalities directly under the central government in the middle-and-western regions may be complemented after approval of the state. The items in the list may enjoy the treatment the encouraged class in the Master list for Foreign Investment Industries; if they import self-use device that can't be made domestically or whose functions can't satisfy their need, as well as the supporting technology, accessioning and attachments, the import tariff and import tax may be exempted according to the Information for Adjusting Import Device Tax Policy by the state council.

2. Broaden the condition limits for the middle-and-western regions to establish foreign investment enterprises and broaden the field of their attracting foreign investment, breaded the stock proportion limit for foreign investors in establishing foreign investment enterprises in the middle-and-western regions.

3. For the state-encouraging foreign investment enterprises in the middle-and-western regions during the 3years after the expiration of current preferential tax policies, their business income tax can be collected at a lower late of 15percent.

4. If foreign investment enterprises reinvest in the middle-and-western regions and the foreign funds amount to 25per cent of the total of item, they may enjoy the treatment as foreign investment enterprises.

5. Permit the coastal foreign investment to go to the middle-and-western regions to contract and operate foreign investment enterprises and domestic-funded enterprises.

6. Permit provinces autonomous regions and municipalities directly and the central Government in the middle-and-western regions to choose a built development zone in their capital cities, applying for a national-grade economic and technical development zone.

(IV) perfect the administration and service for foreign investment enterprises

1. Readjust the Master hist for Foreign Investment Industries at proper time according to the development of economy. In order to meet the demands of broadening the opening up and of drawling foreign Investment, we should reduce the items which demand Chinese to keep stock and don't permit foreigners to invest solely in the above-mentioned list.

2. All the foreign investment items belonging to the encouraged and don't need the synthetic balance may be approved by provincial people's government and report to the State Planning Commission the State Economic and Trade Commission and the Foreign Economics and Trade Administration for arecord. After the three national authorities receive the report, they should give an answer within a month if there is any question. The relevant authorities and local people's governments should further simplify the approval procedure for foreign investment items and establishment of enterprises, and accelerate the approval.

3. Perfect the network checking system of bills of entry checking the authentity of exchange sale wider current account, and shorten the check time; ender special conditions, there may be no possibility of network check system of entry bill, and only correspondence can be used, the check should be speeded up. Foreign investment enterprises may change the deposit in foreign exchange account into fixed deposit within the limited range. According to lex Sinus, the approval rights of the settlement for capital item exchange in come may be sent out and cancel the record and registration system for the settlement of capital item exchange income.

4. Minimize the restrictive evaluation scope for foreign investment enterprises to import device and perfect ways of appraisal; don't implement restrictive evaluation for foreign-funded enterprises in importing device. Normalize the Customs administration, raise the efficiency and

accelerate the customs passing. Stop the arbitrary charge. unformed check and unjustified financial levies, for foreign investment enterprises.

5. Foreign investment enterprises which attain land-use right in the way of selling needn't hand in land-use charge.

6. Clear the policies and regulations about foreign investment enterprises, be quick to readjust the policies and regulations not good for drawing foreign funds and perfect the policies and regulations about foreign investment.

Circular on Regulating the Limits of Authority Concerning Examination and Approval of Guaranteeing Foreign Bodies to Observe Contract

Each branch and sections of State Administration of Foreign Exchange, Sections of Administration of Foreign Exchange in Beijing and Chongqing, the branches in Dalian, Qingdao, Ningpo, Xiamen and Shenzhen:

In order to regulating the limits of authority concerning examination and approval of guaranteeing foreign bodies to observe contract, the handling principles are issued to you now and you should observe them when dealing with the affairs.

1. Legitimate and regular guarantee of foreign bodies to observe contract should be examined and approved by the local branch according to the regulations and the dependency principle settled down in the locality and at the same time copy and report the contents of the examination and approval to State Administration of Foreign Exchange to be put on file.

2. The guarantee of foreign bodies to observe contract with the substantial disobedience to the regulations (means that a guarantor's guarantee action for a foreign body ought to be approved by an administration of foreign exchange, but the guarantor is not approved before signing the guarantee contract) should be examined primarily by the local branch of State Administration of Foreign Exchange and then report State Administration of Foreign Exchange to examine and approve.

3. The guarantee of foreign bodies to observe contract with the procedural disobedience to the regulations£¨only limited to that a guarantor's guarantee action for a foreign body has already been approved by an unit of administration of foreign exchange or needs no approval, but fails to register at an administration of foreign exchange according to the regulations£©should be examined and approved after a relevant penalty referencing to the circumstance of the disobedience by the local branch of State Administration of Foreign Exchange, and at the same time report the penalty and the examination and approval of the guarantee to State Administration of Foreign Exchange to examine and approve and to be put on file..

FOREIGN TRADE

MOFTEC and GOC (General Office of Custom) issuing jointly Notice of administering proceedings about EU textile processing trade in China and export to EU, certificate of Original textile producing area.

In order to further standardize the endorsement and administering of export certificate of EU textile, we specify the related regulations of administering proceedings about EU textile processing and trade in China and export to EU, certificate of original textile producing area as follows:

First, about processing and trade product exported to EU

1.According to the regulation of the double-sided agreements made by China and EU on textile and on silk hemp, if the textile is processed in China by Chinese enterprises and will be exported to EU up to the EU`s current regulations of exterior processing, it won't be restricted by the passive quota set by the double-sided agreements, just applying to the outward processing trade and tradable quota (OPT quota for short in the following) self-administered by EU. As to the again-import that meets the MOFTEC`s processing and trade regulations, EU will endorse the PRIOR AUTHORIZATION FOR ECONOMIC OUTWARD PROCESSING to EU importer in advance.

2. When Chinese enterprises export textile in the item of OPT quota, they shall apply to affiliated department vising textile export certificate for certificate of original producing area with the copy of PRIOR AUTHORIZATION FOR ECONOMIC OUTWARD PROCESSING (two copies) provided by importer and related export documents; the number of PRIOR AUTHORIZATION FOR ECONOMIC OUTWARD PROCESSING shall be indicated in column No. 9 of certificate of original producing area.

3.Visa department shall issue the certificate of original producing area for the export enterprises after checking the copy of PRIOR AUTHORIZATION FOR ECONOMIC OUTWARD PROCESSING provided by importer and related export documents. At the same time, visa department shall seal the badge of EU textile export certificate visa in one copy of the PRIOR AUTHORIZATION FOR ECONOMIC OUTWARD PROCESSING and send it back to the export enterprises; the other copy of the PRIOR AUTHORIZATION FOR ECONOMIC OUTWARD PROCESSING remained in visa department.

4. When export enterprises ask customs for the approval of exporting textile in the term of OPT quota, they shall put in the sealed copy of the PRIOR AUTHORIZATION FOR ECONOMIC OUTWARD PROCESSING and need not take the certificate of textile export The customs transacts the export clearance on the sealed copy of the PRIOR AUTHORIZATION FOR ECONOMIC OUTWARD PROCESSING.

Second, about certificate of original producing area

1. According to the double-sided agreements between China and EU, when Chinese enterprises export textile in the term of double-sided agreements to EU (including quota and non-quota), they shall distinguish different products either to apply to visa department for textile certificate of original producing area, or to apply to visa department that vise general beneficial certificate of original producing area for general beneficial certificate of original producing area or declared in invoices or other bills that products are originally made in China. The above two kinds of certificate of original producing area only are to be checked by EU customs at the time of import. If enterprises export textile in the term of OPT quota, they shall apply for textile export license at the same time.

2. When export enterprises ask our customs for approval of exporting textile to EU, the custom needn't check the certificate of original producing area, but need to check the textile export license for textile in the term of OPT quota.

Every branch of MOFTEC must inform concerned proceedings to local textile export enterprises in time. The following two documents cease to use on Transmitting MOFTEC's Notice of stopping using certificate of non-quota shipment kinds of ECC (S.G. [1995] No.22) issued by Supervising Department of GOC, and Notice on customs clearance for textile exported to EU (P.L. [2000] No.124) issued by policies and Law Department of GOC. If any of the previous documents differ from this notice, this one is the standards.

THE URGENT NOTICE ABOUT FURTHER ENHANCING THE PROCESSING TRADE APPROVAL AND EXAMINATION MANAGEMENT AND STRICTLY PROHIBIT TO ENGAGE IN ANY PROCESSING TRADE BUSINESS OF DEREGULATION AND IRREGULARITY

To every province, autonomous region, municipality directly under the central government and city foreign economic and trading committee(office and bureau) ,mapping departments in charge, news publish bureau, Guang Dong Customs Branch administration, each directly under customs(subjection) listed on the planning sheet:

Recently, there appeared some severe political problems which obey Chinese principles in some of our export products most of which are in the way of processing trade to product and export.

The map on the commodities like some stationary, some globe and audiovisual products, presswork mark our mainland and Tai Wan in different colors and make out Tai Bei a legend of "National Capital" , moreover, some provinces of China are made as color mark as other country's, and some even print so-called "Republic of China" territory. So the exports of these products have formed a severe political impact on our foreign cause.

In order to further strengthen processing trade management and prevent such sort of event happen again , at the time of handling seriously these problems, the Trade Customs General Administration and News Publish Bureau hereby inform on the relevant items as followed:

1. The foreign economy and trade approval management department in all rank must stick to the correct political direction and stand during the course of checking and approving the processing trade business, and must improve the political acuity and discriminability and reinforce the enterprise education and management. For instance, to make clear that on the product which it produces(including product specification and packing), there strictly prohibit any mark and typeface to obey the Chinese principles.

2. When the processing trade operated units and the processing enterprises are taking on and developing the business, they must abide by our constitution and every related law and rules as well as prohibiting strictly to engage in any disobey our country's regulation referenced, and maintain our country's benefit self-consciously.

3. As for the products like the map products, globe and audiovisual products and others attached with map in a manner of processing trade to produce and export , the enterprises must apply to the national mapping bureau through the provincial mapping departments to get examination and approval, in the meantime, provide the sample to record. While the products like the audiovisual (cassette recorded some contents, tape, disc, player, laser player and visual disk) ,presswork(newspaper, magazine and books) in a manner of processing trade to produce and export , the enterprises must apply to the provincial news publish and administrative organization to get examination and approval, in the meantime, provide the sample to record.

4. When the enterprises apply for developing the processing trade business toward the foreign economy and trade approval management departments, they must defy whether the businesses are map concerned or are belong to the audiovisual products and presswork in the 25th and 26th selective columns of the <<Processing Trade Business Approval Certificate Application>> as followed:

1) The products under the items of the contract do not concern map content and belong to audiovisual product and presswork.

2) The products under the items of the contract do concern map content and have obtained the approval document from the National Mapping Bureau.

3) The products under the items of the contract belong to audiovisual product and presswork and obtained the approval document from the provincial news publish administrative organization.

Give clear indication of the following contents in the 25th column:

Proposer declaration: The products produced and operated and processed by our enterprise accord with national laws and rules.(See Appendix1)

5. As for the processing business of products like the map products, globe and audiovisual products and others attached with map, all-leveled processing trade approval management department must check and approve according to the approval document of the National Mapping Bureau; and examine and approve the processing trade business of the products that

belong to the audiovisual ones and presswork depending on the approval document of provincial news publish bureaus as well as giving a clear indication accordingly in the remark column of <<Processing Trade Business Approval Certificate>>

6. The map content concerned of this contract products under the items of this <<Approval Certificate>> have been approved by the National Mapping Bureau(See Appendix2); or this contract products under the items of this <<Approval Certificate>> belong to the audiovisual ones and presswork which have been approved by the provincial news publish administrative organization(See Appendix 3); The products concern simultaneously the above two situations must be examined and approved on the basis of the above two department approval document. and give a clear indication of relevant content accordingly in the remark column of <<Processing Trade Business Approval Certificate>>(See Appendix 5).

All-leveled processing trade management must further actively intensify the work of checking and approving management together with departments related, and censor strictly, and not grant to exam and approve one and all for the enterprises which do not make clear or declare the above selective items in the 25th and 26th columns of the <<Processing Trade Business Approval Certificate Application>>.

7. The processing trade business conducted by the enterprises of either the map product concerned, globe and other export products attached with map or the products which belong to the audiovisual ones and presswork.
Notice issued by the Foreign Economic and Trading Department of related problems about foreign investment research and developing center
Issued by the economic cooperative branch of the Foreign Economic and Trading Department, April,18th,2000

1. Format and operation scope of foreign investment research and developing center

1) The format of foreign investment research and developing center may be either joint-venture, cooperative and foreign enterprises established by foreign investors (including the investment companies established by foreign firms) as per the law, or the independent departments and branches inner the foreign enterprises.

2) The research and developing center is an institute engaging in the research and development or experiment development(including the middle experiment serving for research and developing activities) in natural science and relevant science and technology fields. The content of which may be basic research, high tech research and social commonweal research, and the subjects of which do not include those items prohibited in<<Foreign investment industry guidance catalog>>. In addition, the center must not engage in other technical trade of which the research and developing technical harvest not belonged to this center and production activities except that of the middle experiment. The center may transfer its research and developing technical harvest and entrust or unite to cooperate with civil science and technology institutions to do. The center does not include training center.

2. Establishment condition of foreign investment research and developing center

1) To possess definite research and developing fields and concrete research and developing projects and fixed sites, apparatus and equipment required in the scientific research and other scientific conditions required, the investment of which for researching and developing should be no less than 20 million dollars.

2) The center must prepare full time management personal and research and developing personal, on the other hand, the percentage of persons engaging in research and developing activities with bachelor degree or above should make up 80% of the total percentage in the

center.

3. Establishment program of foreign investment research and developing center

1) Foreign firms which invest to set up the research and developing center by means of joint-venture, cooperative and independent investment must be checked and approved by provincial examining and approving departments

2) Establishment of research and developing centers inner the foreign enterprises(include investment companies)

A. To establish the research and developing branches or independent departments which must be approved by the examining and approving organs by foreign enterprises according to corresponding popedom, but if they belong to Class A enterprises beyond the limitation, they must be checked and approved by provincial examining and approving departments(or handle as per the following clauses)

B. As for the independent departments inner the foreign enterprises having been established by foreign enterprises, if their operation scope has composed of "research" and "developing" business, they must make a supplementary related data report of independent research and developing departments[see the 3rd item of the clause] as well as record at primary examining and approving organs; if the enterprises do not include the above business, they must modify contracts and rules and be approved by the primary examining and approving organs. The condition of qualification cognizance of recorded and item-added enterprises is the same as the second item.

3. Application report reported to the examining and approving organs must add the following contents:

1) The direction ,domain, main task and implement scheme of research and development

2) The status of the site, personal and related scientific research condition

3) The capital source required by the research and development, concrete usage and amount and corresponding accounting budget report.

4) Import self-used equipment and necessary techniques, fittings and spare part within the investment total sum or self-owned capital as well as the research sample in the course of research and development and chemical reagent bill.

5) Specifications for the progress of research and developing content and the arbitrary of the research and developing fruit.

4. Other related rules

1) The research and developing center established by foreign firms must engage in the relative operation activities according to the law, the investment of which must be used for research and developing activities.

2) The required fee of the center in a way of independent departments or branches must conduct accounting and business accounting independently in annual financial budget in enterprises which set up the center.

3) To limit the investment of Class A foreign enterprises which set up independent departments an branches of the center should not be more than 50% of the enterprise total sum.

4) The research and develop center must report up to the examining and approving organs the status of their last year's progress and operation activities of research and development every year before the date of March,31st.

5) The research and developing center share the favorable policies according to our country's relevant rules.

Appendix

Policies of Foreign investment research and developing center

1. The import of self-used equipment and necessary techniques ,fittings and spare parts within the total sum of investment(exclusive the products stipulated in <<Import product catalog without bestowing exempt tax in foreign investment items>> and shipping , airplane, special type vehicles ,construction machinery, etc. And products just limit in the range of the labs which do not shape production scale or middle experiments can be exempt the import tax and section tax.

2. Technical improvement making use of self-owned capital for importing the self-used equipment and necessary techniques and spare parts and fittings according with the previous conditions within primarily approved operation scope can be exempt the import tax and import section tax depending to <<Notice issued by the General Customs Bureau of import tax policy about further encouraging foreign investment>>[No.791[1999] bureau tax]

3. The transfer income of self- research and developing technology can be exempt business tax.

4. The technical developing expenses which increase above 10% (including 10%) than that of last year may commute 50% of technical actual fee into the required taxpaying sum the same year.

5. Other favorable policies stipulated by our country.

ANNOUNCEMENT ON RELEASING THE CATEGORY OF PRODUCTS (THE FIRST BATCH) WHOSE PROCESS AND ASSEMBLY WITH BROUGHT-IN RAW MATERIALS FROM OVERSEAS ARE ENCOURAGED BY THE CHINESE GOVERNMENT

The Economy and Trade(economy, economy planning) Committees of all the provinces, autonomous regions, directly supervised cities and planning -independent cities, the Foreign Trade and Economy Committee (Bureau) , and all the concerned departments of the State Council and the State Bureau of Industry supervised by the Economy and Trade Committee:

In order to put into practice 'The Announcement Transmitted by the Office of State council on the proposal by the Foreign Trade and Economy Committee , the State Trade and Economy Committee and the Ministry of Financial to encourage enterprises to process and assemble products with brought-in materials from overseas' (Office of State Council, issue No. [1997] 17), the category of products (the First Batch) whose process and assembly with brought-in raw materials from overseas are encouraged by the Chinese government has been worked out on the bases of the proposal of the departments conserved. Now they are issued for you and be sure to implement.

The Category of Products (the First Batch) whose process and assembly with brought-in raw materials from overseas are Encouraged by the Chinese Government

1.Machines

1) Loading machine, fork vehicle, grab, tractor
2) Tape ,transportation machine,smash machine, screening machine, hand gourd, electrical gourd, weight lift, industrial bump,

3)Ordinary machine tool,mechanical compressive machine, measurement machine, tools for measurement, blade tools, grinding machines.
4) Axeletree, tightening pieces, chains, steel wires and rope of steel wires.
5)Automobile,motocycle
6)Electrical meter, water meter, optical devices, camera ,duplicating machine.
7)Devices for storage and facilities for large scale supermarket.

2.Products of Electronics
1) Personal computer, display , printer machine, software.
2) Remote control exchange machine, telephone, graphical fax, satellite TV receiver, sending set for broadcasting and TV program.
3)Laser disc film machine, video cape recorder, radio, tape recorder, color TV, white and black TV.
4)Louder hailer, resistance, electrical receptacle, electrical plate for printing, magnetical head, fluorescence lamp.
5)Systemic engineering

3.Products of light industry
1)Washing machine, refrigerator, air conditioner, microwave oven, electrical fan, dust absorber, electrical iron, electrical cooker.
2)Bike and its components, sewing machine, clock and watch.
3) House-hold kitchen range, lampblack-repelling machine, lighter.

4)Common battery, re-chargeable battery, storage battery, solar energy battery.
5)Compound detergent powder, triple sodium phosphate.
6)Matches.
7)Pencil, fountain pen.
8)Plastic intertexture bag, blown plastic film.
9)Toys.
10)Glass for daily use, porcelain for daily use.¡¡¡
¡
4.Textures
1)Closes.
2)Dying, needle weaving work
3)Machines for texturing.
4)Chemical fibers.

5.Tobacco
1)Cigarette
2)Tobacco filament.
3)Machine for making cigarette

FURTHER DEEPENING OF CHINA'S FOREIGN ECONOMIC AND TRADE SYSTEM REFORM IN 1999

With the advance of china's socialist market economic system reform and the acceleration of the negotiation process for china's entry into the WTO, the reform of china's foreign economic and trade system was deepened further in 1999

Firstly, the reform of foreign economic and trade system was deepened and a new mechanism "Lenient Approval and Strict Control" was established.

1. Promoting the registration system for individual import and export rights. We further broadened the scope of application for the registration system of individual import and export rights and by the end of 1999,we had finished the exercise of the registration of self-operated import and export rights nationwide for either state-owned or collective-owned scientific research in situations, high-

tech enterprises and manufacturing enterprises meeting conditions.

2. Further relaxing the approval criterions of various enterprises and simplifying the approval procedure. Since January, 1999,we had transferred the approval powers in clouding the renaming of import and export enterprises and the supplement of import and export rights, begun to endow individual manufacturing enterprises and scientific research institutions self operated import and export rights, and entrust a large number of enterprises border trade operation power.

3. Reforming the operation system in which some national organizations operated export commodities untidily. Since January, 1999,we relaxed the operation power of cotton yarn, polyester-cotton yarn, cotton Grey cloth and polyester-cotton Grey cloth("two yarn and two cloth in short)

4. Establishing a yearly-check system for credentials of import and export enterprises so that a new mechanism of lenient approval and strict control was established 2n1999,we established a yearly-checking system for credentials of import and export enterprises and enhanced the control of the enterprises which had attained import export operation power.

Secondly, the reform the import and export commodity control system was positively propelled so that the management of import and export commodities was scientific and open.

1. further perfecting the control system of import and export licenses. According to the principles "policy formulating severed from execution, quota administration severed from license signing and issue" and "government's macro policy control function enhanced and micro routine control function weakened", since April1,1999,we have realized the separation of government administration form enterprise management as well as the separation of management and license issue, so that license control system became scientific and normalized. We have also executed united network management for licenses, set up quota license data information feedback system so that the quota utilization ratio was raised.

2. Adjusting the kinds of commodities controlled with export licenses and departments issuing licenses, so the operation was opened further. Since January, 1999the number of commodity controlled with license has decreased from 115to 59,47percent less than before; and we have executed the management of named license issue deportment and named export port so that the normal operation order could be protected .

3. Further perfecting quota distribution mechanism of export commodities and upholding and perfecting quota tender offering. Break the lifelong tenure" in the distribution of export commodity quota develop dynamic management, and favor the enterprises with good export benefit, high export extraualue and powerful economic power. The reform of textile negative quota distribution was a great measure of the reform of foreign economic and trade management system, on the one hand, increase the textile quota distribution proportion of self-operated export manufacturing enterprises, and in 1999,the block proportion already reached to 30percent;on the other hand, we increased tender offering number of textile negative quota from 7in 1998to 21in 1999,since we executed tender offering distribution for quota commodities in 1994,the present number of tender offering commodities has come to 37and the number of bidding enterprises has forereached 4,000

4. Strengthening the reform of import electromechanical products control system and enhancing the unitarily and transparency of import policies. Mainly are as the following: perfect laws and regulations controlling electromechanical product import to minimize the management scope and product description of administration; research and formulate technology standards to manage the import of electromechanical products, and draw close to current international technology standard control pattern from former singly by administrative means; enhance the international bidding and procure of specified electromechanical products.

Thirdly, formulate new policies and enhance drawing foreign investment .

In order to further draw foreign investment, suice the latter part of August, some relevant national departments have published series of new policies encouraging foreign investment in tax, finance, insurance, land-use right and so on. For example ,permit the encouraged class foreign-investment enterprises, foreign-investment research and development centers.

Product exported enterprises and advanced-tech enterprises to import renewed equipment's free of duty beyond the total sum of investment, but enterprises of Class B have no such rights; permit the Chinese-fund commercial banks to endow the foreign-investment enterprises domestic fund circulation with foreign stokers' guarantee; give foreign investors, who invest in energy, transportation and so on emphatically encouraged by the government, insurance service including political risk, performance insurance, guarantee insurance and etc. In order to further the harmonious development of regional economy and promote the development and opening up of middle and western areas, particular stipulations were made in new policies to encourage foreign businessmen to invest in middle are western areas.

Fourthly, readjust the operation order of foreign projects contract and labor service cooperation; deepen the reform of foreign aid pattern and strengthen item control.

In order to normalize the operation order of foreign projects contract and labor service cooperation, we executed level-to-level and class-to -class management for enterprises which mainly operated this kind of business, and positively readjusted operation markets, especially the fisherfolk market towards Taiwan.

We've achieved new progress in developing concessional loan and foreign aid joint and cooperation. Enhance the management of foreign aid items and reformulate and publish over 10regulations in foreign aid management; stick to the principle "fair open and beneficial and enroll good enterprises to undertake foreign aid; entirely introduce and implement the ISO Internet. Quality System Standard in foreign aid projects, practices whole-process control in item quality and the quality of foreign aid projects has been evidently improved.
Fifthly, perfect the macro control and management system in foreign trade, adjust foreign trade mainly by means of tariff, interest rate, exchange rate and policies in accord with current international economic regulations.

1. readjust the tariff rate of import commodities and reduce the general tariff rate level, since january1,1999,the government has dropped the import tariff rate of 1041tax-item commodities, with the tax level drown form 17per cent to 16.23per cent. In order to favor the production development of domestic enterprises and reduce import cost, the government also decided to practice the transient tax rate lower than specified rate for 196tax-item import commodities so that the government's industry management policy could be embodied.

2. The government implemented macro regulation and control for foreign export through tax policies, mainly the readjustment of export drawback rage of some goods. In 1999, in order to enhance the support for export and strengthen the export's promotion for economy, the government raised the export drawback rage of some goods twice. At present, the synthetic drawback rate of export commodities has risen from 12.5percent formerly to 15per cent or so.

Sixthly, separate government administration from enterprise management and transform the operation system of state-owned foreign economic and trade enterprises.

1. In accordance with the Central spirit about that the Central party and government offices should disconnect with the economic unites and enterprises directly subordinate to than the Foreign Economic and Trade Administration has fundamentally finished disconnecting with the

enterprises directly under the department. The separation between government administration and enterprise management is a great measure to adapt to the socialist market economic system, which helps to form a market arrangement of fair competition.

2. Transform the internal operation mechanism. Through reform, reorganization and transformation the state-owned foreign enterprises accelerated transforming the internal operation mechanism and optimizing property composition, fundamentally realized the transition to market principals of self-operation, self-development, self-restriction and responsible for their own profits and losses, formed enterprise groups adapting to international market competition, among which some have become large Trans-industrial Trans-regional and transnational enterprise groups integrating trade, industry, technology, finance and information into one body.

3. The stock system transformation of foreign enterprises. In the way that internal enterprise workers hold stocks was of joint-stock system and going on domestic or over sea stock markets some state-owned foreign enterprises perfected company legal person government system, broadened the funds circulation and enhanced the aftereffect of development. Foreign enterprises nave formed "Foreign Trade Block" original in style in the domestic stock market.

4. Implement closed loans for losing state-owned foreign enterprises. In order to support the commodity export and foreign projects contract of these kinds of enterprises which have order forms, benefits and markets, the people's Bureau jointly issued information that demand local banks giving this kind of enterprises closed loans, fixed sums for fixed purposes, to help the enterprises to reduce losses and increase benefits, and support the reform and development of state-owned foreign enterprises.

Last ,enhance the functions of foreign intermediary organizations with import and export trade unions as an example, give full scope to roles as bridges and ties between the organizations the government and enterprises, and strengthen the construction of foreign-trade information network.

1. Strengthen the construction of social intermediary organizations. Promote the reform of import and export trade unions; further give scope to information service function of research and advisory bodies; set up and perfect intermediary bodies such as law, accountancy and auditing to serve the development and reform of foreign economy and trade.

2. Strengthen the information network construction of foreign economy and trade. The network linking system for import and export license approval has passed the acceptance check and the test run for the customs Bureau computer network-linking has also succeeded, since may1,1999, we have realized the approval management for processing trade with computer system we also built liking computer network of checking and electronic systems for textile export license, primarily established a check and feedback system about import and export commodities the quota practice of

REPLY TO ESTABLISHMENT OF EXPERIMENTAL EXPORT PROCESSING ZONES BY THE GENERAL OFFICE OF THE STATE COUNCIL

(April 27, 2000)

General Administration of Customs:

The "Report on Establishment of Experimental Export Processing Zones" (taxation No. [2000] No. 84) and its Additional Remarks submitted have been received. With the approval of the Leaders of the State council, the Reply is given as follows:

1. In accordance with the fundamental principle on establishment of export processing zones approved by the State council, the under-mentioned zones are approved to set up the first experimental export processing zones: Dalian Export Processing Zone in Liaoning Province, Tianjing Export Processing Zone, Beijing Tianzhu Export Processing Zone, Yantai Export Processing Zone in Shangdong Province, Weihai Export Processing Zone in Shangdong Province, Kunshan Export Processing Zone in Jiangsu Province, Suzhou Industrial Park Export Processing Zone in Jiangsu Province, Shanghai Songjiang Export Processing Zone, Hangzhou Export Processing Zone in zhejiang Province, Xiamen Xinglin Export Processing Zone in Fujian Province, Shenzhen Export Processing Zone in Guangdong Province, Guangzhou Export Processing Zone in Guangdong Province, Wuhan Export Processing Zone in Hubei Province, Chengdu Export Processing Zone in Sichuan Province and Huichun Export Processing Zone in Jilin Province.

2. Establishment of export processing zones must avoid new reconstruction of redundant projects. Area of each export processing zone shall be strictly limit to 2~3 square kilometers. With the economic development in the years to come, the expansion of area shall be approved according to procedures.

3. The newly established processing trade enterprises should be firstly introduced into the export processing zone to progressively carry out integrated and standardized management in accordance with the policy to optimize stock, control increment, standardize management and improve level.

4. Please inform relative local governments to seriously organize the construction of separation facilities and administrations. When it is possible, General Administration of Customs shall conduct acceptance check together with relevant departments.

5. General Administration of Customs shall organize the work of the experimental export processing zones together with relevant departments. And supervision shall be executed in accordance with relative laws and rules to promote the healthy development of processing trade and contribute to expansion of foreign trade.

REPLY TO "INTERIM PROCEDURES OF SUPERVISION ON EXPORT PROCESSING ZONES BY CUSTOMS OF THE PEOPLE'S REPUBLIC OF CHINA" BY THE STATE COUNCIL

(April 27, 2000)

General Administration of Customs:

The State council hereon approves the "Interim Procedures of Supervision on Export Processing Zones by the Customhouse of the People's Republic of China" and that General Administration of Customs shall be responsible of publication and implementation.

Attachment:
Interim Procedures of Supervision on Export Processing Zones by the Customs of the People's

Republic of China
(Approved by the State council on April 27, 2000 and issued by General Administration of Customs on (month) (date), 2000.)

Chapter One General Principles

Article 1
In accordance with the "Customs Law of the People's Republic of China" and other relative Chinese laws, rules and regulations, this Interim Procedures hereby is formulated in order to strengthen and improve administration on processing trade, normalize supervision of customs on export processing zones, promote healthy development of export processing zones and encourage expansion of export trade.

Article 2
To avoid construction of redundant projects, the export processing zones (hereinafter referred to as the Processing Zone) in the People's Republic of China can only be set up in current economic and technological development zones having been approved by the State council. And the government of local provinces (autonomous regions or municipalities directly under the Central Government) shall ask the State council for approval.

Article 3
The Processing Zone is a special area supervised by customhouse. The customhouse shall establish agebcies in the Processing Zone to execute 24-hour supervision on goods transferring in and out and relative places inside the Processing Zone in accordance with the Interim Procedures.

Article 4
Separation facilities and close-circuit television monitoring system meeting the supervision requirements of the customhouse shall be set up between the Processing Zone and other regions of the People's Republic of China (hereinafter referred to as the Outside). Relative businesses inside the Processing Zone can be carried out only after the separation facilities of the Processing Zone have been approved by General Administration of Customs through acceptance check.

Article 5
Processing Zone Administration, export processing enterprises, storage enterprises specially offering services to export processing enterprises and transport enterprises verified by the customhouse specially engaged in transportation of goods in the Processing Zone shall be set up. Except security personnel and persons on duty in the enterprises, no other persons are permitted to live in the Processing Zone. No money-earning facilities for personal consumption are permitted to be set up in the Processing Zone.

Article 6
Retail business, general trade, entrepot trade and other irrelevant businesses are prohibited.

Article 7
Enterprises set up inside the Processing Zone (hereinafter referred to as the Inside Enterprise) should be registered at the customhouse.

Article 8
The Inside Enterprises should establish account books and report forms meeting the requirements of the customhouse in accordance with the "Accounting Law of the People's Republic of China" and other relative Chinese laws, rules and regulations. Book-entry and accounting should be done with legal and effective vouchers to record the storage, conveyance, transfer, sale, process, application and wastage of goods transferring in or out the Processing Zone of the enterprise.

Article 9
Computer networking management system and customs inspecting system shall be carried out in the Processing Zone. The Inside Enterprises should establish computer management databases conforming to the supervisiory requirements of the customhouse and link up with the computer system of the customhouse for electronic data interchange.

Article 10
When the Inside Enterprises do processing trade, they won't carry out machine account system of bank cash deposit for processing trade and the customhouse won't perform management of "Registration Handbook for Processing Trade".

Article 11
The customhouse has right to inspect and check the goods, articles, conveyances, persons in or out and any relevant places in the Processing Zone in accordance with the "Customs Law of the People's Republic of China".

Article 12
The state will not levy VAD on processed products in the Processing Zone.

Article 13
Goods and articles prohibited by the state for import and export are not permitted in or out of the Processing Zone.

Chapter Two Supervision on Goods Transferred Between the Processing Zone and Overseas

Article 14
The owner of goods transferred between the Processing Zone and overseas or his agent should make out a bill for export or import goods to file at the customhouse in accordance with the approval of the Processing Zone Administration Commission.

Article 15
The customhouse shall supervise the goods transferred between the Processing Zone and overseas with methods of straightway type or entrepot transportation.

Article 16
Except that export passive quota administration is executed for export and import goods between the Processing Zone and overseas, import and export quota administration and license management shall not be executed.

Article 17
Unless there are additional stipulations by laws and regulations, the import tariff and import link tariff of goods entering the Process Zone from overseas shall be levied according to following regulations:

1. Taxes on machines, equipment for construction of projects of productive infrastructure or capital construction materials for workhouses and warehouses shall be exempted;

2. Taxes on machines, equipment, models or parts needed by Inside Enterprises for production shall be exempted;

3. Taxes on raw materials, parts, components, packing materials and consumptive materials needed by Inside Enterprises for processing of export products shall be exempted;

4. Taxes on office articles with reasonable amount for the Inside Enterprises and administration authorities shall be exempted;

5. Customs entry on vehicles and consumer goods for the Inside Enterprises and administration authorities shall be handled according to relative regulations on import goods. Taxes shall be levied by the customhouse.

Article 18
Unless there are additional stipulations by laws and regulations, export duties shall be exempted on finished products and leftover bits and pieces, offcuts, defectives and wastes during the process of production of the Inside Enterprises.

Chapter Three Supervision on Goods In/Out between the Processing Zone and the Outside

Article 19
Customs entry for goods carried from the Processing Zone to the outside shall be handled in accordance with relative regulations on import goods of the customhouse. And taxes shall be levied according to finished products. In case the goods are of license management, effective import licenses shall be presented to the customhouse.

Article 20
Processed products and their leftover bits and pieces, offcuts, defectives and wastes during the process of the Inside Enterprises shall be exported over again. In case they should be carried to the Outside under special conditions, the enterprise shall make an application to the customhouse in charge. With approval, taxes on assessment according to use value shall be levied. In case they are license administering goods, effective import licenses shall be presented to the customhouse. In case the leftover bits and pieces, offcuts, defectives and wastes without commercial value need to be carried to the Outside for destroy by melting or burning, formalities for ceasing the Processing Zone shall be handled at the customhouse in charge with the approvals of the Administration Commission and Environmental Protection Bureau. Import license and taxes shall be exempted by the customhouse.

Article 21
The Inside Enterprises are prohibited to entrust the outside enterprises for processing products. In case the technology and process can't meet the requirements of the products and entrustment for certain process to the outside enterprise is needed, it should be approved by the customs head on the premise that the basic shape and quantity of the original products are not changed. The formalities for leaving the Processing Zone shall be handled after a deposit equivalent to the goods has been paid to the customhouse in charge in the Processing Zone by the entrusted enterprise in accordance with the administrative provisions on temporary import goods. The duration of entrustment is 6 months and there should be no delay. After processing is finished, the processed products including defectives and wastes should be transported back to the Processing Zone. Formalities for clearance and cancellation after verification shall be handled at the customhouse in charge with the entrusting application and relative documents.

Article 22
Sales of machines, equipment and models to the Outside from the Inside Enterprises shall be treated according to the current national import policy and relative regulations.

Article 23
With the approval of the customhouse in charge, the Inside Enterprises may conduct test, inspection and demonstration of the products Outside. Formalities on products for test, inspection and demonstration out the Processing Zone shall be handled in accordance with administrative provisions on temporary import goods of the customhouse.

Article 24
In case the machines, equipment, models and office articles used in the Processing Zone need to be repaired, tested or checked Outside, the Inside Enterprises should fill in the "Connection Form for Examination on Goods Carried Outside for Repair" and make application to the customhouse in charge. After being approved, recorded and examined by the customhouse in charge, the machines, equipment, models and office articles can be carried to the Outside for repair, test or check. When the Inside Enterprises carry models to the Outside for repair, test or check, samples of the products manufactured with the models shall be kept for examination and verification on the models carried back to the Processing Zone by the customhouse. Machines, equipment,

models and office article carried to the Outside for repair, test or check can't be used for process and application outside.

Article 25
The machines, equipment, models and office articles carried to the Outside for repair, test or check should be carried back to the Processing Zone within 2 months since day they are carried out. In case they can't be carried back on time because of special conditions, the Inside Enterprise should explain and make application for delay to the customhouse in charge within 7 days before expiration of the duration. There is only one application for delay and the extended period should not exceed 1 month.

Article 26
When the machines, equipment, models and office articles repaired in the Outside are carried back to the Processing Zone, it is impossible for the customhouse to identify whether they are the original or new parts, new fittings or new accessories of the same specifications. In case the parts, fittings or accessories have been changed, the original parts, fitting and accessories should be carried back to the Processing Zone together.

Article 27
Entry of goods into the Processing Zone from the Outside shall be regarded as export. Customs clearing procedure for export shall be handled. Unless there are additional stipulations by laws and regulations, the tax reimbursement for export shall refer to the following regulations:

1. Customhouse clearing procedure for export shall be handled for entry of homemade machines, equipment, raw materials, parts, fittings, components, and packing materials with reasonable quantity for the Inside Enterprises from the Outside, and materials or capital construction of infrastructures, workhouses and office buildings of the processing enterprises and administrative agencies. And the customs declaration for the tax reimbursement for export shall be issued. The outside enterprises shall apply for tax reimbursement for export or free export and handle the formalities at tax authorities with the form for tax reimbursement for export of the customs declaration. The specific administrative provisions on tax reimbursement or exemption shall be issued later by the General Tax Bureau.

2. The customhouse will not issue customs declaration for tax reimbursement for export for consumer goods and vehicles entering into the Process Zone for the Inside Enterprises and administrative authorities from the Outside.

3. The Inside Enterprise shall present documents on imported machines, equipment, raw materials, parts, fittings, components, packing materials and materials for capital construction entering into the Processing Zone from the Outside and handle customs clearing procedures for export. And they will be examined by the customhouse. The paid import link tariff for the above-mentioned goods or articles will not be returned.

4. In case it is necessary to carry some prohibited export commodities or commodities under unified management by the state into the Processing Zone for certain process because the

domestic technique is unable to meet the requirements of the products, it must be submitted to the Ministry of Foreign Trade and Economic Cooperation (MOFTEC) for approval. The customhouse shall supervise it in accordance with the administrative provisions on processing with exported materials. The customs declaration for tax reimbursement for export shall not be issued to these goods carried into the Processing Zone.

Article 28
The goods and articles from the Outside shall be carried to the warehouses or places appointed by the customhouse. And the outside enterprises shall fill in export declaration and handle customs clearing procedures for export at the customhouse in charge with domestic purchase invoices and packing list.

Article 29
Goods from the Outside can be exported only after they have been substantively processed by the Inside Enterprises.

Chapter Four Supervision on Goods in the Processing Zone

Article 30
The Inside Enterprises should accurately declare goods in or out of Processing Zone to the customhouse in charge. The customhouse shall examine the goods, give clearance and cancel after verification with lists on record and relevant documents. Procedures as record, entry, examination, clearance and cancellation after verification for goods in or out of the Processing Zone shall be handled inside.

Article 31
After the concrete name, quantity and amount of the goods in the Processing Zone have been filed at the customhouse by both parties concerned, they can be transferred or shifted between the Inside Enterprises.

Article 32
The processors inside the Processing Zone shall not sell the imported raw materials, parts and fittings to the Outside before they are substantively processed. The Inside Enterprise engaged in warehouses shall not supply raw materials, parts and fittings in the warehouses to the Outside enterprises.

Article 33
Since the day of starting export processing or warehouses business, the Inside Enterprise shall handle procedures for cancellation after verification at the customhouse in charge with the account book and relative vouchers every half-year.

Article 34
In case goods in the Processing Zone are short or destroyed due to force majeure during the period of process or storage, the Inside Enterprises shall report to the customhouse in charge

and explain the reasons within 10 days since the day of discovery. After being verified by the customhouse, they are permitted to be deducted from the account books.

Chapter Five Supervision on Goods Transferred between Processing Zones

Article 35
The receiving party and the delivery party shall jointly make an application for transfer of goods between the Processing Zones to the customhouse in charge in the Processing Zone where the delivery party is in. Procedures shall be handled according to relative regulations on entrepot transportation.

Article 36
When goods are transferred to other Processing Zones, the customhouse in charge in the Processing Zone where the receiving party is in shall check the goods. If the seal is intact and the goods accord with the list, they shall immediately be given clearance by the customhouse to enter the enterprise or warehouse.

Article 37
In case procedures can't be handled for goods transferred between Processing Zones according to regulations on entrepot transportation, the receiving party shall pay deposit equivalent the goods to the customhouse in charge in the Processing Zone where it is in. After the goods have arrived in the destination Processing Zone and been checked by the customhouse in charge, the deposit shall be returned to the receiving party within 10 working days.

Chapter Six Supervision on Vehicles/Personal Effects In/Out of the Processing Zone

Article 38
Vehicles and individuals shall go in or out of the Processing Zone through special channels appointed by the customhouse.

Article 39
Processed products transported to overseas and goods carried to the Outside from the Processing Zone shall be examined by the customhouse. After clearance is given, they shall be ratified by the customhouse and undertaken by special transportation enterprises in the Processing Zone. The following goods can be carried by persons specially assigned or transported by the enterprises themselves after they have been examined by the customhouse:

1. Articles with value of US10,000 and the below;

2. Articles returned to the Outside for exchange due to poor quality;

3. Articles whose taxes have been paid for import;

4. Other articles verified by the customhouses.

Article 40

The principal of the vehicles transporting goods in and out of the Processing Zone shall handle procedures and file at the customhouse with business license for incorporated enterprise and list of names of vehicles, quantity, wagon numbers and names of drivers. All the operators of the transportation enterprises undertaking transportation of goods in/out the Processing Zone and entrepot transportation shall abide by the administrative provisions on vehicles and the goods carried by the customhouse and bear relevant legal responsibilities.

Article 41

Without approval from the customhouse, vehicles and individuals from the Processing Zone to the Outside are prohibited to transport or carry any goods inside the Processing Zone to the Outside.

Chapter Seven Supplementary Articles

Article 42

Goods imported to the Processing Zone and goods exported from the Processing Zone shall be listed in import and export statistics. Goods from the Outside to the Processing Zone and goods from the Processing Zone to the Outside shall be recorded in statistics one by one. The statistical methods shall be worked out by General Administration of Customs later.

Article 43

Persons or units violating the Interim Procedures shall be punished in accordance with relative stipulations of the "Customs Law of the People's Republic of China" and the "Implementing Rules on Administrative Penalty of the Customs Law of the People's Republic of China".

Article 44

The Interim Procedures shall be construed by General Administration of Customs.

Article 45

The Interim Procedures shall come into force on May 1, 2000.

PRACTICAL INFORMATION FOR CONDUCTING BUSINESS[3]

DOING BUSINESS IN CHINA

MARKET OVERVIEW

• China's exceptional economic growth continues as the country further integrateswith the global economy. U.S. companies are benefiting, as evidenced by rapid and sustained increases in U.S. exports to China. Over the past several years, increases of U.S. exports to China averaged well over 20 percent. In 2007, the U.S. exports to China increased by 5.7 percent according to the Census Bureau, helping to make China the fastest growing foreign market for U.S. goods. China-U.S. total trade is USD 354.1 billion, placing China as our second biggest trading partner behind Canada. Although U.S. imports of Chinese goods greatly exceed U.S. exports to China, China is our third largest export market. U.S. exports of goods to China are USD 58.3 billion for the year in 2007.

• China's robust economy had a growth rate of 11.5 percent in 2007, according to Xinhua News Agency. China's inflation surged to 6.9 percent, its highest rate in 11 years for the period January-November 2007. Chinese policy makers will have a tough time in 2008 battling inflation, according to China's Vice Finance Minister Li Yong in January 2008. China's manufacturing base helped the country hit record trade surplus levels of USD 262.2 billion in 2007, according to China's Customs statistics. Foreign investment is strong with China remaining as one of the main destinations for foreign capital investment. The nation's rate of consumer consumption increased by an estimated 16.3 percent for the period January through September 2007, according to a report by the Chinese Academy of Social Sciences (CASS). China's economic miracle is tempered by a number of looming threats, namely a rapidly aging population and a perilously deteriorating environment.

• Despite these remarkable changes, China is still a developing country, albeit one with vast potential. Spread over a population of 1.3 billion, China's colossal economy does not represent a large amount of disposable income for each person. Per capita income in China is around USD 1,700. Yet, surprisingly, China stands as the world's third largest market for luxury goods behind Japan and the United States. The income distribution within the country is highly uneven with urban centers, such as Beijing and Shanghai, enjoying a per capita income of more than double the nation's average. Some studies estimate that Chinese citizens with a per capita income over USD 8,000 to be more than 200 million. That said, China's per capita income figures are poised to change dramatically. Over the next several years, many economists predict a surge in the number of people achieving middle class status. (China has not yet released its Statistics of per capita income in 2007.)

MARKET CHALLENGES

American companies continue to have mixed experiences in China. Many have been extremely profitable, while others have struggled or failed. To be a success in China, American companies must thoroughly investigate the market, take heed of product standards, pre-qualify potential business partners and craft contracts that assure payment and minimize misunderstandings between the parties. The problems of doing business in China can be grouped in four large categories:

[3] This section based in part on materials of the US Department of Commerce

• China often lacks predictability in its business environment. A transparent and consistent body of laws and regulations would make the Chinese market more predictable. However, China's current legal and regulatory system can be opaque, inconsistent, and often arbitrary. Implementation of the law is inconsistent. Lack of effective Chinese government protection of intellectual property rights is a particularly damaging issue for many American companies, both those that operate in China and those that do not, have had their products stolen by Chinese companies.

• China has a government that practices mercantalistic style policies. China has made significant progress toward a market-oriented economy, but parts of its bureaucracy still protect local firms, especially state-owned firms, from imports, while encouraging exports. WTO accession will mitigate these tendencies over time – but progress is only gradual.

• China retains much of the apparatus of a planned economy. A five-year program sets economic goals, strategies, and targets. The State and the Communist Party directly manage the only legal labor union. In many sectors of the Chinese business community, the understanding of free enterprise and competition is incomplete. Certain industrial sectors are prone to over-investment. Excessive investment leads to over production, bad debt and declining prices in affected industries.

• Foreign businesses tend to under-estimate the challenges of market entry in China. Encouraged by a government eager for foreign capital and technology, and entranced by the prospect of 1.3 billion consumers, thousands of foreign firms have charged into the Chinese market. These companies often do not sufficiently investigate the market situation - common pitfalls involve carefully reviewing product standards and conformity assessments, such as China's Compulsory Certification (CCC); fully understanding legal issues, like protecting intellectual property rights; and properly vetting local business partners.

It is important to understand that while continued reform is absolutely essential for China to achieve the economic growth it requires and to fully participate in the world trading community, in many areas, the necessary changes have not yet taken place. Companies must deal with the current environment in a realistic manner. Risk must clearly evaluated. If a company determines that the risk is too great, it should seek other markets.

MARKET OPPORTUNITIES

• The growth of imports from the United States in many key sectors, such as energy, chemicals, machinery, telecommunications, medical equipment, construction, financial services, and franchising suggests that China will remain an important and viable market. If China implements its commitments under the WTO in a thorough and systematic manner, the number of sectors with market potential accessible to American companies will continue to expand dramatically.

MARKET ENTRY STRATEGY

• The U.S. Embassy and the U.S. Department of Commerce welcome contact with American companies to initiate or expand exports into the China market. Two of the primary objectives of U.S. policy with regard to China are (a) growing the American economy by increasing exports thereby reducing the bilateral trade imbalance and (b) ensuring that the Chinese government fully complies with its commitments to the WTO in order to expand our companies' ability to compete on a more level playing field.

• A company should visit China in order to gain a better perspective and understanding of its potential market and location. Especially given China's rapidly changing market and large area, a visit to China can provide a company great insight into the country, the business climate, and its people. Chinese companies respect "face-to-face" meetings, which can demonstrate a U.S.

company's commitment to working in China. Prospective exporters should note that China has many different regions and that each province has unique economic and social characteristics. One should be careful not to generalize about such a large country.

• Continued long-term relationships are key to finding a good partner in China. To maximize its contacts, companies should aim at forming a network of relationships with people at various levels across a broad range of organizations.

• U.S. companies commonly use agents in China to initially create these relationships. Localized agents possess the knowledge and contacts to better promote U.S. products and break down institutional, language, and cultural barriers. The U.S. Commercial Service China offers a wide array of services to assist U.S. companies with U.S. exports in finding Chinese partners. U.S. companies are strongly encouraged to carefully choose potential Chinese partners and take the time to understand their distributors, customers, suppliers, and advisors. For more information on CS programs geared to assisting US companies please see: http://www.buyusa.gov/china/en/howhelpus.html.

• China is a very large country with multiple economic sub-regions. In 2005, the Department of Commerce established fourteen "American Trade Centers," field offices in coordination with the China Council for the Promotion of International Trade (CCPIT). These offices cover the important regional markets in China. They are designed to assist American exporters to identify possible agents, buyers, importers or distributors in these markets through the normal DOC services at standard DOC prices.

INVESTMENT AND BUSINESS CLIMATE - STRATEGIC INFORMATION AND CONTACTS FOR STARTING BUSINESS

China maintains a more restrictive foreign investment regime than its major trading partners, including the United States. While China became the world's top destination for foreign direct investment (FDI) in 2014, according to the United Nations Conference of Trade and Development (UNCTAD), broad sectors of the economy remain closed to foreign investors. China relies on an investment catalogue to encourage foreign investment in some sectors of the economy, while restricting or prohibiting it in many other industries. China's investment approval regime appears designed to foster economic growth but may also shield inefficient or monopolistic Chinese enterprises from competition, particularly those China is trying to cultivate as market leaders. Foreign investors cite rising costs, difficulty in finding qualified human resources, market access limitations, and unclear and inconsistent enforcement of laws and regulations as significant challenges to establishing and operating businesses in China. More than half of the U.S. companies surveyed by AmCham China in 2014 believe foreign businesses are less welcome in China than before.

Over the past year, the Chinese central government announced a series of reforms and pledges that could lead to limited improvements in the overall investment climate, both from a market access and a regulatory standpoint if they were implemented. Major developments in 2014 include:

China and the United States worked to narrow differences and reach agreement on the text of a high standard Bilateral Investment Treaty (BIT) that would encourage fairness, openness, and transparency. Both sides committed in November 2014 to continue to pursue the BIT as a top priority in their economic relations and to initiate negotiations over the "negative list" of exceptions to the agreement in early 2015.

The Ministry of Commerce (MOFCOM) released a new draft Foreign Investment Law that would supersede the laws currently governing China's FDI regime. The draft law appears to incorporate some key principles from the U.S. model BIT, including the use of a negative list to enumerate instances where FDI is treated less favorably than domestic investment. The draft would also streamline the approval process for foreign investment in some sectors; however, the proposed law also contains a number of troubling new provisions that could facilitate discriminatory treatment of foreign investors and their investments. The draft law was released for public comment in January 2015.

In December, Premier Li Keqiang announced the establishment of three new Free Trade Zones (FTZs) in Tianjin, Guangdong and Fujian. The FTZs are expected to expand an investment registration regime established in the Shanghai FTZ, which is simpler than the approval process required throughout most of China, and open some previously closed sectors to foreign investment.

Although the Chinese Communist Party says it expects to "fulfill" its Third Plenum market-oriented economic reform agenda by 2020, a detailed reform roadmap and timetable is lacking for many sectors. Foreign investors remain concerned about discriminatory industrial policies, opaque and selectively enforced investment approval procedures, licensing barriers that favor domestic firms, and a lack of effective administrative and legal recourse if investments are restricted. Meanwhile, China's revised Foreign Investment Catalogue, released in March 2015, fell short of meaningful progress toward broader market access for foreign investors. Poor enforcement of intellectual property rights (IPR), the forced transfer of technology, and systemic lack of rule of law are additional concerns. Over the past year, China released new policies to exclude foreign technology from various sectors, including: proposed banking sector guidelines that could disrupt supply chains and increase firms' operating costs, a draft counter-terrorism law which imposes onerous requirements on foreign technology firms, and an intrusive national security mechanism that could be used to hinder or even block foreign investment.

The United States government has raised concerns about China's investment restrictions and discriminatory policies at high levels, in bilateral fora such as the U.S.-China Joint Commission on Commerce and Trade (JCCT), and the U.S.-China Strategic and Economic Dialogue (S&ED). The United States Government emphasizes the need for China to open new sectors to foreign investment, increase transparency, and improve the enforcement of existing laws to protect investors' rights.

1. OPENNESS TO, AND RESTRICTIONS UPON, FOREIGN INVESTMENT

Attitude toward Foreign Direct Investment

The Chinese government has stated that it welcomes foreign investment. China attracted USD 120 billion in FDI in 2014, surpassing the United States as the world's top destination for annual FDI flows for the first time since 2003. China's sustained high economic growth rate and the expansion of its domestic market help explain its attractiveness as an FDI destination. However, foreign investors often temper their optimism regarding potential investment returns with uncertainty about China's willingness to offer a level playing field vis-à-vis domestic competitors. In addition, foreign investors report a range of challenges related to China's current investment climate. These include industrial policies that protect and promote state-owned and other domestic firms, equity caps and other restrictions on foreign ownership in many industries, weak IPR rights protection, a lack of transparency, corruption, and an unreliable legal system.

The American Chamber of Commerce in China's 2014 American Business in China White Paper can be found here:**http://www.amchamchina.org/whitepaper**

Other Investment Policy Reviews

Organization for Economic Cooperation and Development (OECD)

China is not a member of the OECD. The OECD Council decided to establish a country program of dialogue and co-operation with China in October 1995. The most recent OECD Investment Policy Review for China was completed in 2008. The OECD Investment Policy Review noted that the policy changes in China between 2006-2008 tightened restrictions on inward direct investment, including cross-border mergers and acquisitions.

The report can be found at:**http://www.oecd.org/investment/investmentfordevelopment/oecdinvestmentpolicyreviews-china2008encouragingresponsiblebusinessconduct.htm**

World Trade Organization (WTO)

China became a member of the World Trade Organization (WTO) in 2001. WTO membership boosted China's economic growth and advanced its legal and governmental reforms. The most recent WTO Investment Policy Review for China was completed in 2012. The report states that there were few changes to China's policies on inward foreign investment in the period under review (2010-2011).

The report can be found at:**http://www.wto.org/english/tratop_e/tpr_e/tp364_e.htm**

IMF information can be found at:**http://www.imf.org/external/country/Chn/**

FDI Statistics from MOFCOM can be found at:**http://www.fdi.gov.cn/1800000121_10000177_8.html**

Laws/Regulations of Foreign Direct Investment

Overview

China has a legal and regulatory framework that provides the government with discretion to promote investment in specific regions or industries it wishes to develop, and to restrict foreign investment deemed not to be in its national interest or that would compete with state-sanctioned monopolies or other favored domestic firms. Foreign investors report that many regulations contain undefined key terms and standards, and that regulations are often applied in an inconsistent manner by different regulatory entities and localities. Potential investment restrictions in China are thus much broader than those of many developed countries, including the United States.

The Constitution of the People's Republic of China was adopted by the 5th National People's Congress on December 4, 1982, with several revisions through 2004. China's accession to the WTO spurred significant transformations in various areas of Chinese domestic law. The current Chinese leadership has emphasized the need to strengthen the rule of law in China. Nonetheless, foreign investors have expressed concern that the legal system allows regulators significant discretion to adapt decisions to changing circumstances, which results in an unpredictable business climate and rulings that can appear arbitrary or discriminatory. Generally, unlike the United States, the legal system is designed to serve state and Communist Party interests, and as such, does not consistently protect individual rights or effectively resolve disputes. The current system is still being developed as a venue to address investment and commercial disputes.

FDI Laws

Article 18 of the Constitution states that China permits foreign enterprises and other economic organizations or individuals to invest in China. The issuance of the China-Foreign Equity Joint Venture Enterprise Law in 1979 marked the beginning of the establishment of China's foreign investment legal regime. Since then, China has established a foreign investment legal regime based on three central laws. These are: the China-Foreign Equity Joint Venture Enterprise Law, the China-Foreign Cooperative Joint Venture Enterprise Law, and the Foreign-Invested Enterprise Law.

Administrative regulations and regulatory documents governing FDI issued by the State Council include, but are not limited to:

the Implementation Regulations of the China-Foreign Equity Joint Venture Enterprises Law

the Implementation Regulations of the China-Foreign Cooperative Joint Venture Enterprise Law

the Implementation Regulations of the Foreign-Invested Enterprise Law

the State Council Provisions on Encouraging Foreign Investment

the Provisions on Guiding the Direction of Foreign Investment

the Administrative Provisions on Foreign Investment to Telecom Enterprises

There are over 1,000 rules and regulatory documents related to foreign investment in China issued by government ministries. They include, but are not limited to:

the Guiding Catalogue of Foreign Investment Industries

the Provisions on Mergers & Acquisition of Domestic Enterprises by Foreign Investors

the Administrative Provisions on Foreign Investment in Road Transportation Industry

the Interim Provisions on Foreign Investment in Cinemas

the Administrative Measures on Foreign Investment in Commercial Areas

the Administrative Measures on Ratification of Foreign Invested Projects

the Administrative Measures on Foreign Investment in Distribution Enterprises of Books, Newspapers and Periodicals

the Provision on the Establishment of Investment Companies by Foreign Investors

the Administrative Measures on Strategic Investment in Listed Companies by Foreign Investors

In addition, local legislatures and governments also enact their own regulations and rules to regulate foreign investments in their areas, in accordance with national laws and policies; for example, Wuhan's Administration Regulation on Foreign-Invested Enterprises and Shanghai's Municipal Administration Measures on the Land Usage of Foreign-Invested Enterprises.

Under this foreign investment legal regime, China approves foreign investments on a case-by-case basis following review by multiple government agencies. China claims to provide national treatment after an investment has been established, but not before. Foreign investors may only invest where allowed by laws, regulations, and rules, in specified areas or industries, and are required to obtain ratification for planned investment projects and to establish companies. In some industries, such as the telecommunication industry, foreign investors are also required to obtain approval from relevant industry regulators. Separate approval processes govern land use and other administrative areas. Reviews may overlap, resulting in potentially redundant examinations. Low transparency limits the predictability of outcomes.

A list of Chinese laws and regulations, central and local can be found here:**http://www.gov.cn/zhengce/**

FDI Reform Announcements

In November 2013, following the Third Plenum of the 18th Party Congress, the Chinese Communist Party issued a report which is described by the Chinese leadership as one of the largest and most ambitious economic reform programs since Deng Xiaoping's pioneering market-oriented reforms in 1978. Among other things, the report directs China to broaden foreign investment access in China, to explore the possibility of a model for allowing foreign investment that would provide national treatment at all phases of investment, including market access (i.e., the "pre-establishment" phase of investment), and employ a "negative list" approach in identifying exceptions (meaning that all investments are permitted except for those explicitly excluded), and to set up more free trade zones like the newly established and still evolving Shanghai Pilot Free Trade Zone. The report also stated China intends to unify laws and regulations governing foreign and domestic investment. The United States is encouraged by these broad policy pronouncements and will closely monitor China's implementation measures to determine how and to what extent China follows through on them.

The English version of the Third Plenum decision can be found here:**http://www.china.org.cn/china/third_plenary_session/2013-11/16/content_30620736.htm**

In January 2015, China's Ministry of Commerce (MOFCOM) issued a new draft Foreign Investment Law for public comment. When enacted, the law will unify and supersede the three laws governing foreign-invested enterprises (FIEs): the China-Foreign Equity Joint Venture Enterprise Law, the Foreign-Invested Enterprise Law and the China-Foreign Cooperative Joint Venture Enterprise Law. The draft Foreign Investment Law would abolish the case-by-case approach to regulating foreign investment and adopt a system that would treat FDI the same as domestic investment, apart from exceptions to this "national treatment" that would be detailed on a "negative list." Nevertheless, the draft law retains a distinction between foreign and domestic investment, which could invite opportunities for discriminatory treatment of foreign investors and their investments.

Industrial Promotion

Five-Year Plan

China defines its broad economic goals through five-year macro-economic plans. The most significant of these for foreign investors is China's Five-Year Plan (FYP) on Foreign Capital Utilization. The 12th FYP for Utilization of Overseas Capital and Investment Abroad, issued by the National Development and Reform Commission (NDRC) in 2012, promises to guide more foreign direct investment (FDI) to an identified set of strategic and newly emerging industries (SEIs), namely energy efficiency and environmental technologies, next generation information technology, biotechnology, advanced equipment manufacturing, new energy sector, new materials, and new-energy vehicles, while "strictly" limiting FDI in energy and resource-intensive and environmentally damaging industries; encourage foreign multinationals to set up regional headquarters and research and development (R&D) centers in China; encourage foreign investment in production services such as modern logistics, software development, engineering design, vocational skill training, information consulting, technology, and intellectual property services; "steadily open up" banking, securities, insurance, telecom, fuel, and logistics industries; "gradually open up" education and sports; guide foreign capital to enter healthcare, culture, tourism, and home services; and encourage foreign capital to enter creative design. The 13th FYP is expected in 2017.

Innovation

A major goal of China's investment policies, stated in the 12th FYP, is to encourage the domestic development of technological innovation and know-how. Investment projects that involve the transfer of technology or the potential for "indigenous innovation" tend to be favorably received by China's investment authorities. China seeks to promote investment in higher value-added sectors, including high technology research and development, advanced manufacturing, clean energy technology, and select modern services sectors. Foreign investors often must weigh the potential value of accessing China's market against China's inability or unwillingness to protect their intellectual property.

Regional growth

China also seeks to spread the benefits of foreign investment beyond its relatively wealthy coastal areas by encouraging foreign companies to establish regional headquarters and operations in Central, Western, and Northeastern China. China publishes and regularly revises a Catalogue of Priority Industries for Foreign Investment in the Central-Western Regions, which outlines incentives to attract investment in targeted sectors to those parts of China.

The Catalogue of Priority Industries for Foreign Investment in the Central-Western Regions can be found here:**http://www.ndrc.gov.cn/zcfb/zcfbl/201305/W020130516388520815145.pdf**

Limits on Foreign Control

Catalogue for the Guidance of Foreign Investment in Industries

China outlines its specific foreign investment objectives primarily through its Catalogue for the Guidance of Foreign Investment in Industries, most recently revised in March 2015, and maintained by MOFCOM and the National Development and Reform Commission (NDRC). The catalogue delineates sectors of the economy where foreign investment is "encouraged," "restricted," and "prohibited." Investment in sectors not listed in the catalogue is considered permitted. China "encourages" investment in sectors where it believes it will benefit from foreign assistance or technology. Investment is "restricted" and "prohibited" in sectors that China deems sensitive, that touch on national security, or which do not meet the goals of China's economic development plans.

The 2015 edition of the Catalogue lifts foreign investment restrictions on foreign investment in several areas, including in the manufacturing sector, but makes limited progress in services, agriculture, and infrastructure. According to the NDRC, the Catalogue reduces the number of restricted industries from 79 to 38, with direct sales and insurance brokerage companies among the beneficiaries, and limits the number of sectors for which Chinese-controlled joint ventures are required from 44 to 35. Moreover, the new Catalogue reduces the number of industries requiring joint ventures with Chinese partners, but allowing foreign control, from 43 to 15, including in real estate development. The overall reforms to the Catalogue may improve market access in some sectors but the Catalogue also reduces access in others. In general, foreign investment restrictions remain largely unaltered in industries that traditionally face heavy restrictions, such as banking, telecommunications, and cultural industries. On the positive side, the new Catalogue exempts the e-commerce industry from the 50 percent equity cap for foreign investment in value-added telecom services.

The Chinese version of the 2015 Foreign Investment Catalogue can be found here:**http://www.mofcom.gov.cn/article/b/f/201503/20150300911747.shtml**

Problems with the Catalogue

The catalogue reflects China's market access restrictions. Contradictions between the catalogue and other measures have confused investors and added to the perception that investment guidelines do not provide a secure basis for business planning. Even in "encouraged" and "permitted" sectors, regulations apart from the catalogue often detail additional restrictions on the specific forms of investment that are allowed. Chinese regulators have maintained the flexibility to ignore the catalogue's guidance in some instances, and to restrict or approve foreign investment for reasons other than those specified. The government may also adopt new regulations or establish industrial policies that supersede the most recently published edition of the catalogue. Uncertainty as to which industries are being promoted and how long such designations will be valid undermines confidence in the stability and predictability of the investment climate.

Equity Caps

In addition to dividing industries into "encouraged," "restricted," and "prohibited" categories, the catalogue may also require that investment take certain forms (such as a domestic-foreign equity joint venture) and/or that the foreign shareholder's proportion of investment in the enterprise be limited to a minority share. Agency-specific regulations may also require that investment take certain forms.

For example:

In the oil and natural gas exploration and development industry, foreign investment is required to take the form of equity joint ventures and cooperative joint ventures.

In the accounting and auditing sectors, the Chief Partner of a firm must be a Chinese national.

In higher education and pre-school, foreign investment is only permitted in the form of cooperative joint ventures led by a Chinese partner.

In some sectors, the Chinese partners individually or as a group maintain control of the enterprise; for example, construction and operation of civilian airports, construction and operation of nuclear power plants, establishment and operation of cinemas, and the design and manufacture of civil-use satellites.

In some sectors, the foreign shareholder's proportion of the investment may not exceed a certain percentage. For example, foreign stakes are limited to:

50% in value-added telecom services (excepting e-commerce)

49% in basic telecom enterprises

50% in life insurance firms

49% in security investment fund management companies

Mandatory Intellectual Property (IP)/technology transfer requirements

Mandatory joint venture structures and equity caps give Chinese partner firms significant control, often allowing them to benefit from technology transfer. In addition, the relative opacity of the approval process and the broad discretion granted to the authorities foster an environment where government authorities can impose deal-specific conditions beyond written legal requirements, often with the intent to force technology transfer as a condition of market access or to support industrial policies and the interests of local competitors.

Privatization Program

Early indications following China's November 2013 Third Plenum reform pronouncements suggest China will attempt to sell shares in state-owned enterprises (SOEs) to outside investors, improve SOE management structures, emphasize the importance of SOEs meeting financial goals, and take steps to bring private capital into some sectors traditionally monopolized by SOEs, such as energy, telecoms, and finance. Practically, the government must still work out how to implement its SOE reform vision, but a 2014 move to restructure a major state-owned conglomerate, Citic Group, by listing its assets in Hong Kong, where it will be subject to greater transparency rules and heightened regulatory scrutiny, suggests a possible mechanism to improve SOE corporate governance and transparency. The government also committed at the Third Plenum to raise the portion of earnings that SOEs pay out as dividends to the public budget, although here, too, the pace and method of implementation remains uncertain.

Screening of FDI

Overview

As mentioned, foreign investors are required to obtain approvals for their investment projects and to establish an enterprise. In some industries, such as telecommunications, foreign investors are also required to get approval from industry regulators.

Catalogue of Investment Projects Subject to Government Ratification

In July 2004, the State Council issued its Decision on Investment Regime Reform and the Catalogue of Investment Projects subject to Government Ratification (Ratification Catalogue). According to the Ratification Catalogue, all proposed foreign investment projects in China must be submitted for "review and ratification" by the National Development and Reform Commission (NDRC) or provincial or local Development and Reform Commissions, depending on the sector and value of the investment. In 2013, however, the government issued a new catalogue narrowing the scope of foreign investment projects subject to NDRC ratification. Foreign investment which does not require Chinese control according to the Foreign Investment

Catalogue and which is not listed in the Ratification Catalogue requires only "filing for record" with the local NDRC office. The policy shift marked a positive step toward easing bureaucratic barriers to foreign investment.

In November 2014, China released a new edition of the Ratification Catalogue, which eliminates the requirement for NDRC ratification in 15 sectors (out of approximately 50) and delegates ratification authority to local governments in another 23 sectors. The new Ratification Catalogue also raises the threshold of foreign ownership that would trigger the requirement for NDRC approval, as opposed to registration, in several sectors. When announcing the reforms, the NDRC stated the goal of the latest revision to the Ratification Catalogue is to limit ratification to projects relating to "national and ecological security, geographic and resource development," and the "public interest." The NDRC estimated the number of projects requiring ratification from central government authorities would fall by 76 percent following revisions made over the past several years.

The NDRC's approval process for foreign investment projects includes assessing the project's compliance with China's laws and regulations; its compliance with the Foreign Investment Catalogue and industrial policy; its national security, environmental safety, and public interest implications; its use of resources and energy; and its economic development ramifications. In some cases, NDRC also solicits the opinions of relevant Chinese industrial regulators and "consulting agencies," which may include industry associations that represent domestic firms. This can create conflicts of interest that disadvantage foreign investors. The State Council may also weigh in for high-value projects in "restricted" sectors.

The Catalogue of Investment Projects subject to Government Ratification can be found here:**http://www.gov.cn/zhengce/content/2014-11/18/content_9219.htm**

Approvals

Based on the three foreign investment laws, once NDRC approves the foreign investment project, foreign investors must apply to the Ministry of Commerce (MOFCOM) for approval to legally establish a company. Next, foreign investors apply for a business license from the State Administration of Industry and Commerce (SAIC), which allows the firm to operate. Once a license is obtained, the investor registers with China's tax and foreign exchange agencies. Greenfield investment projects must also seek approval from China's Environmental Protection Ministry and its Ministry of Land Resources. The actual implementation of China's foreign investment approvals process may vary in specific cases, depending on the details of a particular investment proposal and local rules and practices.

The U.S. Chamber of Commerce's report on China's Approval Process for Inbound Foreign Direct Investment can be found here: **http://www.uschamber.com/sites/default/files/reports/020021_China_InvestmentPaper_hires.pdf**

Draft Foreign Investment Law

As mentioned, the Ministry of Commerce (MOFCOM) in January 2015 proposed a new Foreign Investment Law, which reflects key principles from the U.S. model BIT, including the use of a negative list to enumerate instances where FDI is treated differently than domestic investment. The draft would also streamline the approval process for foreign investment in some sectors but contains a number of troubling provisions that could facilitate discriminatory treatment of foreign investment. The draft law was released for public comment in January 2015.

Anti-monopoly Review and National Security Review

MOFCOM conducts anti-monopoly and/or national security reviews of proposed mergers or acquisitions of domestic enterprises by foreign investors. The anti-monopoly review is detailed in the section below, on competition policy. Article 31 of China's Anti-monopoly Law also notes that if a merger or acquisition of a domestic enterprise by a foreign investor poses national security concerns, a separate national security review is also required. MOFCOM's Rules on Mergers and Acquisitions of Domestic Enterprises by Foreign Investment Article 12 stipulates that parties are required to report transaction to MOFCOM if:

foreign investors obtain actual control, via merger or acquisition, of a domestic enterprise in a key industry;

the merger or acquisition affects or may affect national economic security;

the merger or acquisition would cause the transfer of actual control of a domestic enterprise with a famous trademark or a Chinese time-honored brand.

If MOFCOM determines that the parties did not report a merger or acquisition that affects or could affect national economic security, MOFCOM, together with other government agencies, may require the parties to terminate the transaction or adopt other measures to eliminate the impact on national economic security.

In February 2011, China released the State Council Notice Regarding the Establishment of a Security Review Mechanism for Foreign Investors Acquiring Domestic Enterprises. The notice established an interagency Joint Conference, led by NDRC and MOFCOM, with the authority to block foreign mergers and acquisitions of domestic firms that it believes may impact national security. The Joint Conference is instructed to consider not just national security but also national economic security and "social order" when reviewing transactions. China has not disclosed any instances in which it invoked this formal review mechanism. Lack of information about China's national security review process reflects the breadth of China's national security concerns, which extend to mechanics of regulatory decisions that are more transparent in the United States and most other developed markets.

Local commerce departments are responsible for flagging transactions that require a national security review when they review them in an earlier stage of China's foreign investment approval process. Some provincial and municipal departments of commerce previously posted on the Internet a Security Review Industry Table listing non-defense industries where transactions may trigger a national security review but MOFCOM has declined to confirm whether these lists reflect official policy. In addition, third parties such as other governmental agencies, industry associations, and companies in the same industry can seek MOFCOM's review of transactions, which can pose conflicts of interest that disadvantage foreign investors. Investors may also voluntarily file for a national security review.

In addition to transforming the current foreign investment regime, the aforementioned MOFCOM draft Foreign Investment Law would also establish a broad and potentially intrusive national security review mechanism. As it is currently envisaged, the national security review could be used to hinder market access and increase the financial burden of foreign investment in China.

Competition Law

Competition Policy, Laws, and Regulations

China has many laws and regulations that concentrate production in certain sectors into monopolies, near-monopolies, or authorized oligopolies. These measures are focused in capital intensive sectors, like electricity and transportation, or in industries such as fixed-line telephony and postal services, in which this approach may be used to ensure national coverage. The measures also target sectors which the government deems vital to national security and economic stability, including defense, energy, and banking. Examples of such laws and regulations include the Law on Electricity (1996), Civil Aviation Law (1995), Regulations on Telecommunication (2000), Postal Law (1986), Railroad Law (1991), and Commercial Bank Law (amended in 2003), among others.

Anti-monopoly Law

China's Anti-monopoly Law (AML) took effect in August 2008 and established an anti-monopoly commission with oversight and coordinating responsibilities. Three agencies share enforcement responsibilities: MOFCOM reviews mergers; NDRC reviews cartel agreements to fix prices, abuse of dominance, and abuse of administrative power involving pricing; and SAIC reviews these same types of activities when they are not directly price-related. After the AML was enacted, MOFCOM, NDRC, SAIC, and other Chinese government ministries and agencies began to formulate implementing regulations, departmental rules, and other measures. Generally, these ministries and agencies have been willing to seek public comment on their proposed measures.

Enforcement

China's enforcement of laws and regulations related to monopolies is uneven. Inconsistent local and provincial enforcement may be exacerbated by local protectionism. Government authorities at all levels in China may also restrict competition with favored firms through various forms of regulation. Official statements frequently suggest these efforts are tied primarily to employment concerns. However, the ultimate beneficiaries of the resulting measures are often unclear. In addition, local governments frequently enact rules that restrict inter-provincial trade, which may also restrict market access for certain imported products, raise production costs, and limit market opportunities for foreign-invested enterprises.

Since the AML went into effect, MOFCOM's oversight of mergers has yielded the most enforcement activity, largely due to the requirement to pre-notify merger transactions. Under the AML, through the end of 2014, China has "unconditionally" approved 961 merger cases and "conditionally" approved 25, according to Chinese statistics. Twenty-one of the 25 cases approved with conditions have involved offshore transactions between foreign parties. The other four transactions involved foreign companies merging with Chinese enterprises. Observers have expressed concern over the speed and inconsistent review process. MOFCOM's March 2014 Provisional Rules on the Applicable Criteria of Streamlined Cases Regarding Concentrations of Undertakings established a procedure for accelerated review.

The NDRC, China's former economic planning agency, enforces the AML's price provisions and launched high-profile investigations of foreign companies in 2014. The majority of cases the NDRC investigated address "horizontal" agreements to set prices or divide the market – a practice that is always illegal in the United States. The smaller number of NDRC investigations into "vertical" price agreements between suppliers and customers and abuse of dominance caused controversy. Seventy-eight percent of NDRC's investigations into "vertical" cases involve foreign firms. There is significant uncertainty about the rules that govern NDRC investigations, which contributes to an impression that they are subject to influence politically and by competitors. In some cases, proposed remedies appear designed not to restore competition, but to compel firms to lower prices regardless of the competitive dynamics of China's market. In

2014, the NDRC reportedly pressured companies it investigated to "cooperate" in the face of unspecified allegations or face steep fines.

At the same time, the NDRC made progress towards greater transparency by releasing aggregate data on investigations and beginning to publicize case decisions. MOFCOM stated it will enforce compliance by Chinese firms with requirements to file notifications for review of proposed mergers and acquisitions. During the U.S-China Joint Commission on Commerce and Trade in December, China's three AML enforcement agencies committed to provide to any party under investigation information about the regulators' competition concerns with the conduct or transaction, treat all business operators equally when enforcing the AML, and allow domestic and foreign legal counsel into AML investigation meetings.

It remains unclear how China will implement the AML with respect to SOEs and government monopolies in industries deemed nationally important. While introductory language in the law says the AML protects the lawful operations of SOEs and government monopolies in industries deemed nationally important, the three AML enforcement agencies have publicly stated that the law applies to SOEs, and have pursued some enforcement actions against them. But concerns remain that enforcement against SOEs will remain limited, especially given China's proactive orchestration of mergers in rail and other strategic sectors that may limit competition and raise prices within China while potentially increasing the competitiveness of Chinese firms in overseas markets.

On the positive side, Anti-monopoly Law provisions restricting regulators from abusing administrative monopolies, which also appear in NDRC's and SAIC's implementing regulations, could help promote the establishment and maintenance of increasingly competitive markets in China if they are enforced. In addition, China amended its Administrative Procedure Law in 2014 to allow private parties to sue government regulators for restricting competition through abuse of administrative power.

Additional Laws Related to Foreign Investment

China's State Secrets Law gives the government broad authority to classify information as a "state secret," creating uncertainty and potential risk for investors negotiating with SOEs or operating in sensitive sectors. The Contract Law encourages contractual compliance by providing legal recourse for a breach of contract, although enforcement of judgments continues to be a problem. Additional investment-related laws include, but are not limited to: the Administrative Permissions Law; the Arbitration Law; the Corporate Income Tax Law; the Enterprise Bankruptcy Law; the Foreign Trade Law; the Government Procurement Law; the Insurance Law; the Labor Contract Law; the Law on Import and Export of Goods; and the Securities Law.

Investment Trends

U.S. – China Bilateral Investment Treaty

The United States resumed negotiations of a bilateral investment treaty (BIT) with China in October 2012. At the 2014 U.S.-China Strategic and Economic Dialogue, China agreed to narrow differences and to reach agreement on core issues and major articles of the treaty text with the United States by the end of 2014, and commit to initiate the "negative list" negotiation early in 2015 based on each other's "negative list" offers. President Obama and President Xi publically highlighted the importance of reaching a U.S.-China Bilateral Investment Treaty (BIT) during President Obama's state visit to Beijing in November 2014 and committed to dedicate all necessary resources to the negotiations.

Table 1

Measure	Year	Index or Rank	Website Address
TI Corruption Perceptions index	2014	100 of 175	transparency.org/cpi2014/results
World Bank's Doing Business Report "Ease of Doing Business"	2015	90 of 189	doingbusiness.org/rankings
Global Innovation Index	2014	29 of 143	globalinnovationindex.org/content.aspx?page=data-analysis
World Bank GNI per capita	2013	USD 6,560	data.worldbank.org/indicator/NY.GNP.PCAP.CD

2. CONVERSION AND TRANSFER POLICIES

Foreign Exchange

Foreign-invested enterprises in China do not need pre-approval to open foreign exchange accounts and are allowed to retain income as foreign exchange or convert it into renminbi without quota requirements. Foreign exchange transactions on China's capital account no longer require a case-by-case review by the State Administration of Foreign Exchange (SAFE). Instead, designated foreign exchange banks review and directly conduct foreign exchange settlements. The Chinese government registers all commercial foreign debt and limits foreign firms' accumulated medium- and long-term debt from abroad to the difference between total investment and registered capital. However, China has been gradually liberalizing foreign exchange controls, and in April 2014, announced new rules (the Regulations on Forex Capital Pooling Operations and Management of Multinational Companies) that provide greater flexibility in transferring foreign currency for large domestic and foreign multinational firms. Foreign firms must report their foreign exchange balance once per year. In April 15, SAFE announced a further loosening of capital controls for foreign-funded firms, which are now allowed to convert up to 100% of their registered foreign-currency capital into renminbi based on business needs.

Remittance Policies

The following operations do not require SAFE approval: purchase and remittance of foreign exchange as a result of capital reduction, liquidation, or early repatriation of an investment in a foreign-owned enterprise, or as a result of the transfer of equity in a foreign-invested enterprise to a Chinese domestic entity or individual where lawful income derived in China is reinvested.

This would include profit, proceeds of equity transfer, capital reduction, liquidation, and early repatriation of investment.

3. EXPROPRIATION AND COMPENSATION

Chinese law prohibits nationalization of foreign-invested enterprises except under "special" circumstances. Chinese officials have said these circumstances include national security and obstacles to large civil engineering projects, but the law does not define the term. Chinese law requires compensation of expropriated foreign investments, but does not describe the formula to be used in calculating the amount. The Department of State is not aware of any cases since 1979 in which China has expropriated a U.S. investment, although the Department has notified Congress of several cases of concern.

4. DISPUTE SETTLEMENT

Legal System, Specialized Courts, Judicial Independence, Judgments of Foreign Courts

Chinese officials typically urge firms to resolve disputes through informal conciliation. If formal mediation is necessary, Chinese parties and the authorities typically promote arbitration over litigation. Many contracts prescribe arbitration by the China International Economic and Trade Arbitration Commission (CIETAC). CIETAC, established by the State Council in 1956 under the auspices of the China Council for the Promotion of International Trade (CCPIT), is China's most widely-utilized arbitral body for foreign-related disputes. Some foreign parties have obtained favorable rulings from CIETAC, while others question CIETAC's procedures and effectiveness. Other arbitration commissions exist and are usually affiliated with the government at the provincial or municipal level. The Beijing Arbitration Commission and the Shanghai Arbitration Commission have emerged as serious domestic competitors to CIETAC. For contracts involving at least one foreign party, offshore arbitration may be adopted. Arbitration awards are not always enforced by Chinese local courts. Investors may appeal to higher courts in such cases.

CIETAC is based in Beijing and has four sub-commissions (Shanghai, Shenzhen, Tianjin, and Chongqing). In 2012, CCPIT, under the authority of the State Council, issued new arbitration rules that granted CIETAC headquarters significantly more authority to hear cases rather than its vis-à-vis its sub-commissions. Expecting a loss in revenue, CIETAC Shanghai and CIETAC Shenzhen declared their independence, issued their own rules, and changed their names. As a result, CIETAC disqualified its former Shanghai and Shenzhen affiliates from administering arbitration disputes.

This jurisdictional dispute between CIETAC in Beijing and the former sub-commissions raised serious concerns in the U.S. business and legal communities, particularly regarding the validity of arbitration agreements specifying particular arbitration procedures and the enforceability of arbitral awards issued by the sub-commissions. In 2013, the Supreme People's Court issued a notice clarifying that any lower court that hears a case arising out of the CIETAC split must report the case to the SPC before making a decision. However, the SPC notice is brief and lacks detail on certain issues, including the timeframe for the lower court's decision to reach the SPC and for the SPC to issue its opinion.

Legal Code

China lacks a unified written "Commercial Law." Rules governing commercial activities are present in various laws, regulations, and judicial interpretations, including China's Civil Law, Contract Law, Partnership Enterprises Law, Security Law, Insurance Law, Enterprises Bankruptcy Law, Labor Contract Law and Implementing Regulations, and Supreme People's Court Interpretation on Several Issues Regarding the Application of the Contract Law. China does not have specialized commercial courts, but recently initiated a three-year pilot program to establish three specialized IPR courts in Beijing, Guangzhou, and Shanghai. These specialized IPR courts will serve as trial courts for certain IPR cases the resolution of which benefits from technical training, including cases related to patents, well-known trademarks, computer software, and trade secrets. The IPR Courts will also hear appeals of other IPR disputes originating in their geographical jurisdiction; the Beijing IPR court will conduct reviews of patent and trademark validity appealed from the responsible IP offices. In addition, many lower level courts outside of these geographic regions have designated specific IPR tribunals to hear IPR disputes.

Lack of Judicial Independence

Formal commercial disputes between investors are heard in economic courts. China's Constitution provides a legal basis for China's courts to independently exercise adjudicative power, and several laws have provisions stating that courts are not subject to interference by administrative organs, public organizations, or individuals. However, in practice, China's court system is not independent of the government or the Chinese Communist Party, which often intervene in disputes. Interference takes place for many reasons, including:

Courts fall under the jurisdiction of local governments.

Courts budgets are appropriated by local administrative authorities.

Judges in China have administrative ranks and are managed as administrative officials.

The Chinese Communist Party is in charge of the appointment, dismissal, transfer, and promotion of administrative officials.

China's Constitution stipulates that local legislatures appoint and supervise the courts.

Corruption may also influence local court decisions.

In practice, China's court system is not independent of the government, and the government often intervenes in disputes. The U.S. business community consistently reports that Chinese courts, particularly the lower courts, are susceptible to outside (political) influence, lack the sophistication to understand complex commercial disputes, and operate opaquely. U.S. companies often avoid challenging administrative decisions or bringing commercial disputes before a local court for fear of political retaliation.

Reports of business disputes involving violence, death threats, hostage-taking, and travel bans involving Americans continue to increase, although American citizens and foreigners in general do not appear to be more likely than Chinese nationals to be subject to this treatment. Police are often reluctant to intervene in what they consider to be internal contract disputes.

Fourth Plenum Reforms

The Chinese Communist Party's (CCP) October 2014 Fourth Plenum Decision called for the strengthening of "rule of law" through top-down judicial, legal, and administrative reforms. The Fourth Plenum Decision set six major tasks: improving the Constitution-centered legal system "with Chinese socialist characteristics" and strengthening the implementation of the Constitution; promoting administration by law and speedily moving toward a government ruled by laws; safeguarding judicial justice; improving judicial credibility; promoting the public's awareness of rule of law; and enhancing and improving the party's leadership in comprehensively promoting the rule of law. Since the conclusion of the Fourth Plenum, the Communist Party has moved forward with several preliminary measures to implement these reforms, including the establishment of some new courts and the promulgation of rules prohibiting official interference in judicial cases. If successful, these reforms could result in fairer judicial procedures and allow companies to pursue judicial or administrative action in a district outside of their base of operations. However, the Communist Party clearly emphasized in the Fourth Plenum that it remains above the law. Many observers say "rule by law" is a more accurate description of the party's Fourth Plenum goals. Ultimately, the implementation of these reforms will be a significant challenge for the Communist Party, and even if the reforms are successful, it could be many years before they begin to have a significant effect.

Bankruptcy

In June 2007, China's new Enterprise Bankruptcy Law came into force. For both foreign investors as well as domestic companies, the bankruptcy process is rarely used to wind down company operations or seek protection from creditors, due to the incomplete nature of the legal regime and judicial inexperience in this area of corporate law.

Investment Disputes

The Chinese government and judicial system do not maintain a public record of investment disputes. The Supreme People's Court maintains a count of the annual number of cases involving foreigners tried throughout China, but does not specify the types of cases, identify civil or commercial disputes, or note foreign investment disputes. Rulings in some cases are open to the public.

International Arbitration

China has bilateral investment agreements with over 100 countries and economies. The majority of these agreements set mediation, domestic remedies and international arbitration as the means to settle disputes. However, investor-state disputes leading to arbitration are rare in China.

There are few precedents where Chinese courts have recognized and enforced foreign court judgments. Articles 281 and 282 of China's Civil Procedure Law covers the recognition and enforcement of the effective judgments of foreign courts by the court system of China. According to these laws, if the courts determine, after reviewing the foreign courts' judgments, China's treaty obligations, reciprocity principles, basic principles of Chinese laws, China's sovereignty, security, and social public interests, the Chinese courts shall issue verdicts to recognize the effectiveness of foreign court judgments and issue enforcement orders if enforcement is needed. China has concluded 27 bilateral agreements on the recognition and enforcement of foreign court judgments, but none with the United States. China's recognition of judgments by U.S. courts can be inconsistent, according to anecdotal reports.

ICSID Convention and New York Convention

China is a member of the International Center for the Settlement of Investment Disputes (ICSID) and has ratified the United Nations Convention on the Recognition and Enforcement of Foreign Arbitral Awards (the New York Convention). The domestic legislation that provides for enforcement of foreign arbitral awards related to these two Conventions include the Arbitration Law, adopted in 1994; the Civil Procedure Law adopted in 1991 and amended in 2012; the Law on Chinese-Foreign Equity Joint Ventures adopted in 1979 and amended most recently in 2001; and a number of other laws with similar provisions. Moreover, Chinese Arbitration Law has embraced many of the fundamental principles of The United Nations Commission on International Trade Law's Model Law on International Commercial Arbitration.

Duration of Dispute Resolution

Article 270 of China's Civil Procedure Law states that time limits in civil cases do not apply to cases involving foreign investment. According to the 2012 CIETAC Arbitration Rules, in an ordinary procedure case, the arbitral tribunal shall render an arbitral award within six months (in foreign-related cases) from the date on which the arbitral tribunal is formed. In a summary procedure case, the arbitral tribunal shall make an award within three months from the date on which the arbitral tribunal is formed. In a domestic arbitration case, the arbitral tribunal shall render an arbitral award within four months from the date on which the arbitral tribunal is formed.

At the request of the arbitral tribunal and with the approval of the Secretary General of the CIETAC, the time period of rendering an arbitral award may be extended..

5. PERFORMANCE REQUIREMENTS AND INVESTMENT INCENTIVES

WTO/TRIMS

When joining the World Trade Organization (WTO) in 2001, China committed to eliminate and cease the enforcement of trade and foreign exchange balancing requirements; local content and export performance offsets; and technology transfer requirements made effective through laws, regulations, and other measures. China also committed to lift within two years all measures applicable to motor vehicle producers that restrict categories, types, or models of vehicles permitted for production, and to increase limits within which investment in motor vehicle manufacturing could be approved by provincial governments.

Investment Incentives

Many localities – including special economic zones, development zones, and science parks – court foreign investors with packages of reduced income taxes, resource and land use fees, and import/export duties, as well as priority treatment in obtaining basic infrastructure services, streamlined government approvals, and funding support for start-ups. These packages may also stipulate export, local content, technology transfer, or other requirements.

Research and Development

There is no express prohibition against foreign firms participating in research and development programs China finances. In certain sectors where China does not possess the expertise to conduct advanced research, foreign participation is generally encouraged. However, a large number of sectors which China deems sensitive to national security, including broadly defined "economic security," are effectively closed to investment from U.S. and other foreign firms.

Performance Requirements

China has committed to eliminate export performance, trade and foreign exchange balancing, and local content requirements. China has also committed to enforce only technology transfer rules that do not violate World Trade Organization (WTO) standards on IP and trade-related investment measures. In practice, however, local officials and some regulators prefer investments that develop favored industries and support the local job market. Provincial and municipal governments often restrict access to local markets, government procurement, and public works projects even to firms that have invested in the province or municipality. In addition, Chinese regulators have reportedly pressured foreign firms in some sectors to disclose IP content or license it to competitors, sometimes at below market rates.

Data Storage

In China, as elsewhere, there are vast opportunities in cloud computing. A broad range of companies are using online data storage to capture cost savings and easier access to data. However, regulatory restrictions, including mandatory source code or IP disclosure requirements in testing and certification regimes related to government procurement, prescriptive technology adoption requirements (often in the form of domestic standards that diverge from global standards), and operational restrictions such as privacy measures, data center colocation, and cross-border data flow restrictions, limit foreign companies' ability to invest in China's emerging cloud industry. For example, a draft counterterrorism law that began working its way through the legislative process in early December 2014 contains troubling requirements for ICT companies, including data-localization provisions. This draft law would require all telecommunications and Internet businesses to place all data-related equipment and store all domestic user data within China. At the 24th U.S.-China Joint Commission on Commerce and Trade in 2013, China agreed to provide foreign enterprises fair and equitable participation in the development of its strategic emerging industries, including cloud computing.

6. RIGHT TO PRIVATE OWNERSHIP AND ESTABLISHMENT

In China, all commercial enterprises require a license from the government. There is no broad right to establish a business. Disposition of an enterprise is also tightly regulated. The Administrative Permissions Law requires reviews of proposed investments for conformity with Chinese laws and regulations, and is the legal basis for China's complex approval system for foreign investment.

7. PROTECTION OF PROPERTY RIGHTS

Real Property

The Chinese legal system mediates acquisition and disposition of property. Chinese courts have an inconsistent record in protecting the legal rights of foreigners.

Tangible Property Rights

All land in China is owned by the State. Individuals and firms, including foreigners, can own and transfer long-term leases for land, structures, and personal property, subject to many restrictions. China's Property Law stipulates that residential property rights will be automatically renewed while commercial and industrial grants shall be renewed absent a conflicting public interest. A number of foreign investors have seen their land-use rights revoked when neighborhoods are slated by the government for development. Investors report compensation in these cases has been nominal.

China's Securities Law defines debtor and guarantor rights and allows mortgages of certain types of property and other tangible assets, including long-term leases as described above. China does not have laws or regulations prohibiting foreigners from buying non-performing debt, which they may acquire through state-owned asset management firms. However, in practice, China uses bureaucratic hurdles that limit foreigners' ability to liquidate assets in order to discourage them from purchasing non-performing debt.

Intellectual Property Rights

China has updated many of its laws and regulations to comply with the Agreement on Trade Related Aspects of Intellectual Property Rights (TRIPS) and other international agreements. However, there are still aspects of China's IPR legal and regulatory regime that the United States believes fall short of international best practices, and, if improved, would provide greater protection to IPR. Furthermore, effective enforcement of China's IPR laws and regulations remains a significant challenge.

In general, criminal penalties for infringement are not applied on a frequent and consistent enough basis to significantly deter ongoing infringement. Furthermore, administrative sanctions are typically non-transparent and are so weak as to lack a deterrent effect. Because of relatively low damage awards, civil litigation against IPR infringement continues to have a limited effect. For detailed information on China's environment for IPR protection and enforcement, please see the following reports:

Office of the United States Trade Representative's (USTR) 2014 Special 301 Report (see section on China): **https://ustr.gov/sites/default/files/2015-Special-301-Report-FINAL.pdf**

USTR's 2014 National Trade Estimate Report on Foreign Trade Barriers in China (see section

on
IPR): **http://www.ustr.gov/sites/default/files/2014%20NTE%20Report%20on%20FTB%20China.pdf**

USTR's 2014 Report to Congress on China's WTO Compliance (see section on IPR):**https://ustr.gov/sites/default/files/2014-Report-to-Congress-Final.pdf**

For additional information about treaty obligations and points of contact at local IP offices, please see WIPO's country profiles at **http://www.wipo.int/directory/en/**.

Resources for Rights Holders
Contact at Embassy Beijing:
Joel B. Blank
Intellectual Property Attaché
86-10-8531-4812
Joel.Blank@trade.gov

8. TRANSPARENCY OF THE REGULATORY SYSTEM

China's legal and regulatory system is complex and Chinese regulators and other government authorities inconsistently enforce regulations, rules, and other regulatory documents. Foreign investors rank inconsistent and arbitrary regulatory enforcement and lack of transparency among the major problems they face in China's market.

The State Council's Legislative Affairs Office (SCLAO) has issued instructions to Chinese agencies to publish all foreign trade- and investment-related laws, regulations, rules, and policy measures in the MOFCOM Gazette, in accordance with China's WTO accession commitment. In addition, it has also issued notices to require its own departments and other central government agencies to post proposed trade- and economic-related administrative regulations and departmental rules on the official SCLAO website for public comment. However, the SCLAO and ministries falling under the State Council continue to post only a fraction of draft administrative regulations and departmental rules on the SCLAO website for a 30-day public comment period. Comment periods can be extremely brief, and the impact of public comments on final regulations is not clear.

Moreover, there are an increasing number of regulatory policies for which public comment is not sought before they are finalized. Foreign investors report that Chinese regulators at times rely on unpublished internal guidelines that nonetheless affect their businesses.

State actions motivated by a perceived need to protect social stability or achieve other political goals can affect foreign investors. Access to foreign online resources, including news, cloudbased business services, and virtual private networks (VPNs), is often and increasingly restricted without official acknowledgement or explanation. Foreign-invested companies have also reported threats of retaliation by the government for actions taken by the U.S. and other foreign governments at the WTO.

9. EFFICIENT CAPITAL MARKETS AND PORTFOLIO INVESTMENT

China's leadership aims to build a modern, developed, multi-tiered capital market. Bank loans continue to provide the majority of credit in China, although other sources of capital, such as corporate bonds, trust loans, equity financing, and private equity financing, are expanding their scope, reach, and sophistication. Regulators use administrative methods to control credit growth, although market-based tools such as interest rate policy play an increasingly important role.

The People's Bank of China (PBOC), China's central bank, has gradually increased flexibility for banks in setting interest rates; the floor on the lending rate was removed in 2013. The PBOC has increased flexibility on deposit rates and has said that the ceiling on deposit rates will be gradually lifted, possibly within the next year. Favored borrowers, particularly SOEs, benefit from greater access to capital and lower financing costs, as lenders perceive these entities to have an implicit government guarantee and hence lower risk profiles. Small- and medium-sized enterprises (SMEs), by contrast, experience the most difficulty obtaining bank financing, and instead, often finance investments through retained earnings or informal channels, including other Chinese firms or private lenders. In recent years, China's "shadow banking" sector, which includes vehicles such as wealth management and trust products, has grown rapidly. The Chinese authorities have taken successive steps to increase the transparency and strengthen the supervision of these activities, while also permitting their continued development, as in many cases, these products increase channels for private firms to obtain capital at market rates. In 2014, the government also announced a pilot program that will allow private investors to establish small commercial banks, with an expansion of this pilot in 2015.

Non-bank financing has expanded over the last few years, including through public listing of stock, either inside or outside of China, and more firms are issuing bonds. Most foreign portfolio investment in Chinese companies occurs on foreign exchanges, primarily in New York and Hong Kong. In addition, China has significantly expanded quotas for certain foreign institutional investors to invest in domestic stock markets, and has approved a two-way cross-border equity direct investment scheme between Shanghai and Hong Kong, which will allow Chinese investors to trade designated Hong Kong-listed stocks through the Shanghai Exchange, and vice versa. Direct investment by private equity and venture capital firms is also rising rapidly, although from a small base.

Money and Banking System, Hostile Takeovers

After several years or rapid credit growth, China's banking sector faces asset quality concerns. The reported non-performing loans (NPL) ratio rose to 1.64 percent at the end of 2014, up from 1 percent at the end of 2013. China's total banking assets hit 172.3 trillion yuan by December 2014, up 13.87 percent from a year earlier, and accounting for over 20 percent of global banking assets. The Big 5 state-owned commercial banks account for almost 50 percent of China's banking sector assets. The People's Bank of China operates as China's central bank.

10. COMPETITION FROM STATE-OWNED ENTERPRISES

China's leading SOEs benefit from preferential government policies and practices aimed at developing bigger and stronger national champions. SOEs enjoy favored access to the most essential economic inputs (land, hydrocarbons, finance, telecoms, electricity) and considerable power in the markets for others (steel, minerals). SOEs have long enjoyed preferential access to credit and the ability to issue publicly traded equity and debt. According to some Chinese academics, provincial governments have used their power to manipulate industrial policies to deny operating licenses in order to persuade reluctant owners to sell out to bigger state-owned suitors.

The November 2013 Third Plenum agenda calls for SOEs to remain a key part of China's economic system, even as China makes them more efficient and transparent by limiting their monopoly power and preferential access to factors of production to improve their contribution to economic development. The Third Plenum meeting called for a "mixed ownership" economic structure, which would allow for private and state-owned businesses to co-exist in the domestic economy and proposed greater balance between private and state-owned businesses, including access to factors of production, competition on a level-playing field, and equal legal protection.

The Third Plenum Decision explains that SOEs will focus resources in areas that "serve state strategic objectives." However, experts point out that SOEs continue to hold dominant shares in their respective industries, regardless of whether they are strategic, which may further restrain private investment in the economy. Moreover, the application of China's Anti-monopoly Law, together with other industrial policies and practices that are selectively enforced by the authorities, protect SOEs from private sector competition.

Investment Restrictions in "Vital Industries and Key Fields"

The December 2006 Guiding Opinions Concerning the Advancement of Adjustments of State Capital and the Restructuring of State-Owned Enterprises called on China to consolidate and develop its state-owned economy, including enhancing its control and influence in "vital industries and key fields relating to national security and national economic lifelines." The document defined "vital industries and key fields" as "industries concerning national security, major infrastructure and important mineral resources, industries that provide essential public goods and services, and key enterprises in pillar industries and high-tech industries."

At the time the document was published, the Chairman of the State-owned Assets Supervision and Administration Commission (SASAC) listed industries in which the State should maintain "absolute control" (aviation, coal, defense, electric power and the State grid, oil and petrochemicals, shipping, and telecommunications) and "relative control" (automotive, chemical, construction, exploration and design, electronic information, equipment manufacturing, iron and steel, nonferrous metal, and science and technology). China maintains that these lists do not reflect its official policy. In some cases, more than 50 percent ownership in some of these industries has been permitted on a case-by-case basis, especially if a particular expertise or technology is deemed important at the time.

China's current agriculture trade rules, regulations, and limitations on foreign agricultural investment severely restrict the contributions of American agriculture companies and, subsequently, the many potential benefits to China's agriculture sector. China's agriculture investment restrictions also appear to be at odds with the objectives of China's 12th FYP, which emphasizes the need to shift more resources to agriculture and food production in order to improve people's lives and meet China's food security and food safety needs. China's State Assets Law is intended to safeguard China's economic system, promote the "socialist market economy," fortify and develop the state-owned economy, and enable SOEs to play a leading role in China's economy, especially in "vital industries and key fields." The law requires China to adopt policies to encourage SOE concentration and dominance in industries vital to national security and "national economic security."

OECD Guidelines on Corporate Governance of SOEs

China's State-owned Assets Supervision and Administration Commission of the State Council (SASAC), the main regulator of central state-owned enterprises (SOEs), participates in the OECD Working Party on State-Ownership and Privatization Practices (WPSOPP). China has indicated to the Working Party that it intends to use OECD guidelines to improve the professionalism of its SOEs, including making boards more independent from political influence. However, despite China's Third Plenum commitments – to foster "market-oriented" reforms in China's state sectors – Chinese officials and SASAC have made minimal progress to fundamentally change regulation and business conduct of SOEs.

Shortly after the annual National People's Congress meeting in 2014, SASAC released a plan to "deepen" economic reforms, entitled "Guiding Opinions for Deepening SOE Reforms." The guidelines were drafted by former SASAC officials. As a next step, SASAC planned to "strategically" define SOEs as either "public-interest" SOEs or "competitive" SOEs; however, these reforms were not carried out during the reporting period. Analysts have discussed the need to push forward a clear separation of SOE administration and policy functions. Reform-oriented supporters suggest that one office should focus on the "administration" of SOEs, to ensure they run efficiently and provide an adequate rate of return, while a separate office should focus on the policy-making role. Currently, both functions are intertwined in SASAC.

Economic analysts have indicated that "vested interests" remain a major impediment to SOE reforms. SOEs enjoy preferential access to a disproportionate share of available capital, whether in the form of loans or equity. SOE executives often outrank their SOE regulators, which minimizes SASAC and other government regulators' effectiveness. Moreover, SOE executives are often promoted to high-ranking positions in the Central Party or local government positions, which further complicates the regulation of Chinese SOEs.

Sovereign Wealth Funds

China's principal sovereign wealth fund is China Investment Corporation (CIC), which was established in 2007. CIC is overseen by a board of directors and a board of supervisors and invests on a 10-year time horizon, using rolling annualized returns to evaluate performance. China's sovereign wealth is also invested by a subsidiary of SAFE, a government agency that reports directly to the PBOC. The SAFE Administrator serves concurrently as a PBOC Vice Governor. While CIC publishes an annual report containing information on its structure, investments, and returns, SAFE does not. China's National Social Security Fund also makes investments using China's sovereign wealth. The Silk Road Fund, established at the end of 2014, is also designed to use China's sovereign wealth to make investments abroad.

11. CORPORATE SOCIAL RESPONSIBILITY

Corporate social responsibility (CSR), or what is increasingly known as sustainability, is a relatively new concept for domestic companies in China, where it is less widely accepted than in the United States. Investors looking to partner with Chinese companies or expand operations with Chinese suppliers face challenges ensuring domestic firms meet internationally recognized, voluntary industry standards in such areas as labor, the environment, and good manufacturing practices. China's 12th FYP highlights sustainability issues as a means to draw attention to the subject. Foreign-invested enterprises tend to follow generally accepted CSR principles, and most report annually on their CSR policies and achievements.

OECD Guidelines for Multinational Enterprises

In the past year China has appeared more willing to engage in dialogue around international standards for responsible investment. For example, in 2014 China signed an MOU with OECD and have indicated possible interest in establishing a National Contact Point, as required of all governments adhering to the OECD Guidelines for Multinational Enterprises. China also participated in OECD's 2014 Global Forum on Responsible Business Conduct (RBC) and plans to participate in the next Global Forum scheduled for June 2015. Additionally, the Chinese Chamber of Commerce of Metals, Minerals and Chemical Importers and Exporters (CCCMC), a government-affiliated chamber, signed a separate MOU with the OECD in October 2014 to help Chinese companies implement responsible business conduct policies in global mineral supply chains.

12. POLITICAL VIOLENCE

The risk of political violence directed at foreign companies operating in China remains small. Every year there are reportedly many tens of thousands of protests. The government is adept at handling them without violence, but given the number of mass incidents annually, the potential for violent flare-ups is real. Violent but unconnected protests that have occurred throughout China generally involved ethnic tensions or local residents protesting corrupt officials, environmental and food safety concerns, confiscated property, and disputes over unpaid wages. In several recent examples, workers and mid-level managers have protested against corporate merger and acquisition decisions on the grounds that employees were not consulted. There have also been a small number of cases of foreign businesspeople being trapped in China during a business dispute.

13. CORRUPTION

Corruption remains endemic in China. The lack of an independent press, as well as the fact that all bodies responsible for conducting corruption investigations are controlled by the Chinese Communist Party, hamper the transparent and consistent application of anti-corruption efforts.

According to Chinese law, accepting a bribe is a criminal offense with a maximum punishment of life in prison or death in "especially serious" circumstances. The maximum punishment for offering a bribe to a Chinese official is five years in prison, except when there are "serious" or "especially serious" circumstances, when punishment can range from five years to life in prison. A February 2011 amendment to the Criminal Law made offering large bribes to foreign officials or officials of international organizations a punishable offense, although there has yet to be a prosecution.

The Supreme People's Procuratorate and the Ministry of Public Security investigate criminal violations of laws related to anti-corruption, while the Ministry of Supervision and the Chinese Communist Party Discipline Inspection Commission enforce ethics guidelines and party discipline. China's National Audit Office also inspects accounts of state-owned enterprises (SOEs) and government entities.

Anti-corruption measures

China is in the midst of the most intensive and large-scale anti-corruption campaign it has seen in decades, with investigations reaching into all sectors of the government, military and SOEs. President Xi Jinping has said that endemic corruption threatens the Party's survival. The Party announced at its annual plenums in 2013 and 2014 its intention to press ahead with judicial and administrative reform and to more thoroughly fight corruption. Key Party meetings in late 2014 and early 2015 pledged to use judicial reforms to institutionalize the fight against corruption, but concrete measures are only just beginning to emerge. To enhance regional anti-corruption cooperation, the 26th Asia-Pacific Economic Cooperation (APEC) Ministers Meeting adopted the Beijing Declaration on Fighting Corruption in November 2014.

In 2014, more than 70 senior SOE officials were investigated for graft by the Party's Organization Department. Several high profile SOE executives were investigated and charged with corruption, including former oil-sector executives and the head of the country's SOE oversight body. Also in 2014, Chinese Communist Party discipline organs have investigated 226,000 cases and disciplined 232,000 officials, of which 12,000 criminal suspects were transferred to judicial authorities. Courts nationwide concluded 31,000 graft and bribery cases involving 44,000 people, and sentenced 2,349 people. China's overseas fugitive-hunting campaign captured 749 fugitives suspected of official crimes.

China's anti-corruption crackdown could curb abuse of administrative powers by government officials colluding with private sector patrons; however, inconsistent and discretionary application of anti-corruption rules may also raise concerns among foreign companies in China. To fight rampant commercial corruption in the medical/pharmaceutical sector, China's health authority issued "black lists" of firms and agents involved in commercial bribery. Several of these "black listed" firms were foreign. Additionally, anecdotal information suggests many government officials are slowing approval of foreign investment projects so as not to arouse corruption suspicions.

The Communist Party is constantly on guard against threats to political or social stability. It views independent criticism of the Party as dangerous, and therefore citizens who have called for officials to disclose their public assets or have campaigned against officials' misuse of public resources have been subject to criminal prosecution.

UN Anticorruption Convention, OECD Convention on Combatting Bribery

China ratified the United Nations Convention against Corruption in 2005 and participates in Asia-Pacific Economic Cooperation (APEC) and Organization for Economic Cooperation and Development (OECD) anti-corruption initiatives. China has not signed the OECD Convention on Combating Bribery.

Resources to Report Corruption

The following government organizations receive public reports of corruption:

Anti-Corruption Reporting Center of the CPC Central Commission for Discipline Inspection and the Ministry of Supervision

Telephone Number: 010-12388

14. BILATERAL INVESTMENT AGREEMENTS

China has bilateral investment agreements with over 100 countries and economies, including Austria, the Belgium-Luxembourg Economic Union, Canada, France, Germany, Italy, Japan, South Korea, Spain, Thailand, and the United Kingdom. China's bilateral investment agreements cover expropriation, arbitration, most-favored-nation treatment, and repatriation of investment proceeds. They are generally regarded as weaker than the investment treaties the United States seeks to negotiate.

A list of China signed BITs can be found here:**http://tfs.mofcom.gov.cn/article/Nocategory/201111/20111107819474.shtml**

China maintains twelve Free Trade Agreements (FTAs) with its trade and investment partners, and is negotiating or implementing an additional eight FTAs. China's FTA partners include

ASEAN, Singapore, Pakistan, New Zealand, Chile, Peru, Costa Rica, Iceland, Switzerland, Hong Kong, Macao and Taiwan. China has recently concluded FTA negotiations with Korea and Australia, both of which include a chapter on investment.

Bilateral Taxation Treaties

The United States and China concluded a bilateral taxation treaty in 1984. In the fall of 2012, the United States resumed negotiation of a bilateral investment treaty.

15. OPIC and Other Investment Insurance Programs

The United States suspended Overseas Private Investment Corporation (OPIC) programs in the aftermath of China's crackdown on Tiananmen Square demonstrators in June 1989. OPIC honors outstanding political risk insurance contracts. The Multilateral Investment Guarantee Agency, an organization affiliated with the World Bank, provides political risk insurance for investors in China. Some foreign commercial insurance companies also offer political risk insurance, as does the People's Insurance Company of China.

16. LABOR

Human resource challenges remain a major concern for American companies operating in China. Labor costs are the problem most often cited, followed closely by difficulties in finding and retaining talent, particularly at the management level and highly skilled technical staff. Navigating evolving labor and social insurance laws and implementation rules also remains a challenge.

In particular, trial implementation regulations issued in November 2014 to clarify new visa rules introduced in 2013 has led to uncertainty rather than clarity for foreign companies trying to obtain visas for their employees traveling to China. Companies continue to cite China's poor air quality and pollution generally as causing difficulties in trying to attract and retain qualified foreign talent. Together, these issues contribute to higher labor costs, and in response, a small but increasing number of foreign companies are planning to move capacity or investments outside of China.

Independent trade unions are illegal in China. The Trade Union Law gives the All-China Federation of Trade Unions (ACFTU) control over all union organizations and activities, including enterprise-level unions. The ACFTU is a Chinese Communist Party organ chaired by a member of the Politburo, and its priority task is to "uphold the leadership of the Communist Party." The ACFTU and its provincial and local branches aggressively organize new constituent unions and add new members, especially in large, multinational enterprises, but these enterprise-level unions do not generally participate actively in employee-employer relations. The right to strike is not protected by law. However, worker protests and work stoppages occur with increasing regularity especially in labor intensive and sunset industries. Official forums for mediation, arbitration, and similar mechanisms of alternative dispute resolution are generally ineffective in resolving disputes.

China has not ratified core International Labor Organization conventions on freedom of association and collective bargaining, but has ratified conventions prohibiting child labor and employment discrimination. Apart from a lack of freedom of association and the right to strike, on paper, Chinese labor laws generally meet international labor standards. Enforcement of existing labor laws and regulations, however, is inconsistent.

17. FOREIGN TRADE ZONES/FREE PORTS/TRADE FACILITATION

China's principal customs bonded areas include Shanghai, Tianjin, Shantou, three districts within Shenzhen (Futian, Yantian, and Shatoujiao), Guangzhou, Dalian, Xiamen, Ningbo, Zhuhai, and Fuzhou. Besides these official duty-free zones identified by China's State Council, numerous economic development zones and open cities offer similar privileges and benefits to foreign investors.

In September 2013, the Shanghai Municipal government and the State Council announced the establishment of the China (Shanghai) Pilot Free Trade Zone (SFTZ), which condensed four previously existing bonded areas into a single free trade zone. The goal of the SFTZ is to provide a trial ground for trade and investment liberalization measures and to introduce services sector reform, especially in financial services, that China expects to eventually introduce in other parts of the domestic economy. Shanghai officials tout the use of a negative list, to spell out sectors where national treatment does not apply, as a key reform introduced in the zone. Shanghai officials released a revised negative list in June 2014 that reduced the number of entries, but many foreign firms complained that this was done by combining entries and reducing barriers mostly in sectors that do not affect foreign firms. According to free trade zone officials, there are over 12,000 entities registered throughout the free trade zone, including 1,600 foreign firms. The municipal and central government have released a number of administrative and sector-specific regulations and circulars that outline the procedures and regulations in the zone, and expanded the zone's area to 120.7 square kilometers, an increase from its original 28.78 square kilometer size.

On December 12, 2014, Premier Li Keqiang chaired a State Council Executive Committee meeting to create three new free trade zones in Fujian, Tianjin, and Guangdong as well as an expanded area for Shanghai's already existing pilot free trade zone. Since then, a draft to adjust relevant laws and regulations on investment in the new free trade zones was discussed in the Standing Committee of the National People's Congress (NPC). On December 28, the NPC Standing Committee authorized the State Council to offer preferential policies in the new free trade zones. The three new zones are expected to be announced in 2015. The effect of the investment climate will depend on the package of reforms included in the announcement of the FTZs, the scope of the negative lists, details on bonded warehouses and customs duties, and specifics on financial reforms and incentive policies.

18. FOREIGN DIRECT INVESTMENT AND FOREIGN PORTFOLIO INVESTMENT STATISTICS

Table 2: Key Macroeconomic Data, U.S. FDI in Host Country/Economy

	Host Country Statistical source*		USG or international statistical source		USG or International Source of Data: BEA; IMF; Eurostat; UNCTAD, Other
Economic Data	Year	Amount	Year	Amount	
Host Country Gross Domestic Product (GDP) ($M USD)	2013	8,523,829	2013	9,240,270	www.worldbank.org/en/country
Foreign Direct Investment	Host Country Statistical source*		USG or international statistical source		USG or international Source of data: BEA; IMF; Eurostat; UNCTAD, Other
U.S. FDI in partner country ($M	2013	73,010	2013	61,534	Bureau of Economic Analysis

USD, stock positions)					
Host country's FDI in the United States ($M USD, stock positions)	2013	21,899	2013	8,073	Bureau of Economic Analysis
Total inbound stock of FDI as % host GDP	2013	16%	N/A	N/A	N/A

* National Bureau of Statistics of PRC; China Commerce Yearbook; MOFCOM

Table 3: Sources and Destination of FDI

According to MOFCOM's 2013 China Commerce Year Book, the top five destinations for China's Outward Direct Investment from 2003-2012 are: Hong Kong, British Virgin Islands, Cayman Islands, United States, and Australia.

Direct Investment from/in Counterpart Economy Data From Top Five Sources/To Top Five Destinations (US Dollars, Millions)

Inward Direct Investment			Outward Direct Investment		
Total Inward	2,068,027	100%	Total Outward	N/A	100%
China, P.R.: Hong Kong	1,112,242	48%			
Virgin Islands, British	330,624	14%			
Japan	147,594	6%			
Singapore	101,619	4%			
United States	76,465	3%			
"0" reflects amounts rounded to +/- USD 500,000.					

Source: IMF Coordinated Direct Investment Survey

Contact for More Information

Bridget Davis
Investment Officer
Economic Section

55 Anjialou Road, Chaoyang District, Beijing, P.R. China
0086-10 8531-3000
Beijinginvestmentteam@state.gov

Other useful online resources:

Chinese Government:
Chinese Embassy in Washington, D.C.: **http://www.china-embassy.org/eng/**
Ministry of Commerce: **http://english.mofcom.gov.cn/**
Invest in China: **http://www.fdi.gov.cn/pub/FDI_EN/default.htm**
National Development and Reform Commission: **http://en.ndrc.gov.cn/**

State Administration of Foreign Exchange: **http://www.safe.gov.cn/**
State Administration of Taxation **http://www.chinatax.gov.cn/n6669073/index.html**
United States Government:
U.S. Embassy in Beijing (Doing Business in China): **http://beijing.usembassy-china.org.cn/business.html**
U.S. Department of State travel information: **http://travel.state.gov/**
U.S. Trade Representative: **http://www.ustr.gov/**
U.S. Department of Commerce: **http://www.export.gov/**
U.S. Department of the Treasury: **http://www.treasury.gov/Pages/default.aspx**
Export Import Bank: **http://www.exim.gov/**
Overseas Private Investment Corporation (OPIC): **http://www.opic.gov/**
U.S. Trade and Development Agency: **http://www.ustda.gov/**

LOCAL LAWYERS

BEIJING

U.S. law firms

Frederick W. Hong Law Offices
Suite 11-D, Building 1, Majestic Towers (baifu guoji), No.20 Gongti Donglu
Chaoyang Beijing, 100020
Tel: (010) 6506-1180
Fax: (010) 6506-1720
Email: beijing@fwhonglaw.com
www.fwhonglaw.com
Specialty: corporate and commercial, IP, US Visa, M&A, contacts

Garvey Schubert Barer
820 South Tower, Kerry Center
1 Guang Hua Road
Chaoyang District Beijing, PRC 100020
Tel: (101) 8529-9880
Fax: (010) 8529-9881
www.gsblaw.com
Specialty: full service

Gide Loyrette Nouel (French speaking)
Suite 3501, Jingguang Center
Hu Jia Lou
Chaoyang District Beijing 100020
Tel: (010) 6597-4511
Fax: (010) 6597-4551
www.gide.com
Specialty: Banking and finance, foreign direct investment, M&A, dispute settlement

Hogan & Hartson LLP
10/F, South Tower, Kerry Center Office
Building, 1 Guanghua Road,
Chaoyang District, Beijing 100020
Tel: (010 6598-8600
Fax: (010) 8529-7408
www.hhlaw.com

Specialty: Corporate and commercial aw, mergers and acquisitions, project financing, IP, technology transfer law

Morrison & Foerster LLP
22nd Floor, Tower 3,
China Central Place,
No. 77, Jianguo Road,
Chaoyang District,
Beijing 100025 China
Tel: (010) 5909-3399
Fax: (010) 5909-3355
www.mofo.com; www.mofo.com.cn
Specialty: Corporate, real estate, technology

Orrick, Herrington & Sutcliffe LLP
22/F South Tower, Kerry Center
1 Guanghua Road, Chaoyang
Beijing 100022
Tel: (010) 8595-5600
Fax: (010) 8595-5700
www.orrick.com
Specialty: Intellectual property

Sidley Austin LLP Beijing
Suite 608, Tower C2, Oriental Plaza
No.1 East Chang An Ave.,
Beijing 100738
Tel: (010) 6505-5359
Fax: (010) 6505-5360
www.sidley.com
Specialty: Corporate finance, securities, securities litigation

Vinson and Elkins LLP
20/F, Beijing Silver Tower
No. 2 Dong San Huan Bei Lu
Chaoyang District, Beijing 100027
Tel: (010) 6410-6300
Fax: (010) 6410-6360
http://www.velaw.com
Specialty: Business law, international business transaction, cross-border mergers, acquisition

Skadden, Arps, Slate, Meagher & Flom LLP
30th Floor, Tower 2, China World Trade
Center, 1 Jianguomenwai Avenue,
Beijing 100004
Tel: (010) 6535-5500
Fax: (010) 6535-5577
www.skadden.com
Specialty: Corporate, particularly M&A, finance and investments

Bingham McCutchen
China World Tower 3,
1 Jianguomenwai Avenue, 50th floor,

Beijing, 100004 China
Tel: (010) 6535-2888
Fax: (010) 6535-2899
www.bingham.com
Specialty: Corporate and commercial law, mergers and acquisitions, financial services, investment management, life science

Chinese Law Firms (most have English-speaking lawyers)
Suite 711, Jing Guang Centre Office Building
Hujialou, Chaoyang District, Beijing 100020
Tel: (010) 6597-5044
Fax: (010) 6597-5202
www.atzp.com
Specialty: IP Law

Beijing Tianbo Law Firm (English-speaking)
F1 11/E, North Bldg.3, Sunny Plaza (Yangming Guangchang),
No. 10 Xiaoying Rd, Chaoyang District, Beijing 100101
Tel: (010) 8464-3018
Fax: (010) 8464-9785
Mobile: 13910064337
Email: law@tianbolawfirm.com
www.tianbolawfirm.com
Contact: Tianli (Jenny) Zhang
Specialty: General practice

Beijing Globe Law Firm
(English-Speaking)
19F, Golden Land Building, 32 Liang Ma Qiao Rd., Chaoyang District, Beijing 100016
Tel: (010) 8451-2800
Fax: (010) 8451-2790
www.globe-law.com
Specialty: IP law, Corporate, real estate, arbitration and litigation

Beijing Tian Yuan Law Firm (English-speaking)
11/F, Tower C, Corporate Square (Guoqi Dasha),
No. 35 Financial Street, Xicheng Dist., Beijing, 10003
Tel: (010) 8809-2188
Fax: (010) 8809-2150
www.tylaw.com.cn/en
Specialty: M & A, FDI & securities

Bright & Right (English, German, Japanese, French & Russian Speaking)
Suite 1008-1009, 10/F, Kuntai International Mansion, B-12 Chaowai Avenue, Chaoyang District, Beijing 100020
Tel: (010) 5128 7593
Fax: (010) 5128 9296
www.brightandright.com
Specialty: Civil commercial, M & A, International investment & arbitration

B & D Law Firm (English-speaking)
10/F, Botai Plaza, No.221 Wangjing Xiyuan, Chaoyang District, Beijing 100102
Tel: (010) 6478-9318

Fax: (010) 6478-9550
www.bdlawyer.com.cn
Specialty: Marriage, inherit, divorce, labor law, FDI (Foreign Direct Investment), JV(joint-venture), Representative Office, M&A (Mergers and Acquisitions), securities and corporate law, legal due diligence investigation, IP infringement, disputes resolution/arbitration and litigation

Gaopeng & Partners (English-speaking)
28/F, Silver Tower, 2 Dongsanhuan Rd., Beijing 100027
Tel: (010) 5924-1129
Fax: (010) 5924-1199
www.gaopenglaw.com
Specialty: Corporate, investment, dispute solution, arbitration

Han Kun Law Offices (English-speaking)
Suite 906, Office Tower C1, Oriental Plaza, No. 1 East Chang An Avenue Beijing 100738,
Tel: (010) 8525-5500
Fax: (010) 8525-5511, 8525-5522
http://www.hankunlaw.com
Specialty: Foreign direct investment, M & A, Public & Private financings, IP

Kingfield Law Firm (English-speaking)
#406, CYTS Plaza, 5 Dongzhimen South Ave.,Dongcheng District, Beijing 100007
Tel: (010) 5815-6278
Fax: (010) 5815-6270
Contact: Nancy Zhang
www.kingfieldlaw.com
Specialties: Real estate, merger & acquisition, general corporate, criminal

Lehman, Lee & Xu (English-speaking)
10-2 Liangmaqiao Diplomatic Compound #A, No.22 Dongfang East Road,Chaoyang District, Beijing 100600
Tel: (010) 8532-1919
Fax: (010) 8532-1999
Email: mail@lehmanlaw.com
www.lehmanlaw.com
Specialty: Full services

TransAsia Lawyers (English-speaking)
Suite 2218, China World Tower #1,No.1 Jianguomenwai Dajie, Beijing 100004
Tel: (010) 6505-8188
Fax: (010) 6505-8189/6505/8198
E-mail:Beijing@TransAsiaLawyers.com
www.TransAsiaLawyers.com
Specialty: marriage, inherit, divorce, labor law, FDI (Foreign Direct Investment), JV(joint-venture), Representative Office, M&A (Mergers and Acquisitions), securities and corporate law, legal due diligence investigation, IP infringement, disputes resolution/arbitration and litigation

Beijing Zhongyin Law Firm (English-speaking)
SOHO-A 31st F 39 East 3rd-ring Rd.
Chaoyang District Beijing
Tel: (010) 58698899
Fax: (010) 58688666
E-mail: gwh-office@zhongyinlawyer.com

http://www.zhongyinlawyer.com/
Specialty: TMT, commercial, IPR, labor

Beijing PangBiao Law Firm (English-speaking)
Rm2103 SOHO Shangdu South Tower
No. 8 Dongdaqiao Rd., Chaoyang District Beijing
Tel: (010) 57495709
Fax: (010) 59005719
E-mail: pangbiaolaw@163.com
http://www.legalservicescenter.cn
http://www.qianquanlaw.com
Specialty: contract & employment, infringement, real estate, marriage & family, labor dispute, criminal defense

Beijing Jin Tian Cheng Law Firm (English, Japanese, German and French-speaking)
6F C1 Oriental Plaza
No. 1 East Chang'an Ave.
Dongcheng District Beijing
Tel: (010) 85230688
Fax: (010) 85230699
Mobile: 13910062778
E-mail: susanguo@allbrightlaw.com
http://www.allbrightlaw.com
Specialty: disputes, criminal & civil cases, economic law suits & arbitration, M&R, securities market, banking & finance, risk investment, real estate & construction, international trade, IPR

Beijing Yingke Law Firm (English-speaking)
6F Tower C, Dacheng International
Center No. 76 East 4th Ring Middle Road, Chaoyang District Beijing 100124, China
Tel: (010) 59626906
Fax: (010) 59626918
E-mail: international@yingkelawyer.com
http://www.yingkelawyer.com
Specialty: full service including corporate law, commercial law, international arbitration, IP, real estate, investment, securities & capital markets, and mergers & acquisitions

Beijing Liangbe Law Firm (English-speaking)
Room 307 South Building Huakang Tower 78 Maizidian Street, Chaoyang District, Beijing
Tel: (010) 88259898
Fax: (010) 65618828
E-mail: zhiquan_lawyer@126.com
shenliangyin@126.com
http://www.liangbe.com
Specialty: criminal Law, corporate law and securities law

King & Capital Law Firm
Beijing Office:
23F Building C Yuanyang Guanghua Guoji NO. 5 Jinghua South Street, Chaoyang District, Beijing
Tel: (010) 8525 3900/ 5709 6000

Shanghai Office:
Suite 3903A Nanzheng Building, 580 West Nanjing Road, Shanghai

Tel: (021) 5234 1066
Fax: (021) 5234 1011
www.king-capital.com
Specialty: criminal matters

TIANJIN

Tianjin Jason Law Firm (English-speaking)
Rm. F, 21 Floor, Yitingyuan Mansion
No. 22, Liuwei Rd.,
Hedong District, Tianjin, China
Tel: (022) 2421-8883, 2421-8333
Fax: (022) 2421-9555
Email: jasonlawfirm@sina.com
Specialty: Company laws, contract laws and labor laws

Divine Land Precede Law Firm (English-speaking)
B908 Sunny Building 11th, longitude,
Hedong district, Tianjin, China
Tel: (022) 2433-5619
Fax: (022) 2433-5617
www.huayinlawyer.com
Specialty: Civil lawsuit, IP, Merger and acquisition insurance, investment funds

Jun Yue Law Firm (English-speaking)
Room 2204, Evening Paper Mansion,
#358 Nanjing Road, Tianjin, China
Tel: (022) 2750-0134
Fax: (022) 2750-0124
Email: havemelove@163.com
www.junyuelaw.com
Specialty: Civil & commercial law, contact, corporation, real estate

Jin Bin Zheng Tong Law Firm (English-speaking)
3rd Floor, Building 2, Xunyuang XiaoQu, No.76 Dong Ting Road
Economic-Technological Development Area, Tianjin, China
Tel: (022) 6529-9710 ext. 83
Fax: (022) 6529-9710 ext.85
Specialty: Contract, corporation, real estate, white collar crime

Tianjin Si Fang Jun Hui Law Firm (English-speaking)
20F Tower A Fenghui Plaza
No. 103 Weidi St. Hexi District
Tianjin, China
Tel: (022) 27305678
Fax: (022) 27309385
Email: sfjh@join-highlaw.com
http://www.join-highlaw.com/
Specialty: Contract, IPR, corporation & foreign investment, real estate, labor

Shaanxi

Shaanxi Sheng Di Law Firm (English-speaking)

Shenye Mansion 819, Jiefang Rd. 25, Xi'An City, Shaanxi, China
Tel: (029) 8740-7363
Email: fengdong911911@yahoo.com.cn
Specialty: Contract, corporation, real estate, Security

Shaanxi Xu Xiao Ping Law Firm (English-speaking)
B7-1 Kai Ai Plaza, No. 1 Xi Hua Men, Xi'An City, Shaanxi, China
Tel: (029) 87201100
Fax: (029) 87201870
Email: xuke@lawres.com
http://www.lawres.com/
Specialty: real estate & construction, corporate & foreign investment, banking & finance, IPR, environmental protection, criminal defense

GANSU

Gansu Yongsheng Law Firm (English-speaking)
1-5-201 Anju Beishan Rd., Wudu District Longnan City Gansu, China
Tel: (0939) 9212721
Fax: (0939) 8212431
Mobile: 138-3091-9411
Email: 1078835770@qq.com
Specialty: Civil litigation, criminal defense, individual legal consultation

Gansu Zhengding Law Firm
Tower B 24F Century Plaza, 350 Qingyang Rd. Chengguan District, Lanzhou City, Gansu, China
Tel: (0931) 8441636; 8441888
Fax: (0931) 8441888
www.zdlawyer.com
Specialty: real estate & construction, IPR, banking & finance, other legal services

HEBEI

Hebei Taipingyang Century Law Firm (English-speaking)
5F No. 128 Zhonghua N. Ave.
Shijiazhuang City, Hebei, China
Tel: (0311) 87899558
Fax: (0311) 87890768
Mobile: 138-3091-9411
Email: zhmlawyer@126.com
http://www.heblawyer.com.cn/
Specialty: banking & finance, M&R, assets, bankrupt, high-tech & risky investment, IPR protection, other legal issues

Hebei Yanzhao Zhongcheng Law Firm (English-speaking)
12F Tower A Jinyuan Plaza
No. 3 Zhonghua N. Ave. Shijiazhuang City, Hebei, China
Tel: (0311) 87660090
Fax: (0311) 87614149
Email: yzzc01@126.com
http://www.yz-zc.cn/
Specialty: foreign legal issues, company law, real estate, criminal defense, marriage, inherit, other legal issues

Hebei Haiyue Law Firm (English-speaking)
No. 1 Jianshe N. Ave. Cangzhou City, Hebei, China
Tel: (0371) 3071791; 3580148
Tel: (0371) 3071702; 3071707
Tel: (0371) 3071772; 3510123
Tel: (0371) 3071711; 3071719
Fax: (0371) 3071791; 3071702
Email: haiyue-lawyers@163.com; wangjicang-lawyer@163.com
http://www.haiyue-lawyers.com.cn/
Specialty: foreign legal issues, legal consultation and all related services

HENAN

Henan Yandongfang Law Firm (English, Japanese-speaking)
10F Tower A Riyuexing Plaza, No. 238 West Ave.
Zhengzhou City, Henan, China
Tel: (0371) 88885148
Tel: 400-666-5148
Fax: (0371) 66268288
Email: 18638276688@163.com;
http://www.yandongfang.com/
Specialty: legal consultation, company investment, real estate, company contract, international business, IPR, banking & finance, foreign exchange market, issuance, civil and criminal defense, other legal issues

HUBEI

Hubei Yingda Law Firm
Rm 1801 Fuxing International Plaza, No. 186 Xinhua Rd.
Wuhan City, Hubei, China
Tel: (027) 85350032; 85350997
Fax: (027) 85350833
Email: info@yingdalaw.com
http://www.yingdalaw.com
Specialty: corporate & foreign investment, international practice, banking and finance, capital market, M&A, civil litigation & dispute resolution, employment, real estate & reconstruction, administrative law, anti-monopoly, international maritime law, state-owned enterprise (SOE) reconstruction and privatization, environment and energy, criminal defense

HUNAN

Hunan Qinxiyan United Law Firm (English-speaking)
9F Weiyi Xingcheng International Plaza, No. 216 Shaoshan N Rd. Changsha City, Hunan, China
Tel: (0731) 84150066; 84155918
Fax: (0731) 84180608
Email: qin_xiyan@163.com
http://www.qinxiyan.com/
Specialty: law suits & arbitration, other legal services

Hunan Jinzhou Law Firm (English-speaking)
20F Xinshikong Plaza No. 398 San Duan Furong Middle Rd.
Tianxin District, Changsha City, Hunan, China
Tel: (0731) 85012988

Fax: (0731) 85231168
Email: 35182569@qq.com
http://www.hnjzlaw.net/
Specialty: civil litigation, criminal defense

Hunan Tiandiren Law Firm (English, Japanese-speaking)
15F Hunan Wenhua Mansion
No. 139 Shao Shan North Rd., Changsha City, Hunan, China
Tel: (0731) 82767188
Fax: (0731) 82767150
Email: lawyerzhouzhengping@foxmail.com
http://www.titanlaw.com
Specialty: criminal defense, legal consultation, contact and company business, real estate, foreign marriage, international trade, international investment, overseas listing, anti-dumping, dispute on personal violence, visa and other foreign affairs

INNER MONGOLIA

Inner Mongolia Jianzhong Law Firm(English, Japanese, Mongolian, Italian, German, Russian and Spanish-speaking)
Jianshe Zhong Duan, Baotou City, Inner Mongolia, China
Tel: (0472) 7155359
Fax: (0472) 7155474
Email: sjz@jzlawyer.com.cn
http://www.jzlawyer.com.cn/
Specialty: capital & stock market, M&R, International trade, arbitration, joint-venture enterprises, law suits

JIANGXI

Jiangxi Qiuzheng Wode Law Firm (English-speaking)
6F Xinfeng Holiday Inn
No. 29 Huizhan Rd. Hong Gu Tan, Nanchang City, Jiangxi, China
Tel: (0791) 8620098
Fax: (0791) 3850881
Email: qz.jx.lawfirm@163.com
http://www.jxqzwd.com/
Specialty: all related legal services

Jiangxi Ganxing Law Firm
No. 79 Yangming Rd.
Nanchang City, Jiangxi, China
Tel: (0791) 6833571; 6818020
Tel: (0791) 7525901
Fax: (0791) 6833571
Email: ganxing20000101@126.com
http://jxgxyzh.com/
Specialty: legal consultation and related legal services

NINGXIA

Ningxia Fude Law Firm
15F Zhongyin Plaza

No. 187 Xinchang E Rd., Jinfeng District, Yinchuan City, Ningxia, China
Tel: (0951) 6989216
Fax: (0951) 6989220
Email: fude_lawfirm@163.com
http://www.fudelawyer.com/about.html
Specialty: civil litigation, criminal defense, legal consultation

QINGHAI

Qinghai Jingfan Law Firm
12F Chuangxin Plaza
No. 128 Changjiang Rd.
Chengzhong District, Xining City, Qinghai, China
Tel: (0971) 8587800; 8587816
Fax: (0971) 8587819
Email: jfslawyer@yahoo.com.cn
http://www.jflaw.cn
Specialty: company & stock market, banking & finance, real estate, trade & investment, IPR, environmental protection, medication, arbitration, civil litigation, criminal defense, legal consultation

Qinghai Shuren Law Firm (English-speaking)
6F Building 1 Dingxiang Jiayuan, No. 32 Xinning Rd. Xining City, Qinghai, China
Tel: (0971) 6111958; 6111968
Tel: (0971) 6111858; 6111998
Fax: (0971) 6111123
Email: qhshuren@163.com
Specialty: M&R, mining resources, banking & finance, stock market, energy & electricity

SHANDONG

Shandong Qilu Law Firm (English-speaking)
16F Xiqu Building 8 Shuntai Plaza
No. 2000 Shunhua Rd. High-Tech Zone, Jinan City, Shandong, China
Tel: (0531) 62323888
Fax: (0531) 62323887
Email: qilu@qilulawyer.com
http://www.qilulawyer.com/
Specialty: stock market, banking & finance, investment, real estate & construction, IPR, international trade, maritime business, criminal defense, civil business, arbitration, legal consultation, American & Canadian business immigration, Hong Kong business immigration, passport services

Shandong Qilu Law Firm (Yantai office)
Rm607 Dianzi Plaza No. 202 Changjiang Rd.
Developing Zone Yantai City, Shandong, China
Tel: (0535) 6116600
Fax: (0535) 6116600
Email: qilulawyer@126.com
http://www.qilulawyer.com/
Specialty: stock market, banking & finance, investment, real estate & construction, IPR, international trade, maritime business, criminal defense, civil business, arbitration, legal

consultation, American & Canadian business immigration, Hong Kong business immigration, passport services

Shandong Qilu Law Firm (Qingdao office)
No. 87 Donghai Rd. Laoshan District
Qingdao City, Shandong, China
Tel: (0532) 88259666
Fax: (0532) 80955360
Email: qilulawyer@126.com
http://www.qilulawyer.com/
Specialty: legal services and construction

Shandong Zhongcheng Renhe Law Firm (English, Korean and Russian-speaking)
11F Building 11 Shuntai Plaza
No. 2000 Shunhua Rd. High-Tech Zone
Jinan City, Shandong, China
Tel: (0531) 66590816; 66590909
Fax: (0531) 66590906
Email: zhongchenglawyer@163.com
http://www.zclawyer.com/
Specialty: foreign investment, international trade, IPR, stock market, banking & finance, real estate & construction, marriage & inheritance, traffic accident, medical dispute, criminal defense, labor dispute, foreign arbitration, other legal services

Shandong Qindao Law Firm (English-speaking)
22F North Tower Huangjin Plaza
No. 20 Hong Kong Middle Rd.
Qingdao City, Shandong, China
Tel: (0532) 85023100
Fax: (0532) 85023080
Email: qindao@qindaolaw.com
http://www.qindaolaw.com/
Specialty: complex legal services

SHANXI

Shanxi Kebei Law Firm
20F High-Tech Dongli Tower
High-Tech Developing Zone , No. 226 Changzhi Rd.
Taiyuan City, Shanxi, China
Tel: (0351) 8330241; 8330242
Tel: (0351) 8330243; 8330244
Fax: (0351) 8330240
Email: szd.xx@tom.com
http://www.kebeilaw.com/
Specialty: M&R, international investment, big project tender, IPR, stock market, foreign legal services

XINJIANG

Xinjiang Tianyang Law Firm (English-speaking)
24&25F Tower A Shiji Baisheng Plaza, No. 36 Xinhua S Rd.
Urumqi City, Xinjiang, China

Tel: (0991) 2842887; 2818102
Fax: (0991) 2825559
Email: bgsxj@tianyanglaw.com
http://www.tianyanglaw.com/
Specialty: M&R, international investment, constructive project tender, IPR, stock market, internet & e-business, arbitration, legal consultation

Xinjiang Tianyang Law Firm (Beijing office) (English-speaking)
12F Tower A Guoxing Plaza, No. 22 Shouti S Rd. Beijing, China
Tel: (010) 88355211
Fax: (010) 88355208
Email: bgsbj@tianyanglaw.com
http://www.tianyanglaw.com/
Specialty: M&R, international investment, constructive project tender, IPR, stock market, internet & e-business, arbitration, legal consultation

Xinjiang Zhengjia Law Firm (English-speaking)
12F Xiangcheng Plaza
No. 527 Kezi Duwei Rd.
Kashi City, Xinjiang, China
Tel: (0998) 2879696; 2879715
Mobile: 86-15886887888
Fax: (0998) 2879696
Email: bgsxj@163.com
Specialty: all kinds of legal services

SHANGHAI

Baker & McKenzie, Shanghai Office
Attorney Contact: Danian Zhang
Address: 88 Century Avenue, Jin Mao Tower – Unit 1601, Shanghai 200121
Tel: 021-6105-8585
Fax: 021-5047-0020
E-mail: danian.zhang@bakermckenzie.com
Website: www.bakermckenzie.com
Main Practices: Insurance, Banking/Financial, Commercial/Business, Foreign Investment, Marketing Agreements, Intellectual Property, Civil Law, Damages, Contracts, Transportation, Corporation, Foreign Claims, Taxation, Labor Relations, Immigration, Mergers and Acquisitions, Securities and Initial Public Offerings, Dispute Resolution and Arbitration, Real Estate, Anti-Trust, Environmental.
English speaking staff.
Offers free initial consultation by phone.

Faegre Baker Daniels LLP, Shanghai Office
Attorney Contact: John V. Grobowski
Address: 1601 Nanjing Road West, Park Place – Suite 2702, Shanghai 200040
Direct Tel: 021-6171-6588
Office General Tel: 021-6171-6600
Fax: 021-6171-6601
Email: john.grobowski@faegrebd.com
Website: www.faegrebd.com
Main practices: Insurance, Banking/Financial, Commercial/Business, Foreign Investment, Marketing Agreements, Intellectual Property, Civil Law, Contracts, Transportation, Corporation, Taxation, Government Relations, Labor Relations, Immigration, Anti-Trust, Architecture &

Engineering
Specializes in: corporate law.
English Speaking Staff
Offers free initial consultation by phone.

Hogan Lovells International LLP
Attorney Contact: Andrew McGinty
Address: 1601 West Nanjing Road, Park Place-18th Floor, Shanghai 200040
Tel: 021-6122-3800
Fax: 021-6122-3899
E-mail: andrew.mcginty@hoganlovells.com
Website: www.hoganlovells.com
Main Practices: Insurance, Banking/Financial, Commercial/Business, Foreign Investment, Marketing Agreements, Intellectual Property, Contracts, Transportation, Corporation, Government Relations, Labor Relations
Specializes in: litigation, corporate and employment matters
English speaking staff
Offers free initial consultation by phone

Chinese Law Firms in Shanghai

GANUS Law Offices
Attorney Contact: Erex Chen
Address: 855 South Pudong Road, World Plaza – 21st Floor, 200120
Tel: 021-5877-2770 (ext. 706) or 133-9105-2852
Fax: 021-5877-0160
Email: erexchen@cnlawoffices.cn, erexcxl@gmail.com
Website: www.ganuslaw.com
Main Practices: Family Law, Adoptions, Child Custody, Parental Child Abduction, Child Protection, Marriage/Divorce, Insurance, Banking/Financial, Commercial/Business, Foreign Investment, Marketing Agreements, Patents/Trademarks/Copyrights, Civil Law, Criminal Law, Damages, Narcotics, Collections, Commercial Law, Contracts, Transportation,, Corporation, Aeronautical/Maritime, Foreign Claims, Estates, Taxation, Government Relations, Labor Relations, Immigration, Auto/Accidents.
Specializes in: criminal law, corporate, commercial law, intellectual property, trade and settlement
English speaking staff
Offers free initial consultation by phone

Han Kun Law Offices Shanghai Branch
Attorney Contact: Yinshi Cao
1266 Nanjing West Road, Plaza 66-Tower 1- Suite 5709, Shanghai
Tel: 021-6080-0909
Fax: 021-6080-0999
E-mail: Yinshi.Cao@hankunlaw.com
Website: www.hankunlaw.com
Main Practices: Commercial/Business, Foreign Investment, Marketing Agreements, Intellectual Property, Civil Law, Contracts, Corporation, Foreign Claims, Estates, Government Relations, Labor Relations.
Specializes in: capital market, dispute resolution
English speaking staff
Offers free initial consultation by phone

Shanghai Li Xiaohua Law Firm
Attorney Contact: Xiaohua Li

Address: Royal Court Hotel, Suite 201, 7 Middle Huaihai Road – Lane 622, Shanghai 200020
Tel: 021-6385-8668 (ext. 239)
E-mail: lxh@lxh-lawfirm.com
Website: www.lxh-lawfirm.com
Main Practices: Family Law, Adoptions, Marriage/Divorce, Insurance, Banking/Financial, Commercial/Business, Foreign Investment, Marketing Agreements, Intellectual Property, Civil Law, Criminal Law, Damages, Narcotics, Contracts, Corporation, Estates, Taxation, Government Relations, Labor Relations, Immigration, Auto/Accidents, Legal Counselor
Specializes in: criminal law
English speaking staff
Offers free initial consultation by phone

Watson & Band Law Offices
Attorney Contact: George Fu
Address: 755 Weihai Road, Wen Xin United Press Tower – 26th Floor, Shanghai, 200041
Tel: 021-5292-1111; 021-6350-0777
Fax: 021-5292-1001; 021-6272-6366
Email: mail@watson-band.com.cn
Website: www.watson-band.com.cn
Main Practices: Intellectual Property, Unfair Competition, Antitrust & Competition, FCPA & Anti-Commercial Bribery, Custom Practice, Liquidation & Bankruptcy, Compliance, Commercial/Business, Contracts, Foreign Investment, Taxation, Government Relations, Insurance, Banking/Financial, Civil Law, Labor Relations, Criminal Law.
Offers free initial consultation by phone
Specializes in: general law
English speaking staff
Offers free initial consultation by phone

Zhong Yin Law Firm, Shanghai Office
Attorney Contact: Haiying Shen
Address: 1 Pudong Avenue, China Marine Tower – Suite 1207, 12th Floor, Shanghai 200120
Tel: 021-6887 1787
Fax: 021-6886 9532
Email: tianjie@zhongyinlawyer.com ; doroto@163.com
Website: www.zhongyinlawyer.com
Main Practices: Family Law, Marriage/Divorce, Commercial/Business Law, Foreign Direct Investments, Civil Law, Damages, Commercial Law, Contracts, Corporations, Estates, Labor Relations, Auto/Accidents, Real Estate, Sports Law, Litigation and Arbitration. Specializes in: litigation, arbitration and settlement
English speaking staff
Offers free initial consultation by phone

HANGZHOU

T & C Law Firm – Zhejiang Office
Address: 1 Hangda Road, Dragon Century Square- 11F Block A, Hangzhou, Zhejiang 310007
Tel: 0571- 8790 1111
Fax: 0571-8790 1500
E-mail: patrickwlx@tclawfirm.com
Website: www.tclawfirm.com
Main Practices: Family Law, Insurance, Banking/Financial, Commercial/Business, Foreign Investment, Intellectual Property, Civil Law, Criminal Law, Contracts, Transportation, Corporation, Foreign Claims, Estates, Government Relations, Labor Relations, Securities Law, Legal Risk Management

Mostly Chinese speaking staff
Offers free initial consultation by phone

CHENGDU

ZANE International Law Firm, PLLC (Chengdu Branch)
Attorney Contact: Richard L. Zane, JD, Esq.
Address: Room 2016 Unit C Shang Pu International Fortune Centre, #6 Da Ye Road, Jin Jiang District, Chengdu, Sichuan
Tel: 028-6559-5002; 400-617-6663
Cell: 186-0283-0911 (China) +1-888-355-0226 (US)
Website: http://www.uszane.com/
E-mail: rich@uszane.com

Grandway Law Office (Chengdu & Chongqing)
Attorney Contact: Stewart Zhang
Address: Room 602, Tower E, China Overseas International Center, #333 Jiao Zi Avenue, Chengdu, Sichuan
Tel: 028-6558-5333
Fax: 028-6626-6533
E-mail: zhangyu@grandwaylaw.com
Website: http://www.grandwaylaw.com/cn/

King & Wood Mallesons (Chengdu & Chongqing)
Attorney Contact: Luo HaoFei/罗浩斐
Address: Unit G, 22nd Floor, City Heart, #86 1st Section South Ren Min Road, Chengdu, Sichuan
Tel: 028-8620-3818/15882012489 (Cell)
Fax: 028-86203819
E-mail: luohaofei@cn.kwm.com
Website: http://www.kingandwood.com/office.aspx?language=en&id=Chengdu

Young, Keen & Hua LLP
Attorney Contact: Diao Hong/刁红
Address: 10th Floor, No. 1 Building, Bo Jin Mansion, No. 27 Qing Long Street, Chengdu, Sichuan
Tel: 028-86282930
Cell: 130-7600-3277
Fax: 028-86282233
E-mail: Contactus@youngkeeuhua.com

Sichuan Hoke Law Firm
Attorney Contact: Regan Ferrell
Address: No. 11 11th Floor, Unit C, Jin Sha Wan Rui Center, No.1 Shu Jin Road, Chengdu, Sichuan
Tel: 028-8733-8318; 8733-9068; 8733-5868
Fax: 028-8774-8898
Website: http://www.heqilaw.com/index.asp

Sichuan Canway Law Firm
Attorney Contact: Mr. Li, Hao
Address: Hangxing International Plaza, No.66 Tianfusijie, Middle Section of Tianfu Avenue, South Hi-Tech Zone, Chengdu, Sichuan 610041
Tel: 028-8521-0123

Cell：139-0804-1406
Fax: 028-8521-7227
E-mail: canway@canwaylaw.com
Website: http://www.canwaylaw.com/ (Only in Chinese仅中文)
Practice Areas: Corporation Law

Sichuan Sifangda Law Firm
Attorney Contact: Mr. Wang, Shang/王上
Address: A-24F, Xiyu Mansion, No.8 Xiyu Street., Chengdu, Sichuan 610015
Tel: 028-8611-9970 (ext.71,72,73)
Cell：135-6880-6573
Fax: 028-8611-9827
E-mail: sfd@scsfd.com
Website: http://www.sifangda.com/
Practice Areas: International Law, Corporation Law, and Labor Dispute

Sichuan Grandall Law Firm
Attorney Contact: Mr.Zhao,Junxi
Address: A-24F, Xiyu Mansion, No.8 Xiyu Street., Chengdu, Sichuan 610015
Tel: 028-8612-1678
Cell：138-8181-6953
Fax: 028-8611-9827
E-mail: grandallcd@grandall.com.cn
Website: http://www.grandall.com.cn/index.htm
Practice Areas: International Business Law

Sichuan Zhigao Law Firm
Attorney Contact: Ms. Wu, Qiaoya
Address: 21th Floor, Unit 9-2, Tianfuxingu, No.399 West Section of Fucheng Avenue, Hi-Tech Zone, Chengdu, Sichuan 610041
Tel: 028-6155-8181
Cell：139-8223-7238
Fax: 028-8515-1003
E-mail: zg@sczhigao.com
Website: http://www.sczhigao.com/ (Only in Chinese中文)
Practice Areas: International Finance and Investment

Sichuan Zhongyi Law Firm
Attorney Contact: Ms. Gao, Xiaodong
Address: 10th Floor, Unit 6, Tianfuxingu, No.399 West Section of Fucheng Avenue, Hi-Tech Zone, Chengdu, Sichuan 610041
Tel: 028-8531-2773;8531-2779;8531-2270
Cell：138-8221-9411
Fax: 028-8531-1163
E-mail: zyls@zy_ls.com
Website: http://www.zy-ls.com/ (Only in Chinese中文)
Practice Areas: Finance and Contract Law

Sichuan Tahota Law Firm
Attorney Contact: Mr. Zhang, Tiankui
Ms. Ma, Chunyan
Address: A-25F, 27F,International Trade Center, No.117 South Gulou Street., Chengdu, Sichuan
Tel: 028-8662-5656, Ext: 804 (International dept.)
Cell：139-8218-5501（Mr. Zhang, Tiankui）139-8192-7908 (Ms. Ma, Chunyan)

Fax: 028-8676-1128
Website: www.tahota-lawyer.com (Chinese & English)
Practice areas: Finance and Commerce

Sichuan Yingji Law Firm
Attorney Contact: Mr. Wang, Nengchun
Mr. Gu, Jinyan
Address: No.18, Section 3, Middle Renmin Rd. Chengdu, Sichuan 610017
Tel: 028-8625-1610
Cell: 139-0801-4894
Fax: 028-8625-7918
Website: http://www.yingjilf.com/
Practice areas: Corporation Law, and labor law
Intellectual Property, and foreign proceedings

Sichuan Provincial Legal Aid Centre
Address: No. 24 Shangxiang Street, Chengdu, Sichuan
Tel: 12348 / 028-867-50814

KUNMING

Yunnan Qianhe Law Firm
Attorney Contact: Nie, Yuxuan
Address: 5th Floor Sports Mansion, No. 11 Middle Ren Min Road, Kunming, Yunnan
Tel: 0871-6317-2192/186-6921-7899（ Cell）
Cell: 186-6921-7899
Fax: 0871-6317-2192
Email: ynqhlawyer@vip.tom.com

Yunnan Jian Guang Law Firm
Attorney Contact: Zhang, Hui
Suite A 7th Floor, Society Science Research Institute, #577 Huang
Cheng Xi Road, Kunming, Yunnan
Tel: 0871-6364-4502
Fax: 0871-6364-4501
Cell: 133-5495-1488
E-mail: zhanghlawyer@163.com

Yunnan Shangyi Law Firm
Attorney Contact: Wang, Jianyong
Address: 26th Floor Zhengquan Mansion, #62 Chun Cheng Road, Kunming, Yunnan
Tel: 0871-6311-5820/6311-5542
Cell: 136-0885-5848
Fax: 0871-6317-4516
E-mail: jianyongwang99@yahoo.com.cn

Yunnan Datao Law Firm
Attorney Contact: Yan, Li
Yang, Zhengfa
Address: 11th Floor, Dan Tong Mansion, #548 Bai Yun Road, Kunming, Yunnan
Tel: 0871-6571-09550/6571-9544
Cell: 136-0885-5939（Yan, Li）/137-0061-3138 (Yang, Zhengfa)

Fax: 0871-6571-9533
E-mail: dataolawyer@126.com

Beichuan Law Firm
Attorney Contact: Liu, Liu
Address: 14F, Guangye Mansion, No. 2 Huguo Rd., Kunming, Yunnan Zip code: 650011
Tel: 0871-6311-6515
Cell 手机 13888787780
Fax: 0871-63116521
Website: www.beichuan.cn (Chinese & English Version)
Practice areas: Civil cases

International Lawyers Inc. China
Address: A1,B1 Zone, 16/F, Dantong Plaza, No. 548, Baiyun Rd., Kunming, Yunnan 650224
Tel: 0871-6573-2100
Fax: 0871-65731269
Cell: 138-8811-5950
Email: attorneys@china.com
Practice areas: Company law, marriage Law, and property law

Yunnan Zhenxu Law Firm
Attorney Contact: Mr. Jiang, Wenju
Mr. Zhang, Zhiyong
Address: 10F, #5 Bldg, Shulin Garden, Shulin St., Kunming, Yunnan 650011
Tel: 0871-6318-4701 / 6313-5726
Fax: 0871-6310-4024
E-mail: zhenxu@zhenxu.com.cn
Tel: 0871-6318-9864, Cell: 138-8880-1611 (Jiang, Wenjun/蒋文军)Practice areas: Company Law, financial law, civil law, and Mining Act
Tel: 0871-6313-7533, Cell: 1370-841-9766 (Zhang, Zhiyong/张智勇)
Practice areas: Sino-foreign joint venture, International investment

Yunnan Provincial Legal Aid Centre
Address: No. 26 Xichang Road, Kunming, Yunnan
Tel：12348 / 0871-4189036

CHONGQING

Solton & Partners
Address: Enrich International Plaza, 12 FL, #162, 3rd Zhongshan Rd., Yuzhong District, Chongqing
Tel: 023-63892901, 023-6363-1830
Fax: 023-6363-1834
Cell: 130-0231-6210（Zhang, Tao）
Practice areas: Investment, and Import/Export Trade
Cell: 139-8306-7186（Sheng, Jie）
Practice areas: Investment, Import/Export Trade, and civil dispute
Website: www.solton.com.cn

Chongqing Yuanbing Lawyers Office
Attorney Contact: Jiang, Min
Address: Hilton Hotel (12th Floor of Business Center), 3rd Zhongshan Road. Yuzhong District, Chongqing

Tel: 023-6387-4080, 023-8903-8518
Fax: 023-8903-8567
Cell: 134-5246-7886 (Jiang, Min)
Practice areas: Civil case

Chongqing Zhonghao Lawyers Office
Attorney Contact: Guo, Jia
Yang, Qing
Address: No. 68 Zourong Rd., 22 Fl. Daduhui Plaza, Yuzhong District, Chongqing
Tel: 023-6371-6888
Fax: 023-6371-6888
Cell: 185-2302-0548 (Guo, Jia)
182-0309-3176 (Yang, Qing)

Chongqing Zhihao Lawyers Office
Attorney Contact: Zhang, Zhiyong
Address: 22nd Floor Suite B, Xin Gan Xian Mansion, Liang Lu Kou, Yuzhong District, Chongqing
Tel: 023-6360-8269; 133-1024-0199
Cell: 133-0838-2919 (Zhang, Zhiyong)
Fax: 023-6360-8269
E-mail: zhihaolaw@sina.com
Practice Areas: Criminal Law in China

Chongqing GuoYan Law Firm
Attorney Contact: Yang, Xiaoying
Address: No. 66 East City Garden, Sha Ping Ba District, Chongqing
Cell: 150-2549-1085 (Yang, Xiaoying)
Practice Area: Foreign Affairs Case

Chongqing Municipal Legal Aid Centre
Address: No. 4 Huanglong Road, Yubei District, Chongqing
Tel: 12348 / 023-6708-6155

GUIYANG

Guizhou Beidouxing Law Firm
Attorney Contact: Huang, Yun
Address: 17th Floor, You Zheng Mansion, Middle Zhong Hua Road, Guiyang,

Guizhou
Tel: 0851-690-1517 / 690-1734
Cell: 138-8501-0933 Huang, Yun
Practice areas: Civil Action

Guizhou Xinhai Law Firm
Attorney Contact: Ren, Wu
Address: 10/F North Suite, Tianheng Mansion, No. 66 Fushuibei Road. Guiyang,

Guizhou
Tel: 0851-521-2510
Fax: 0851-521-2509
Cell: 138-8518-0351 (Ren, Wu)
Practice areas: Company Law, and Intellectual Property

Guizhou Xingke Law Firm
Attorney Contact: Shang, Bailing
Address: 22nd /F Suite B, Triumphal Arch Mansion, #60 North ZhongHua Road, Guiyang, Guizhou
Tel: 0851-681-3676 / 685-8316
Fax: 0851-681-3676
Cell: 182-5814-6512 (Shang, BaiLing)

Guizhou Gongxin Law Firm
Attorney Contact: Lu, Hao
Address: 5th Floor Jing Yuan Mansion, No.9 Wei Qing Road, Yun Yan District, Guiyang, Guizhou
Tel: 0851-652-6777
Fax: 0851-652-6777
Cell: 139-812-8677 (Lu, Hao)

Guizhou Provincial Legal Aid Centre
Address: No. 188 Dusi Road, Guiyang, Guizhou
Tel: 12348 / 0851-584-1580

LHASA

Tibet FaJian Law Firm
Attorney Contact: Yao, Kai
Address: No. 5 N. Deji Road, Lhasa
Tel: 0891-681-2161
Fax: 0891-681-8616
Cell: 139-8908-5416 (Yao, Kai)
Summer Working Hours: 08:30am – 1:00pm / 1:30pm – 6:00pm
Winter Working Hours: 09:30am – 1:00pm / 1:30pm – 6:00pm
Practice areas: Foreign related Law case

Tibet ZiChan Law Firm
Attorney Contact: Sun, Guilin
Address: No. 18 BeiJing Dong Road, Lhasa
Tel & Fax: 0891-634-9562
Cell: 139-8908-1556 (Sun, Guilin)
Summer Working Hours: 08:30 – 13:00 / 15:30 – 18:00
Winter Working Hours: 09:30 – 13:00 / 15:30 – 18:00
Practice area: Foreign related law case

Chomolungma Law Firm
Attorney Contact: Jeekme
Address: Jinzang Linkka A-11, No. 54 West Jinzhu Road, Lhasa
Tel: 0891-682-5168 / 682-5398 / 682-5578
Fax: 0891-6825288
Cell: 138-8900-3661(Jeekme)
E-mail: heyyak@yahoo.com.cn

Tibet Hengfeng Law Firm
Attorney Contact: Ousang Qunpei Baiga
Address: No.25 Dang Re Rd., Lhasa, Tibet
Tel: 0891-683-8899 (9:30am-1:00pm, 3:30pm-6:00pm)
Lawyer: Ousang Qunpei (English Speaker),

Cell: 139-0891-8861
Practice areas: International Law / Securities & Finance Law
Lawyer: Baiga (English Speaker) Cell: 13908991580
Practice area: Chinese Civil Law

Tibet Yuanshang Law Firm
Attorney Contact: Zhang, Yuehui
Address: No.1 De Ji Zhong Road., Lhasa, Tibet
Tel: 0891-683-0566 (9:30am-12:30pm, 2:30pm-6:00pm)
Cell: 138-8909-7044 Zhang, Yuehui
Practice area: Chinese Civil Law

Tibet Autonomous Region Legal Aid Centre
Address: No. 8 South Duodi Road, Lhasa, Tibet
Tel: 12348 / 0891-6325214

GUANGZHOU

Deacons Guangzhou Office
Address: Room 1808, 18/F South Tower, Guangzhou World Trade Center, 371-375 Huanshi Road East, Guangzhou, Guangdong
Tel: 020-8778-5678, 8778-7378
Fax: 020-8777-0488
Web site: www.deacons.com.hk
Specialty: Assists clients with investment and business transactions covering all industry sectors in China, including foreign investments, technology transfer and licensing; energy and natural resources; infrastructure and construction projects; telecommunications, land transactions and property development; securities; intellectual property protection; transportation, etc.
Languages spoken: English, Chinese, and French

Dezan Shira & Associates – Guangzhou office
Address: Unit 1005, 10/F, Tower B, Center Plaza, 161 Linhexi Road, Tianhe District, Guangzhou, Guangdong 510620
Tel: 020-3825-1526 Fax: 020-3825-1367
E-mail: guangzhou@dezshira.com Specialty: Provides assistance to foreign companies doing business in China including establishing and restructuring, legal and financial due diligences and M&A; advising on commercial contracts and IPR; full Corporate accounting services including bookkeeping, tax filling, payroll and internal reviewing, tax compliance and practice in the P.R.C.
Languages spoken: English, Mandarin, Cantonese, French, Italian and Spanish.

GFE Law Office
Address: 18/F Yuehai Mansion, 555 Dong Feng Road East, Guangzhou, Guangdong 510030
Tel: 020-8315-1955
Fax: 020-8315-0222
Specialty: Economic and civil cases.
Languages spoken: Chinese, English

Guangdong Hong An Xin Law Firm
Address: Room 1901-1903, 19/F Yuehai Mansion, 555 Dong Feng Road East, Guangzhou, Guangdong
Tel: 020-8384-9409
Fax: 020-8384-9799
E-mail: jianhua@21cn.com

Website: http://www.HonganLaw.com
Specialty: Economic, civil and criminal cases; also provides a wide range of other legal services
Languages spoken: Chinese, English

Guangdong Qi Yuan Law Office
Address: 3/F Guang Xin Peony Court, 187 Huang Pu Da Dao West, Guangzhou, Guangdong
Tel: 020-3831-2200, 3831-2188 Lawyers list 12/2013 3
Fax: 020-3831-2211
Specialty: Cases involving foreign trade, economics, maritime law and real estates
Languages spoken: Chinese, English

Guangzhou Guang Zhi Zhou Law Office
Address: Room 1506 Dong Bao Mansion, Dong Feng Road East, Guangzhou, Guangdong
Tel: 020-3821-0345, 3836-1035
Fax: 020-3821-0457
Specialty: Cases involving civil, economic, criminal matters and maritime law
Languages spoken: Chinese, English

Guangzhou King Pound Law Firm
Address: Room 3803 Fuli Yinglong Plaza, 76 Huang Pu Da Dao West, Guangzhou, Guangdong
Tel: 020-3839-0333
Fax: 020-3839-0218
Specialty: Economic, civil and criminal cases; also provides a broad range of legal services
Languages spoken: Chinese, English

H.J.M. International Law Offices
Address: Unit 2303 Hui Mei Building, 3 Jin Sui Road, Zhujiang New Town, Guangzhou, Guangdong
Tel: 020-8755-6610
Fax: 020-8755-6687
E-mail: webmaster@hjmlawyer.com
Specialty: International business, real Estate, finance and Insurance, administration and Criminal law, Intellectual Property
Languages spoken: English, Chinese

Law Offices of Frederick W. Hong
Address: Room 1503 North Tower, Guangzhou World Trade Center, 371-375 Huanshi Road East, Guangzhou, Guangdong
Tel: 020-8760-9933, 8760-9856
Fax: 020-8760-9896
Specialty: Provides legal services that include pre-investment planning, business negotiations, formation and structuring of joint ventures, wholly foreign-owned enterprises and representative offices, securing permits and licenses, government relations, international finance, commercial contracts, taxation, arbitration, litigation, intellectual property rights protection, as well as U.S. immigration and visa matters.
Languages spoken: English, Chinese

Law Offices of K. C. Li, American Attorneys at Law
Address: Room 906, Bldg B, Tian Yu Garden (Phase II), 142 Lin He Zhong Road, Tianhe District, Guangzhou, Guangdong
Tel: 020-3885-3644
Fax: 020-8121-6947
E-mail: gzomega@public.guangzhou.gd.cn or kacheungli@hotmail.com Lawyers list 12/2013 4

Specialty: Corporate / commercial law, immigration law and general practice
Languages spoken: Chinese, English

Wang Jing & Co. Law Firm
Address: 11/ F, Block D, G. T. Land Plaza, 8 Zhujiang Road West, Zhujiang New Town, Guangzhou 510623
Tel: 020-8393-0333
Fax: 020-3808-2990
Email: info@wjnco.com
Website: www.wjnco.com
Specialty: Assist predominantly foreign clients (European, Japanese, Hong Kong and U.S.A.) in their business activities in China, focusing on corporate investment and transactions, commercial contracts and dispute resolution, intellectual property rights protection (registration and enforcement).
Languages spoken: Chinese, English, Japanese, French, and Dutch.

SHENZHEN

Guangdong Shengfang Law Firm
Address: 8/F, Zhuoyue Plaza No. 98 Fuhua 1st Road, Futian District, Shenzhen, Guangdong 518048
Tel: 0755-8287-7888
Fax: 0755-8287-7778
Email: sflawyer@126.com.cn
Web Site: www.sflawyers.cn
Specialty: Legal consultancy and business legal issues, finance and security, intellectual property rights, foreign investment and international business, civil litigation and arbitration, criminal cases
Languages spoken: English, Mandarin and Cantonese.

Guangdong Harbor Law Firm
Address: Guangdong Harbor Law Firm Mansion, Ming Shang Golf Club, 111 Sha He Road East, Nanshan, District, Shenzhen, Guangdong
Tel: 0755-8299-0380 or 8608-4066
Fax: 0755-8299-0246
Specialty: Providing legal services in relation to domestic and foreign commerce, real estate, finance, securities, merger and acquisition, investment, intellectual property, criminal matters, litigation and arbitration.
Languages spoken: Chinese, English

TAISHAN

Guangdong Xiong Jun Law Firm
Address: No. 3 Jin Xiu Garden, Sha Gang Hu Road, Tai Cheng Town, Taishan, Guangdong
Tel: 0750-552-1181
Fax: 0750-553-0123
Language spoken: Chinese Lawyers list 12/2013 5

Guangdong Zhi Xin Law Firm
Address: 2/F, 37 He Bin Road Central, Tai Cheng Town, Taishan, Guangdong
Tel: 0750-552-1998
Fax: 075-552-1900
Language spoken: Chinese

ZHONGSHAN

Dezan Shira & Associates – Zhongshan office
Address: Room 921, West Bldg, Yi Hua Commercial Center, Zhongshan Road, Zhongshan, Guangdong, 528400
Tel: 0760-8826-9592
Fax: 0760-8830-7592
Email: zhongshan@dezshira.com
Specialty: Provides assistance to foreign companies doing business in China including establishing and restructuring, legal and financial due diligences and M&A; advising on commercial contracts and IPR; full Corporate accounting services including bookkeeping, tax filling, payroll and internal reviewing, tax compliance and practice in the P.R.C.
Languages spoken: English, Mandarin, Cantonese, French, Italian and Spanish.

FUZHOU

Fujian Chuang Yuan Law Office
Address: 28/F Block A Zhongshan Building, 154 Hu Dong Road, Gu Lou District, Fuzhou, Fujian 350003
Tel: 0591-8785-0803
Fax: 0591-8781-6904
Specialty: Civil, criminal and economic lawsuits and non-litigation cases; other legal matters such as commissions and investment. They also represent enterprises, institutions as permanent legal consultants
Languages spoken: Chinese, English

Fujian Jian Da Law Office
Address: 17/F West Area, 338 Hua Lin Road, Gulou District, Fuzhou, Fujian
Tel: (0591) 8767-6169
Fax: (0591) 8767-6123
Specialty: Civil, criminal, economic, finance and real estate lawsuits.
Languages spoken: Chinese, English

Fujian Rong Cheng Law Office
Address: 16/F, World Finance Building, Wu Si Road, Gulou District, Fuzhou, Fujian
Tel: 0591-8337-7794
Fax: 0591-8334-5707
Specialty: Civil, criminal and economic lawsuits and non-litigation cases; other legal matters such as commissions and investment. They also represent enterprises, institutions as permanent legal consultants Lawyers list 12/2013 6
Languages spoken: Chinese, English

Fujian Century Law Firm
Address: 6/F Jin Xiu Building, 145 Yang Qiao Zhong Road, Gulou District, Fuzhou, Fujian
Tel: (0591) 8377-2571, 8377-5687
Fax: (0591) 8377-2571
Website: www.lawyer86.com
Email: gaojianxun@sina.com
Specialty: International trade and investment, civil and commercial investigation, real estate, litigation, legal document translation, etc.
Languages spoken: Chinese, English

XIAMEN

Lian He Xin Shi Law Office
Address: Room 134 1/F Law Institute, Xiamen University, Xiamen, Fujian 361005
Tel: 0592-208-6165, 218-2409
Fax: 0592-208-6182
Specialty: Civil, criminal and economic lawsuits and non-litigation cases; other legal matters such as commissions and investment. Most of the lawyers of this Office also teach on the law faculty of Xiamen University. They also represent enterprises, institutions as permanent legal consultants.
Languages spoken: Chinese, English

Wang Jing & Co. Law Firm – Xiamen
Address: Suite 1606, Bank Center, 189 Xia He Road, Xiamen, Fujian
Tel: 0592-268-1376
Fax: 0592-268-1380
Email: Xiamen@wjnco.com
Website: www.wjnco.com
Specialty: Assist predominantly foreign clients (European, Japanese, Hong Kong and U.S.A.) in their business activities in China, focusing on corporate investment and transactions, commercial contracts and dispute resolution, intellectual property rights protection (registration and enforcement).
Languages spoken: Chinese, English, Japanese, French and Dutch.

Fujian Titan & Partners
Address: 7/F, Hualong Building, 6 Hu Bing Dong Road, Xiamen, Fujian
Tel: 0592-238-8618
Fax: 0592-238-8608
Website: www.Chinalegaladvice.com
Email: Stephen@chinalegaladvice.com
Specialty: Banking/financial, commercial/business law, foreign investments, patents/trademarks/copyrights, civil law, contracts, corporations, foreign claims.
Languages spoken: Chinese, English, Minnan dialect

Haikou

Hainan Hai Da Ping Zheng Lawyers Office
Address: Room 201 Block C She Ke Qun Lou, Hainan University, Haikou, Hainan 570228
Tel: 0898-6626-1295
Fax: 0898-6626-1295
Specialty: Civil, criminal and economic cases. Most of the lawyers also teach on the law faculty of Hainan University.
Languages spoken: Chinese, English

Hainan Wei Te Law Firm
Address: 4/F Shenzhen Development Building, 22 Jin Long Rd., Haikou, Hainan 570125
Tel: 0898-6853-3819, 6853-3919, 6855-4427, 6855-4437
Fax: 0898-6853-3516
E-mail: weitelawyer@vip.sina.com
Specialty: International trade, real estate, taxation, customs, intellectual property rights, financial, etc.
Languages spoken: Chinese, English

NANNING

Jin Gui Bei Dou Law Office
Address: 19/F Tai An Building, No. 38-2 Minzu Da Dao Central Section, Nanning, Guangxi 530022
Tel: 0771-586-7696, 586-7609
Fax: 0771-586-7661
Website: http://gxjgbd.com/
Specialty: Cases involving foreign and domestic trade and economics, as well as other legal matters.
Languages spoken: Chinese, English

Guangxi Guang He Law Office
Address: 15/F De Rui Building, 143 Minzu Da Dao, Nanning, Guangxi
Tel: 0771-551-6950; 551-6951; 551-6952
Website: www.gh-lawyer.com/
Languages spoken: Chinese, English

Beijing Dacheng (Nanning) Law Office
Address: 19/F Block D Jin Yuan CBD Xiandaicheng, 63 Jin Hu Road, Nanning, Guangxi
Tel: 0771-551-1820
Website: nanning.dachenglaw.com/about/?siteid=112
Languages spoken: Chinese, English Lawyers list 12/2013 8

Guilin

Guangxi Jun Jian Law Firm
Address: Room 801 Guilin Big World Mansion, 36 Zhongshan Road Central, Guilin, Guangxi
Tel: 0773-288-2826
Fax: 0773-288-2827
Website: http://www.junjianlaw.com/
Specialty: Litigation, non-litigation, all legal matters
Languages spoken: Chinese, English

Gold Hope Law Firm
Address: 6/F Mingcheng Hotel, 6 Zheng Yang Road, Guilin, Guangxi
Tel: 0773-281-9519
Website: www.gllawyer.com/index.php
Languages spoken: Chinese, English

LEADING SECTORS FOR US EXPORTS AND INVESTMENTS

AGRICULTURAL EQUIPMENT

U.S. manufacturers hold a 43.5 percent share of China's import market for agricultural equipment. Taking in into account domestic production, however, ITA estimates that imports from the United States represent less than two percent of a total Chinese market that may be worth as much as $8.8 billion. Despite their substantial position in the import market, strong and growing competition from domestic manufacturers and well-established third-country competitors challenge U.S. suppliers across all major categories of agricultural equipment sold in China.

In 2014, China was United States' sixth-largest export market for agricultural equipment, worth $376.1 million. Machinery and equipment for producing grains, oilseeds, and other commodity row crops represented 38.1 percent of total U.S. exports, valued at $143.2 million. Exports related to livestock and fresh produce represented 18.8 and 9.0 percent of total exports respectively, amounting to $70.8 million and $33.7 million. Exports of parts, at 34.2 percent of the total and with a value of $128.8 million, are proportional to global U.S. exports in this category. Exports of agricultural sprayers and tractors in the 40- 100hp and less-than-40hp ranges together accounted for less than one percent of U.S. exports.

Exports to China fell sharply in 2014, declining by 23.3 percent from the previous year. This followed the steep decline in global grain prices that began in 2011- 2012. It is consistent with falling exports in other markets where machinery and equipment for producing grains and oilseeds and other row crops are a large portion of U.S. exports.

U.S. shipments of agricultural equipment parts fell at almost the same rate in 2014—22.4 percent—as total agricultural equipment exports to China. Export performance in the broad parts segment varied widely in 2014, with strong growth in parts for highly specialized equipment such as milking machinery, seeders and planters, and certain tractor components. Weak 2014 results notwithstanding, exports of parts have grown strongly in recent years, at annual rate of more than 27 percent from 2009 to 2014.

Parts exports reflect not only the demand for after- market parts and components, but also the rapidly evolving character of China's agricultural equipment manufacturing sector. A downturn in domestic demand certainly contributed to this. However, the global decline in agricultural equipment trade—and Chinese exports— is also likely to have reduced Chinese demand for imported parts.

Total U.S. agricultural equipment exports to China will likely fall again in 2015, although not as sharply as last year, due to continued weakness in global grain prices. Stabilizing commodity prices will improve prospects for U.S. exporters in 2016. Exports of equipment for the livestock sector will remain a growth area for U.S. exporters. Fresh produce and other high-value food products represent an area of opportunity, especially as Chinese producers position themselves to comply with the U.S. Food Safety Modernization Act (FSMA). Significant risk will continue to characterize the Chinese market for U.S. exporters – even as the world's largest agricultural economy mechanizes itself at a rapid pace.

	United States Export Statistics Commodity: 8701, Tractors (Other Than Works Trucks Of Heading 8709)							
Rank	Partner Country	United States Dollars			% Share			% Change 2015/ 2014
		2013	2014	2015	2013	2014	2015	
	World	2305306046	2141220942	1808239435	100	100	100	- 15.55
1.	Canada	1186568048	1091491414	1060135556	51.47	50.98	58.63	- 2.87
2.	Australia	208279621	153479905	106873550	9.03	7.17	5.91	- 30.37
3.	Mexico	86061017	106205490	89012754	3.73	4.96	4.92	- 16.19
4.	Germany	65357959	47754758	41551240	2.84	2.23	2.30	- 12.99
5.	United Kingdom	42146876	27731013	35441632	1.83	1.30	1.96	27.81
6.	South Africa	82267308	95438015	34456348	3.57	4.46	1.91	- 63.90
7.	France	49749080	30418525	33293913	2.16	1.42	1.84	9.45
8.	Belgium	41086850	19852976	32934364	1.78	0.93	1.82	65.89
9.	Turkey	4348158	10933273	32643877	0.19	0.51	1.81	198.57
10.	Saudi Arabia	45699636	92391549	31609414	1.98	4.31	1.75	- 65.79
11.	Netherlands	31335425	45630265	28470701	1.36	2.13	1.57	- 37.61
12.	China	10024723	25574824	22214711	0.43	1.19	1.23	- 13.14

Source: Global Trade Atlas

Rank	United States Export Statistics Commodity: 8433, Harvesting Or Threshing Machines; Grass Or Hay Mowers; Machines For Cleaning, Sorting Or Grading Eggs, Fruit Or Other Produce, Nesoi; Parts Thereof							
Rank	Partner Country	United States Dollars			% Share			% Change
		2013	2014	2015	2013	2014	2015	2015/2014
	World	1495013897	1352199607	1292105230	100	100	100	- 4.44
1.	Canada	643506102	531634646	492028978	43.04	39.32	38.08	- 7.45
2.	Mexico	83896881	72648700	78450755	5.61	5.37	6.07	7.99
3.	Netherlands	46323364	36162314	70386476	3.10	2.67	5.45	94.64
4.	Australia	63902365	69009553	68783986	4.27	5.10	5.32	- 0.33
5.	China	40997487	23811792	65237866	2.74	1.76	5.05	173.97
6.	France	75703386	72052556	63564543	5.06	5.33	4.92	- 11.78

Source: Global Trade Atlas

	United States Export Statistics Commodity: 8432, Agricultural, Horticultural Or Forestry Machinery For Soil Preparation Or Cultivation; Lawn Or Sports Ground Rollers; Parts Thereof							
Rank	Partner Country	United States Dollars			% Share			% Change 2015/2014
		2013	2014	2015	2013	2014	2015	
	World	448999329	422735989	300765507	100.00	100.00	100.00	- 28.85
1.	Canada	226400608	205764021	159620029	50.42	48.67	53.07	- 22.43
2.	Australia	12639560	7260588	12258278	2.82	1.72	4.08	68.83
3.	Russia	41906724	35408142	10102954	9.33	8.38	3.36	- 71.47
4.	Mexico	12336056	9131571	9428369	2.75	2.16	3.13	3.25
5.	Germany	10607724	11990663	9180589	2.36	2.84	3.05	- 23.44
6.	Brazil	7632759	8581766	8394607	1.70	2.03	2.79	- 2.18
7.	Ukraine	30856401	34801119	7859333	6.87	8.23	2.61	- 77.42
8.	United Kingdom	6057884	6788969	7166638	1.35	1.61	2.38	5.56
9.	South Africa	7612570	7375097	7146052	1.70	1.74	2.38	- 3.11
10.	Kazakhstan	6564277	3285413	6938796	1.46	0.78	2.31	111.20
11.	China	10805207	10357340	5446228	2.41	2.45	1.81	- 47.42
12.	Japan	3550295	3508882	5093440	0.79	0.83	1.69	45.16

Source: Global Trade Atlas

	United States Export Statistics Commodity: 8434, Milking Machines And Dairy Machinery, And Parts Thereof							
	Partner Country	United States Dollars			% Share			% Change
		2013	2014	2015	2013	2014	2015	2015/2014
	World	46138256	53844761	59375026	100.00	100.00	100.00	10.27
1.	Canada	13209371	19504301	19711969	28.63	36.22	33.20	1.06
2.	China	3101271	1724177	7986479	6.72	3.20	13.45	363.21
3.	Saudi Arabia	4195166	7033762	6634669	9.09	13.06	11.17	- 5.67
4.	Netherlands	898845	4603739	5004762	1.95	8.55	8.43	8.71
5.	Germany	1574024	2981304	3406121	3.41	5.54	5.74	14.25
6.	Mexico	1066539	1710378	2973080	2.31	3.18	5.01	73.83
7.	Japan	1641085	1845629	1900525	3.56	3.43	3.20	2.97

Source: Global Trade Atlas

Opportunities

The country is in the midst of an historic transformation from traditional, labor-intensive farming practices to mechanized, high-technology agriculture. A variety of forces drive this transformation. The Chinese Government, which effectively owns and operates the country's farm sector, has made mechanizing agriculture and moving rural inhabitants to urban areas a top policy objective. Behind this policy lie China's changing demographics, limited agricultural land and water resources, the Chinese population's increasingly varied dietary preferences, and the high priority the government continues to attach to food security.

A major influence driving mechanization of Chinese agricultural is the need to make the most of scare agricultural land and water. Although China has roughly 20 percent of the world's population, it possesses only nine percent of the world's farmland and six percent of its freshwater. Freshwater per capita in 2009 was one-third the global average at the time.

Land and water are also located disproportionately in different parts of the country. Sixty-five percent of China's agricultural land is in northern China, which produces half the country's grain and nearly all of its wheat and corn, along with numerous other commodities. Yet, only 20 percent of China's freshwater resources are located in the north.

The opportunities presented by the rapid mechanization of the world's largest agricultural economy have to be balanced against the challenges faced by U.S. exporters doing business in China. These challenges include an array of Chinese Government policies, local business practices, and the cost—and attendant business risk—of simply establishing business operations in China before significant sales can be realized.

Market Entry

There are no specific market-access restrictions. However, subsidy policies do pose a challenge to U.S. exporters. The competition between local Chinese suppliers of low-end and mid-range equipment is fierce. This leaves the high-end technology/equipment market as a practical target for U.S. manufacturers.

In 2005, the Chinese government began to subsidize agriculture machinery for farmers. The government does not subsidize all equipment; only what it determines to be eligible for "government promotion." Eligible categories include: tractors, harvesting machines, planters, land preparation machines, crop care machines, and dairy machines. Provincial and local governments decide on which equipment they want to subsidize. There are no subsidies for imported products.

Market Demand

Domestic agricultural machinery production and sales maintained strong growth, but not for all sectors. Sales of soil tillage machinery, grain combines, rice transplanting and corn harvesting machinery were 1,578,000 units, 222,000 units, 97,000 units, and 52,000 units respectively in 2012.

In 2012, for agricultural machinery industry sales, Shandong Province ranked first with a 22% share; Henan Province ranked second with 19%; Jiangsu Province ranked third with 10%; and Zhejiang Province ranked fourth with 6%. Large-scale enterprises (with sales revenue of at least $3.2 million) produced the majority of China's agricultural machinery in these four provinces alone.

According to the China Agricultural Machinery Distribution Association (CAMDA), the agricultural machinery industry's top five manufacturers comprised only 24.8% of the industry market shares in 2011.

Market Obstacles

Inadequacies in China's protection and enforcement of intellectual property rights (IPR) continue to present serious barriers to U.S. exports. China was again placed on the Priority Watch List in the 2015 Special 301 report, and several online and physical markets were named in USTR's 2013 Out-of-Cycle Review of Notorious Markets, which identifies Internet and physical markets that exemplify key challenges in the global struggle against piracy and counterfeiting.

The protection and enforcement of trade secrets in China is also a serious problem. Thefts of trade secrets that benefit Chinese companies occur both within China and beyond its borders. The Chinese Government frequently has failed to recognize serious infringements of IPR that violate Chinese law. Entities affiliated with the Chinese Government and the Chinese military have infiltrated the computer systems of U.S. companies, stealing huge amounts of data, including intellectual property.

For more details on China's IPR environment, please refer to the materials located in the "China IPR Toolkit" located at: http://beijing.usembassy-china.org.cn/ipr.html

For more information on these and other concerns, see the "2014 National Trade Estimate Report on Foreign Trade Barriers," published by the United States Trade Representative, athttps://ustr.gov/sites/default/files/2014%20NTE%20Report%20on%20FTB.pdf.

Web Resources

Ministry of Agriculture, China
www.moa.gov.cn
Ministry of Water Resource, China
www.mwr.gov.cn
Chinese Academy of Agricultural Mechanization Sciences
www.caams.org.cn

Contacts

U.S. Embassy in Beijing
Feng Tan, Commercial Specialist
(86-10) 8531-3000
Feng.tan@trade.gov

U.S. Consulate in Shenyang
Yang Liu, Senior Commercial Specialist
(86- 24) 2322-1198
Yang.liu@trade.gov

U.S. Consulate in Chengdu
Liping Lin, Senior Commercial Specialist
(86- 28) 8598-6633
Liping.Lin@trade.gov

U.S. Consulate in Shanghai
Ken Shen, Commercial Specialist
(86- 21) 6279-8789
Ken.Shen@trade.gov

U.S. Consulate in Guangzhou
Sophie Xiao, Commercial Specialist
(86- 20) 3814-5613
Sophie.Xiao@trade.gov

Ackles Zhu, Commercial Assistant
(86-20) 3814 – 5886
Ackles.Zhu@trade.gov

AGRICULTURAL SECTORS

The United States Department of Agriculture, through the Foreign Agricultural Service (FAS), operates six offices in the People's Republic of China for the purpose of expanding exports of U.S. agriculture, fishery, and forestry products. U.S. agricultural, fishery, and forestry exports to China from January to December 2014 were $28 billion, down 2percent from 2013. That said, China remains the United States' No.1 largest market for agricultural exports. Soybeans are the largest agricultural export to the Chinese market ($14.7 billion), accounting for over half of the total, followed by distiller grains ($1.2 billion), hides and skins ($1.1 billion), and dairy products ($697 million). China accounted for 17 percent of total U.S. agricultural exports in 2014.

These figures continue to underline a shift in Chinese agricultural imports away from products for processing and re-export, to finished products for consumption at home. While overall exports of U.S. consumer-oriented food products to China slowed by 19% in 2014, to $2.4 billion, this level of exports is still well above the five year average. Exports of fruits & vegetable juices and snack foods rose to peak imports. Stronger export growth continued for inputs into China's burgeoning animal husbandry sector. Delays in China's approval of biotech corn varieties strongly impacted U.S. corn exports. However, after its first year of commercial exports of sorghum to China, U.S. exports of sorghum skyrocket in 2014.

Key consumer trends over the past year have highlighted, in addition to growth in animal husbandry, continued consumer concern for food safety, and the expansion of e-commerce. The former has been a driving factor for imports, which are seen as being more heavily inspected and generally safer than local products. The impact has been particularly strong for dairy products, especially those for children, and food ingredients for Chinese manufacturers seeking to avoid problems with locally sourced ingredients.

E-commerce was the other major trend for food imports, as growth rates for e-commerce far exceeded those for any other sales format. This is also being affected by consumer concerns over food safety: in general, e-commerce products are seen as more authentic and safer than those purchased through traditional stores. Logistics for e-commerce matured, with products as delicate as fresh cherries and pears from the U.S. and live seafood being promoted and shipped through these channels quite successfully.

Since 2013, China has embarked on a comprehensive review of its food safety and agricultural standards, including an extensive overhaul of its National Food Safety Law. Due to the changing regulatory environment in China, U.S. exporters are advised to carefully check import regulations. Individuals and enterprises interested in exporting U.S. agriculture, fishery, and forestry commodities to China should contact the FAS offices (listed below) as well as USDA Cooperator organizations. Exporters of U.S. agricultural commodities should also review the FAS website (http://www.fas.usda.gov), which features general information about trade shows and other promotional venues to showcase agricultural products, FAS-sponsored promotional efforts, export financing and assistance, and a directory of registered suppliers and buyers of agricultural, fishery, and forestry goods in the United States and abroad.

The Animal Plant Health Inspection Service also operates an office in Beijing.

Best Prospects

Animal Feed
Hides and Skins
Dairy Products
Fish and Fish Products
Processed Food Products
Tree Nuts
Soybeans
Fresh Fruit
Wood and Wood Products

Offices

Agricultural Affairs Office
AgBeijing@usda.gov

Agricultural Trade Office - Beijing
ATOBeijing@usda.gov

Agricultural Trade Office - Guangzhou
ATOGuangzhou@usda.gov

Agricultural Trade Office - Shanghai
ATOShanghai@usda.gov

Agricultural Trade Office - Chengdu
ATOChengdu@usda.gov

Agricultural Trade Office - Shenyang
ATOShenyang@usda.gov

Animal and Plant Health Inspection Service
Elia.P.Vanechanos@aphis.usda.gov

Annual GAIN Reports
FAS publishes a wide range of reports on agriculture, agricultural markets and market access issues and regulations. These reports are available on the FAS webpage at:http://gain.fas.usda.gov/Pages/Default.aspx

AUTOMOTIVE COMPONENTS MARKET

The Government of China has viewed its automotive sector, including the auto parts industry, as a pillar industry for many years. China continues to be the World's largest automobile market in 2014. Auto sales grew at a compound annual rate of nearly 17% between 2003 and 2014, according to PricewaterhouseCoopers. According to the statistics released by China Association of Automobile Manufacturers in January, 2015, the total annual automobile output in China was 23.72 million a 7.26% year on year growth, the total sales was 23.49 million, a 6.86% year on year growth. The total annual output of passenger vehicles was 19.91 million, a 10.15% year on year growth. The total sales were 19.70 million, a 9.89% year on year growth, which SUV's sales were 4.08 million (a 36.4%y-on-y growth), MPV's sales were 1.91 million (a 46.8% y-on-y growth), sedan's sales were 12.38 million (a 3.1% y-on-y growth), cross passenger car's sales were 1.33 million units (a 18.1% y-on-y decline). It is projected that the total annual sales in 2015 will reach 25.13 million units, which 24.27 million units are for domestic sales, 0.86 million units for export. (Source: China Association of Auto Manufacturers)

China's top ten passenger car manufacturers in 2014 were: FAW-Volkswagen, Shanghai GM, Shanghai Volkswagen, Beijing Hyundai, Nissan-DFM, Shenlong, Chang'an Ford, Dongfeng Yueda Kia, FAW Toyota and Guangzhou Auto Honda. In 2014 these ten companies accounted for 69.82% of total auto sales in China.

The total import and export trade for automobile and its components valued 182.9 billion U.S. $, with a year on year growth of 15% in 2014, which import valued 100.3 billion U.S. $, export valued 82.6 billion U.S. $, with a trade deficit of 17.8 billion U.S. $.

The China Association of Automobile Manufacturers expects passenger-vehicle sales to rise 8% to 21.3 million vehicles in 2015, compared with 9.9% growth in 2014. China Automotive Industry Association predicts the sales volume of saloon car will be 12,510,000 and the growth rate will be 1% in 2015. This data for SUV and MPV are 5,100,000, 25% and 2,580,000 and 35%. 1,060,000 and -20% are the data for multi-purpose passenger cars. The total sales volume of passenger car in 2015 will be around 21,250,000 and the growth rate will be 8%.

Sub-Sector Best Prospects

Best prospects in China's auto industry include electric vehicles (EVs) and new energy vehicles (NEVs) as well as recreational vehicles (RVs).

Electric Vehicles (EVs) and New Energy Vehicles (NEVs)

China is the world's largest market for automobiles and the world's top auto producer. China plans to grow its production of new energy autos and parts by 35 percent annually, dedicating more than $18 billion in government support to the sector through 2020. If achieved, China will very likely become the world's leading producer of electric and hybrid vehicles and their key components by 2030.

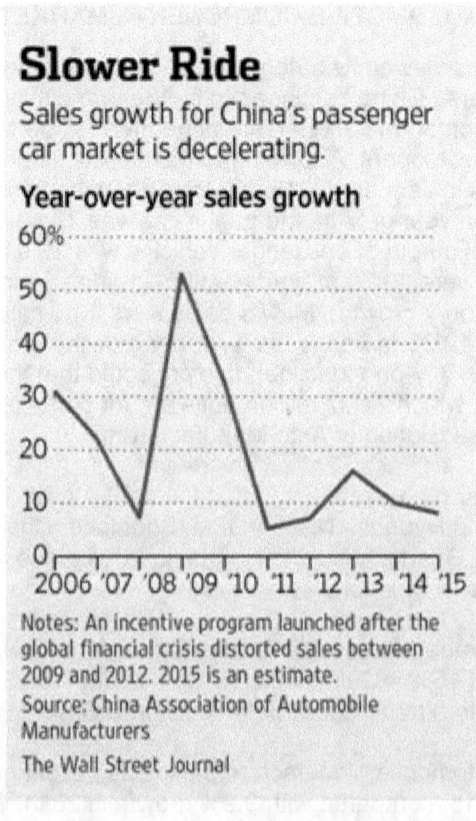

Facts on automotive industry sales in China

(Source: The Statistics Portal, in Chinese Renminbi

Automobile Sales Figures	Values
Trade value of cars in China in Mar 2015	268.4bn
Growth rate of vehicle sales in China in 2014	6.86
Forecast for the number of passenger cars sold in China in 2025	27.6m
Volkswagen market share in China	13%
SAIC Motor revenue	565.81bn
Customers and Users	**Values**
Number of drivers in China 2013	217.43m
Privately owned vehicles in China 2013	105.02m
Length of car ownership of 2 to 4 years	56%
Foreign brands as most recently purchased car brand in China	81%
Luxury Car Market	**Values**
Number of Mercedes Benz cars sold in China	198,520
Number of Lexus cars sold in China	56,000
Audi ad spend	2,240m
BMW ad spend	1,427m
Used Car Market	**Values**
Trade volume of used cars in China in 2014	367.57bn
Used car unit sales in China	4.79m
Number of used cars sold in China in 2014	6.05m

The total sales of NEVs in 2014 were 75 thousands units with a year on year growth of 324%, which pure electric vehicles' sales were 45 thousands units with a year on year growth of 208%, plug-in electric vehicles' sales were 30 thousands units with a year on year growth of 878%.

16 NEV related policies were released in 2014 to support the NEV industry development, the "Fiscal Subsidy to NEVs for 201-2020 Notice" has recently been issued, according to the Notice, with the exception of fuel cell NEVs, subsidies for all other types of NEVs will be reduced by 20% during 2017-2018 from the levels in 2016, and 40% during 2019-2020. The 2013-2015 plan provided a national subsidy of RMB 35,000-60,000 ($5,656-$9,696) for consumers who purchase NEVs. Vehicles qualify for the subsidy as long as they are in a Ministry of Industry and Information Technology (MIIT) catalogue restricted to locally-produced models. According to the "Government and Public Institutions New Energy Vehicle Procurement Plan, at least 30% of Official Used Vehicles must be NEVs between 2014 and 2016.

The Chinese government 12th Five-Year-Plan (2011-2015) includes specific directives to steer the nation toward energy-efficient vehicles, specifically New Energy Vehicles (NEVs), as a way to combat petroleum imports and oil dependency, as well as to build new industrial capacity. For example, during the 12th FYP, the central government initiated the "Ten Cities, 1,000 Vehicle Program" to stimulate electric vehicle development in ten cities. Shenyang, Changchun, Harbin and other 23 cities are pointed as the second bunch of NEV demonstration cities, in addition to the 28 areas/cities jointly announced by the Ministry of Industry and Information Technology,

National Development and Reform Commission, Ministry of Finance and Ministry of Technology in November, 2013. This Plan now includes 88 areas/cities.

The "Notice on exception from Vehicle Purchase Taxation of NEVs" released by the Ministry of Finance, National Taxation Bureau and Ministry of Industry and Information Technology except NEVs' from Vehicle Purchase Taxation, this applied not only to domestic made NEVs, but also pure electric vehicles, hybrid and battery electric vehicles imported from overseas.

According to China's 2014 draft Catalogue Guiding Foreign Investment (CGFI), foreign investment in the NEV industry is "encouraged," meaning that there are few restrictions on such activities. Nevertheless, a 50 percent ownership cap remains in battery manufacturing—a crucial component for NEVs—mirroring the 50 percent ownership caps across the auto industry.

The New BEV Passenger Car Production Enterprise Investment Projects and Rules on the Production Admission Administration has completed opinion collection in March 2015 and is expected to be introduced within the year. In accordance with the opinion draft, there is hope of loosening electric car production qualification in China, Then parts manufacturing firms (e.g. Wanxiang), internet companies (e.g. Letv), low-speed electric car companies (e.g. Yogomo) and other non-traditional car companies are likely to get the electric car production license, and Chinese electric vehicle market will present the characteristics of diversification.

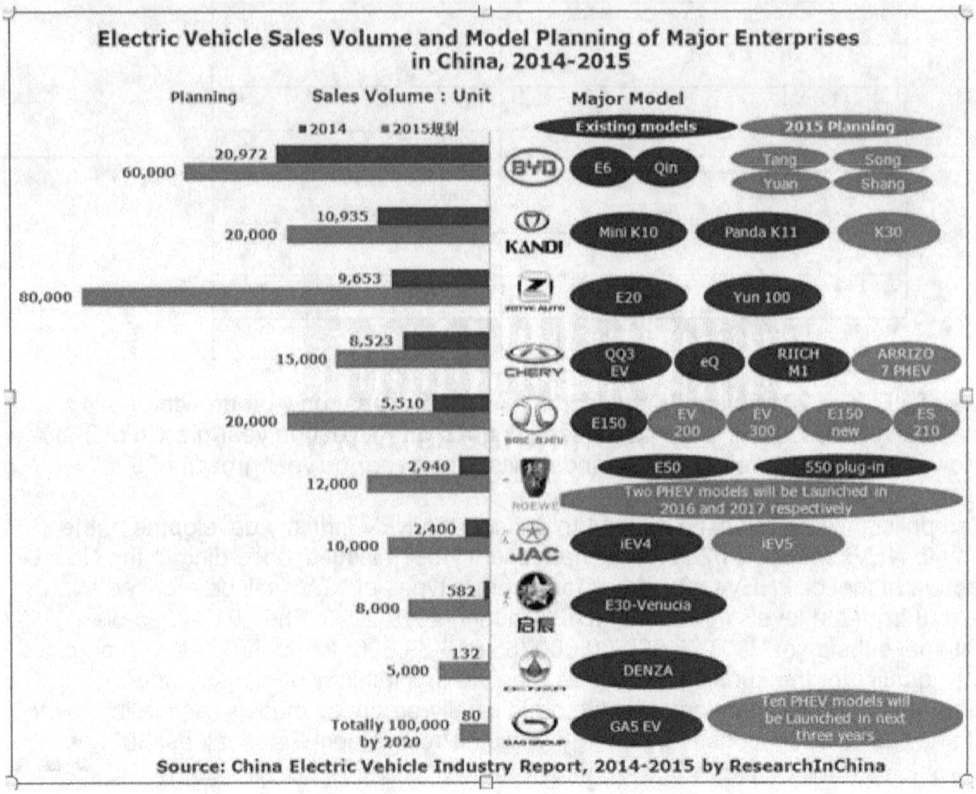

Number of Chinese Charging Stations and YoY Growth Rate, 2010-2016 E

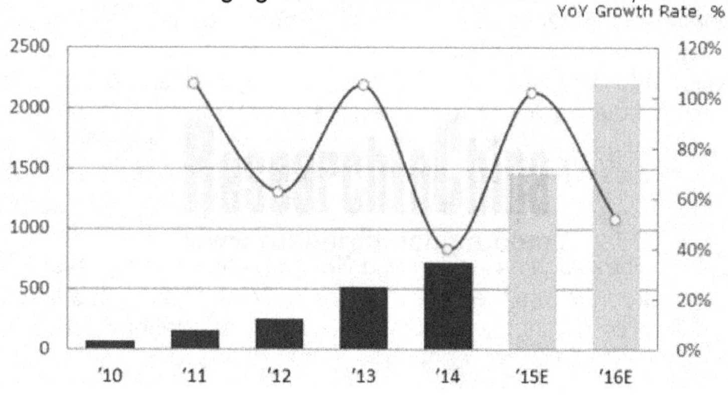

Recreational Vehicles

China's RV market has undergone significant changes over the past several years, including a national focus on the development of tourism, campgrounds and the RV industry. With a growing demand for RVs and a shift in consumers' travel preferences, tourism experts in China anticipate a surge of RV-related businesses in the coming years. While currently there are roughly 10,000 RVs in China, the Shanghai Tourism Administration predicts that this number could reach three million in the coming decade. China's rapidly growing economy and rising middle class are fueling an unprecedented demand for leisure-related goods and activities, such as RVs and RV camping.

China ranks second only to Canada as a destination market for U.S. RV exports. While exports to China are small compared to Canada, they are expected to grow considerably over the next three years. Some industry associations estimate that U.S. RV exports to China will increase to $80.2 million in 2017, with an annual growth rate of 22 percent.

China currently has about 40 RV manufacturers, comprising mainly of converters and specialty vehicle makers. Domestically produced RVs dominate the marketplace, accounting for about 60 percent of overall RV sales in China. Chinese manufacturers offer a variety of products, from towable RVs to motorhomes, ranging in price from about RMB 44,500 to over RMB 1 million ($7,100 USD to over $159,000 USD). It is believed that none of the Chinese manufacturers make an RV that is exportable to the United States.

Despite the growing popularity and demand for RVs, China has only about 100 campgrounds nationwide. Less than 50 of these are RV-ready. The lack of an adequate RV infrastructure has led to unrealized potential for exports of downstream goods and services needed by RV travelers (such as camping equipment, clothing, gasoline, food, leasing, etc.)

In addition to the shortage of campgrounds, growth of the RV industry has also been hampered by the lack of a standards and a regulatory framework governing the manufacture and use of RVs. Although some government agencies have adopted their own rules and regulations for RVs, these are not uniform across agencies. Existing standards and regulations are primarily based on motor vehicle-related standards without regard to the unique characteristics of RVs.

China has made a push in recent years to develop domestic tourism. China's State Council circulated an opinion in December 2009 on accelerating development of the tourism industry. The document specified that China should vigorously support the emerging tourism industry, including RVs and outdoor lifestyle activities.

Campground development has received strong support from the government in China. In August 2014, the State Council called for the development of campgrounds and campground standards, and to update existing requirements on travel trailers. In October 2014, the State Council specified the need for auto campsites and RV-ready campgrounds and it included RVs and camping among one of the six growth areas the government is focusing on in an effort "to promote consumer spending on tourism and leisure activities." In addition, the Chinese automotive industry has listed RVs as a key emerging sector to boost healthy, rapid and stable development.

At the local level, large cities such as Beijing and Shanghai are actively involved in efforts to develop tourism, campgrounds and the RV industry. In October 2014, the first campground for RVs in Shanghai opened on Chongming Island. It features recreation facilities that offer a range of activities for RV owners and visitors wanting to rent RVs onsite.

Newly developed campgrounds are emerging monthly across China. These include sites in Anhui, Guizhou, Heilongjiang, Hebei, Henan, Liaoning, Ningxia, Sichuan, Yunnan, and Zhejiang provinces. National and local tourism officials have plans to develop other campgrounds in a number of other locations as well, including RV service centers in the Yangtze River Delta.

China hosts two major RV trade shows -- the China Beijing International RV and Camping Exhibition (March) and All In Caravaning (AIC) (June). The Beijing International RV and Camping Exhibition is hosted by the Beijing Tourism Development Commission, People's Government of Fangshan and the Beijing China RV & Camping Association. Exhibitors include manufacturers and suppliers from a range of motorized and towable RVs, parts and accessories, outdoor/camping products, and representatives from the campground and park industries.

Key Auto Parts and Technologies

China is the third largest market for U.S. auto parts exports. In 2014, there were $2.5 billion in exports with an increase of 13% from the previous year. China exported $16 billion in auto parts to the United States in 2013, an increase of 9%.With the rapid growth in automobile market in China, auto parts and technologies are also developing rapidly. There are more than 10,000 auto parts enterprises in China (which scaled enterprises no more than 6,000), enterprises with foreign background counts for 20% of the scaled enterprises (45% wholly foreign owned, 55% JV), but its market share is over 70%. Enterprises with foreign background (40% wholly foreign owned, 35% JV) occupies ¾ of the key and core auto parts manufacturing market.

China Association of Automobile Manufacturers has set up 12 auto (motorcycle) parts manufacturing basis to further promote auto parts manufacturing development in China. Those 12 auto parts manufacturing basis are located in Zhejiang, Guangxi, Jiangsu, Sichuan, Anhui, Hebei provinces and Dalian, Chongqing and Wuhan cities.

Shanghai and its surrounding provinces (Zhejiang, Jiangsu, and Anhui) are the centers for component manufacturing, representing around 44% of national production. Shanghai is home to Shanghai General Motors, Delphi, Visteon, and other notable American automotive companies. Therefore, Shanghai provides a good starting point for American automotive component exporters to explore the Chinese market. In addition to Shanghai, other major automotive centers in China include: Beijing (Capital), Guangzhou (South China), Chongqing (West China), and Changchun (North China).

New auto-related regulations and policies in China continue to be developed as the market grows. In late 2014, there were some new announcements related to the distribution of aftermarket parts, requirements for automakers sharing technical information with independent repair shops, and establishing minimum service requirements for independent repair shops. This may allow non- original equipment manufacturers to sell to dealers and end users.

The following automotive segments in China are considered to be highly competitive and will be relatively difficult for low-tech automotive goods segments to penetrate, unless they have a unique competitive advantage. For example, these segments are dominated by low-cost producers:

1. Fabric for seats/interiors
2. Seat covers
3. Floor mats
4. Curtains
5. Aluminum die casting
6. Rubber bumpers
7. Electronic harness cables
8. Antennas
9. Speakers
10. Electric starters
11. Vehicle cleaning products
12. Window films
13. A/C compressors
14. Fuel, air and oil filters

Key auto parts and technologies are facing the following challenges:

1. Key auto parts import increased, low end products export declined.
2. Foreign auto parts manufacturers occupy China's high end auto parts market, which challenge local brands' development.
3. Lack of policy support on auto parts
4. Technology innovation needs more fiscal support
5. IP protections on auto parts and counterfeit auto parts

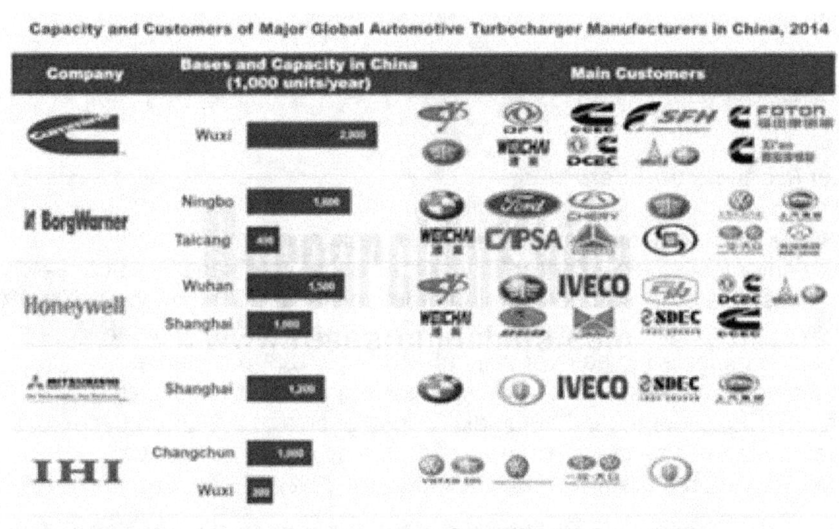

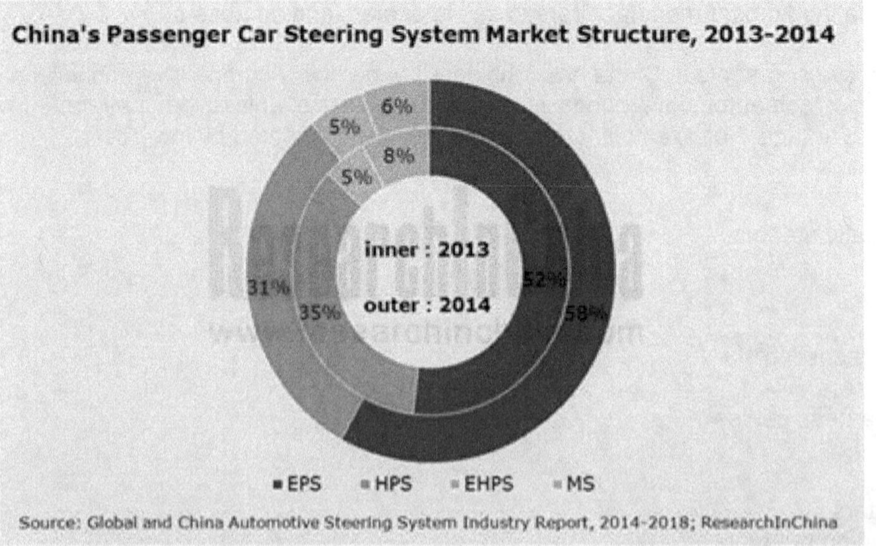

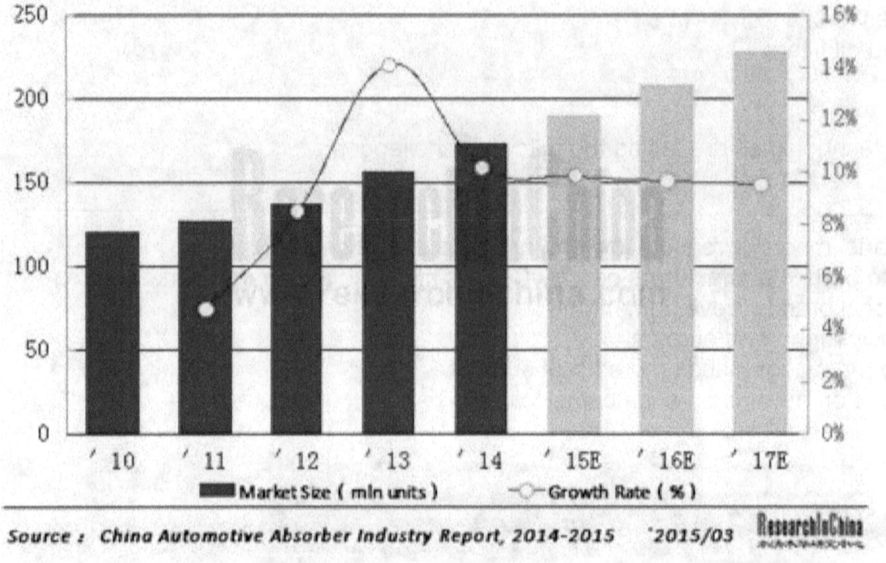

Automotive Aftermarket Products and Services

Automotive Aftermarket includes automotive component sales, repair and maintenance, modification, second hand automobile sales, car rental, car insurance, car finance and car e-commerce etc. It is the most stable profit source in the automotive industrial chain, about 60-70% profit is from the automotive aftermarket. The market size in 2014 reached 600 million RMB, an increase of 30%. This figure is expected to be over trillion RMB by 2018. Four markets are expected to grow fast in the next few years, which are: car maintenance (a market size of 1.7 trillion by 2020, a growth of 19%), second hand auto sale (a market size of 2.1 trillion by 2020, a growth of 33%), car rental (a market size of 122 billion by 2020, a growth of 23%), auto remanufacturing (a market size of 38.3 billion by 2020, a growth of 22%).

Beginning on January 1, 2015, automakers are required to provide maintenance and technical information for all models with independent repair shops. In addition, original equipment suppliers will be allowed to sell their products directly to consumers and non-authorized dealers. These changes will encourage greater competition and will allow component manufacturers more access to aftermarket sales.

Currently, China's aftermarket is still in its development stage, with immense opportunities for growth. The average age of the country's vehicle fleet is three years old, and after-sales services haven't become a major issue for cars, which are still under warranty. By 2017, the average age of China's fleet is projected to rise to 5 years, and after-sales services will become increasingly important.

Overall, this industry is still in its early stages of development, industry patterns varied, standards confusion, the user consumption habits has not been formed. Consumers' challenges in various fields are broken down below:

Second hand automobile sales:

Data show that the trading volume of the used car market increased from 251,700 to 5,203,300, an increase of nearly 20 times the amount of the transaction has reached 291.649 billion yuan of scale between 2000-2013. According to China Automobile Dealers Association statistics, second-hand car trading volume of up to 6,052,900, an increase of 16.33% in 2014, an turnover of 367.565 billion yuan, an increase of 26.03%. There are professionals predict that by 2020, China's second hand car market trading volume is expected to reach 40 million, the market value will exceed 1 trillion RMB.

There are three types of second hand automobile sales in China, which are C2C, C2B and B2B. Credibility of second hand car dealers, identification standard and evaluation system are not unified.

Car maintenance:

It is difficult to identify whether the component are original OEM product or counterfeit, the maintenance technologies are also various, the 4S shops charge too much money for labor cost.

Car modification:

Car modification businesses are famous in some developed cities as Shanghai, Shenzhen, Beijing, Guangzhou and Kunming. China's "Road Traffic Safety Law" prohibits modification; there is neither no "market access qualifications", nor "quality assurance qualifications" for modified cars which brings safety concerns, the "Opinions on Strengthening and Improving the motor vehicle inspection work" jointly released by Ministry of Public Security and State Administration of Quality Supervision, Inspection and Quarantine allows vehicles registered after September 1st, 2010 to be inspected every six years instead of every year, which stimulate the car modification market, however, car owners need to change the cars back to its original outlook once the car needs to be inspected.

Even though car modification businesses are facing challenges, foreign tuning companies have seen the market potentials and some of them have started their businesses in China, e.g. German tuning company specializing in Mercedes-Benz "Lorinser" and German Babs, AMG Mercedes, as well as Porsche's professional conversion companies Gemballa.

Permitted modifications	Modification needs to be filed	Prohibited modifications
Luggage rack	Change of engine serial number	Add lighting device
Pedals	Change car frame serial number	Installation of Xenon lights
Anti-collision devices	Change of car owner	Modification of vehicle mufflers and shock absorbers
	Change of car color more than 1/3 than the original car color	

Car rental:

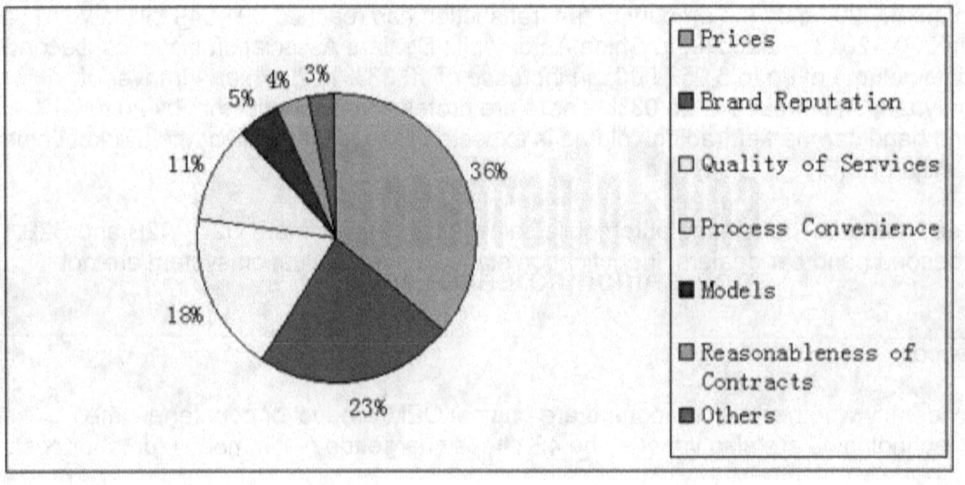

Specialty

Currently China has regulations which prohibit many vehicle modifications, constraining U.S. specialty auto equipment exports. ITA has helped to inform Chinese industry and government representatives about how the United States safely regulates the U.S. aftermarket, including specialty equipment.

The Specialty Equipment Market Association (SEMA) has a Market Development Cooperator Program (MDCP) award with ITA to help U.S. specialty parts companies increase their exports to China. Each fall, SEMA organizes an event in China where U.S. specialty parts companies can explore the market and meet potential buyers.

Opportunities

Despite the competitiveness of the market and trade disputes, opportunities exist for American auto makers and parts suppliers. All of the major U.S. automakers are opening up new plants, primarily to serve the growing domestic market. Other opportunities exist in energy efficient vehicles and technology, particularly with battery swap and plug-in hybrid vehicles (which are being actively promoted by the central government). There is also the potential for JV partnerships between U.S. and Chinese firms to develop these technologies for the Chinese domestic market, however, strategies for protecting IP must be considered.

2015 Trade Shows and Events:

CIAAF 2015 - China International Auto Aftermarket Fair & the 12th China Int'l Auto Accessories and Replacement Fair
Zhengzhou International Convention and Exhibition Centre
June 26-29, 2015

Auto Chongqing 2015 – The 16th Chongqing International Auto Industry Fair
June 10-16, 2015
Chongqing International Convention & Exhibition Center

AIC 2015 – All in CARAVANING
June 26-28, 2015
Beijing, Beijing Exhibition Centre (BEC)

EV CHINA 2015 - The 8th China International New Energy and Electric Vehicles Exhibition
June 11-14, 2015
Beijing New China International Exhibition Center (NCIEC)

Auto Show 2015 - China (Beijing) International Automobile Exhibition 2015
June 11-14, 2015
Beijing New China International Exhibition Center (NCIEC)

AIT 2015 - All in TUNING
June 12-14, 2.15
China National Convention Center (CNCC)

AMTS 2015 - Shanghai Int'l Automotive Manufacturing Technology & Material Show 2014
August 26-28, 2015
Shanghai New International Expo Centre (SNIEC)

Automotive Testing Expo China 2015
September 15-17, 2015
Shanghai Everbright Convention & Exhibition Center (SECEC)

Car Auto Salon CAS
September 18-21, 2015
Shanghai Auto Conference Center

CIAPE 2014 - China International Auto Products Expo 2014
September 19-22, 2015
Shanghai National Exhibition and Convention Center (Shanghai) (NECC)

SIAAF 2015 - Shanghai International Automotive Aftermarket Fair 2014
September 23-25, 2015
Shanghai New International Expo Centre (SNIEC)

RA China 2014 - The 10th RA China Auto Salon
October 9-11, 2015
Shanghai World Expo Exhibition & Convention Center (SWEECC, Formerly Shanghai World Expo Theme Pavilion)

2014 SAECC/CAEMEX - 2014 SAE-China Congress & China Automotive Engineering and Manufacturing Expo

October 27-29, 2015
Shanghai Automobile Exhibition Center (SAEC)

Shenzhen Convention & Exhibition Center (SZCEC)
November 3-7, 2015
Shanghai National Exhibition and Convention Center (Shanghai) (NECC)

CIAAR 2015 – China International Auto Air-conditioning & Transport Refrigeration ExhibitionNovember 16-18, 2015
Shanghai Everbright Convention & Exhibition Center (SECEC)

Auto Guangzhou 2015 – 13th China (Guangzhou) International Auto Parts & Accessories Exhibition
November 23 – December 2, 2015

Automechanika Shanghai 2015
December 2-5, 2015
Shanghai New International Expo Centre (SNIEC)

AAITF 2015 – 11th China International Automotive Aftermarket Industry and Tuning Trade Fair
February 26-28, 2016
Shenzhen Convention & Exhibition Center (SZCEC)

Web Resources

Ministry of Transport of China (MOT)
http://www.mot.gov.cn

China Associations of Automobile Manufacturers
http://www.caam.org.cn/

China Automobile Dealers Association
http://www.china-cada.org.cn

China Automotive Technology and Research Center (CATARC)
http://www.catarc.ac.cn/ac_en/index.htm

Department of Mechanic, Electronic and Hi-Tech Industry, MOFCOM
http://cys.mofcom.gov.cn/

Certification and Accreditation Administration (CCC Certification)
http://www.cnca.gov.cn/

Ministry of Information and Technology, Department of Industries
http://cys.miit.gov.cn/

AVIATION

Aircraft, Spacecraft, and related parts (HS Code 88) Unit: USD millions

	2012	2013	2014
Total Exports	1,560	1,941	2,704
Total Imports	17,727	23,183	28,503
Imports from the U.S.	7,590	13,580	15,517
U.S. share of total imports	43%	59%	54%

Source: World Trade Atlas

China is the world's second largest and one of the world's fastest growing civil aviation markets. The industry has grown at double-digit rates for several years. Industry forecasts expect growth to remain strong over the medium term, averaging 7% over the next 20 years. Commercial opportunities in the civil aviation market include final assembly and tier-one suppliers, small niche parts manufacturers, airport design and construction companies, and general aviation among others.

As stated in China's 12th Five Year Plan, China plans to build 56 new airports, re-locate 16 airports, and renovate/expand 91 airports with investment totaling $68.5 billion during the 2011 – 2015 period. At the end of 2014, the total number of civil airports in China was 202. China will have more than 230 airports by 2015, accessible by 83% of the population, including 3 national hubs, 5 regional hubs, and 24 medium hubs.

The commercial air fleet will grow along with the number of airports, with passenger traffic increasing at a rate of 6.6 percent per year. Given that there are only about 2,310 commercial jets operating in China in comparison to roughly 7,000 in the United States, industry analysts predict that Chinese airlines will need to add 6,020 aircraft, valued at $870 billion (RMB 5.39 trillion) to their fleets over the next two decades to meet projected demand. Not surprisingly, Boeing and Airbus have identified China as the single most important market for sales over the next 20 years, and both companies are working hard to win orders from Chinese airlines. China's top three airlines, i.e., Air China, China Southern, and China Eastern, are now among the world's top 10 carriers.

China's aviation industry is a national priority, and the Chinese government is expending significant resources to develop domestic manufacturing capabilities, build new airports, train new pilots, and increase domestic maintenance capacity. In 2013, China was the largest overall export market for U.S. aerospace products at nearly $13.5 billion. Most of that figure was complete aircraft; a fairly low percentage of China's aerospace imports from the United States over the past decade were aircraft parts (22 percent). However, that figure is likely to change as China's fleet ages and China does more maintenance at home.

The expansion of China's market creates both opportunities and challenges for U.S. companies. Companies that supply spare parts to aircraft operators and maintenance and overhaul shops should consider the growth of China's aircraft fleet in their sales and marketing plans. U.S. parts suppliers might also find new opportunities as suppliers to Chinese manufacturing programs. However, since aerospace manufacturing is a national priority in China, U.S. companies may face substantial localization pressures or may be disadvantaged by government policies in favor of local firms.

Sub-Sector Best Prospects

Aircraft Parts: Manufacture and Repair

Aircraft parts (HS Code 8803) Unit: USD millions

	2012	2013	2014
Total Imports	1,737	2,081	2,338
Imports from the U.S.	590	620	714
U.S. share of total imports	34%	30%	31%

China is working to develop a globally competitive manufacturing industry.

China's import market for aircraft parts and components exceeded $2.3 billion in 2014, an increase of around 12% compared with year 2013. China's demand for aircraft parts can be attributed to a number of factors including an increasing capacity utilization rate, the age and expansion of China's aircraft fleet, and the domestic production and assembly of aircraft.

The best immediate opportunity for U.S. companies will be in supplying parts for China's commercial aircraft fleet. It is the largest and most well-established segment of China's aviation market and is currently dominated by western aircraft with many U.S. suppliers.

In addition, the Chinese government is supporting the development of indigenous Chinese aircraft, most notably the ARJ21 regional jet and the C919 large civil aircraft. While the aircraft structures are often made by Chinese firms, most of the major subsystems are being supplied by manufacturers headquartered in the United States and Europe.

China's domestic aircraft part and assembly manufacturing sector is also growing. In addition to approximately 200 small aircraft parts manufacturers, there are also a number of regionally-based major manufacturers concentrated in Shanghai, Chengdu, Xi'an, Jiangxi and Shenyang. China's domestic manufacturing base is developing, as reflected by the commitments of large aircraft and engine manufactures to expand procurement in China over the long term. However, most highly technical and sophisticated parts and assemblies will continue to be imported until production quality meets international standards. At the present time, domestic manufacturers do not have the ability to produce all of the qualified materials and parts.

Airports

China currently has 202 civil aviation airports, including the world's second busiest in Beijing, with plans to expand aggressively to more than 230 by 2015. The expansion will place 83% of China's population and 96% of its GDP within 100 kilometres (roughly 60 miles) of the nearest airport, greatly enhancing the potential for aviation growth.

The airport system at present is highly concentrated, with top airports suffering from major congestion. The top three airports, Beijing, Shanghai and Guangzhou, account for 1/3 of all traffic, while the top 14 airports handle 2/3 of total traffic nationwide. Local industry estimates indicate that 40 of China's airports are already at or near capacity, with another 29 expected to reach this limit within the next one year.

International companies will have opportunities to participate in both the airport design and in the infrastructure construction. Qualified companies can bid for design, consultation, surveillance, management, and construction of designated civil airport projects. China intends to build 56 new airports and expand 101 existing ones by the end of 2015. This presents tremendous opportunities for U.S. companies to sell equipment and services from airport design and construction to air traffic management and environmental consulting. In particular, companies that provide the following equipment and services to airport development have great opportunities: airport design, green construction, energy efficiency equipment, airport security equipment, ground support and terminal related equipment, and airport management.

Ground service is another area in which foreign companies can actively participate. Beijing

Capital Airport, Guangzhou Baiyun Airport, and Chengdu Shuangliu Airport have all established joint ventures with foreign partners (Singapore, Indonesia and UK) in ground services. Shanghai Airport Ground cooperated with Cargo Warehouse and Lufthansa set up a joint venture. China Air Oil Supply Corporation (CAOSC) has established many joint ventures with foreign companies to provide airport oil supply services.

General Aviation (GA)

In China, the airspace is tightly controlled by the Chinese military and the airspace class system does not segment out its GA air activities. Strict military control over roughly 70% of all Chinese airspace is the largest single factor limiting growth of this industry. GA is still underdeveloped in China in terms of GA aircraft numbers, GA professionals and GA facilities.

China is a growing market for business aircraft, helicopters, and other general aviation aircraft. The fleet grew 14.3 percent between 2012 and 2013, and the number of operating hours increased by 28.5 percent.

Though the total current fleet is still relatively small, the potential importance of this industry to the Chinese economy in the long-term has led aircraft OEMs and Chinese government officials to devote significant resources towards capacity-building for general aviation.

A welcome change came in November 2010 when civilian and military authorities issued a joint reform document calling for liberalization of low altitude airspace under 4,000 meters (13,000 feet), setting the goal of opening up airspace below 1,000 meters by 2015 and airspace below 3,000 meters by 2020. Implementation of the reform will roll out in three stages, starting with an Experimental Phase in Guangzhou and Shenyang. The policy outlines a national rollout by 2015, and a final deepening and consolidation by 2020.

Since then, GA has been developing at a fast pace with new players coming to this market and the more involvement of local governments. GA has big potential market driven by the state and local economy development plan, the public demand for business jet, and the need for public services and individual recreations.

China currently has 123 operators registered with the Civil Aviation Administration of China (CAAC), the main stakeholder formulating policies and regulations concerning the safety and economics of GA in China. However, about 80% of Chinese operators have only 2 or 3 aircraft thus struggle to achieve operating scale and profitability. In addition, GA aircrafts are very costly to use in China due to airspace access, flight approval procedures, and operation charges such as airport charges, plus maintenance services. All of these factors contribute to low profitability for Chinese operators.

Helicopters

China will further open up its low-altitude airspace (below 1,000 meters) across the board by 2015 to unleash a vastly untapped general aviation market, valued at trillions of RMB. With the rise of the General Aviation market here, China could become the fastest-growing helicopter market in the world. It is both exciting and challenging. In China, two-thirds of the country is covered by hard to reach mountains and high plateaus.

In 2008, an earthquake in the Sichuan region of China resulted in many casualties, and Chinese officials cite the failure of emergency teams to reach inaccessible areas as the reason. This has convinced China's leaders that they must dramatically increase their helicopter fleet.

For a country similar in geographical size to the United States, China operates comparatively few helicopters, most of which are built abroad, with the rest built locally under license. But with demands growing in both military and civil sectors, change is on the horizon for China's relatively small helicopter industry. The main civil helicopters are supplied by Airbus Helicopters, Sikorsky Aircraft Corporation, Bell Helicopters, Agustawestland Helicopters, Russian Helicopters and Robinson Helicopter Co. The local suppliers are Changhe Aircraft Industry Corporation and Harbin Aircraft Manufacturing Corporation. In 2013, Chongqing Helicopter Investment Co. Ltd acquired Enstrom Helicopter Corporation and entered into China market.

China's fleet of helicopters grew by 29 percent in 2014 to reach 655 aircraft in total.. Over the next ten years, China's civil helicopter needs are expected to rise up to about 1,500 helicopters. China has realized the importance of helicopters for disaster relief work and medical rescues, and the country has become a bright spot in the struggling helicopter industry.

The Chinese government has also loosened its control on helicopter manufacturing to allow local private firms and foreign companies to co-operate in developing and manufacturing civil helicopters. The growing Chinese economy provides a huge potential market for helicopters of all classes.

Below is a partial yet representative list of best sales prospects:

Air Data & Inertial Reference System (ADIRS)	Fuel hydraulics
Airfield buses	Fuel System
Automatic Flight Control System (AFCS)	Fuel Tank Inserting System
Auxiliary power unit, door system	High Lift System
Avionics	Hydraulic System
Bearings	Integrated flight deck panel
Baggage sorting systems and handling equipment	Integrated Supervise & Control System
Baggage x-ray machines	Interior components
Crew seats	Landing gear
Composite Materials	Lighting equipment
De-icers/ Refuellers	On-board Maintenance System
Electric power system	Oxygen fuelling vehicles
Emergency evacuation equipment	Radio remote control apparatus
Engine vibration monitoring system	Runway friction testers
Flight Data Recording System	Pilot training
Flight Control Actuation System	Signalling & Safety equipment for airfields
Flight deck control suite	Telecommunication and Navigation System
Fire fighting vehicles	Towing tractors
Fire protection equipment	Turbofan Engines
Food loaders	Windshield heater control & wiper system
	Windshields and opening windows

Opportunities

In July 2012, China's "State Council Opinions on Promoting Civil Aviation Development" set several key development targets for the industry including a transport growth rate of 12.2 percent for 2011-2020, an improved safety record, general aviation growth of 19 percent, and increased access to air services for more of the population. China's civil aviation system is forecasted to be as large as the U.S. system in approximately two decades.

Meaningful cooperation between the United States and Chinese governments on aviation is essential to realizing these business opportunities. The U.S. Federal Aviation Administration (FAA) and the Civil Aviation Administration of China (CAAC) continue to enjoy a close partnership that has benefited both sides for many years. The U.S.-China Aviation Cooperation Program (ACP) brings together U.S. industry and government agencies from both countries - CAAC, FAA, the U.S. Trade and Development Agency (TDA), and the U.S. Transportation Security Administration (TSA) in a unique and active forum for bilateral cooperation.

Efforts to reduce constraints on the healthy and sustainable development of civil aviation in China have been largely successful. However, significant challenges remain. Further efforts are needed to open up and modernize China's airspace system, reduce inefficiencies and congestion, realize environmental benefits, and accommodate growth.

U.S. firms without an existing China presence may want to consider hiring a local distributor or representative. This partner generally helps establish access to decision makers and gain timely commercial information about the market. They also traditionally leverage personal connections to promote the U.S. product, and develop sales leads. While this is a common global practice, successful exporters comment on the need to invest significant time and attention to maintaining and managing relationships with Chinese partners. Some U.S. firms decide to enter into a Joint Venture (JV) relationship with Chinese partners, exchanging technological know-how for market access. This should only be done after significant due- diligence and cost/benefit analysis.

U.S. firms often use training programs to establish productive partnerships with Chinese clients. Industry associations such as the U.S.-China Aviation Cooperation Program (ACP) can serve as valuable vehicles for American firms to leverage similar opportunities.

Web Resources

Government Authorities

- Civil Aviation Administration of China (CAAC) www.caac.gov

- Air Traffic Management Bureau: www.atmb.net.cn
- Center of Aviation Safety Technology: www.castc.org.cn

Airlines

- Air China: www.airchina.com.cn/en
- China Eastern Airlines: http://en.ceair.com/
- China Southern Airlines: www.csair.com/en
- Spring Airlines: www.china-sss.com
- Hainan Airlines: www.hnair.com
- Sichuan Airlines: www.scal.com.cn
- Xiamen Airlines: www.xiamenair.com.cn
- Shenzhen Airlines: www.shenzhenair.com
- Chengdu Airlines: www.chengduair.cc
- Tibet Airlines: www.tibetairlines.com.cn

Aircraft Manufacturers

- Aviation Industry Corporation of China (AVIC): www.avic.com.cn
- Commercial Aircraft Corporation of China (COMAC): www.comac.cc
- AVIC Commercial Aircraft Co.

MRO Facilities

- Aircraft Maintenance and Engineering Corporation (AMECO): www.ameco.com.cn
- Shanghai Technologies Aerospace Co. (STARCO): www.staero.aero/starco.html
- Guangzhou Aircraft Maintenance Engineering Co. (GAMECO): www.gameco.com.cn
- Taikoo Aircraft Engineering Company Limited (TAECO): www.taeco.com
- MTU Maintenance (Zhuhai): www.mtuzhuhai.com/en
- GE Engine Services (Xiamen)
- Sichuan Services Aero-Engine Maintenance Company (SSAMC): www.snecma.com/-chengdu-

Aircraft Trading Companies
- China Aviation Supplies Corporation (CASC): www.casc.com.cn/eng

Other
- CAAC news: www.caacnews.com.cn
- Civil aviation industry analysis report: bit.ly/10kub4X
- China Civil Aviation Report: www.uniworldusa.com

Contacts

U.S. Embassy in Beijing
Ida Peng, Senior Commercial Specialist
(86 10) 8531 3947
Aiqun.Peng@trade.gov

U.S. Consulate in Shanghai
Vivien Bao, Commercial Specialist
(86 21) 6279 8766
Vivien.Bao@trade.gov

U.S. Consulate in Chengdu
Fan Li, Commercial Specialist,
(86 28) 8598 6546
li.fan@trade.gov

U.S. Consulate in Guangzhou
Senior Commercial Specialist, Lena Yang
(86 20) 3814 5173
Lena.Yang@trade.gov

U.S. Consulate in Shenyang
Dongmei Sun, Commercial Specialist
(86 24) 2322-1198
dongmei.sun@trade.gov

COAL MINING EQUIPMENT

Coal Consumption and CO2 Emissions

	2011	2012	2013	2014 (Jan-Nov)
Coal Consumption in China (bn tonnes)	3.48	3.52	3.61	3.52
China's total energy consumption	70%	69%	65.7%	63.2%
CO_2 emissions per capita in China (tonnes)	7.2	6.5	7.1	6.8

Source: China Coal Association (http://www.chinacoal.gov.cn/templet/3/) and the U.S. Department ofCommerce in China.

China is the world's largest energy consumer and the leading emitter of greenhouse gases. In 2014, coal accounted for 63% of China's overall energy consumption, and the most coal-dependent country amongtop energy consumers. As a consequence, China's major cities have long endured high levels of air pollution. In 2013, 92% of Chinese cities failed to meet national ambient air quality standards. This has not held back the construction of new coal-fired plants or factories. Coal burning is responsible for almost half of the country's PM 2.5 pollution (particulate matter of 2.5 micrometers in diameter).

In 2014, the impact of China's clean air and renewable energy policies began to have an impact on the country's coal industry as coal production fell for the first time this century. In addition, government restrictions on the export of low-quality coal hit the market and coal prices fell by around 20% in 2014.

The Chinese government continues to promote the clean and efficient development of conventional fossil energy production and utilization. The Development Plan for Coal Industry During the 12th Five- Year Plan Period, which has been issued and implemented, calls for the vigorous development of clean coal technology and the efficient and clean utilization of coal.

Clean coal is the process of chemically washing coal of its minerals and impurities, removing sulfur dioxide, and making the carbon dioxide in the flue gas economically recoverable. The coal industry usesthe term "clean coal" to describe technologies designed to enhance both the efficiency and the environmental acceptability of coal extraction, preparation, and usage. Present day clean coaltechnologies include several generations of technological advances that have led to a more efficient combustion of coal with reduced emissions of sulfur dioxide and nitrogen oxide.

Clean coal technologies currently being developed in China include advanced coal utilization, highefficiency combustion and advanced power generation technologies, coal conversion technologies,integrated gasification combined cycle and carbon capture(*pre-combustion capture, post –combustion capture, oxy-combustion capture*), utilization and storage.

Sub-Sector Best Prospects

Carbon Capture, Utilization and Storage (CCUS)

CCUS technology has been considered an important strategy of China's clean coal technology strategyin both the short and the long term. The International Energy Agency (IEA) forecasts that by 2050, CCUS could become the biggest contributor to emissions reduction among any one single technology. As such, China is emerging as a major influence on CCUS deployment, with several planned andoperational demonstration projects. The country has adopted an encouraging policy framework and hasincreased the support for research and development projects.

As a pioneer in CCUS, the United States has developed cutting edge technology through various R&D projects. The U.S. Department of Energy (DOE) administers a Clean Coal Technology program to encourage and support public/private partnerships to research, develop, and demonstrate clean coaltechnologies that can be ultimately brought to large-scale commercial deployment.

Advanced Coal Gasification Technology

China is the largest coal gasification market in the world. In this respect, the National EnergyAdministration has laid out plans to produce 50 billion cubic meters of gas from coal by 2020, enough to satisfy more than 10% of China's total gas demand. However, there are two major problems with coalgasification. Coal gasification produces more CO_2 than a traditional coal plant, and it is one of the morewater-intensive forms of energy production. New technology and equipment to solve these two problems are good prospects for U.S. companies.

Coal Gasification with carbon capture and storage

Combining coal gasification with carbon capture and storage in the power sector remains a critical pathway towards low-carbon power generation. With the huge demand in using gasification, China has high demand in developing new coal co-generation systems with CO_2 capture including new coal-to- chemical co-generation, new CO_2 capture processes, and co-generation system with combined pyrolysis, gasification, and combustion.

CO_2 -EOR (Enhanced Oil Recovery)

CO_2 -EOR is an oil production technique through which CO_2 is injected into previously developed oilfields to recover additional oil not obtainable by primary and secondary techniques. CO 2-EOR is widelyconsidered to be a method to increase domestic oil production by using CO_2 captured from power plants and industrial sources. China is in the developing stage to adopt this technology to local oil fields.

The United States has more than 40 years of experience in CO_2 -EOR which gives U.S. companies a leg up in China's growing EOR market.

Opportunities
The bestselling opportunities in the clean coal technology sector include:

- CO_2 capture technology exports/licensing
- Pipeline fabricators for CO_2 transportation
- Information technology companies, materials suppliers, and engineering contractors for CO_2utilization
- Storage monitoring service suppliers and Emergency Response services suppliers for CO_2 Storage
- Coal gasification technology exports/licensing

Web Resources
U.S. China Clean Energy Research Center
http://www.us-china-cerc.org/Advanced_Coal_Technology.html

Clean Coal Working Group, Energy Cooperation Program
http://www.uschinaecp.org/en/Outcomes/CleanCoal.aspx

Climate Change Working Group
http://www.state.gov/r/pa/prs/ps/2013/07/211768.htm

China NDRC Climate Change Division
http://en.ndrc.gov.cn/

National Center for Climate Change Strategy and International Cooperation
http://www.ncsc.org.cn/

US Commercial Services Contact Information in China

US Embassy in Beijing
Wenjuan Zhan, Commercial Specialist
(86 10) 8531-4819
wenjuan.zhan@trade.gov

US Consulate in Shanghai
Scott Yao, Commercial Specialist
(86 21) 6279-7630
scott.yao@trade.gov

US Consulate in Guangzhou
Lena Yang, Commercial Specialist
(85 20) 3814-5000
lena.yang@trade.gov

US Consulate in Chengdu
Haiyan Hua, Commercial Specialist
(86 28) 8558-3992
haiyan.hua@trade.gov

US Consulate in Shenyang
Liu Yang, Commercial Specialist
(86 24) 2322-1198
yang.liu@trade.gov

CONSTRUCTION AND GREEN BUILDING

	2013 (estimated)	2014 (estimated)	2015 (forecast)	2016 (forecast)	2017 (forecast)
Total Construction Market Value (USD billion)	634.2	692.3	734.4	784.2	838.4
Construction Industry Value, Real Growth (% year to year)	7.30	6.78	6.28	4.52	4.21

Source: "China Infrastructure Report: Q2 2015" Business Monitor International (2015).

In the last several years, the construction market in China has grown exponentially although more modestly since two years ago. According to China Infrastructure Report (Q2, 2015), China's construction industry will face a gradual slowdown, with a forecast of growth rate by 6.3% in 2015, a slowdown from 6.8% in 2014. But as the government's 'Belt and Road' initiative provides opportunities for this industry, China remains an attractive market, and is expected to maintain its position as the world's largest construction market for the near future and account for a significant share of all new global construction between now and 2020.

With the urbanization of China expected to continue to grow, green building will be relied on to fulfill the demand for new energy efficient buildings. On March 16th 2014, the Chinese government issued the National New-type Urbanization Plan for 2014 to 2020, which aims to lift the proportion of Chinese citizens living in cities from the present 53.7% to 60% by 2020.

In the same year, the State Council Green Building Action Plan of 2014, government mandated that public buildings such as schools, hospitals, museums, stadiums and affordable housing, as well as any single building area over 20,000 square meters such as airports, railway stations, hotels, restaurants, shopping malls, offices and other large public buildings must meet the green building standards of China's 3-Star Rating System administered by the Ministry of Housing and Urban-Rural Development (MOHURD).

To support the market trend, the Chinese government initiated a green building incentive program. National level financial subsidies will provide 50 million RMB to projects that meet Green Building Demonstration Town (GBDT) standards as stipulated by MOHURD. In order to qualify as a GBDT project, new construction projects must be over 200 square meters and the construction period must be less than two years. For two-star green building projects the central government will subsidize 45 RMB per square meter, for three-stars and above 80 RMB per square meter.

Besides China's 3-Star rating system, the U.S. Leadership in Energy and Environmental Design (LEED) certification is also prevalent in China. In June, 2014, the U.S. Green Building Council (USGBC) announced that 29 of China's 34 provinces are home to LEED-certified projects, according to its newreport "LEED in Motion: Greater China", a full showcase of all LEED activity in China, Hong Kong, Taiwan and Macau. To date, Greater China is home to 1,961 LEED-registered and -certified projects, totaling 111 million gross square meters of construction space. Mainland China was also announced as the second largest market in the world for LEED green building activity. Mainland China has projects that have pursued both LEED certification along with China Green Building Label or Three Star Rating.Additional sectors have developed in order to support the growth in green building, such as Energy Service Companies (ESCs), and consulting companies that can identify greater efficiencies in design and construction.

The United States is China's second largest source of imports for the construction industry, with a 13 percent import market share. U.S. exports to China are expected to continue to grow in all subsectors through 2017.

Sub-Sector Best Prospects

Green building products that meet the new energy efficiency standards in new, unique or economically competitive ways have a potential market in China. Some of the best prospects for China's market are:

- Green building design
- Building energy efficiency retrofits
- Green building material production and supply
- Integrated energy efficiency solutions
- Green building operation and energy efficiency management
- Low-carbon neighborhood development design and energy solution

Looking at the Sector as a whole, U.S. exporters took the lead over all international competitors, notably edging ahead of Japan, which long had occupied the leading import market share position. Japan now trails the U.S. slightly at 11 percent market share, followed by Germany (9.7 percent), Russia (7.5 percent), and Canada (5.7 percent). A view of each subsector gives a more informed sense of the competitive environment.

HVACR

China is the world's largest HVACR market. There is strong demand for high-quality HVACR products in China, with exporters from Germany, Japan, the U.S. and Korea claiming 60 percent of the import market. The United States is the third largest source of subsector imports, with a 12 percent market share. Germany leads the market, with just over 20 percent, followed by Japan, at nearly 19 percent. Korean products rank fourth.

Lighting

Lighting represents an enormous area of opportunity for U.S. exporters. Government authorities throughout China are working to encourage energy efficient retrofits of buildings, in which lighting is widely viewed as a "low hanging fruit" investment option to increase energy performance. U.S.

lighting exporters have room to grow their share of the China market, currently at just 6.5 percent. Performing ahead of U.S. exporters are Japan (24 percent share), Germany (17 percent), Korea (8.9 percent) and Taiwan (8.7 percent).

Wood
China represents an enormous market opportunity for U.S. wood products exporters, who currently claim 13.3 percent of the import market and are the second largest source of imports after Russia (16 percent) and just ahead of Canada (12 percent). China's demand for wood and wood products has shown extremely strong growth, with that trend expected to continue through 2017. While Chinese importers have shown strong interest in importing logs or least-processed wood and undertaking value-added production in China, U.S. exporters have tremendous opportunities in higher value-added wood product sales.

Plumbing
There is ample room for growth in U.S. plumbing exports to China, which are the fifth largest foreign source of imports with 8 percent of the market. Plumbing imports in China are dominated by Japan, which holds a 22 percent market share, followed by Korea (13.2 percent), Germany (13 percent) and Taiwan (9.5 percent).

Insulation
U.S. exporters have steadily been gaining import market share in China's insulation market and now stand a close second to Japan at 19.4 percent market share. Japan leads the import market with just over 20 percent share, and Taiwan (10.3 percent), Germany (6 percent) and Korea (5.8 percent) round out the top five foreign sources of subsector imports.

Windows and Doors
There are solid opportunities for growth in U.S. window and door exports to China, which currently rank sixth in import market share at 5.7 percent. Germany leads the import market, claiming fully 30 percent, followed by Korea (9.2 percent), Taiwan (8.9 percent), Norway (8 percent), and Italy (6.3 percent).

Glass
U.S. exporters enjoy a healthy 22 percent share of China's glass import market, ranking third as the source of imports. Japan and Taiwan out-compete U.S. exporters, with 30 percent and 28 percent of the import market respectively.

Opportunities

One sector with a significant foreign presence is architectural design, which is dominated by many well-known architectural firms from the US and Europe. Other opportunities exist in consulting on green building designs, as well as on energy saving strategies for both new and old buildings. Both of these sectors require skills and expertise that are not yet fully developed in the Chinese domestic market and can help lower energy intensity in line with the 12th Five-Year Plan. More than 95% of existing buildings in China are not green buildings, creating good potential opportunities in retrofitting old buildings with green building technology.

The 18th Chapter of the National New-type Urbanization Plan indicated that the following three sectors of construction will be the key developing sectors in China from 2014 to 2020:

•New-type city construction: The key projects will be focused on building with green energy, green building, green traffic, innovation in industrial parks and the urban environment.

•Smart city construction: Cities should use information technology to manage the development of the city, such as extending the broadband information network, and promoting cloud computing and large data centers. Promoting cross-sector, regional government information sharing and business collaboration is also encouraged.

•Humanities city construction: The Plan encourages localities to focus on protecting historical and cultural heritage in old cities and to incorporate traditional cultural elements into new city construction.

In addition, as of April 23, 2014, the Chinese government also started allowing private in public infrastructure projects. The state council selected 80 infrastructure projects and opened them to public tender bidding in order to encourage and attract private capital in joint ventures, wholly foreign owned enterprises, and franchises. The projects include railways, ports, other transportation infrastructure, new generation information infrastructure, major hydropower, wind power, photovoltaic power generation and other clean energy projects, oil and gas pipelines and storage facilities, and modern coal chemical and petrochemical industries. In the future, the government's next step will be to open investments to oil and gas, utilities, water, airports and other sectors.

According to MOHURD, China plans to build large scale affordable housing. The plan includes 36 million apartment units to be built in 2015 throughout China. Many provinces and cities have already drafted their own development plans.

Following are some major construction project plans:

- By the end of 2015, Guangdong Province plans to invest $225 billion in infrastructure construction and complete 294 projects.
- Wuhan City plans to invest $483 million in the renovation of the old city.
- Beijing plans to build 100 Sunny Schools using solar energy for electricity, water, and heating system.
- According to the National Airport Allocation Plan, China will upgrade, expand and build 244 airports by the end of 2020, including Beijing's second capital airport which will be located in Daxing County, Beijing. The airport is expected to be completed by 2017 and in operation by 2018. It will serve 600 million passengers per year.
- According to MOHURD's Qinghai branch, Qinghai province plans to invest $11.2 billion (75 billion RMB) in real estate development by 2015
- By 2015, Nanchang City plans to build 231 key projects, with a total investment estimated to reach $23 billion (155.2 billion RMB), the projects will include fast transportation systems with modern transportation hubs, bio-landscape gardens, and a renewable development demonstration city.
- By 2015, Hubei Province plans to turn 1,000 towns and villages into eco-demonstration projects. The water supply pipe line will reach 98% of the province, the garbage treatment rate will reach 85%, and the urbanization rate will reach 52%.
- According to MOHURD of Ningbo city in Zhejiang province, there will be 129 key construction projects between 2014 and 2016, and the total investment will be $12.6 billion (78.3 billion RMB), which include 57 city traffic networking projects, 25 city center construction projects and 47 affordable- housing projects.
- Shandong Province will invest $330 million to build demonstration green towns each year from 2014 to 2016.
- By 2015, Hainan province will build 894,000 square meters of new buildings and renovate 49,000 square meters of old buildings.
- Anhui province will invest $6.5 billion to renovate old buildings.

Web Resources

Ministry of Housing and Urban-Rural Development

http://www.mohurd.gov.cn/
See also: https://www.uschina.org/policy/ministry-housing-and-urban-rural-development-mohurd

China Building Materials Industries Association
http://cbmia.cbminfo.com/english/eindex.htm

Ministry of Environmental Protection of China
http://www.mep.gov.cn/

CS China Design Construction Webpage
http://export.gov/china/doingbizinchina/industryinfo/designconstruction/index.asp

U.S.-China Energy Cooperation Program
http://www.uschinaecp.org

US Commercial Services Contact Information in China

US Embassy in Beijing
Grace Yue Cao, Commercial Specialist
(86 10) 8531-4796
yue.cao@trade.gov

US Consulate in Chengdu
Sunny Cui, Commercial Specialist
(86 28) 8558-3992
cui.shiyang@trade.gov

US Consulate in Shanghai
Scott Yao, Commercial Specialist
(86 21) 6279-8780
juliet.lu@trade.gov

US Consulate in Shenyang
Liu Yang, Commercial Specialist
(86 24) 2322-1198
yang.liu@trade.gov

US Consulate in Guangzhou
Jericho Li, Commercial Specialist

EDUCATION AND TRAINING

China has become by far the largest single source of international students studying in the United States. In 2013-14, China sent 274,439 students to the United States, an increase of 17 percent over its total in 2012-2013. Chinese students make up a commanding 31 percent of all international students in the United States and have accounted for about two-thirds of the increase in total international student enrollments coming to the United States since 2003. The economic impact of these students on the U.S. economy is significant, and the Bureau of Economic Analysis reports that in 2013 (the most recent data available) U.S. exports of education services (tuition, fees, and living expenses) to China reached $8.0 billion.

Figure 1: Chinese Students in the United States (1998-2014)

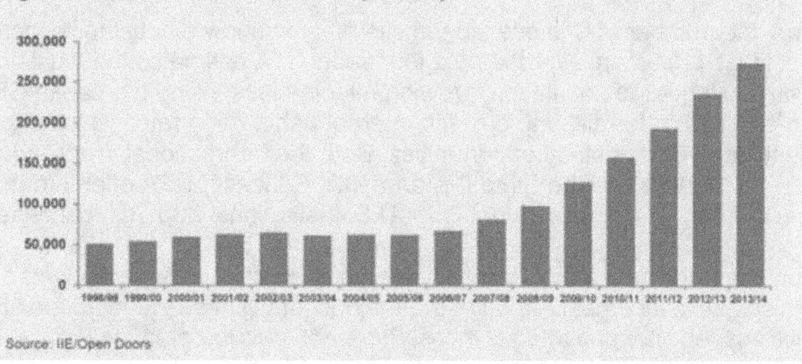

Source: IIE/Open Doors

Figure 2: Chinese Students in the United States (2009-2018)

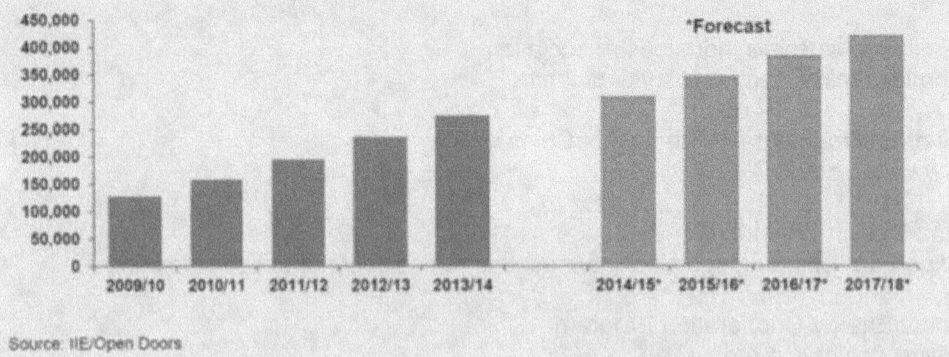

Source: IIE/Open Doors

Chinese students are fairly evenly split with 42 percent of Chinese students in the United States studying at the graduate level while 40 percent are undergraduates. The remainder of Chinese students is enrolled either in "Optional Practical Training" or "Other." As with many other countries, the STEM fields are the largest field of study for Chinese students. STEM fields attracted 42 percent of Chinese students. Business and management attract 28 percent, and the social sciences, eight percent. There does not seem to be a geographic concentration of Chinese students among the top 10 states hosting international students. While each of these top 10 states hosts in excess of 25,000 international students, Chinese students only comprised more than 40 percent of all international students in Ohio, where Chinese students comprise 42 percent of all international students, and in Indiana, where they represented 41 percent. Chinese students are also increasingly attracted to U.S. boarding schools, in the belief that a year or two of study at a U.S. boarding school will facilitate acceptance at a U.S. college or university.

Sub-Sector Best Prospects

Short-term training programs, technical schools and workshops in specialized fields as well as business education are particularly sought after. In December 2011, China's National Development and Reform Commission (NDRC) along with the Ministry of Commerce (MOFCOM) jointly released a revised edition of the Guiding Catalogue on Foreign Investment in Industry, replacing the 2007 edition. The 2011 revised Catalogue adds "training and vocational education" to the so-called "encouraged" list of industries for foreign direct investment. (The Catalogue includes four categories: "encouraged," "restricted," "prohibited" and "permitted".) U.S. educational organizations can also sell teaching materials and equipment, convey the latest methodologies and case studies, exchange faculty, and provide educational consulting services.

Opportunities

In the near term, the number of Chinese students is likely to show a substantial increase, estimated as at least 11 percent over the next four years. ITA estimates that sustained growth will result from: rising college-age population, growing middle-class, rising per capita GDP, continued growth in word-of-mouth referrals, and growing internet penetration rates which expose more potential students to overseas study opportunities. Both the International Trade Administration's (ITA's) Commercial Service and the State Department's EducationUSA offer information and guidance on recruitment of Chinese students for U.S. institutions. http://educationusachina.com/

There's no doubt that the desire by Chinese students to enroll in U.S. institutions is high, fueled by increasing disposable incomes. Although the majority of Chinese students are still pursuing degrees in business, engineering and sciences, there appears to be an increase in demand for vocational classes, and utilization of community colleges. There is also a marked increase in the number of students interested in high school and summer programs to upgrade skills to increase earning potential as well.

U.S. institutions will have to remain active in the promotion of American education in China. Competition for Chinese students from other English-speaking countries has increased, along with an expansion of the domestic education market which has created greater opportunities for students to pursue higher education without leaving China. A common approach used by U.S. schools to recruit Chinese students is through local education agents. Over one thousand education agents are estimated to exist in China, with about 301 of them having obtained proper licensing from the Ministry of Education (down from around 400 the previously). U.S. schools are encouraged to vet education agents carefully before engaging their services. The Commercial Service education specialists can offer guidance regarding how to use reputable, licensed education agents.

The Internet and social media are significant parts of recruitment efforts, despite Chinese restrictions on some uses of the Internet in China. One way for U.S. institutions to more effectively promote their programs is by taking advantages of the U.S. Commercial Service social media (Weibo) platform, which is focused on promoting studying in the U.S. http://www.weibo.com/useducation

In China, and many other parts of Asia, it is important to supplement online recruitment efforts with face-to-face recruitment efforts such as student fairs because Chinese parents (many of whom do not possess strong English-language capability), play a large role in determining whether and where their son or daughter will attend university. ITA has not organized a recent trade mission to China, as many U.S. institutions want to diversify their foreign student body and seek missions targeting other countries. Furthermore, several private sector organizations offer help in recruiting students in China.

Web Resources

Ministry of Education, Department of International Cooperation and Exchanges Tel: 86-10 6609-6275http://www.moe.gov.cn/publicfiles/business/htmlfiles/moe/moe_2792/index.html

Contacts

U.S. Embassy in Beijing
Maggie Qiu, Commercial Specialist
(86-10) 8531-4157
Email: jing.qiu@trade.gov

U.S. Consulate in Shanghai
Yuan Liu, Commercial Specialist
(86-21) 6279-8958
Yuan.Liu@trade.gov

U.S. Consulate in Guangzhou
Veronica Liang, Commercial Specialist
(86 20) 8667-4011 ext. 628
Veronica.Liang@trade.gov

U.S. Consulate in Chengdu
Lily Lin, Commercial Specialist
(86 28) 8558-3992 ext.6633
Lin.Liping@trade.gov

U.S. Consulate in Shenyang
Andrea Shen, Commercial Specialist
(86 24) 2322-1198 ext. 8145
andrea.shen@trade.gov

ENVIRONMENTAL TECHNOLOGY

China is the largest and fastest growing emerging market for environmental technologies. It is estimated that China's environmental investment in the coming years will around USD $1.3 – 1.6 trillion (MEP, March 2015). About $286 billion will be spent on air pollution sector and $315 billion will be spent on water sector and another $315 billion spent on soil pollutions sector. The Chinese environmental industry has kept 20% growth rate annual from 2004 to 2014 (MEP 2014). It is expected that the development trend of the industry will keep going in the coming years.

Recently, China has fundamentally restructured its approach to environmental regulatory enforcement with the introduction of the amended Environmental Protection Law on January 1, 2015. This could yield greater adherence to environmental rules if incentives and penalties therein are greater than the cost of non-compliance. Although China's environmental regime has improved with the development of national legal framework, enforcement remains weak in many areas. Market barriers, particularly those related to protection of intellectual property, continue to make China a challenging market to operate.

Sub-Sector Best Prospects

Air Pollution Control

China's State Council released its Action Plan for Air Pollution Prevention and Control on September 12, 2013. The Action Plan sets the road map for air pollution and control for the next five years in China with a focus on three key regions: Beijing-Tianjin-Hebei Area (BTH), Yangtze River Delta (YRD) and Pearl River Delta (PRD). The Action Plan is a detailed implementation plan of the National 10 Measures:

- Reduction of emission of multi-pollutants
- Promotion of industry upgrades and restructuring
- Acceleration of companies' technology upgrade
- Acceleration of energy restructuring
- Enforcement of energy-saving and environmental protection in market entrance requirements
- Application of market-oriented instruments and environmental economic policies
- Improvement of the legal framework, implementation and enforcement
- Establishment of regional collaboration mechanisms
- Establishment of monitoring, alerting and emergency response systems for air pollution episodes
- Definition of responsibilities and engagement with government, private sector and the public for environmental protection.

The goal of the new plan is to improve the air quality of the entire country by 2017, while imposing stricter air pollution reduction guidelines in three key industrial areas surrounding Beijing, Shanghai and Guangzhou. Specifically, the plan pledges to:

- Reduce PM 10 levels in cities nationally by at least 10% from 2012 levels
- Reduce PM 2.5 levels in Beijing/Tianjin/Hebei (BTH) by 25%, in the Yangtze River Delta (YRD) by 20%, and in the Pearl River Delta (PRD) by 15%
- Control coal consumption by establishing medium and long term targets for coal consumption
- Prohibit the approval of new coal-fired power plants in BTH, YRD and PRD areas (with the exception of combined heat and power plants), while requiring existing coal consuming projects to implement coal reduction and substitution projects
- Reduce the proportion of coal in the energy consumption mix to 65% by 2017 (from around 67% in 2012)
- Achieve negative coal consumption growth in the three key air pollution areas (BTH, YRD and PRD) by replacing coal with electricity generated from natural gas and non-fossil fuel energy
- Cut iron-making and steel-making capacity by 15 million tons in 2015
- Control the number of automobiles on its roads: Beijing, Shanghai, Guangzhou and other large Chinese cities should strictly restrict the number of vehicles to curb pollution while other cities should have reasonable controls on the number of vehicles
- Increase usage of non-fossil fuel (wind, solar) from 9.1% in 2012 to 13% by 2017 and increase shale-gas production.

Water

China's water pollution is the byproduct of three decades' rapid economic development. Remediating this will cost time and money before any fundamental improvement, especially considering the fact that the polluted water has entered the underground water cycle. In terms of regulatory development, due to lack of government incentives and enforcement in the past, the industry continues to build low-cost solutions despite the availability of more advanced technology solutions.

Chinese government released Clean Water Action Plan in April 2015 and according to the plan China seeks to improve the quality of water in China's seven major river valleys and coastal areas so that 70 percent is "good" by 2020 and over 75 percent of the water is "clear" by 2030.

The Plan pledges to shut down small, "outdated" factories in 10 polluting industries -- including paper making, production of agricultural chemicals and fertilizer, printing and dyeing, and tanning -- by the end of 2016. Bigger plants will be required to reduce emissions and upgrade technology, and new projects will be controlled more carefully. The plan also says that impact on water resources will become a key factor in future city planning and industrial project location, with restrictions on constructing new petrochemical and iron and steel plants in major river basins.

The plan also says that the results of annual pollution checks will be taken into account when reviewing the performance of provincial officials and the allocation of government funds will depend on the results. And it requires all Chinese cities to release water quality statistics to the public by next year, and all county level governments to release figures by 2018.

The opportunities for companies looking to share knowledge and expertise in the water sector are both broad and comprehensive. In the short term, if stricter government control is enforced and intellectual property issues are resolved, wastewater treatment, water efficiency solutions, and water recycling technologies will be a significant potential market.

Soil remediation

The National Soil Pollution Prevention and Treatment Action Plan of China was approved by the MEP in early 2014 and is waiting for further approval from the central government before being released to the public. MEP will start with six soil remediation demonstration projects and the investment for one demonstration project will be around 1 to 1.5 billion RMB. Those demonstration sites have been selected and they are located at Taizhou, Zhejiang Province, Huangshi, Hubei Province, Changde, Hunan Province, Shaoguan, Guangdong Province, Hechi, Guangxi Province, Tongren, Guizhou Province..

Soil and groundwater protection are both inseparable cycles. MEP has issued the National Groundwater Contamination Pollution Prevention and Remediation Plan (2011-2020) which allocated 37 billion RMB ($6 billion) to support the implementation of new measures. With regulatory developments, it is expected that the soil and groundwater remediation markets will grow in the coming years, especially under two sub-sectors: arable land and brownfield sites in urban areas. The People's Daily newspaper has suggested that as many as 300,000 brownfield sites are in need of treatment before redevelopment. But there is still a big concern on the market opportunity in the short term due to the lack of standards and funding.

Opportunities

AIR POLLUTION CONTROL

Ambient Air Monitoring

In late 2013 the State Council issued the Airborne Pollution Prevention and Control Action Plan. The state air plan stipulates a 25 percent reduction in particulate matter for the Beijing-Tianjin-Hebei region, a 20 percent reduction for Shanxi and Shandong, and a 10 percent reduction for Inner Mongolia. With the exception of Beijing, no other cities included in the plan have sufficient monitoring networks to establish the baseline for reductions or to monitor progress.
Implementation of the state plan will thus require development of a series ambient air monitoring networks across the five regions identified in the plan and should yield opportunities for U.S. air pollution monitoring and instrumentation companies.

Technologies and Services in Demand:

- Continuous emissions monitoring systems
- Ambient air quality monitoring equipment
- Source emissions measurement technologies
- Analytical and laboratory testing goods and services
- Air pollution control equipment
- Fuel vapor control systems

Industrial Air Pollution Reduction

The Beijing Air Pollution Control Action Plan includes a budget of US$ 163 billion of measures to reduce airborne pollutants by 2017. Among the stated goals for industry is a 30 percent reduction in criteria pollutants and a 50 percent reduction of Volatile Organic Compounds (VOCs) from the iron, steel, cement, chemical, and petrochemical industries. If enforced, this ambitious emissions reduction effort will require the immediate implementation of control technologies at industrial sites. Industries that will be of the highest interest for the application of control technologies include iron and steel plants, oil refineries, non-ferrous metallurgical plants, coal boilers, and petrochemical plants.

Key Technologies in Demand:

- Wet/dry scrubbers (particularly systems that remove multiple pollutants)
- Carbon injection systems (for reduction in mercury and organics)

- Particulate matter control systems (particularly new bagging systems)
- NOx, mercury, CO2, and particulate matter monitoring and continuous monitoring systems
- Selective catalytic and non-catalytic reduction controls
- Oxygen enrichment, fuel injection, and other efficient combustion technologies
- Innovative specialty cements
- Mixing technologies
- Pumping and fluid handling equipment
- Engineering and plant design
- Leak detection equipment
- Alternative fuel technologies used to fire cement kilns

Power Plant Emissions Reduction

The Chinese power generation sector is heavily reliant on coal and in the past has applied few if any central measures to reduce particulates and other criteria pollutants such as Sulfur oxides (SOx), nitrogen oxides (NOx), and mercury. Coal-fired power plants generated 67.5 percent of China's energy in 2013,[ii] significantly contributing to air quality issues in the region. Thus reducing coal-fired based emissions is a key pillar in the 2013 State Council plan for air pollution control.

The Hebei region relies heavily on coal-fired power to fuel the nation's steel industry, but has committed nonetheless to a reduction in coal consumption of 40 million tons. Maintaining production while reducing coal consumption will require switching to cleaner burning fuels and administering control technologies. Similarly, the Beijing Air Pollution Control Action Plan stipulates an approach to power generation that includes fuel switching to natural gas.

The Chinese Government has also ratified the Minamata Convention on Mercury. The convention is an international and legally binding instrument to reduce mercury use and emissions. The text of the Minamata Convention was adopted by over 150 countries, including China, in January 2013. Given that coal-fired power plants represent a major source of airborne mercury (and other toxins); the implementation of this instrument will further foster Chinese interest in air pollution control emission control technologies. Furthermore enforcement of the new reduction targets is expected to increase. The Ministry of Environmental Protection dedicated a team in November 2013 to investigate and audit coal-burning heat plants exclusively.

Key Technologies in Demand:

- Continuous emissions monitoring systems
- Dry sorbent injection technologies
- Flue gas desulfurization equipment
- Activated carbon injection technologies
- Inspection, adjustment, maintenance, repair services
- Selective catalytic reduction technologies

WASTE MANAGEMENT AND RECYCLING

Solid Waste and Recycling

Outlined in China's Five Year Plan (2011 – 2015), goals for recycling and solid waste include comprehensive resource recovery from bulk solid waste such as public associated mineral resources, coal powder, coal gangue, industrial by-product gypsum, refining and chemical waste, tailings, construction waste, as well as straw, livestock wastes, and waste wood. The government of China would like to achieve a comprehensive utilization rate of 72 percent by the end of the

Five-Year Plan period.

Key Technologies in Demand:

- Waste piles
- Composting equipment
- Sorting machines
- Crushing and grinding machines
- Materials handling equipment
- Collection services, containers, and vehicles
- Recycling process expertise

Recycling of Discarded Electronics

In 2011, the Chinese government implemented a series of regulations to guide the domestic processing of discarded electronics and electrical appliances called the *Rules on the Administration of the Recovery and Disposal of Discarded Electronic and Electrical Products (or China WEEE)*. The Ministry of Environmental Protection estimates that 1.7 million tons of electronic scrap was generated domestically in China in 2006, which would increase to 5.4 million tons by 2015. China's current electronic scrap recycling infrastructure is dominated by small-scale collection operations, informal recycling facilities, and outdoor recycling markets.

Guided by the Ministry of Environmental Protection and funded by a levy on electronics sold throughout the country, the current recycling infrastructure will be replaced by a large network of sophisticated electronics recycling facilities. In 2011 the Institute for Scrap Recycling Industries (ISRI) estimated that 6 percent of U.S. export sales of scrap equipment were destined for China.

The relatively sudden explosion in Chinese demand for equipment and recycling services present opportunities to U.S. companies with experience in providing equipment or services used in the safe and efficient recovery of valuable materials from discarded electronics.

Key Technologies in Demand:

- Sorting machines
- Crushing and grinding machines
- Materials handling equipment
- Collection services, containers, and vehicles
- Recycling process expertise

Hazardous Waste Management

In November 2012, the Chinese government adopted an action plan to address mounting environmental and health issues related to improperly managed hazardous waste (medical, chemical, and heavy metal). The Chinese Ministry of Environmental Protection estimates 60 million tons of hazardous waste will be produced annually by 2015.

With current disposal capacity at approximately one third of that amount, there is an urgent need to develop disposal capacity commensurate to the scope and size of waste production. Four billion dollars have been set aside to construct 300 hazardous waste disposal facilities and initiate brown field remediation projects throughout China.

Key Technologies in Demand:

- Waste handling equipment
- Waste treatment technologies
- Brownfield site remediation design and equipment
- Soil contamination testing and monitoring equipment

WATER AND WASTEWATER TREATMENT

The Ministry of Environmental Protection is currently drafting a Clean Water Action Plan in the same vein as the State Council's Clean Air Plan. The plan will seek to address pervasive and persistent pollution problems with both ground and surface waters. Key themes under consideration are improved industrial effluent management, municipal wastewater treatment, and treatment approaches for rural areas.

Municipal Water and Wastewater Treatment and Plant Development

Aggressive construction of water treatment plants continues as China works to improve water quality and enhance access to drinking water and sanitation services. The Ministry of Environmental Protection (MEP) announced in 2014 it would invest US$ 329 billion in addressing water pollution which will include treating municipal and industrial wastewater. In the coming years, China hopes to protect the drinking water sources and improve the water quality in centralized drinking sources. The government hopes to expand and promote the protection and management of important water resources.

The China Greentech Initiative (CGTI) reports that 40 billion cubic meters of urban water supply capability will be added by 2015. Furthermore, the South-to-North Water Diversion Project mandates the construction of 426 wastewater treatment plants along the eastern route to treat heavily polluted surface waters. Tightening of national regulations will provide retrofit opportunities for existing plants to move beyond mechanical treatment alone and introduce improved chemical and biological methods. In the 2015 – 2016 tender period the total value of wastewater and desalination projects expected to be tendered is US$528 million across 13 projects.

Key Technolgies in Demand:

- Waste handling equipment
- Engineering, procurement, and construction services
- Advanced filtration
- Membrane filtration
- Waste to energy technology
- Anaerobic digestion
- Nitrification
- Biological denitrification
- Monitoring equipment
- Testing equipment

Sludge Treatment

China discharges approximately 22-30 million tons of untreated sludge annually, a growing and persistent environmental challenge. Recent government action has led to the development of technology standards for sludge treatment, a requirement that municipalities install sludge treatment systems, and a central government capital development investment of RMB 60 billion (US$ 9.6 billion) for sludge treatment facilities. Nonetheless, lack of domestic operational expertise and technology for sludge treatment remains a challenge for China that could provide sludge treatment opportunities for U.S. firms.

In February 2011, the National Development and Reform Commission (NDRC) and Ministry of Housing and Urban-Rural Development (MOHURD) issued plans for developing sludge treatment demonstration projects using advanced technologies. U.S. involvement in those demonstrations could enhance down-stream export opportunities. The municipalities of Beijing, Guangdong, Hebei, and Hubei are top prospects, having set 100 percent treatment targets by 2015.

Key Technologies in Demand:

- Engineering and design
- Anaerobic digestion
- Bio-gas/natural gas recovery

Groundwater Monitoring, Pollution Prevention, and Remdiation

Much of China's groundwater resources have been degraded by pollution, limiting their use as a reliable source for drinking water. The Ministry of Land Resources reports that 57 percent of ground water ranks 'bad' or 'very bad' in quality estimates. The *National Groundwater Contamination Prevention and Remediation Plan* calls for an RMB 34.7 billion (US$ 6.2 billion) investment through 2020. Groundwater protection efforts are focused on monitoring, source control, and remediation.

The 12th Five-Year Plan delineates the study of pollution assessment, monitoring, and simulation in order to establish a national monitoring system and quality standards. Source control research focuses on hazardous waste storage, landfill contamination, oil and gas extraction, mining, agriculture, and underground piping and disposal systems to establish control techniques and rules. China seeks to address contaminated groundwater by conducting a groundwater pollution remediation pilot study that will inform national approaches to groundwater remediation and lead to subsequent large-scale remediation projects. U.S. Superfund experience in environmental remediation creates a competitive advantage for U.S. companies.

Key Technologies in Demand:

- Monitoring equipment
- Source pollution control technologies
- Sparging
- Bioremediation
- Chemical treatment
- Flushing
- In-situ air stripping
- Multiphase extraction
- Permeable reactive barrier
- Phytoremediation
- Pump and treat

Water efficiency and reuse

China's scarce fresh water resources have made water efficiency and reuse a national priority designed to limit further economic disruptions due to water shortages. These priorities will be a boon to membrane, non-revenue water management, and industrial water efficiency technologies. It is estimated that water reuse will lead to 30 percent annual growth over the next five years in the membrane technology market.

Key Technologies in Demand:

- Engineering and design
- Monitoring equipment
- Non-revenue water control software
- Membranes
- Advanced filtration
- Low-loss distribution equipment
- Storage equipment

Process and Produced Water

New effluent standards and better enforcement thereof are driving growth in produced water treatment, while continued industrial expansion and water reuse targets promote the process water market. China anticipates strengthening pollution control in many of its water-intensive industries, particularly in pulp and paper, printing and dying, chemicals, leather and large-scale livestock and poultry. Investments in improved effluent management are expected to reach RMB 125 billion (US$ 20.1 billion) by 2015.

The State 12th Five-Year Plan targets nine sectors for improved produced water treatment: paper and pulp, raw chemicals, petroleum refining, textiles, dyeing, pharmaceuticals, ferrous metals processing, food processing, and power generation. The China Greentech Initiative has developed a list of top tier client industries using government prioritization, pollution reduction targets, discharge volumes, and treatment profitability measures. They include pharmaceuticals, beverages, paper and pulp, raw chemicals, textiles, agricultural food processing, and coal mining and washing. Second tier industries include ferrous metal processing, petroleum refining, tobacco, food manufacturing, and chemical fibers.

Key Technologies in Demand:

- Engineering and design
- Monitoring equipment
- Membranes
- Advanced filtration

Soil remediation

A result of weak or non-existent waste management strategies including the failure to develop sanitary landfills has led to prevalent soil pollution. The Ministry of Environmental Protection and the Ministry of Land Resources report that 16.1 percent of China's soil is polluted and of this total, 19.4 percent of arable land is polluted. Much of this contamination is non-organic with the most prevalent pollutants being cadmium, nickel, and arsenic. Soil pollution threatens the safety of agricultural products and contributes to groundwater pollution through leaching.

The government is in its early stages of planning a national effort to address soil pollution but in the coming years a substantial remediation effort should yield opportunities for U.S. providers of remediation technology and services.

Key Technologies in Demand:

- Engineering and design
- Monitoring equipment

Environmental Engineering and Consulting

The new Environmental Protection Law stipulates that all new construction projects must undergo an Environmental Impact Assessment (EIA) before construction permits can be issued. Similar to the U.S. National Environmental Policy Act (NEPA) if fully implemented EPL will develop a massive industry for EIAs, and area where U.S. environmental engineering and consulting firms have substantial expertise.

Key Technologies in Demand:

- Environmental Impact Assessment

Web Resources

Ministry of Environmental Protection Environmental http://www.mep.gov.cn/
China National Environmental Monitoring Center http://www.cnemc.cn/
China Environmental News http://www.cenews.com.cn/
China Solid Waste http://www.solidwaste.com.cn/
Water China http://www.h2o-china.com/
China City Water http://www.chinacitywater.org/

Contacts

U.S. Embassy in Beijing
Jiangyao Zhang, Commercial Specialist
(86 10) 8531-3000
jiangyao.zhang@trade.gov

U.S. Consulate in Chengdu
Mengyue Xu, Commercial Specialist
(86 28) 8558 3992 ext. 6546
Cui.Shiyang@trade.gov

U.S. Consulate in Shanghai
Sophia Chen, Commercial Specialist
(86 21) 6279-7630
shiqiao.chen@trade.gov

U.S. Consulate in Shenyang
Xiaolei Zhou, Commercial Specialist
(86 24) 2322 1198 - 8146
Evelyn.Zhou@trade.gov

U.S. Consulate in Guangzhou
Cathy Wang, Commercial Specialist
(86 20) 3814-5000
cathy.wang@trade.gov

U.S. Consulate in Wuhan
Jing Wang, Commercial Specialist
(86 27) 8555 7791 - 808
Jing.wang@trade.gov

FRANCHISING SECTOR

Franchising shows promise in China. Statistics from China Chainstore & Franchise Association (CCFA) show that the country's top 100 franchises generated a total sales of RMB428 billion with the total number of stores across these 100 franchises is 124,086. 90% of these franchises believed that their sales will continue to grow in 2015. China has over 4,500 franchises and chain store companies creating more than 5 million jobs nationwide.

Challenges to U.S. franchise firms include a relatively weak regulatory system, increasing costs of labor and real estate and a lack of qualified Chinese franchisee candidates. The most recent legislation released by the Ministry of Commerce stipulates that franchise firms can start franchising in China as long as they own and operate two company-owned stores for one year in any part of the world. In addition, franchise firms must file with the local commercial authority for record within 15 days after the execution of the initial franchise contract.

Sub-Sector Best Prospects

The Chinese franchising market is dominated by traditional franchise operations like food and beverage (F&B) and retail outlets. According to CCFA, nearly 40 percent of all franchisers in China are engaged in such industries. U.S. franchisers established a particularly strong foothold in the F&B market.

Franchising opportunities abound in non-F&B industries. The best prospects in this form of franchising include sectors such as car rental and services, education and youth learning, and health and fitness.

Major international franchise firms have established the following best practices for doing business in China:

1. Register the brand in China before entering the China market.
2. Find local partners who can help navigate the local business environment.
3. Understand the cultural differences and adjust market access strategies accordingly.
4. Have an ability and willingness to localize your product if necessary, without changing the core product.
5. Minimize the price of the final product and the franchising fee to achieve rapid expansion and mass acceptance.
6. Manage government relations by establishing and maintaining solid working relationships with relevant Chinese Government agencies.

Opportunities

Foreign franchise brands are receiving greater interest from second and third-tier market developers as markets in Beijing and Shanghai become more saturated. It's noteworthy that some major locations that were abandoned by foreign multinationals over the past few years were almost all in first-tier cities where their Chinese story began. High rent is expected to hit more foreign franchises in Beijing and Shanghai. However, there is room for growth in China's west and inland regions that boast advantages such as lower labor costs, reasonably-priced real estate facilities and untapped consumer spending.
Additionally, we are seeing an increase in F&B companies entering the market as wholly owned enterprises to manage their brand, demonstrate proof-of-concept and create a strong foothold prior to expanding into the franchise model.

Per Capita Disposable incomes at China's 1st and 2nd tier cities (figures in $)

City	2011	2012	2013
Beijing *	5,193.02	5,853.65	6,583.23
Shanghai *	5,718.11	6,450.77	6,802.56
Chengdu**	4,021.62	4,365.00	4,833.41
Dongguan**	6,326.26	6,893.09	7,515.15

Source: National Bureau of Statistics

Web Resources

International Franchise Association www.franchise.org

China Chain Store and Franchise Association Website: http://www.ccfa.org.cn

Ministry of Commerce (MOFCOM) Website: http://www.mofcom.gov.cn

Shanghai International Franchise Show

Every September
Shanghai International Exhibition Center, China http://sh.ccfa.org.cn/

US Commercial Service Offices in China:

U.S. Embassy in Beijing
Mr. Shen Yan, Commercial Specialist
(86 10) 8531-3554
Email: yan.shen@trade.gov

U.S. Consulate in Shanghai
Ms. Janet Li, Commercial Specialist
(86 21) 6279-8775
Email: janet.li@trade.gov

U.S. Consulate in Guangzhou
Roya Xie, Commercial Specialist
(86-20) 020 3814 5807
Email: roya.xie@trade.gov

U.S. Consulate in Chengdu
Ms. Fan Li, Commercial Specialist
(86 28) 8558-3992
Email: li.fan@trade.gov

U.S. Consulate in Shenyang
Liu Yang, Commercial Specialist
(86 24) 2322-1198
yang.liu@trade.gov

INFORMATION AND COMMUNICATIONS TECHNOLOGY EQUIPMENT AND SOFTWARE

IDC (a well-known professional IT consulting firm) estimated the 2015 Chinese information and communications technology (ICT) total market size to be $465.6 billion, an increase of 11.4% over 2014. According to the firm, the 2014 IT market totaled $205 billion with a 14.2% increase over the previous year, and is estimated to reach $211 billion in 2015. The 2015 telecommunications market is estimated to reach $254 billion, an increase of 31.8% compared with 2014. Chinese government statistics reported via the Ministry of Industry and Information Technology (MIIT) and presented below reflect higher numbers, but similar growth trends.

SUB-SECTOR BEST PROSPECTS

Semiconductors

China represents the largest and fastest growing country market for U.S. semiconductors. China is the third largest country market for U.S. semiconductor manufacturing equipment and the fastest growing market for such equipment.

Although China is the top market for semiconductors, U.S. companies face IPR problems, and issues stemming from China's program to develop its indigenous integrated circuit industry.

Semiconductors
China ranks number one in our study based on semiconductor demand in its electronics manufacturing industry. China is the largest and fastest growing semiconductor market in the world, representing 50 percent ($168 billion) of the $336 billion global market in 2014. China's

market is forecast to grow ten percent per year from $168 billion in 2014 to $203 billion in 2016. In 2014, U.S. companies had 51 percent of worldwide semiconductor sales, while Chinese companies only had a 4 percent share.

Growth is being propelled by an increase in domestic consumption of consumer electronic products, as well as consumer electronics assembled for export; growth in the manufacturing of automobiles which are increasingly reliant on electronics; and expanding demand for medical and healthcare electronics. Semiconductor demand growth is forecast to remain in the double digits for years to come. U.S. companies have been successful in selling into the Chinese market, but dark clouds loom over the horizon as the Chinese government has started an initiative to pour up to $150 billion into developing its domestic semiconductor industry over the next ten years.

Semiconductor Manufacturing Equipment
China ranks third as a market for U.S. semiconductor manufacturing equipment. The country's domestic semiconductor industry is still relatively small but growing. Total global sales of semiconductor manufacturing equipment in China reached $4.4 billion in 2014 (12 percent of the $37.5 Billion world market), up 57 percent over 2013. China is increasing semiconductor production/fabrication facility (fab) capacity and buying more equipment, but the majority of new facilities are for Light-Emitting Diodes (LEDs), not integrated circuits (ICs).

In addition to wafer processing equipment for ICs and LEDs, China also buys a significant amount of machinery for semiconductor packaging/final assembly and testing. China represents 27 percent of the world's floor space for semiconductor packaging and testing in the world. China produces a nominal amount of semiconductor manufacturing equipment, less than 0.5 percent share of the world market.

Opportunities for U.S. Companies

Most semiconductors and semiconductor manufacturing equipment have duty-free access to the Chinese market under the existing WTO Information Technology Agreement. If the WTO Information Technology Agreement expansion is successfully concluded, certain types of semiconductors and semiconductor manufacturing equipment, accessories, and parts whose coverage is in question under the original Agreement will be eligible for duty free trade. This would ensure that U.S. exporters compete on level terms with non-U.S. suppliers, creating potential opportunities for U.S. companies.

Semiconductors
China accounts for over 50 percent of the world's electronics production, which is the main driver of semiconductor demand. However, not all of the buying decisions for semiconductors are made in China. Such decisions are often made by the foreign companies that contract out electronic goods production to China. The supply chain is global and semiconductors in different stages of completion are transshipped and re-exported from numerous markets. The U.S. Commerce Department thus encourages U.S. companies to target large Chinese consumer electronics companies manufacturing in China. Lenovo and Huawei, for example, are among the top ten buyers of semiconductors globally, and other Chinese companies including ZTE, Datang Telecomm, Xiaomi, and Haier are also major purchasers.

Semiconductor Manufacturing Equipment
Overall sales of equipment in China are forecasted to grow by 57 percent in 2015 to $5.1 billion due to fab equipping. Sales are expected to slow later in 2015 as the fab building frenzy declines, and fall to $4.6 billion in 2016 (down 10 percent year-on-year) with China dropping to become fourth largest market behind Japan. China's market is volatile and not as big as those of Taiwan or Korea. The National IC Industry Development plan creates opportunities but the projects funded may spur artificial demand for semiconductor manufacturing equipment. In addition, there are some IPR issues. However, overall, the U.S. semiconductor manufacturing equipment

industry currently enjoys good access to the Chinese market.

Cloud Computing

Although China is a fast-growing, important market for global cloud computing, the country presents serious challenges for U.S. cloud providers and ranks only 13th in the listing. Regulatory restrictions, some aspects of governmental decision making, and local competition make China a problematic market for even large, experienced U.S. providers. Operating in China therefore requires substantial resources, flexibility, and a long-term outlook.

While in some keys ways China is at an earlier stage in cloud adoption than other large economies, it is clear that the market is expanding notably and poised for significant future growth. Estimates of the size and growth rate of the domestic cloud computing sector vary widely. The Ministry of Industry and Information Technology (MIIT) has reported that China's public cloud market was worth approximately 4.8 billion RMB ($771.2 million at current exchange rates) in 2013 and expects 36 percent growth for 2014. Gartner projects the public cloud market to reach $20.7 billion by 2018, with an annual growth rate of 31.5 percent (while IDC notes sustained annual growth of over 40 percent in the Chinese public cloud market).

As for the broader market, the state-run China Software Industry Association previously predicted the overall cloud value chain would be worth at least $122 billion by 2015, although some more recent estimates have trended lower.

As in other sectors, the main challenge for U.S. firms in seizing cloud-related opportunities in China is its regulatory environment. For example, foreign cloud providers are required to partner with local companies to serve customers in China, raising questions about how much control foreign providers will ultimately have over their joint ventures, given that their Chinese partners may fully manage daily operations. Moreover, certain regulatory requirements impact the cloud services and threaten to present additional restrictions in the future. To deal with these challenges, U.S. companies have found it necessary to completely isolate their China cloud systems from their global ones, creating likely technical inefficiencies and other operational complications.

Other key regulatory developments rose to prominence at the close of 2014 and in the first few months of 2015.

The first is a planned security rating system to be used in assessing the "trustworthiness" of cloud providers vying for public contracts. Foreign firms are expected to be able to participate in the review process, though in doing so they may be required to turn over proprietary source code. Secondly, reports indicate that the central government may be aiming to by 2020 have removed foreign-made software and hardware from major segments of the economy, such as the military, banks, some government bureaus, and the country's massive state-owned enterprises.

Mainland China's Internet download speeds also present issues. The penetration of broadband access, which is critical to the meaningful use of cloud services, is only about 14 percent. Average download speeds are only 3.14 to 4 megabits per second. The average download speed in Hong Kong, by contrast, exceeds 44 megabits per second, while the developed world standard is 17.4 megabits per second.

Although some point out that local players currently lack some of the larger U.S. firms' key advantages (e.g., scale, technical skill, innovative services), there can be no doubt that these gaps will close to varying degrees over the next several years.

OPPORTUNITIES

Smart City Development in China

"Smart City" is a term applied to everything from urban design to higher education policy. But the most accepted definition is the use of information technology to address urban issues. Database and network systems are now being connected to objects in the physical world such as meters, sensors, cameras, and control systems in pilot projects around the world. Smart city systems are managing traffic, stabilizing electric grids, allocating and coordinating emergency services, and providing more city information to people and managers than has ever been available before. In China, this issue is still in the beginning stages of discovery.

A big bet on smart cities

China's 12th Five-Year Plan, which guides broad economic policy through 2015, specifically calls on smart city technology as a sector to be strengthened and encouraged, and ministries are jostling to sponsor programs and industry alliances. In 2012, the Ministry of Science and Technology (MOST) organized the China Strategic Alliance of Smart City Industrial Technology Innovation. Last year, the Ministry of Industry and Information Technology (MIIT) sponsored another group, the China Smart City Industry Alliance, and this year announced a ¥50 billion ($8 billion) fund to invest in smart city research and projects. A third group, the Smart City Development Alliance was formed this spring by the National Development and Reform Commission (NDRC). Some companies are working with only one of these new groups, and some are involved with all three. At present there is little connection between the groups, which apparently exist to improve communications between industry participants and between industry and government and, in the case of at least the MIIT group, to coordinate investment. Additionally, there are more than 300 pilot sites in China nationwide including local governments and economic development zones. Many of these were chosen by MOHURD.

There is no standard definition of the sector, but some estimates foresee ¥2 trillion ($320 billion) of investment into smart city development projects over the next 10 years. These enormous sums, rapid technology advances, and vigorous marketing of smart city products from both domestic and international companies, have created a booming and chaotic marketplace. In Beijing the effort now is to create standards and guidelines to manage this flood of new projects. This spring, all the ministries involved in smart cities issues joined with the Standardization Administration of China to create working groups whose job is to manage and standardize smart city development, though their activities have yet to be publicized.

The private sector: smart city suppliers

The smart city sector is not a single industry, but an emerging collection of technologies cutting across many industries – transportation and utility infrastructure, network equipment, telecom and wireless, data analytics, electronics equipment, and software applications. To manage the massive quantity of information generated, applications rely heavily on new IT technologies such as cloud computing and "big data" analytics.

For multinational corporations, huge potential in the China market is tempered by real challenges. The Chinese government is raising increasing concerns about data security concerns. The recent announcement from the State Information Office that it would be testing the security (as yet undefined) of foreign information technology products and services, and barring those that do not pass, only further underscores the difficulties that international firms may face in China.

Another significant challenge may be China's rapidly maturing domestic competition. China is no longer a developing-nation market in which international companies compete only with one another. Chinese firms are mastering technologies and becoming price competitive. China's two electric grid companies, State Grid and Southern Grid, as well as all three of its major telecoms, are actively developing smart grid policies and products and sponsoring pilot projects.

In China, there are many stand-alone projects based on a few core applications such as energy, transportation and government management platforms, but even at the pilot level there are not yet any comprehensive smart cities. But China has committed to its cities and is placing large hopes on technology to make them manageable and livable.

POLICIES

Multi-Level Protection Scheme (MLPS)
In 2010, MPS, the leading ministry tasked with combating cybercrime and protecting critical infrastructure, implemented the Multi-Level Protection Scheme (MLPS). Designed to secure critical Chinese infrastructure information systems, MLPS classifies information networks in China according to their relative impact on national security, social order and economic interests if the system is damaged or attacked. The classification levels range from one to five, one being the least critical and five being the most critical. A level five ranking indicates extremely significant networks, such as for military and defense. According to MLPS regulations, systems classified at level three or above must procure IT security products containing only domestic IP. MLPS also requires that traditional IT products at level three or above be subject to rigorous testing and review guidelines under the China Compulsory Certification for Information Security Products (CCCi) for government procurement. As a result of the 2014 JCCT discussions, companies are no longer required to use Chinese encryption for MLPS. In general, foreign companies are not allowed to sell above level 3, without submitting to testing. Very few U.S. companies have done the MLPS classification testing or CCCi, because foreign ICT products are not supposed to be allowed to sell to organizations above level three or to the government.

Telecom Services Catalog
According to the existing Chinese Telecom Services Catalog, cloud computing service providers are required to obtain a value-added telecom services license to launch cloud services in China. To obtain this license, a partnership is required with a Chinese company. The 2013 draft revision of the Catalog of Telecommunications Services signaled China's intention to expand value-added telecom services licensing requirements to include a host of Internet-based business activities and services that have generally been unregulated in China, and are unregulated in most other markets. The draft Catalog relies on very specific definitions of service categories, classified as either basic or value-added telecom services. Once a business's services are classified as value-added, various licenses are required, all of which compel partnership with a Chinese company.

CBRC Guidelines
China issued an official notice (CBRC/MIIT Joint Circular #57) to its banking sector April 13, including Chinese and foreign-owned banks, suspending for revision its earlier Guidelines for Secure and Controllable Information Technology in the Banking Industry for 2014-2015 (CBRC Circular [2014] 317, the Guidelines). The Guidelines, as previously written, would have required banks in China to ensure that at least 75% of their ICT products and services are "secure and controllable," i.e. are indigenous and Chinese-controlled, by 2019. First, this would conflict with China's WTO obligations and commitments it has made at the JCCT and S&ED. Second, forcing an overhaul of banks' ICT systems in favor of inferior products would impose huge costs and create real security vulnerabilities. Third, the Guidelines, if carried out, could become the template for other key sectors. We do expect a revised version to come out, possibly not requiring the divulgence of source code or other requirements, but still requiring "secure and controllable" to some degree. We also have concerns that this concept will spread to other industries in addition to banking, such as telecommunications.

Counterterrorism Law (CTL)

Post has been monitoring the draft Counterterrorism Law. The draft is reportedly being revised, in response to concerns expressed by foreign industry and governments. However, we have not seen a revised draft, and it remains unclear what China's timeline is and whether it will publish a draft for public comment. In general, the CTL if passed will impose onerous requirements on all ICT product and service providers in China, and grant authorities unfettered access to company data. Requirements in the initial draft included data localization, installation of an interface that the government can access, and source code divulgence. Regardless of where one stands on the security vs. privacy debate in the United States, China's approach is extreme, and could make it impossible for U.S. and other foreign ICT companies to continue to do business in China.

Cybersecurity Review Regime

We are aware that a finalized draft of China's National Cybersecurity Review Regime has been released internally by the Cyberspace Administration of China (CAC). We expect the necessary law for this review regime will pass this year, yet we are unclear on what new controls it will impose. A news report published by the Shanghai-based newspaper Liberation Daily and posted on the official CAC website clarified certain aspects of the regime as:

- Scope of application: key technologies, products, and services used in systems related to national security and public interest
- Key contents for review: security and controllability of products
- Objectives: to prevent illegal control, interference and interruption of user systems by product providers, and to prevent illegal collection, storage, processing and utilization of user-related information.
- Management: products and services that do not meet relevant safety requirements will be prohibited from entering Chinese territory.

Web Resources

Ministry of Industry and Information Technology (MIIT)
http://www.miit.gov.cn/

Ministry of Science and Technology
http://www.most.gov.cn/

China Academy of Information and Telecommunications Technology (CAICT)
http://english.catr.cn/

China Electronics Standardization Institute (CESI)
http://www.cesi.cn/

China Institute of Electronics (CIE)
http://www.cie-info.org.cn/

China Communications Standards Association (CCSA)
http://www.ccsa.org.cn/

China Electronics Chamber of Commerce (CECC)
http://www.cecc.org.cn/

Contacts

Commercial Service in Beijing:
Liting Bao, Commercial Specialist
Tel: (86 10) 8531-3889

Liting.Bao@trade.gov

Commercial Service in Chengdu:
Haiyan (Helen Hua) Hua, Commercial Specialist
Tel: (86 28) 8558-3992 ext. 6738
Haiyan.Hua@trade.gov

Commercial Service in Shanghai:
Jane Shen, Senior Commercial Specialist
Tel : (86 21) 6279-7630 ext. 8718
Jane.Shen@trade.gov

Commercial Service in Guangzhou :
Sophie Xiao, Senior Commercial Specialist
Tel : (8620) 8667-4011 ext. 619
Sophine.Xiao@trade.gov

Commercial Service in Shenyang :
Dongmei Wang, Commercial Specialist
Tel : (8624) 2322-1198 ext. 8142
Dongmei.Sun@trade.gov

MARINE INDUSTRIES

Sales and manufacturing of Ships, Boats and Floating Structures in China (USD millions)

(USD millions)	2011	2012	2013	2014
Total Market Size	66,809	75,551	77,025	79,000
Total Local Production	108,605	102,341	98,784	104,266
Total Exports	43,687	38,819	29,006	25,202
Total Imports	1,810	1,783	2,033	1,315
Imports from the U.S.	46	67	63	39

Source: Global Trade Atlas/IBIS World/China Association of the National Shipping Industry

This section covers the use and development of sea-related industries including shipbuilding, ports, pleasure boats, sea communications and transportation.

As the world's largest exporter, China has become a center of maritime activity, and China's major state-owned shipping and shipbuilding companies are among the world's largest. According to the Ministry of Land and Resources of the People's Republic of China, the marine industry will gradually become one of the pillars of China's economy.

According to Global Trade Atlas statistics, the total value of China's sea freight-based imports and exports reached $26 billion in 2014, of which ship imports accounted for $1.3 billion. Trade volume reached a historic high of approximately $45 billion in 2011. However, oceanic pollution, a 44% tax rate on imported yachts, underdeveloped ports, and cost increases continue to present challenges for the development of the marine industry.

Sub-Sector Best Prospects

Best prospects in China's marine industries include shipbuilding and related accessories, recreational marine, port related accessories and sea transportation.

Shipbuilding

Firms operating within the Ship Building industry in China primarily manufacture ships, ship bodies and boats from metals such as steel and aluminum. The ships and boats manufactured by this industry are intended for civil and military use, and exclude non-metal ships and boats for entertainment and sport.

In 2013, the weak economy around the globe led to decreases in international trade and resulted the corresponding decline in marine industry exports. In 2014, the Ship Building industry in China has been slowly recovering. Chinese shipbuilders' production volume was 36.29 million Deadweight Tonnage (DWT) from January to December of 2014. The market share of Chinese shipbuilding output, new ship orders and ship orders in hand, respectively accounted for 39.9%, 46.5% and 47.2% of world totals in 2014. *(Source: Analysis on China's Shipbuilding Industry by China Shipbuilding Industry Association)*

Over the past five years, the Ship Building industry in China has been growing at an annual rate of 2.5% to reach a total production value of $79.4 billion in 2014. This industry's activities are highly concentrated in Jiangsu, Zhejiang, Shandong and Shanghai. Foreign-owned enterprises generate 29.4% of industry revenue. The largest two shipbuilding groups, CSSC and CSIC, produce over 30.0% of domestic metal ships. During 2009 to 2019, industry value-added growth is expected to be lower than GDP growth. Further, due to fierce market competition the number of enterprises in the industry is expected to decrease 2.3% per year over the period.

The industry is dominated by three types of ships: oil tankers, bulk cargo carriers and container carriers, which in total accounted for 71.2% of shipping exports in 2013 in China. This indicates that product variety in this industry is low, which assists companies in standardizing processes and developing efficiencies.

The best sales prospects for U.S. exports to China's shipbuilding market include: raw materials, coating equipment and coating materials, computer aided design (CAD) software and associated technologies for ship design and construction, equipment maintenance, Global Positioning Systems (GPS), navigation and on-board computer systems, and cutting and welding technology.

Recreational Marine Industry

China has become a force to be reckoned with in the global recreational marine market. The total value of yachts and other vessels for pleasure or sport imported by the country in 2014 has increased to more than $150 million, compared to less than $11 million back at 2004. United States is ranked the world's third largest exporter of yachts and pleasure boats to China and the total export value reached close to $28 million last year (Source: Global Trade Atlas). Over the next five years, China's yacht and pleasure boat industry is projected to have an annual growth of 30% to reach $2.4 billion in 2018. Industry experts also foresee continued growth of opportunities for yachting accessories and equipment, as well as marine planning and construction materials.

According to the China Cruise & Yacht Industry Association, as of November 2014, China had 7 provincial-level yacht associations based in Shanghai, Hainan, Guangdong, Liaoning, Fujian, Tianjin and Zhejiang; 10 municipal-level yacht associations, and 3 of which are located in Shenzhen in South China. The Number 30 Decree of the State Council of the People's Republic of China on promoting the reform and development of tourism industry in 2014 has emphasized the importance of encouraging cruise and yachting tourism. Unlike many western countries, China's current marine industry is still at an early stage. So far, there are 6,404 marina berths nationwide, while Shenzhen in particular, has almost 1,000 berths which is the highest in the country. The Chinese government is also devoting resources to improve the marine infrastructure and build more public wharfs, the lack of which has restricted the rapid development of yacht and recreational boat market. Private investors and marinas have also begun to increase the number of marine berths in order to attract more yacht owners. For instance, the Shanghai government has decided to build marinas and cruise ship centers along the downtown riverfront as part of the effort to remake Shanghai into a world-class city. The Guangzhou municipal government is also expediting polices to shape the marine sector as the city's strategic industry, and is planning to build over 3,000 new berths in the coming years.

Maritime Emergency Response and Port Safety

China is one of the world's largest maritime markets with a coastline of 32,000 kilometers and over 1,400 harbors. From North to South along China's eastern coastline, there are five established coastal port groups: the Bohai Bay Rim Port Cluster, the Yangtze River Delta Port Cluster, the Southeast Coast Port Cluster, the Pearl River Delta Port Cluster, and the Southwest Coast Port Cluster. These ports are administered by their respective local Port Authorities, together with the Maritime Safety Administration, which are both agencies under the Chinese Ministry of Transport.

Under the 12th Five-Year Development Plan of Transportation Safety and Emergency, by 2015, China expects to make significant advancement in the areas of regulations and emergency plans, equipment and facilities, information technology, workforce quality and infrastructure safety capabilities. The Chinese government also announced that it will spend over $450 billion on maritime environmental protection and oil spill response with a focus on importing advanced equipment for emergency management and enhancing maritime safety soft skills.

Port Construction and Sea-Transportation

China is allocating significant capital for port and waterway construction to meet significant growth in freight volume. China's port flow is increasing at exponential rates, reflecting foreign trade growth. Eight ports in mainland China -- Ningbo-Zhoushan, Shanghai, Tianjin, Tangshan, Guangzhou, Suzhou, Qingdao and Dalian -- are among the 10 largest ports in the world in terms of port cargo throughput. In 2014, total port cargo turnover in China exceeded 12.4 billion tons, rising 5.8% from 2013, and container throughput reached 202 million twenty-foot equivalent units (TEU), with an annual increase of 6.4%. With cargo turnover exceeding 870 million tons, an annual increase of 7.9%, the port of Ningbo-Zhoushan port is by far the busiest in the world. *(Source: chineseport.cn)*.

To facilitate global trade, most ports in China are placing emphasis on expanding capacity, upgrading port facilities, and modernizing operations. The products and technologies in high demand are vessel traffic management information systems, laser-docking systems, terminal tractors, dredging equipment and security equipment for ports and vessels to enable them to comply with the International Ship and Port Security Code (ISPS).

China is building more deep-water berths to handle the larger fifth and sixth-generation container vessels. The largest project is the construction of Yangshan deep-water port, approximately 20 miles offshore from Shanghai and linked to the mainland by a 20-mile causeway bridge. The master plan calls for the completion of 50 berths by 2020, which will cost over $10 billion. It also includes a logistics park and new harbor city on mainland China.
Lianyungang, a northern port city in Jiangsu Province, is racing to build an international port after winning State Council approval to construct a 300,000 DWT deep-water channel and a 300,000 DWT berth for handling crude oil and ore.

The sea freight transport industry in China is mainly engaged in shipping exported items to their destination countries and territories from China. Therefore, industry performance is extremely sensitive to the global economic climate, which determines demand for Chinese goods. Over the past five years, industry revenue has been increasing at an annual rate of 4.1%. In 2015, industry revenue is set to reach $35.9 billion, up 7.0% from 2014. The industry plays a significant role in China's international trade, delivering products between China and other countries by sea. Therefore, industry operators are highly concentrated in coastal provinces. Further, the coastal provinces are more economically developed, with higher demand for international trade. Shanghai accounts for 23.1% of China's total international freight shipment volume. *(Source: IBISWorld)*

Opportunities

China's marine economy currently accounts for about 10% of the national economy as a whole and its importance is expected to grow in the future, which will bring more businesses to the industry.

The relatively young Marine Services industry in China has developed strongly along with China's booming marine economy. In the past five years, industry revenue has increased at an average annual rate of 10.4% despite the negative effects of the global recession in late 2008 and 2009. Industry revenue totaled $308.4 million in 2014, up 10.2% from 2013. The Marine Services industry in China comprises establishments that provide a wide range of specialized marine and offshore services, including marine management, marine evaluation, marine and polar expeditions, marine weather forecasting, marine pollution control and other marine services. Most marine services are highly specialized and require advanced technologies and industry expertise. Therefore, it is crucial for new entrants to this market to have a team of experienced and professional technicians. *(Source: IBISWorld)*

China's marine equipment industry currently lags behind the shipbuilding industry. Equipment that is in high demand includes machinery, key electric-mechanical equipment, communications systems, diesel engine crank-shafts and components, high-powered diesel engines, ship superstructures, deep-sea exploration ship products, high-grade steel plates and section bars, and environmentally friendly paint. Other potential prospects for shipbuilding can be seen in markets for coating equipment, computer-aided design software and associated technology for ship design and construction, equipment maintenance, high-tech equipment (such as GPS, navigation and on-board computer systems), and cutting and welding technology.

China has routinely sought foreign design support for large marine engineering projects, but to date has relied heavily on European and Asian firms. With marine engineering projects as a targeted area of growth in the industry revitalization plan, and with United States expertise in offshore energy projects, there will be increasing opportunities for American design firms in this segment.

Pleasure boats are one of the best prospects for exporters. China's recreational marine industries are poised to expand rapidly in the coming years. China's provincial governments, property developers and boat builders are all investing heavily in this expanding industry, presenting significant opportunities for United States exporters of pleasure boats, accessories, marina planning services, and construction materials.

Maritime emergency response and port safety equipment and services have also begun attracting attention in China. There are good opportunities for equipment, technology, and services related to communication and supervision systems, flight supervision and maritime rescue, marine oil spills, salvage, mapping, waterway maintenance, and public security.

Web Resources

China Port Association
www.port.org.cn

China Shipbuilding Engineering Association
www.csname.org.cn

China Association of the National Shipbuilding Industry
www.cansi.org.cn

China Cruise & Yacht Industry Association
www.ccyia.com

MEDICAL DEVICES

The medical device market is one of the fastest growing market sectors in China. It has an average growth rate of 20% over the last decade. That leads to the fact that, in 2013, China surpassed Japan to become the second largest medical device market in the world.

In 2014, the market scale of the medical device market reached Rmb255.6 billion, an increase of 20.5% when compared to 2013. 76% of this growth is fueled by hospitals. Based on the target policy set by China's Health and Family Planning Commission, 70 to 75% of the medical devices in Tier-3 hospitals and 66% of that in Tier-2 hospitals should be imported from foreign countries. With an increasingly aging population and increasing health awareness, there is a great potential for the medical device industry on the mainland.

The government has invested heavily in the healthcare infrastructure and the provision of basic health insurance for all of its citizens. In 2013, China's public healthcare spending amounted to Rmb954 billion. However, it only accounted for 5.6% of China's GDP, which is far lower than countries like the US (18%), Germany (12%), Canada(11%) and Japan (9%), given the sheer size of China's economy. In fact, globally, the medical device market is equal to about 42% of the pharmaceutical market. In China, however, the percentage is much lower, about 14%. This signals enormous room for continued growth.

Currently China's medical device market has two distinct categories: 1) domestic manufacturers who supply low to mid-range products. Over 80% of the domestic manufacturers belong to this category 2) foreign-sourced, high-end products supplied by large companies like GE, Philips, and Siemens. According to the 2014 China Medical Device Industry Development Bluebook issued by China Medical Pharmaceutical Material Association, by the end of 2014 there were a total of 15,700 domestic medical device manufacturers. China's total sales volume was RMB 255.6 ($40.57) billion in 2014 representing a growth of over 20% since the close of fiscal year 2013. It is worth noting that the sales volume through E-Commerce platforms has reached 1.58 billion RMB, approximately 25.8% of the total retail market.

The United States ranks #1 in the import medical device market, followed by Germany and Japan. These three countries represent the majority share of China's imports.

Table I below shows an analysis of medical device imports during 2012-2014 based on HS codes under the medical device categories.

Table I: 2012-2014 China's Import of Medical Device by HS code from the Top 3 Countries (USD millions)

				Share			Change %	Change %
	2012	2013	2014	2012	2013	2014	2012-2013	2013-2014
World	15,31	17,136	18,08	100%	100%	100%	11.92%	5.56%
U.S.	5,219	5,918	6,059	34.09%	34.54%	33.50%	13.39%	2.38%
Germany	2,713	3,132	3,183	17.72%	18.28%	17.60%	15.44%	1.63%
Japan	2,359	2,210	2,313	15.41%	12.90%	12.79%	-6.32%	4.66%

China has about 25,509 hospitals, 52.3% are public hospitals. Compared with 2013, the number of public hospitals was decreased by 98 and that of private hospitals was increased by 1,137. In 2014, China announced it would allow foreign investors to wholly own hospitals in seven cities and provinces (Beijing, Shanghai, Guangdong, Fujian, Hainan, Jiangsu and Tianjin), further opening up the country's fast-growing private hospital sector. Of the USD 41.3 billion medical devices sales market in 2014, 76.1% of purchases were by hospitals, and 23.9% were retail.

The Chinese hospitals consider U.S. products to be of superior quality as well as the most technologically advanced and they particularly welcome medical equipment and products with high-technology content. U.S. firms garner nearly three-quarters of their local revenues from tier 3 hospitals and the remainder from tier 2 hospitals. In an effort to capitalize on China's burgeoning medical device market, U.S. firms have expanded their local presence in China while also targeting the country's rural population. At the same time, domestic medical device companies are consolidating, upgrading quality, and beginning to compete in medium- level technology niches. With the government policy of supporting and encouraging medical device innovations, some domestic manufacturers such as Shenzhen Mindray are growing stronger and are already competing with foreign suppliers.

Given the status of the Chinese medical device market, significant potential exists for U.S. companies interested in entry or expansion in the Chinese market. China continues its healthcare reform under the new Administration which has entered into the stage of deepening public hospital reform at all levels. In 2014 the Chinese government invested RMB1, 007 billion ($167 billion) in the healthcare sector, an increase of 9.6% year-on-year. The total healthcare expenditure is likely to increase from 5.56% of the GDP in 2013 to 6.5 or 7% by 2020. While the newly-released State Council's guideline about pilot reform on urban public hospitals and the foreseeable cost increase after charging the new *CFDA registration fee* signal difficulties to U.S. companies, opportunities still exist for U.S. companies with high technology and quality products.

(Note: The State Council's guideline encourage public hospitals to purchase China's domestic high-end medical disposables and to share large-size medical equipment which indicates a reduction of the overall procurement).

Companies interested in entering the Chinese market should realize they must overcome existing barriers in an uncertain and changing regulatory environment. China's State Council announced changes in the Regulation for Supervision and Administration of Medical Devices (Order 650), implemented 2014. Order 650 is the revision of the old regulation, Order 276, which was implemented in 2000. Compared with the old regulation, noticeable changes include extending validity of the registration certificate to five years; adopting a notification system to replace the registration system for all Class I products; requiring Chinese language in product manuals, on labels, and packaging. It also requires clinical trials to be done inside China for the Class II and Class III medical devices that are not on the CFDA's exemption catalog. As the regulator of medical devices, China Food and Drug Administration (CFDA) issued a number of implementation rules for this new regulation, including "Measures for the Administration of Medical Device Registration", "Regulations on the Administration of Instructions and Labeling of Medical Devices", "Guidance on Clinical Evaluation of Medical Devices", Class II Medical Device Clinical Trial Exemption List and Class III Medical Device Clinical Trial Exemption List. Significant achievement was made in last year's Joint Commission on Commerce and Trade (JCCT) on Medical Devices and Pharmaceutical Access. Goals include reducing the time-to-market for medical devices, accelerating the regulatory review and approval system, minimizing application backlog and expanding the scope of medical devices that can be exempted from conducting clinical trials. CFDA also committed to providing a 60-day comment period for all draft medical device rules and regulations under relevant WTO rules. Additional issues and challenges that the U.S. exporters will face include registration fees, pricing, tender, and bar code systems that are delaying entry into the Chinese medical device market.

Sub-Sector Best Prospects

The best-selling prospects in the medical device sector include:

- In vitro diagnostic equipment and reagents: Clinical and diagnostic analysis equipment, diagnostic reagents, medical test and basic equipment instruments, and point of care testing (POCT).
- Implantable and intervention materials and artificial organs: Interventional materials, implantable artificial organs, contact artificial organs, stent, implantable materials, and artificial organ assisting equipment.
- Therapeutic products: Tri-dimensional Ultrasonic-focused therapeutic systems, body rotary Gamma knife, simulator, linear accelerator, laser diagnostic and surgical equipment, nuclide treatment equipment, physical and rehabilitation equipment.
- Medical diagnostic and imaging equipment: Black & white and colored supersonic diagnostic units, sleeping monitor, digital X-ray system, MRI, CT, DR, and ultrasound equipment.
- Surgical and emergency appliances: Anesthesia ventilation systems and components: high frequency surgical equipment, high frequency and voltage generators.
- Healthcare Information Technology related equipment and products: Medical software, computer-aided diagnostic equipment, and hospital information systems (HIS, CIS, and HLT).
- Medical equipment parts and accessories.

Web Resources

China Food and Drug Administration (CFDA)
http://eng.sfda.gov.cn/WS03/CL0755/

The National Health and Family Planning Commission (NHFPC)
http://en.nhfpc.gov.cn/

China Association of Medical Device Industry (CAMDI)
http://www.camdi.org/en/

China Chamber of Commerce for Medicines and Health Products (CCCMHPIE)
http://www.cccmhpie.org.cn/English/default.aspx

Contacts

U.S. Embassy in Beijing
YANG Ming
Senior Commercial Specialist
Email: Ming.Yang@trade.gov
Tel: 8610-8531-4006

SHI Huiling
Senior Commercial Specialist
Email: Huiling.Shi@trade.gov
Tel: 8610-8531-3419

U.S. Consulate in Shanghai
PAN Xiaoli
Senior Commercial Specialist
Email: xiaoli.pan@trade.gov
Tel: 86-21-6279-8750

U.S. Consulate in Guangzhou
Angela HAN
Senior Commercial Specialist
Email: Angela.han@trade.gov
Tel: 86-20-8667-4011 ext. 612

U.S. Consulate in Chengdu
Mini TIAN
Senior Commercial Specialist
Email: Mini.Tian@trade.gov
Tel: 86-28-8558-3992 ext. 6567

U.S. Consulate in Shenyang
LIU Yang
Senior Commercial Specialist
Yang.liu@trade.gov
Tel: 86-24-23221198 ext.8143

U.S. Consulate in Wuhan
Wang Jing
Senior Commercial Specialist
Jing.Wang@trade.gov
Tel: 86-27-8555-7791 ext.808

NUCLEAR

The Chinese government is actively promoting nuclear energy as a clean, efficient and reliable source of electricity generation. It is on pace to triple its nuclear capacity to 58 GWe by 2020 and 150 GWe by 2030. In this regard, China has 23 operational nuclear power reactors, 26 under construction. China plans to ramp up its construction of reactors in the coming years and build an estimated 10 reactors per year after 2020.

China also plans begin marketing its indigenously designed reactors for export in 2015.

As China has becomes increasingly self-sufficient for its nuclear power technology needs, imports of nuclear power related equipment will decline. However, ample opportunities exist for U.S. industry in new builds and all aspects of the fuel cycle. Nuclear fuel assemblies are fabricated and supplied indigenously and the country's energy policy states that PWRs will be the primary but not sole reactor type, and that domestic manufacturing of plants and equipment will be maximized.

Nuclear currently constitutes less than only 2% of installed electricity capacity in China but is projected to constitute 7% by 2040. According to the China Nuclear Energy Association (CNEA), investment in China's nuclear industry reached $9.2 billion in 2014, 6.6% lower than in 2013.

	2011	2012	2013	2014	2015
Nuclear power plants in operation	14	15	20	21	23
Nuclear power plants under construction	25	24	22	28	26
Nuclear power plants in operation growth (year on year)		1	5	1	2

Source: International Atomic Energy Agency (IAEA); World Nuclear Association

Much of this growth in power generation will come not only from the construction of new nuclear sites, but also from the development of more advanced plant designs. Whereas most plants currently in operation have a production capacity of 2 GW, the vast majority of reactors currently under construction are using more advanced designs. The designs most favored in current construction plans are the CPR-1000 and American designed AP1000 generators, which have a production capacity of around 1.25 GW. In the case of the AP1000, this imported design is forming the main basis of China's move towards 3rd generation nuclear technology.

While China recognizes the need to import foreign technology, it also wants to localize as much of this technology as possible and China continues to demand full technology transfer and localization whenever possible. As a result, many U.S. power equipment manufacturers and related construction and engineering firms have formed joint-ventures in this market.

China has the fastest growing nuclear energy program in the world. Its reactors under construction comprise just over one-third of the global nuclear power capacity being built. The government suspended approvals for new nuclear plants following the Fukushima accident in March 2011, but new plant approvals and construction resumed in October 2012. China also intends to build strategic and commercial uranium stockpiles through overseas purchases and continues to develop domestic production. The country is also in the process of developing nuclear fuel reprocessing facilities that are expected to come online by 2017.

China has become largely self-sufficient in reactor design and construction, as well as other aspects of the fuel cycle, but it is making full use of western technology while adapting and improving upon it. The country aims to expand its nuclear technology exports, including heavy components in the supply chain. Despite high levels of government support for new nuclear builds due to intense pressure to find new sources of clean electricity, public opinion regarding nuclear energy is complex. Several cases of public opposition have resulted in delays or suspensions of planned projects, though strong public sentiment toward achieving clean air goals may make the public more supportive. In February 2015, China announced the merger of two of its key nuclear power firms - China Power Investment Corp (CPI) and State Nuclear Power Technology Corp (SNPTC) – a consolidation that will support China's nuclear expansion plans.

Regulatory Environment

In contrast to the situation in much of the rest of the world, China's regulatory environment is supportive of nuclear development. The Chinese government has a strong interest in diversifying the country's energy supply and in promoting the cleaner production of energy. Indeed, in the government's 12th Five Year Plan the country's leaders committed themselves to several ambitious targets including a 16-17% reduction in energy and carbon intensity and a 11.4% share of non-fossil fuel in energy mix by 2015. Given these regulatory incentives, it seems that China will continue to support the development of the nuclear industry in the future.

The Fukushima Daiichi reactor incident event had a heavy impact on the advancement of the nuclear power industry, stalling the approval process for all new nuclear sites and mandating an immediate safety review for all existing nuclear facilities. In addition, the government committed itself to the development of a new safety plan and improved regulatory oversight of the industry.

To this end, the government released the Nuclear Safety Radioactive Pollution Prevention 12th Five Year Plan and Vision for 2020, which seeks to belay concerns that China will forego safety procedures as it seeks to rapidly develop its nuclear industry. This plan, which was developed by the National Energy Administration, places a far more rigorous set of safety criteria upon each stage of nuclear development. In addition, it calls for the deployment of the more advanced nuclear technology and better safety management systems to minimize future risks.

As of October 2012, the State Council has resumed approval of construction for new nuclear plants, albeit at a slower pace and with a greater emphasis on safety. The Mid and Long-Term Plan for Nuclear Power (2011-2020) emphasizes that construction of new sites will, up to 2015, be limited to coastal areas where the chances of earthquakes remain small. While this framework has brought some clarity to the picture, a degree of uncertainty will linger until China releases a complete atomic energy law.

Sub-Sector Best Prospects

Given the enormous growth in the Chinese nuclear industry, foreign companies looking to conduct businesses in the local market have several avenues of approach. As development of new nuclear plants continues, surveying, construction and construction equipment services will be in high demand. Furthermore, as domestic energy firms are looking to improve reactor design, U.S. companies with a specialty in advanced reactor technology have opportunities to cooperate in reactor production.

Besides opportunities to supply AP1000 projects in China, Chinese power utilities have been collaborating with U.S. Company Westinghouse in the development of the new CAP1400 reactor, capable of producing an output of 1.5 GW, based on the Westinghouse AP1000 design. China's State Nuclear Power Technology Corporation claimed in 2013 that they were ready to start exploration of the global market for CAP1400. The first CAP1400 demonstration reactor started construction in Shidaowan, Shandong province, this year and it is expected to be commissioned in late 2018. In addition, while most current designs including the AP1000 are Pressurized Water Reactors, China is looking to move towards the construction of more Fast Neutron Reactors (FNR). Beyond standard technologies, Chinese firms are also eager to explore alternative nuclear reactor designs including "pebble bed reactors" and "molten salt reactors."

Following the international trend at the present, China is also ready to develop and deploy Small Modular Reactors (SMR) technology, now that it has sufficient financial support from the government and enough investment from power companies. In 2011, the CNNC signed an agreement with Zhangzhou municipal government in Fujian Province to host the first ACP-100 demonstration site. China is a potential site for many international designers and developers of SMRs, as its goal is to export rather than appeal to the domestic market.

In the wake of the Fukushima Daiichi nuclear disaster, efforts have been focused on improving safety standards across the industry. China currently operates several types of nuclear reactors using multiple technologies, making safety management a significant challenge. The Ministry of Environmental Protection (MEP) has suggested that China may have to spend as much as $13 billion to achieve 3rd generation safety standards across all of its existing plants, since China will only be approving 3rd generation projects over the next three years. Given this expected outlay, U.S. companies with significant experience in nuclear safety management, retrofits and extensive upgrade technology will have significant opportunities in China over the next few years.

Sources: "SMRS in China: An Exciting New Sector" Yun Zhou and Jonathan Hinze (The Ux

Consulting Company, LLC); "China Power Forecast Scenario" and "Industry News Nuclear Sector on the Path to Criticality" Business Monitor International; "China's Nuclear Inustry in 2015 – Moving Forward" Nicobar Group

OPPORTUNITIES

Running the world's largest new build program safely and successfully continues to require significant investment in all areas. Opportunities for U.S. nuclear firms with experience, advanced technologies, and strong quality and performance reputations exist and should be pursued aggressively. The Chinese industry will face challenges as the country pushes to build the first-of-a-kind units of new 3G reactor designs while quickly localizing the production of major components. There are opportunities in following areas:

Services (front- and back-end): Opportunities for probabilistic risk assessment and regulatory advisory services.

Licensing Support: Opportunities to support China's Nuclear Safety Administration (NNSA).

Design, Construction and Operations: Significant opportunities for new PWR plant construction.

Components: Significant opportunities for nuclear pumps and valves, breakers, large forging parts, and other components.

Fuel Management: China is not fully self-sufficient in the upstream market of raw materials used in NPPs. Chinese mines produce 70% of the uranium used in Chinese reactors and Chinese firms have actively acquired mines overseas. Chinese imports of U.S. graphite moderator rods recently increased, making China the third largest buyer of U.S. graphite after Japan and Canada. Westinghouse is providing the first cores for the Sanmen and Haiyang AP1000 units, and although China will take over fuel fabrication at the Baotou facility, there may be room to sell fuel to the Chinese market given front-end fuel cycle capacity.

China intends to become self-sufficient in most aspects of the nuclear fuel cycle, which will limit opportunities for foreign exporters. However, the country still relies on foreign suppliers for all stages of the fuel cycle, from uranium mining through fabrication and reprocessing. As China rapidly increases the number of new reactors, it has initiated a number of domestic projects, often in cooperation with foreign suppliers, to meet its nuclear fuel needs. Local content requirements are a key barrier for U.S. civil nuclear exports. Although there is strong foreign competition, the size of China's market is so large and the industry is developing so rapidly that China will remain a strong market for U.S. exports for years to come in all areas of the civil nuclear supply chain.

ECP Nuclear Power Working Group

Launched in May, 2012, the Nuclear Power Working Group (NPWG) is the newest addition to the public-private partnership platform of the U.S.-China Energy Cooperation Program (ECP). As part of ECP, the NPWG is a commercially led platform that currently represents American companies who work across the entire nuclear value chain. Bi-lateral advocacy efforts focus on improving technical standards, specifications and requirements in the aspects of safety, control valves and fuel resourcing, etc. Those efforts, in the medium-term, aim to create market entry opportunities for advanced U.S. technologies and products to China, and support the development of world-class protocol. Website:http://www.uschinaecp.org/

Web Resources

Government Authorities

China Atomic Energy Authority - http://www.caea.gov.cn

National Energy Administration - http://www.nea.gov.cn/
National Nuclear Safety Administration - http://nnsa.mep.gov.cn/
State-owned Assets Supervision & Administration Commission - http://www.sasac.gov.cn/

Chinese Corporations
State Nuclear Power Technology Corporation – http://www.snptc.com.cn/en/
China National Nuclear Corporation – www.cnnc.com.cn
China General Nuclear Power Group – http://www.cgnpc.com.cn/
China Power Investment Corporation - http://www.cpicorp.com.cn/

Additional Information
Civil Nuclear Trade Advisory Committee - http://trade.gov/mas/ian/nuclear/
Civil Nuclear Guide to Exporting - http://export.gov/civilnuclear/
Nicobar Group - http://www.nicobargroup.com/
World Nuclear Association - http://www.world-nuclear.org/

U.S. & Foreign Commercial Service and Department of Energy Nuclear Industry Contacts in China

U.S. Embassy in Beijing
Hongying Cai, Commercial Specialist
(86 10) 8531-3000
hongying.cai@trade.gov

Department of Energy
Ms. Shao Jun
Nuclear Nonproliferation Analyst
(86 10) 8531-3403
ShaoJ@State.gov

U.S. Consulate in Shanghai
Scott Yao, Commercial Specialist
(86 21) 6279-7630
scott.yao@trade.gov

U.S. Consulate in Guangzhou
Lena Yang, Commercial Specialist
(86 20) 8667-4011
lena.yang@trade.gov

U.S. Consulate in Chengdu
Cui Shiyang, Commercial Specialist
(86 28) 8558-3992
cui.shiyang@trade.gov

U.S. Consulate in Shenyang
Evelyn Zhou, Commercial Specialist
(86 24) 2322-1198
evelyn.zhou@trade.gov

OIL AND GAS

According to the Oil & Gas Journal (OGJ), as of January 2014, China holds 24.4 billion barrels of proven oil reserves, up over 0.7 billion barrels from the 2013 level and the highest in the Asia-

Pacific region. China's total oil and liquids production, the fourth largest in the world, has risen by about 54% over the past two decades and serves only its domestic market. However, production growth has not kept pace with demand growth during this period. In the past five years, China's crude oil production has averaged 4 million barrels per day (bbl/d). In 2014, China produced 4.21 million bbl/d of crude oil, an increase of 0.7% over the previous year. In the long term, the EIA projects a steady growth for China's oil and liquids production, reaching 4.6 million bbl/d in 2020 and 5.6 million bbl/d by 2040.

China's oil consumption growth has eased after a high peaking in 2009 and is a continuing reflection of the lingering effects of the global financial and economic downturn. China's oil demand growth hinges on several factors, such as domestic economic growth and trade, power generation, transportation sector shifts, and refining capabilities. In 2014, China's oil consumption registered a growth rate of 3.7% to 10.4 million bbl/d. Despite the slower growth, China still made up nearly a third of global oil demand growth in 2014, according to EIA estimates. China's market demand for oil was 10.7million bbl/d in 2014 and it is expected to continue growing moderately in the coming years.

In 2009, China became the second-largest net oil importer in the world behind the United States, and average net total oil imports reached 6.2 million bbl/d in 2013. Notably, for the fourth quarter of 2013, China actually became the largest global net importer of oil. EIA projects that China is likely to have surpassed the United States in net oil imports on an annual basis in 2014. This is due to the boom in U.S. domestic shale oil production and the simultaneous increase in China's demand. China's net oil imports in 2014 reached 6.18 million bbl/d compared to 5.5 million bbl/d for the United States.
Source: EIA, China's Ministry of Land and Resources. CNPC ENTR

Natural gas currently makes up a relatively small portion of China's primary energy mix. However, the discovery of huge domestic shale gas reserves has inspired the government to prioritize the development of this resource for the sake of energy security as well as to reduce its reliance on coal. As such, China has developed an ambitious plan to develop natural gas and shale gas in particular. China plans to produce between 200-250 billion cubic meters of natural gas per year by 2020. China consumed 183 billion cubic meters of natural gas in 2014, according to a report released by CNPC's economic and technology research center. The research center predicted that this number will go up to 200 billion cubic meters in 2015, representing 6.6% of China's total energy consumption in the year.

China's oil and gas market is dominated by four national and provincial oil companies: PetroChina, Sinopec, China National Offshore Oil Corporation (CNOOC), and Yanchang Oil (a Shaanxi Provincial-level state-owned company). Sinopec controls 46% of total crude refining capacity, while PetroChina accounts for 31%. The remainder is processed by smaller refineries. CNOOC focuses on offshore oil development and has limited refining capacity in the market.

China manufactures a great majority of oil and gas equipment domestically. China's State-Owned Enterprises (SOEs) control around 66% of the market for well-drilling equipment. Small- and medium-sized private Chinese companies make up 19% of the market. Foreign companies make up 10% of the market and supply advanced complete-set equipment. Chinese privately owned oil and gas equipment companies are catching up quickly. Among them, Sichuan based HongHua Group and Shandong based Jereh Group and Kerui Group are among the leading suppliers of such equipment.

International Oil Companies (IOCs) and service companies have established their presence in China mostly through partnering with Chinese companies. At present, IOCs mostly team up with CNOOC in offshore oil development while service companies are hired by the big three oil giants on both onshore and offshore projects, which oftentimes are complicated and complex drillings. IOCs and international service companies have started working with Sinopec, PetroChina and

Yanchang to develop shale gas and tight oil and gas in Sichuan and the Erdos Basin, and Xinjiang.

The following chart explains the market size and penetration of foreign products in this industry including drilling and refinery equipment, compressed vessels and offshore engineering equipment. U.S. manufactured oil and gas equipment represents 50%-60% of China imports in his sector. This will likely increase in the future as China looks to more fully develop its shale gas resources, much of which is in more complex geology than that of the United States.

Oil and Gas Equipment Unit: USD Billions

	2011	2012	2013	2014	2015 estimated
Total Market Size	29	46	70	77.98	75.5
Total Local Production	45	57	82	89.98	90
Total Exports to the World	23	19	19	18.9	21
Total Imports from the World	6.5	6.7	6.9	6.9	6.5

Source: China Petroleum and Petrochemical Equipment Industry Association (CPEIA website:www.cpeia.org.cn) and the U.S. Commercial Service in China.

SUB-SECTOR BEST PROSPECTS

In general, areas with high government support and low domestic product maturity offer the best prospects for foreign companies. Oil and gas exploitation technologies enjoy strong government support, specifically steam-assisted gravity drainage (onshore), geologic exploration equipment, position navigation systems, deep-water drill systems (offshore), and fracturing technology (shale gas) are technologies and equipment that enjoy high demand.

Shale Gas

The Chinese shale gas industry is poised to expand rapidly over the coming decade. According to the Ministry of Land and Resources (MLR), China holds more shale gas assets than any other country, having around 25 trillion cubic meters of technically recoverable reserves. The Chinese government is eager to promote the development of the domestic shale gas energy.

The country has set itself ambitious targets for cleaner growth and the government believes that tapping its large unconventional gas resources might be a way of reducing its reliance on coal, which produces significant CO2 emissions. In addition, China wants to improve its energy security by becoming less reliant upon foreign imports. The central government aims to produce 6.5 billion cubic meters of shale gas by 2015, rising to 100 billion by 2020.

In an effort to kick-start the industry, the Chinese government has taken a number of proactive steps. The government released its first Five Year Plan for the industry in 2012, mandating ambitious production targets, establishing market entry conditions, and defining the scope for foreign cooperation. As part of this plan, the government developed an incentive plan to encourage investment in shale gas. In November 2012, the Ministry of Finance (MOF) announced that they would provide a subsidy of RMB 0.4 ($0.06) for every cubic meter of gas produced. Furthermore, in recognizing the need for foreign technology and expertise, the government has recently relaxed regulations surrounding the shale gas industry. Most significantly, MLR announced in September of 2012 that foreign companies would be allowed to take part in the bidding process for shale gas exploration licenses. Whereas this bidding was previously limited only to domestic firms, new rules permit Chinese-controlled foreign joint ventures to take part in the tender process.

Despite these efforts, China has failed to reach the ambitious targets set in the 2012 plan. Last year, for example, China only produced 1.2 billion cubic meters and it is widely acknowledged that the country will have a hard time reaching the 5 billion cubic meter mark in 2015. There are a number of factors that have hindered the development of the shale gas industry. In particular, Chinese shale gas reserves are located in regions that will make extraction very difficult. Not only are these areas often mountainous and inaccessible, but the resources are often located at depths beyond those which have previously been considered viable. This point is exemplified by the conditions surrounding the Sichuan Basin. Although this area holds massive shale gas reserves, it is both prone to significant seismic activity and a great deal of geological structural complexity. Furthermore, China lacks a developed pipeline network that is able to transport potentially massive amounts of shale gas to the more energy demanding regions on the East coast. Finally, the water intensive nature of shale gas extraction will pose a strong challenge to the industry as China already faces water shortages in many of the areas where shale gas reserves exist.

OPPORTUNITIES

With China struggling to meet its defined targets for natural gas production, U.S. companies are expected to find significant opportunity in investment and exploration. This situation has the potential to create substantial sales for American companies across the shale gas value chain. For example, firms that have developed significant advantages in extraction technologies – particularly in water efficiency and deep extraction - are well positioned. Companies that specialize in drilling, extraction equipment, or provide operational services for shale gas developers may also benefit from the growth of the Chinese shale gas market.

In addition, U.S. firms that have technologies and expertise in other unconventional gas sector such as tight gas, coal-bed methane and coal gasification will also have sales opportunities in the market as China is trying to cope with the increasing demand for gas and searching for alternative and cleaner ways for the use of the country's coal resources.

Web Resources

Government Authorities
National Energy Administration: http://www.nea.gov.cn
Ministry of Land Resources: http://www.mlr.gov.cn
National Development and Reform Commission: www.ndrc.gov.cn
Ministry of Environmental Protection: www.mep.gov.cn

Additional Information
China Greentech Initiative Reports: http://www.china-greentech.com/publications
Gas Technology Institute: http://www.gastechnology.org
Energy Information Administration: http://www.eia.gov
United States Energy Association: www.usea.org

Contacts

U.S. Embassy in Beijing
Jianhong Wang, Commercial Specialist
(86 10) 8531-3424
jianhong.wang@trade.gov

U.S. Consulate in Chengdu
Helen Hua, Commercial representative
(86 28) 8558-3992
Haiyan.hua@trade.gov

U.S. Consulate in Shanghai
Scott Yao, Commercial Specialist
(86 21) 6279-8727
scott.yao@trade.gov

U.S. Consulate in Shenyang
Evelyn Zhou, Commercial Specialist
(86 24) 2322-8146
evelyn.zhou@trade.gov

U.S. Consulate in Guangzhou
Lena Yang, Commercial Specialist
(86 20) 3814-5000
lena.yang@trade.gov

RAIL AND URBAN

Railway Industry

China's Rail Investment/Operating Mileage/Total Freight Volume

	2012	2013	2014
Total Fixed Asset Investment *(exchange rate: $1 = RMB6.3)*	$100 billion	$103 billion	$117 billion
Total Operating Mileage	98,000 kilometers	100,000 kilometers	112,000 kilometers
Total Freight Volume	3.9 billion tons	3.97billion tons	3.07bilion tons

(source: China Railway Corporation official website http://www.china-railway.com.cn/)

Railway transportation plays a key role in China's economic development. During China's 12th Five Year Plan, the total fixed assets' investment on railway will be over $460 billion. By 2015, China's total railway operating mileage is planned to increase from the current 100,000 kilometers to around 120,000 kilometers. After rapidly developing its passenger network, the China Railway Corporation (C.R.) is performing feasibility studies on increasing the freight transportation volume, i.e. heavy haul.

By the end of 2014, China's national railway operating mileage reached 112,000 kilometers, ranking first in the world; while its high-speed railway operating mileage reached 10,000 kilometers, ranking first in the world. China's railway passenger turnover, freight volume, cargo turnover, and conversion volume all rank first in the world. China is now considered technologically advanced in high-speed rail, high-altitude rail, and heavy-haul freight rail.

China's high-speed rail network is expected to reach 20,000 kilometers by 2015. High-speed railways are incorporated as part of the country's "express railway network," which is expected to reach 45,000 kilometers by 2015. The express railway network includes railways of three speeds: arterial rail lines at a speed of 300 km/h, intercity and extension and linking lines at 200-250 km/h, and railways in western China with speeds of 160-200 km/h.

Chinese railway authorities and operational organizations are willing to learn new technologies, best practice and international standards on heavy haul rail in order to continue to improve the cargo shipping efficiency and lower operating costs. The U.S. freight rail network is widely considered one of the most dynamic freight systems in the world, with a rail network of 225,000 kilometers. With the largest heavy haul railroad network in the world, U.S. has broad experience in heavy haul operation. U.S. companies own proprietary technologies and technical expertise with a demonstrated track record of success. The U.S. rail industry, organized in China through the U.S. Embassy Commercial Section's American Railway Working Group (ARWG), is actively engaged in collaborating with Chinese partners to assist in developing China's freight rail sector.

Urban Rail Transit Industry

Currently, China is the world's largest urban rail market. To date, National Development and Reform Commission (NDRC) has approved urban rail projects in 36 cities, with plans for around 5,800 kilometers. Beijing, Shanghai, Guangzhou, and Shenzhen share 70% of the built urban rail transit mileage in China. By 2015, 37 cities in China will have metro/light rail. The total investment on the urban rail sector will be around RMB 1 trillion. The largest OEM in China for the urban rail sector is China Southern Rolling Stock (CSR), occupying 54% of the market in 2013. The second largest OEM is China Northern Rolling Stock (CNR). Opportunities exist for American companies as the suppliers to CSR and CNR.

SUB-SECTOR BEST PROSPECTS

Rail Industry technology and equipment:

1. Rail safety
2. High speed Electric Multiple Unit
3. Communication, signaling, and IT systems
4. Track maintenance for high speed rail
5. Traction power supply in high speed rail
6. Passenger station design and construction
7. Heavy haul transport
8. High-altitude rail
9. Energy conservation and environmental protection

Metro industry technology and equipment:

10. Urban rail vehicles
11. Communication and signaling
12. Power supply and distribution
13. Electromechanical systems
14. Safety supporting
15. IT system
16. Intelligent AFC
17. Engineering and construction, survey, and design
18. Earthquake disaster prevention

Opportunities

Railway Industry Opportunities

The investment scale of the new railway line during 12th Five Year Plan (12FYP) from 2011-2015 should reach 30,000 kilometers. By the final phase of the 12FYP, the total railway operating mileage is planned to increase from the current 100,000 kilometers to around 120,000 kilometers. 60% of lines will be electrified, while 50% will be double-track lines. The high speed railway will reach 16,000 kilometers. Railways in western China area could reach 50,000 kilometers. The number of new and renovated railway stations will reach a total of 1,015. At the same time, there will be a large number of advanced technical equipment put into use.

During the 12FYP, the total railway investment is expected to reach RMB 2.8 trillion. Compared with railway new line investment during the 11FYP, new line investment during the 12FYP period is expected to increase by 88%, with total investment to increase 41%.

It is estimated that by 2020, an additional RMB 2 trillion will be invested, of which RMB 600 billion will be for development of infrastructure related to passenger-dedicated lines, the coal corridor, lines in western China, and inter-regional connections. China's total rail network will exceed 120,000 kilometers in length, possibly reaching 150,000 kilometers, and 17,000 kilometers of rail will accommodate double-decker trains.

Urban Rail (Metro) Industry Opportunities

By 2015, there will be around 158 urban rail lines in total. By 2020, China is expected to have 7,000 kilometers of urban rail lines.

Example of Metro Projects in Key Cities:

City	Current Metro Lines	Current Metro Mileage (KM)	2020 Planned Metro Lines	2020 Planned Metro Lines (KM)
Shanghai	14	548	20	887
Beijing	18	527	30	1050
Guangzhou	9	260.5	19	570
Shenzhen	5	177	16	585
Tianjin	4	139	14	470

American Rail Working Group (ARWG)
The U.S. Embassy Commercial Section in Beijing launched an American Rail Working Group (ARWG) in January 2009 to strengthen public-private cooperation in the rail sector. The ARWG features 30 U.S. company members and benefits from close relationships with the Chinese Ministry of Railway, U.S. Department of Transportation, Federal Rail Administration, U.S. Trade and Development Agency, U.S. State Department and the U.S. Export-Import Bank. The group meets regularly in Beijing as well as via conference call. New company members are welcome to join. For ARWG membership enquiries, please contact the U.S. Embassy Commercial Section in Beijing by email: aiqun.peng@trade.gov

Major Shows/Exhibitions:

Metro China 2015
Host: China Communications and Transportation Association
Show dates: November 17-20, 2015
Show venue: China International Exhibition Center, Beijing
www.metro-china-expo.com

Web Resources

National Railway Administration (NRA)
http://www.nra.gov.cn

China Railway Corporation (C.R.)
http://www.china-railway.com.cn/

Contacts

U.S. Embassy Beijing
Ida Peng, Senior Commercial Specialist
(86 10) 8531 3947
aiqun.peng@trade.gov

U.S. Consulate in Shanghai
Vivien Bao, Commercial Specialist
(86 21) 6279 8766

Vivien.bao@trade.gov

U.S. Consulate in Chengdu
Liping Lin, Commercial Specialist,
+86 28 85583992 Ext. 6633
Lin.liping@trade.gov

U.S. Consulate in Guangzhou
Lena Yang ,Senior Commercial Specialist,
(86 20) 3814 5173
Lena.Yang@trade.gov

U.S. Consulate in Shenyang
Dongmei Sun, Commercial Specialist
(86 24) 2322-1198
dongmei.sun@trade.gov

SAFETY AND SECURITY MARKET

Unit: USD thousands

	2013	2014	2015 (estimated)	2016 (estimated)
Total Market Size	7005567	7649071	8290000	9110000
Total Local Production	6639202	7262469	7830000	8540000
Total Exports	577335	768134	960000	1150000
Total Imports	404936	328337	280000	250000
Imports from the U.S.	107266	69618	63000	56000
Exchange Rate: 1 USD	6.1956	6.1238	6.25	6.30

Data Sources: China Customs, Zeefer Consulting

China is an important market for U.S. exporters of Safety & Security equipment. According to the statistics from the China Security & Protection Industry Association (CSPIA), there are about 27,000 Safety & Security enterprises and distributors in China, and a majority are local private enterprises with low-end technology and without dominant market share. Zeefer Consulting estimates that the 2014 total market size is around $7.6 billion, and is expected to grow to $8.29 billion in 2015, an average 10 percent annual growth based on the last 3 years' growth rate. However, U.S. market share in 2014 was around $70 million and U.S. firms face significant U.S. and Chinese licensing control regulations. Some indications suggest the U.S. market share could shrink in the near future.

As one of the world's important economies, China is undertaking numerous large-scale projects nationwide, including airports, sports stadiums, and metro systems that will entail the installation of extensive security systems. In addition, many municipalities continue installing emergency response systems to improve security and bolster response times. On a consumer level, China's growing middle class and the affluent are demanding high-quality residential security products and services to protect their personal and families' safety and security and their property. This segment of the market is particularly open to U.S. products. Before selling in China, U.S. exporters need to be aware of Chinese certification requirements, as well as potential U.S. export controls. Overall, the sector maintains rapid growth and has good export opportunities for U.S. exporters.

Best Prospects

Safety and security products in China are mainly used in public security, transportation, and finance. In recent years, demand for safety and security products in health care, education and civilian fields has experienced strong growth according to the information from CSPIA. Much of the demand for safety and security solutions focuses on high-tech equipment, such as integration and networking technology for inspection control systems, early warning systems, detection equipment, and access control systems. Specific sectors are:

•Integration and networking technology for inspection control systems: Whole systems are in demand for running platforms and managing organizational intelligence. The markets for control systems in transportation, commercial residential buildings, public security, courts, and finance account for about 40 percent of total demand.

• Aviation and transportation market: Two out of three new airports built worldwide are in China. There is strong demand for intelligent airport systems. In addition, the country's public transportation system continues to grow and is a priority for the Chinese government at all levels.

• Early warning systems: Both the Chinese public and private sectors are interested in all types of early warning systems.

• Detection Equipment: Contraband detection, leak detection, and tamper proof technologies, among others, are of strong interest. Since China's domestic manufacturers lack capacity to produce enough equipment, foreign products in this field are in high demand.

• Access control systems: These systems are mainly used in traffic control and management. However, applications for intelligent building operations have enormous market potential. China's domestic manufacturers mainly dominate the access control system market for physical identification, while U.S., German, and Japanese companies dominate this market for high-end products, such as biometric identification.

Opportunities & Obstacles

The safety and security sector remains a highly regulated industry in China. U.S. exporters should look for opportunities to cooperate with qualified and reputable Chinese engineering firms that have close connections with the Chinese government. Having a strong a partnership with a local company provides additional advantages in that these Chinese firms are often better positioned to more readily process and obtain all required certifications.

Chinese government policy encourages the use of Business to Consumer (B2C) e-commerce markets, and more and more safety and security firms are testing the e-commerce market. In the first six months of 2014, 43 percent of 27,000 known Chinese firms have opened online shops. It is thought that the sales volume of safety and security equipment sold through e-commerce could become a significant market share in the near future. (Source: CSPIA)

As the markets in Beijing, Shanghai, Guangzhou, and Shenzhen become more mature, firms are beginning to target second-tier and third-tier cities. In addition to local firms, foreign safety and security firms are also entering and promoting their products in those cities. While the competition between local Chinese suppliers of low-end and mid-range equipment is fierce, the high-end technology/equipment market is a more practical target for U.S. exporters.

In early 2015, the Chinese government issued the Regulation for the Implementation of the Government Procurement Law. This regulation aims to provide a fair and open procurement process and to better define the process for bidding projects in a transparent environment. This regulation has the potential to open more possibilities for U.S. companies to win government projects in conjunction with Chinese partners.

Intellectual Property Rights (IPR): While the Chinese government is working to improve IPR protection, U.S. companies should still take precautions to protect their IPR by ensuring that they have undertaken the proper protections to restrict illegal copying or distribution of their safety and security products.

In addition, it is recommended that U.S. companies establish a clear strategy to handle the challenges of protecting their IPR in a complex legal environment. More specifically, companies should consider how to structure their business transactions to minimize risks of intellectual property theft and how to protect and enforce their rights in the most economical and cost effective way.

For more details on China's IPR environment, please refer to the materials located in the "China IPR Toolkit" located at the following site: http://beijing.usembassy-china.org.cn/ipr.html

MARKET ENTRY

The security industry is still at the center of several regulatory issues. Regarding restrictions imposed by the U.S. government, provisions of the Tiananmen Sanctions against China are still in effect, and, among other things, prohibit the export or re-export of certain U.S. crime control items to China.

In addition, a license must be obtained from the Department of Commerce before exporting or re-exporting certain items to China. The U.S. Department of Commerce's Bureau of Industry and Security (BIS) is responsible for implementing and enforcing the Export Administration Regulations that regulate the export and re-export of purely commercial items, items that have both commercial and military applications (i.e., "dual-use" items), and less sensitive military items. The BIS Office of Exporter Services is responsible for counseling exporters, conducting export control seminars, and drafting and publishing changes to the Export Administration Regulations. It is also responsible for licensing and compliance actions relating to the special comprehensive license and for administering the processing of license applications and commodity classifications.

In terms of restrictions by China's central government, China's Ministry of Public Security oversees the trade of all security products, as well as products for police, fire, and other emergency services departments. Certain intruder alarm systems need the China Compulsory Certification (CCC) mark from the China Certification Center for Security and Protection before they can be sold in China. More details on the CCC mark please visit www.cnca.gov.cn

RESOURCES

U.S Association:
Security Industry Association (SIA)
Website : www.siaonline.org

Chinese Association:
China Security & Protection Industry Association (CSPIA)
Website : http://xh.21csp.com.cn

Major Trade Shows:
The 7th Shanghai International Disaster Reduction and Security Exhibition
Date: Nov 4-7, 2015
Venue: Shanghai World Expo Exhibition Center
http:// www.disasterchina.org

The 15th China Public Security Expo
Date: Oct 29-Nov 1, 2015
Venue: Shenzhen Convention & Exhibition Center
http:// www.cpse.com.cn

2016 China International Exhibition on Public Safety and Security
Date: Oct, 2016
Venue : China International Exhibition Center (New)
http:// www.securitychina.com.cn

TRAVEL AND TOURISM

China is rapidly becoming one of the most important outbound tourism markets in the world. According to the China National Tourism Administration (CNTA), Chinese outbound travelers reached 109 million in 2014, with 10 million more travelers than in 2013.

The United States is becoming an increasingly popular destination for Chinese travelers. In 2014, China ranked as the 6th largest international market (and 4th largest overseas market) for the United States. While 2015 final data is not yet available, an estimated 2.6 million Chinese (excluding Hong Kong) may visit the U.S. in 2015, constituting a 17 percent increase over 2014.

According to the National Travel and Tourism Office within the U.S. Department of Commerce, China is expected to become the largest source of overseas travelers to the United States by 2020. Overseas excludes Canada and Mexico.

The United States welcomed a record 2.19 million visitors from China in 2014, and received more than $24 billion* in spending from Chinese tourists on travel and tourism related goods and services. Travel exports from Chinese visitors to the U.S. set a record in 2014. China is the second largest travel export market for the country. The following charts illustrate how Chinese travelers to the U.S. stacked up against other top markets in 2014 and how their spending compared to their Asian counterparts, respectively.

Top International Arrivals to U.S. in 2014

2014 Rank	Area/Country of Residence	Annual 2014	% change 2013-2014
--	TOTAL ARRIVALS	75,011,080	7.2%
--	OVERSEAS *	34,938,207	9.0%
1	CANADA	23,003,055	-1.6%
2	MEXICO	17,069,818	17.3%
3	UNITED KINGDOM	4,149,129	8.2%
4	JAPAN	3,620,224	-3.0%
5	BRAZIL	2,263,996	9.9%
6	CHINA, PRC	2,189,781	21.2%

* Overseas is all countries excluding Canada and Mexico
Source: U.S. Department of Commerce, National Travel and Tourism Office

Top International Markets for U.S. Travel and Tourism Exports in 2014

2014 Rank	Area/Country of Residence	Annual 2014, in $ m	% change 2013-2014
--	TOTAL Tourism-Related Exports	$220,757	2.9%
--	OVERSEAS *	$175,810	4.0%
1	Canada	$26,282	-3.8%
2	China (PRC)	$24,019	13.6%
3	Mexico	$18,665	3.0%
4	Japan	$17,676	0.3%
5	United Kingdom	$13,496	2.3%
6	Brazil	$13,429	8.1%
7	India	$9,842	9.7%
8	South Korea	$7,799	10.8%
9	Germany	$7,360	1.7%
10	Australia	$6,180	-9.3%

* Overseas is all countries excluding Canada and Mexico
Source: U.S. Department of Commerce, National Travel and Tourism Office

1 - Total Travel and Tourism Exports represents the sum of 'Travel' + 'Passenger Air Transport' exports (what international visitors spent while here + what they spent to get here).
2 - Travel: These accounts cover purchases of goods and services by U.S. persons traveling abroad and by foreign travelers in the United States for business or personal reasons. These goods and services include food, lodging, recreation, gifts, entertainment, local transportation in the country of travel, and other items incidental to a foreign visit.
3 - All travel purposes include 1) business travel, including expenditures by border, seasonal, and other short-term workers and 2) personal travel, including health-related and education-related travel, along with spending on day-trips (less than one night).
4 - Fares received for the transport of nonresidents by U.S. air carriers between the United States and foreign countries and between two foreign points (exports).

Annual 2014 U.S. Travel and Tourism Balance of Trade

Travel & Passenger Air Transport Receipts (Exports)1

[Millions of Dollars]

Country/Region	Receipts (Exports)			
	Travel (all purposes)[2,3]	Passenger Air Transport[2]	Total Travel & Tourism	2014/2013 % Change
Total (All Countries)	$177,241	$43,516	$220,757	3%
Asia and Pacific	$66,277	$11,135	$77,412	7%
China	$21,499	$2,520	$24,019	14%
Japan	$12,116	$5,560	$17,676	0%
India	$8,131	$1,711	$9,842	10%
Korea, Republic of	$7,633	$166	$7,799	11%
Australia	$5,367	$813	$6,180	-9%
Taiwan	$2,098	$9	$2,107	0%
Philippines	$1,018	$81	$1,099	6%
New Zealand	$1,036	$0	$1,036	6%
Singapore	$922	$8	$930	-5%
Hong Kong	$781	$122	$903	0%
Indonesia	$876	$0	$876	9%
Thailand	$729	$9	$738	6%
Malaysia	$697	$0	$697	4%

Source: U.S. Department of Commerce, National Travel and Tourism Office

Source: U.S. Department of Commerce, National Travel and Tourism Office

American tour operators, destination marketing organizations, hotels and airlines will need to cooperate with each other, as well as with government entities, in order to capture more of this highly profitable market.

Sub-Sector Best Prospects

As China rebalances its economy to promote consumerism as a greater driver of economic activity, some best sub-sector prospects for U.S. suppliers include luxury travel to the United States, such as wineries and fine dining, golf courses and leisure activities, MICE (meetings, incentives, conventions, and exhibitions), as well as foreign individual travel. While group tours to American destinations famous in China are still preeminent, more Chinese are becoming interested in visiting places of natural beauty, cultural and historical significance, and venturing off the beaten path.

Opportunities

Several developments bode well for U.S. travel and tourism suppliers in the China market. With the expected year to year continued increase in Chinese travelers to the U.S., the Commercial Service's China Travel and Tourism Team is in the process of coordinating a U.S. Embassy China Travel and Tourism Country Strategic Plan. One of the strategic goals is to encourage Chinese travelers to visit lesser known U.S. destinations in order to spread the benefits of the expected increase in Chinese tourism more evenly throughout the U.S. As part of this strategy, the Commercial Service, working closely with Commercial Service Export Assistance Centers (EACs) and external stakeholders such as BrandUSA and VisitUSA, is creating promotions highlighting these lesser known destinations and all 6 CS offices in Mainland China are programming numerous events and promotions of which U.S. travel and tourism suppliers can take advantage.

In another new development, BrandUSA now has four representative offices in China located in Beijing, Shanghai, Guangzhou and Chengdu. BrandUSA has organized and supported U.S.

pavilions at major travel trade shows around China, runs collaborative and broad-based marketing campaigns, and other tourism events and programs. A third development is the new establishment of a VisitUSA Committee in China, consisting entirely of private-sector entities and companies promoting Chinese travel to the United States. The VisitUSA Committee has also organized numerous roadshows in 2014 and 2015, educational programming and other promotional events. Overall, U.S. destinations and travel and tourism suppliers should consider working with Commercial Service for their initial entry into the market and/or participating in VisitUSA and BrandUSA organized promotional roadshows and seminars.

In regard to long-term entry into the China market, travel and tourism organizations have two ways to enter the market. The first is to establish a direct office in China. To do this the travel and tourism supplier should obtain a registration license from the China National Tourism Administration (CNTA). The second method is to contract with a marketing/PR company to represent and/or promote your organization or destination. The second method is the one used by most U.S. destinations currently represented in the market.

Finally, the new 10 year multiple entry visa available to Chinese travelers has made a huge impact and will drive increasing demand for Chinese travel to the U.S., especially the growing Frequent Individual Travelers market.

It is important to note that as the Chinese government continues to develop its policy interests toward this sector, new policies, guidelines, and regulations may be imposed. For example, this year saw draft e-tourism guidelines proposed by National People's Congress in May 2015 which seemed to be aimed at Chinese provinces, and municipalities setting out a policy touching on a list of nine task areas and meant to integrate the tourism sector, internet, and information security strategy to enhance and upgrade the tourism sector. The impact of this policy on U.S. travel and tourism supplies is not clear.

Major Trade Shows

Beijing: Beijing International Travel Expo (June 26-28, 2015)
http://www.bitechina.com.cn/

Beijing: China Incentive Business Travel and Meeting Exhibition (MICE) (August 5-6, 2015)
http://www.cibtm.com/

Shanghai: China International Travel Mart (CITM) (November 13-15, 2015)
http://www.citm.com.cn/english/index.aspx
Guangzhou: Guangzhou International Travel Fair (February 25-27, 2015)
http://www.gitf.com.cn/en/

Web Resources

Brand USA – http://www.thebrandusa.com/
Discover America – http://www.discoveramerica.com/
Visit USA Committee: http://visitusa-china.com/index.html
U.S. Travel Association (USTA) – http://www.ustravel.org/
National Tour Association (NTA) – http://www.ntaonline.com/
China National Tourism Administration – Chinese regulatory agency, the U.S. does not have an equivalent bureau. http://en.cnta.gov.cn/
Commercial Service China Tourism Team –
http://export.gov/china/doingbizinchina/industryinfo/tourism/index.asp
National Travel and Tourism Office (NTTO) – http://travel.trade.gov/
2014 China Market Profile for Travel and Tourism -

http://travel.trade.gov/outreachpages/download_data_table/2014_China_Market_Profile.pdf
NTTO 2015-2020 Forecast - http://travel.trade.gov/view/f-2000-99-001/forecast/Forecast-COUNTRIES.pdf
NTTO Inbound Data Page - http://travel.trade.gov/outreachpages/inbound.general_information.inbound_overview.html
2015 Country Commercial Guide for China - http://export.gov/ccg/china090765.asp

Contacts

U.S. Embassy in Beijing
Jing Wei, Commercial Specialist
Tel: (86 10) 8531 4296
Jing.Wei@trade.gov

U.S. Consulate in Shanghai
Stellar Chu, Senior Commercial Specialist
Tel: (86 21) 6279 8726
Stellar.Chu@trade.gov

U.S. Consulate in Guangzhou
Barry Zhang, Senior Commercial Specialist
Tel: (86 20) 3814 5442
Barry.Zhang@trade.gov

U.S. Consulate in Shenyang
Andrea Shen, Commercial Specialist
Tel: (86 24) 2322 1198 ext. 8145
Andrea.shen@trade.gov

U.S. Consulate in Chengdu
Flora Fan, Commercial Specialist
Tel: (86 28) 8598 6567
Li.fan@trade.gov

U.S. Consulate in Wuhan
Wang Jing, Commercial Specialist
Tel: (86 27) 8555 7791 ext. 808
Jing.wang@trade.gov

MARKETING US PRODUCTS AND SERVICES

DISTRIBUTION AND SALES CHANNELS

Trading Companies: Generally, foreign companies are not permitted to directly engage in trading in China, with the exception of the direct marketing of a portion of the products manufactured in China, or the establishment of wholly owned foreign trading companies in some free trade zones with limited access to markets outside these zones. Distribution rights may change after WTO accession. Accordingly, U.S. exporters need to use a domestic Chinese agent for both importing into China and marketing within China.

At the time of this writing, only those trading companies authorized by the central government to handle exports and imports are permitted to sign import and export contracts. Since the beginning in 1998, some private and collectively-owned enterprises in the manufacturing sector have been granted this authorization. Some import/export trading firms extend their scope of business to represent foreign manufacturers as their distributors, in arrangements similar to a "manufacturers representative." However, likely in calendar year 2002, WTO accession will bring further changes.

With careful selection, training and constant contact, a U.S. exporter can obtain good market representation from a Chinese trading company, many of which are authorized to deal in a wide range of products. Some of the larger companies have offices in the U.S. and other countries around the world, as well as a network of offices and affiliates in China. However, given transportation and communication difficulties as well as regional peculiarities, most of these trading companies cannot provide diversified coverage throughout China. China's WTO accession promises a three-year phase in of improved trading rights that should improve such conditions for foreign firms.

Local agents: In addition to trading companies, China is witnessing an explosion in local sales agents who handle internal distribution and marketing. Most of these firms do not have import/export authorization. They are the next layer down the distribution chain, buying imported products from those that do. They may be representative offices of Hong Kong or other foreign trading companies, or domestic Chinese firms with regional or partial national networks.

Given China's size and diversity, as well as the lack of agents with wide-reaching capabilities, it makes sense to engage several agents to cover different areas, and to be cautious when giving exclusive territories. China can be divided roughly into at least five major regions: the South (Guangzhou), the East (Shanghai), the Central/North (Beijing-Tianjin), West China and the Northeast.

The U.S. & Foreign Commercial Service's service assist new-to-market firms. The International Partner Search (IPS) will locate, screen, and assess potential qualified overseas sales representatives, agents, distributors, joint venture partners, licensees, franchisees or strategic partners for your products or services. The IPS program locates up to six potential agents or distributors, screened from a large pool of candidate firms. Normal turnaround time is around 15 days after each post receives $600 for each product line and the company's product literature. A report is developed from on-the-spot research by U.S. Embassy staff and provides the contacts needed to launch marketing efforts in China. As a next step, a visit to China can be supported by Gold Key Service for appointments with prospective agents and distributors and key government officials responsible for an industry. IPS clients are eligible for a 25% discount on the Gold Key Service. Regional IPSs and Gold Key services are available from the USFCS offices in Beijing, Shanghai, Guangzhou, Shenyang, and Chengdu, but nation-wide searches are not available.

For those firms unable to travel and seeking potential partners, the Commercial Service in conjunction with IBM now offers BuyUSA.com as a user supported "B2B" web site. Companies seeking foreign partners may list their firm's information for as little as $300 per year and foreign buyers are enlisted worldwide. In China, plans for a Chinese language interface will draw on USASources.com, an existing service in Taiwan and future contributor of content to BuyUSA.com.

Establishing a Representative Office: Representative offices are the easiest type of offices for foreign firms to set up in China, but these offices are limited by Chinese law to performing "liaison" activities. As such, they cannot sign sales contracts or directly bill customers or supply parts and after-sales services for a fee, although most representative offices perform these activities in the name of their parent companies. Despite limitations on its scope of business activities, this form of business has proved very successful for many U.S. companies as it allows the business to remain foreign-controlled.

China's Company Law, which has been in effect since July 1, 1994, permits the opening of branches by foreign companies but, as a policy matter, China still restricts this entry approach to selected banks, insurance companies, accounting and law firms. While representative offices are given a registration certificate, branch offices obtain an actual operating or business license and can engage in profit-making activities.

Establishing a representative office gives a company increased control over a dedicated sales force and permits greater utilization of its specialized technical expertise. The cost of supporting a modest representative office ranges from $250,000 to $500,000 per year, depending on its size and how it is staffed. The largest expenses are rent for office space and housing, expatriate salaries and benefits.

Establishing a Chinese Subsidiary: A locally incorporated equity or cooperative joint venture with one or more Chinese partners, or a wholly foreign-owned enterprise (WFOE), may be the final step in developing markets for a company's products. In-country production avoids import restrictions - including relatively high tariffs - and provides U.S. firms with greater control over both intellectual property and marketing.

The role of the Chinese partner in the success or failure of a joint venture cannot be over-emphasized. A good Chinese partner will have the connections to help smooth over red tape and obstructive bureaucrats; a bad partner, on the other hand, can make even the most promising venture fail. Common investor complaints concern conflicts of interest (e.g., the partner setting up competing businesses), bureaucracy and violations of confidentiality. American companies should bear in mind that joint ventures are time-consuming and resource-demanding, and will involve constant and prudent monitoring of critical areas such as finance, personnel and basic operations in order for them to be a success.

Some companies prefer to establish a wholly foreign-owned enterprise (WFOE, often pronounced "woofy") rather than a joint venture, with a view to retaining greater management control, due to concerns over intellectual property rights (IPR) protection, desire for simplicity, or for other reasons of corporate policy. The law on WFOEs requires that they either provide advanced technology or be primarily export-oriented, and restricts or prohibits them in a number of service and public utility sectors. However, an increasing number of U.S. companies find WFOEs, which now account for roughly 20% of all foreign-invested enterprises (FIEs), to be a viable entry vehicle to the China market, taking much less time and money to set up than a joint venture (see Chapter IV).

Licensing: Technology transfer is another initial market entry approach used by many companies. It offers short-term profits but runs the risk of creating long-term competitors. Due to this concern, as well as intellectual property considerations and the lower technical level prevailing in the China market, some firms attempt to license older technology, promising higher-level access at some future date or in the context of a future joint venture arrangement.

Licensing contracts must be approved by and registered with the Ministry of Foreign Trade and Economic Cooperation (MOFTEC). A tax of 10-20% (depending on the technology involved and the existing applicable bilateral tax treaty) is withheld on royalty payments (see section F of this chapter).

Franchising: China has no laws as yet which specifically address franchising, but many foreign companies are beginning to establish multiple retail outlets under a variety of creative arrangements, including some which for all practical purposes function like franchises. Virtually all of the foreign companies who operate multiple-outlet retail venues in China either manage the retail operations themselves with Chinese partners (typically establishing a different partner in each major city) or sell to a master franchisee which then leases out and oversees several franchise territories within the territory. Within three years of WTO accession, restrictions on equity share, number of outlets and geographical area are to be eliminated.

Direct selling: Major U.S. direct selling companies entered the China market in the early- to mid-1990's, when China's legal and regulatory framework for this industry was not very clear. Direct selling was quickly modeled after by domestic Chinese companies, some of whom abused this legitimate format of doing business and operated scams to rip off consumers and evade taxes. In early 1998, the Chinese government started implementing a series of strict controls over this industry, culminating in the re-licensing of all direct selling companies. Although a few major U.S direct selling companies were re-issued the business license, restrictions are severe and requirements many, resulting in difficult business environment. The U.S direct selling industry is working pro-actively with various Chinese government departments and agencies, as part of an overall effort toward China's WTO accession, to construct a fairer business climate in this industry. The implementation of WTO commitments promises to change this method of marketing in a rapidly changing business environment.

E-commerce: The Chinese government has adopted an open attitude towards the advent of electronic commerce in China. Interest among both Chinese and international businesses focuses on investing and on establishing vertical integration and sales channels on-line. Investment is risky, however, due to the lack of clearly defined regulatory powers over the industry, an effective Chinese certificate authentication system, secure and reliable on-line settlement system, and an efficient physical delivery system. Many U.S. IT sector companies have been actively engaged in jointly developing these systems in China, and WTO accession will increase the speed of these developments.

SELLING FACTORS/TECHNIQUES

Relationships: Personal relationships in business are critical. The Chinese feel more comfortable dealing with "old friends," and it is important for exporters, importers, and investors to establish and maintain close relationships with their Chinese counterparts and relevant government agencies. It is equally important that American exporters encourage strong personal relationships between their Chinese agents or distributors and the buyers and end-users. A web of strong personal relationships will help ensure smoother development of business in China.

Foreign Currency: Chinese companies are not permitted to retain foreign exchange. In business deals with Chinese companies, U.S. companies have been asked to keep a portion of the Chinese companies hard currency earnings in foreign bank accounts to avoid reporting and turning it over to the foreign exchange control authorities. As part of an effort to clamp down on corruption and tighten foreign exchange control, the Chinese government is coming down hard on such practices.

In contrast, FIEs are permitted to retain foreign exchange contributed to or earned by the enterprise. On December 1, 1996, China made its currency convertible on the current trade account. However, foreign exchange balancing requirements remain in effect in other Chinese laws and regulations and in joint-venture contractual arrangements.

Chinese companies are, however, able to purchase the foreign currency necessary for authorized imports and foreign-currency obligations such as licensing fees, royalties, and loans by authorized entities.

ADVERTISING AND TRADE PROMOTION

Advertising: Advertising is an effective way to create product awareness among potential consumers in China. Channels for mass advertising include publications, radio, television, billboard displays, internet, and sports sponsorship. A list of major Chinese publications can be found in the appendix.

China's retail boom and increasing competition among retailers is making China's advertising industry grow even faster than the economy as whole. According to China's National Advertising Association (under the State Administration for Industry and Commerce, or SAIC), over-all advertising spending reached $ 8.7 billion in 2000, a 17% growth over 1999's volume. China has about 70,747 advertising businesses, including more than 380 foreign joint ventures. Foreign advertising firms are limited to taking an equity stake of up to 51% in joint venture enterprises. All of the major international advertising firms are present in China.

Television advertising takes the largest single portion of the Chinese advertising market. China's regular television viewing population is 84% of China's 1.2 billion people. Major articles sold on television include toiletries, foodstuffs, pharmaceuticals, liquor, and home electronics. Television stations in big markets (Beijing, Guangzhou, Shanghai) require advertisers to book and pay for specific spots two to ten months in advance.

Now that China is in the midst of a consumer revolution, foreign products, complete with advanced marketing, advertising and research techniques, are leading the way. Brand awareness is increasingly important and sophisticated advertising is beginning to play a crucial role in charming the Chinese consumer. Foreign products are expected to continue making inroads despite 1999 regulations calling for more control over customer surveys that help foreign firms enhance their marketing effectiveness.

China's 1995 Advertising Law contains guiding principles that set broad requirements. For example, one of the requirements is that advertising should "safeguard the dignity and interests of the State." Comparison advertising is not allowed, nor is the use of superlatives. Chinese restrictions within the advertising sector include requirements for the verification of safety and hygiene from the relevant ministries that monitor various consumer products. Censorship standards vary considerably throughout China.

MOFTEC and SAIC are the primary regulatory organizations for the advertising sector, but many other organizations, such as the Ministry of Culture and the State Administration of Radio, Film and Television, play an active role in controlling what ends up in print or on television.

Trade Shows and Missions: Hundreds of exhibitions are now held annually in China. Most are sponsored or co-sponsored by government agencies, professional societies, or the China Council for the Promotion of International Trade (CCPIT). Shows are also organized by U.S., Hong Kong, and state trade departments, and other professional show organizers. Show participation costs are sometimes high and may only reach a local audience so companies are advised to scrutinize which shows to participate in. A list of trade shows that are screened by the U.S. Department of Commerce are listed in the appendix.

Electronic Commerce and the Internet: The rapid growth of the internet raises interest in using "e-commerce" in China. Though China remains a developing country, the ambitious use of high technology has made inroads with the growth of governmental and business-to-business forms of e-commerce. Government at all levels seeks to use technology to inform the public about laws, deal with customs and simplify procedures, and businesses are beginning to conduct bidding, process sales and handle contacts on-line. In addition, direct marketing and sales-on-line have begun despite the lack of credit card usage and distribution difficulties. Beijing and Shanghai SAICs have begun a licensing process to create a "reasonable and reliable market." In May 2000, nearly 30 internet companies were awarded licenses to sell online advertising.

PRODUCT PRICING AND CUSTOMER SERVICE

Most Chinese consumers are sensitive to price and will usually choose the less expensive product unless they can be swayed by better after-sales service or clearly better product quality. For larger purchases, attractive financing that lowers the effective price is offered by Japanese, European and other foreign governments' companies and may make some U.S. products less competitive.

Foreign companies are normally not permitted to directly provide after-sales service and customer support for their products sold into China. Foreign Invested Companies (FIEs) can provide such services on products that they manufacture in-country. Foreign firms sometimes engage authorized Chinese entities to provide service, often on a contractual basis, or to establish service centers jointly that can provide both spare parts and after-sales service. American companies complain that such arrangements give them inadequate control over the quality of customer service and result in the loss of customer confidence. Some companies opt to provide regular servicing from bases outside of China, such as Hong Kong.

SALES TO THE GOVERNMENT

In 1999, new regulations controlling government procurement were issued by the Chinese State Development Planning Commission (SDPC). While ostensibly making the system more transparent and open, it also centralizes the procedure much more. In the past, government procurement was conducted through state-owned/controlled companies affiliated with a particular ministry. Since these entities will remain the main end-users of the purchases, their participation in the process will probably continue.

China's government procurement practices have often not been consistent with open and competitive bidding and, for the most part, non-transparent. It is unclear at this point how the new regulations will streamline a system that previously was subject to at least one, and usually several, approvals from governments at various levels. While tenders for projects funded by international organizations are usually openly announced, most government procurement is by invitation only. Competition is by direct negotiation rather than by competitive bid but that is supposed to change under the new regulations. Goods and vendors for large projects that are covered in the annual state plan have been frequently designated during the planning process. All information, from solicitation to award, remains secret and is known only to those companies involved or to officials in the planning and industrial ministries.

Direct sales to the Chinese military are also a possibility. While restrictions on this type of business exist both in the United States and in China, U.S. manufacturers have successfully sold a wide variety of products to the Chinese military through the General Logistics Department of the People's Liberation Army (PLA).

INTELLECTUAL PROPERTY RIGHTS (IPR) PROTECTION

The U.S. and China signed an IPR Memorandum Of Understanding (MOU) in 1992, pursuant to which China improved its laws governing IPR protection over the following two years and joined the Berne Copyright and Geneva Phonograms Conventions. The March 1995 extension of the IPR MOU sets out a plan for enforcing IPR and grants market access to certain products. In 1998, in an effort to improve IPR coordination and enforcement, China established a new organization, the State Intellectual Property Office (SIPO). As envisioned, SIPO will eventually have authority over the Patent Office, the Trademark Office, and the National Copyright Administration. At present, however, SIPO only controls the Patent Office, with which it is co-located. The Trademark Office falls under the authority of the State Administration of Industry and Commerce, while the National Copyright Administration is controlled by the State Printing and Publishing Administration.

Chinese leaders have acknowledged that protection of patents, copyrights, and trademarks is needed to promote a "knowledge-based economy" in China. China has committed to full compliance with the Agreement on Trade-Related Aspects of Intellectual Property (TRIPS) upon accession to the WTO. It has completed a revised Patent Law and is now reviewing and revising its trademark, and copyright laws to ensure consistency with TRIPS requirements. In spite of steady, significant progress in improving its intellectual property legal and regulatory regime, IPR protection in China remains weak. Criminal penalties are too seldom applied. Trademark and copyright violations are blatant and widespread. While Chinese officials are increasing enforcement efforts, IPR violations, including growing exports of counterfeit products, continue to outpace enforcement.

China is a member of the World Intellectual Property Organization (WIPO), the Paris Convention for the Protection of Industrial Property, the Berne Convention, the Madrid Trademark Convention, the Universal Copyright Convention, and the Geneva Phonogram Convention. The Chinese Government is still debating, however, whether China's Copyright Law will be brought into full compliance with the WIPO Copyright Treaty and the WIPO Performances and Phonograms Treaty. While China has made no commitments in this regard, the U.S. Government believes that China's signing these treaties would further indicate China's intent to provide a high level of IPR protection.

Enforcement: Large-scale violations of intellectual property rights in China, including counterfeiting and smuggling, often overwhelm enforcement efforts. In recent years, China has had considerable success in closing down factories that produced illegal optical disks (CDs, VCDs, and CD-ROMs) computer software products - only to see an increase in such products smuggled across its borders. The authorities have also conducted thousands of raids at both the manufacturing and the retail level, resulting in the confiscation of counterfeit or smuggled products. In 1999, the State Council issued a decree admonishing government agencies to purchase only legal computer software.

At the same time, in 1998, in reaction to continuing IPR violations, foreign companies in China formed a coalition-now called the Quality Brands Protection Committee (QBPC)-to draw the attention of Chinese and U.S. Government authorities to the counterfeiting problem, and to propose ways of strengthening enforcement. These companies estimate their annual losses due to counterfeiting at over $1 billion. Severely limited market access for products such as foreign movies and computer software provides an additional incentive for smugglers and counterfeiters. Foreign companies have devoted considerable on-the-ground resources to combating IPR violations, with mixed results. In early 2000, the QBPC gained recognition from Chinese authorities as an official organization to protect their products. QBPC has expanded its membership and offers technical and financial support for IPR enforcement in China.

Inadequate enforcement of IPR laws and regulations, through either judicial or administrative means, remains a serious problem. Enforcement of existing IPR regulations is uneven and is sometimes impeded by local interests. Industry associations representing computer software, entertainment, and consumer goods industries report high levels of piracy and counterfeiting of all types of products. They also report increasing exports of IPR-infringing goods to other countries. The Business Software Alliance estimates that more than 90 percent of business software used in China is pirated. Consumer goods companies report that, on average, 20 percent of their products in the Chinese market are counterfeits. Chinese companies experience similar, or greater, problems with piracy and counterfeits. The administrative penalties for IPR violations, often no more than confiscation of the counterfeit products, are generally insufficient to deter counterfeiters. China's criminal sanctions against IPR violations are seldom used, in part, because of restrictions on types of admissible evidence and cumbersome procedures.

Combating IPR violations in China is a long-term, multi-faceted undertaking. China has established special IPR courts in all provinces, major cities, and at the Supreme People's Court. Judges in Chinese courts are charged with fact-finding and have greater discretion in the adjudication of cases than those in the United States. However, the lack of legal training of many trial court judges undermines the effectiveness of these courts. The USG and U.S. companies have provided resources for training judges. Chinese authorities are attempting to address the lack of legal training of court officials by establishing IPR law centers at Beijing University, Qinqhua University, and People's University. Chinese IPR professionals are also studying in foreign countries. The United States and the European Union have made IPR -- and commercial dispute resolution -- a key feature of "Rule of Law" discussions with Chinese authorities.

Enforcement options: The Chinese government agencies most often involved in enforcement actions are the Quality and Technical Supervision Bureau (TSB) (soon to be merged into the General Administration of the PRC for Quality Supervision, Inspection, and Quarantine (AQSIQ) and the State Administration of Industry and Commerce (SAIC). U.S. companies have also reported some success in registering trademarks, patents and copyrights with the Customs General Administration, which can then confiscate infringing products. The Trademark Office and the National Copyright Administration also can take action in cases involving trademark and copyright infringement. In addition, China's court system can be utilized to enforce IP rights. However, the court system is relatively slow compared with the administrative agencies (such as the SAIC and the TSB), which reportedly sometimes conduct raids within hours of receiving a complaint.

Patents: Under China's patent law enacted in 1984, domestic and foreign patent applications have increased steadily. Patent protection was extended in January 1993 to pharmaceutical and chemical products, as well as processes; the period of protection was lengthened to 20 years. The amendments also provide the patent-holder the right of importation and expand the scope of patent infringement to include unauthorized sale or importation of products manufactured with the use of patented processes. Under the provisions of the MOU, China extends transitional administrative protection to some U.S. pharmaceutical and agrochemical products for up to seven-and-a-half years. A revised patent law is now under review.

China acceded to the patent cooperation treaty on January 1, 1994, and will perform international patent searches and preliminary examinations of patent applications. Under the patent law, foreign parties must utilize the services of a registered Chinese agent to submit the patent application. Preparation of the application may be done by foreign attorneys or the Chinese agent.

Copyrights: In March 1992, China established bilateral copyright relations with the U.S. and in October 1992 acceded to both the Berne Convention and the Universal Copyright Convention. China also joined the Geneva Phonogram Convention in April 1993. Following accession to the Berne Convention, China explicitly recognized computer software as a literary work and extended protection to computer programs for 50 years without mandatory registration requirements.

Trademarks. Although problems remain with enforcement, China's trademark regime basically conforms to world standards. In October 1989, China joined the Madrid Pact for protection of trademarks; the latter grants reciprocal trademark registration to member countries. China amended its trademark regime in February 1993 to add special regulations for criminal prosecution for trademark infringement.

Legal framework: China is revising its copyright, trademark and patent laws to meet the requirements of TRIPS and WTO accession. The revised patent law is closest to completion, and the copyright and trademark laws are also likely to be revised.

China has a "first-to-register" system that requires no evidence of prior use or ownership, leaving registration of popular foreign marks open to anyone. The Unfair Competition Law extends IPR protection to trade dress. Under the trademark law, foreign parties must utilize the services of registered Chinese agents to submit the trademark application. Preparation of the application may be done by foreign attorneys or the Chinese agent.

Trade secrets: In September 1993, the Chinese government adopted the Law Against Unfair Competition. This law defines unfair competition to include conduct that infringes the "lawful rights" of another business operator, including acts that violate "commercial secrets" rights. Commercial secrets which can bring economic benefits to the authorized users and which are protected by taking appropriate security measures are defined to include technical and operational information not available to the public. Sanctions under the law include civil remedies such as damages, administrative sanctions such as fines, and criminal penalties for "serious violations." China is further obligated to protect trade secrets under the Paris Convention for the Protection of Industrial Property, to which it is a signatory.

Regulation of Technology Licensing: Technology transfer by foreign companies is governed by 1985 regulations on technology import contracts, which include contract-licensing patents, trademarks, know-how or trade secrets; contracts for technical services; and other technology import contracts. Contracts transferring intellectual property as part of the foreign equity contribution to FIEs are generally regulated by laws concerning foreign investment. Technology licensing contracts must be approved by MOFTEC or its provincial commissions. Some of the issues of particular concern to U.S. companies include:

the licensor cannot require confidentiality beyond the duration of the contract, except where the supplier provides improvements to the technology, and most technology contracts are not to extend beyond 10 years;

the licensor cannot restrict sales channels or impose unreasonable restrictions on the export of products produced with the licensed technology; and

special approval is required for extended confidentiality, export restrictions, and preferential treatment for payment of royalty tax.

PROFESSIONAL SERVICES

The system for regulation of foreign commercial activity in China is difficult to navigate and non-transparent. Companies new to market are strongly encouraged to retain professional services to structure commercial transactions. Establishing a wholly foreign owned subsidiary, joint venture, or representative office requires compliance with complex contract approval requirements, business registration requirements, taxation regulations and statutes, and labor regulations. Many foreign banks, accountants, attorneys, and consultants have established offices in China and are familiar with Chinese requirements. Some Chinese professional service providers also have substantial experience serving foreign clients.

Accountants: Chinese law requires representative offices and foreign invested enterprises to engage the services of accountants registered in China to prepare officials submission of annual financial statements and other specified financial documents. Therefore, only Chinese accountants and joint venture accounting firms may provide these services. All the Big Five accounting firms (KPMG Peat Marwick, Pricewaterhouse Coopers, Deloitte Touche Tohmatsu, Ernst & Young, and Arthur Andersen) have established offices in China and provide services ranging from providing advice on taxation matters and preparation of investment feasibility studies, to setting up accounting systems that are in compliance with Chinese law. Among accounting firm clients, multinationals are shifting their focus from market entry strategies to business operation efficiency. During the past six years, their market share has grown from 2% to 30%.

Attorneys: During the past eight years, many U.S. and international law firms have received approval to register in China as a foreign law firm. Prior to l992, most foreign law firms were registered as consulting firms. More than one hundred foreign law firms currently operate in China, of which nearly thirty are based primarily in the United States. Foreign law firms registered in China are restricted to advising clients on legal matters pertaining to the jurisdiction where they are licensed and general international business practices. Although a foreign lawyer may not offer a legal opinion, clients can obtain assistance with structuring transactions, drafting contracts, and resolving disputes. Only attorneys licensed in China may appear in court and provide legal advice on Chinese legal matters. Foreign law firms are allowed to open only one office in China and are not allowed to employ Chinese lawyers in that firm. Foreign lawyers are not permitted to qualify to practice law in China and are not allowed to form a joint venture with Chinese lawyers

Management Consultants: Foreign companies new to the Chinese market typically engage the services of local consultants to develop market entry strategies, conduct due diligence investigations, and identify potential investment partners, sales agents and customers. More than 100,000 companies are active in the Chinese consulting industry, of which 65% are foreign firms that generate 85% of consulting industry revenue. Licensed and unlicensed firms compete in the market, and the regulatory environment for this services sector is unclear. Only four foreign consulting firms have received a consulting firm license - BCG, Arthur Andersen, China Consulting Association, and the Lei-Da Group of Hong Kong.

Advertising: Approximately 64,000 advertising firms exist in China, of which 500 are foreign invested enterprises. Foreign advertising firms are limited to a 51% maximum equity stake. The major international advertising firms have established a presence in China. Companies new to market can gain valuable advice from top-notch advertising firms on how to effectively craft an effective advertising strategy that is responsive to Chinese consumer preferences and cultural differences. Advertising is strictly regulated in China, and penalties for violation of the law through misleading advertisements, unauthorized use of national symbols, or other prohibited forms of advertising are subject to fines of 100,000 RMB ($12,500).

Commercial Service posts in China maintain lists of U.S. law, accounting, and consulting firms with offices in China, as well as lists of Chinese firms that the Commercial Office or its customers have had favorable dealings.

DUE DILIGENCE

Undertaking a due diligence investigation prior to engaging in a trade or investment transaction can minimize risk of encountering commercial disputes. The primary causes of commercial disputes between Chinese and American companies concern breach of contractual payment obligations, irregularities in accounting practices, financial mismanagement, undisclosed debt, and struggle for control within joint ventures. These problems can be minimized by investigating the financial standing and reputation of local companies before signing contracts with them. Both U.S. and Chinese firms with offices in China conduct due diligence investigations; the former include Dun & Bradstreet, Kroll Associates, PricewaterhouseCoopers and Pinkerton Consulting Services. The fees charged by these companies may be considered a useful investment to ensure that the local customer or partner is financially sound and reliable. The U.S. Foreign Commercial Service's International Company Profile (ICP) is not offered in China at this time.

TRADE REGULATIONS, CUSTOMS AND STANDARDS

The signing of the U.S.-China Bilateral Market Access Agreement on China's Accession to the WTO on November 15, 1999 represents a major victory in the United States' ongoing effort to open China's market to U.S. goods and services. By encouraging structural reform and the rule of law, the Agreement will also support China's own domestic reform process.

China in 2000 completed its bilateral WTO negotiations with all concerned WTO member states except Mexico. The WTO Working Party on China's accession resumed drafting of a Protocol and Working Party Report with a view towards completing the accession process by the end of 2005. WTO membership will build on and strengthen China's implementation of its commitments to the United States in the 15 trade agreements negotiated since 1979.

China restricts imports through a variety of means, including high tariffs and taxes, non-tariff measures, trading rights restrictions, and other barriers. Prohibitively high tariffs, in combination with taxes and other import restrictions, block many imports. Chinese officials are increasingly aware, however, that such protective measures contribute to endemic economic inefficiencies and encourage smuggling. To this end, the Chinese Government has undertaken measures to reduce these barriers. The number of firms with trading rights is continuing to increase; after WTO accession foreign entities will also benefit from this right. China is reforming its tax system to minimize distinctions between domestic and foreign entities according to the WTO principle of national treatment. In addition, China substantially reduced the number of goods subject to import quotas. China is clarifying its licensing procedures in accordance with the WTO's transparency requirement. Finally, in preparation for WTO accession, the Chinese Government cut tariffs on many goods on January 1, 2005.

IMPORT TARIFFS AND CUSTOM REGULATIONS

The most comprehensive guide to Chinese Customs regulations is The Practical Handbook on Import & Export Tax of the Customs of the PRC, compiled by the General Customs Administration. This guide contains the tariff schedule and national customs rules and regulations. It may be obtained for 220 RMB plus shipping and handling from:

Xing Sheng Zhong Hai Fa Xing Zhong Xing Company.
#6 JianNei DaJie
Dong Cheng Qu, Beijing 100730.
Phone: (86-10) 6519-5923 Fax: (86-10) 6519-5616

Tariff Rates: The Customs General Administration (CGA) assesses and collects tariffs. Import tariff rates are divided into two categories: the general tariff and the minimum (most-favored-nation) tariff. Imports from the United States are assessed at the minimum tariff rate, since the U.S. has concluded an agreement with China containing reciprocal preferential tariff clauses. The five Special Economic Zones, open cities, and foreign trade zones may offer preferential duty reduction or exemption. Companies doing business in these areas should consult the relevant regulations.

On top of normal tariff duties, both foreign and domestic enterprises pay either value-added taxes (VAT) or business taxes, depending on the nature of their business and the type of products involved. VAT applies to enterprises engaged in import-export, production, distribution or retailing activities.

China offers a comprehensive program of tax incentives and concessions. The general VAT rate is 17% but necessities, such as agricultural and utility items, are taxed at 13%. Enterprises regarded as small businesses (annual production sales of less than renminbi 1 million or annual wholesale or retail sales of less than renminbi 1.8 million) are subject to VAT at the rate of 6%. Unlike other VAT payers, small businesses are not entitled to claim input tax credits for VAT paid on their purchases. Different standards apply regarding VAT rebates. The applicable rebate method is a function of the establishment date of the enterprise. Certain limited categories of goods are exempt from VAT.

In an attempt to stimulate exports, the State Tax Administration increased VAT rebates several times in 1999, up to 17% (a full rebate) for certain kinds of processed exports. Exporters complain that it takes months to obtain the rebates and amounts are often miscalculated. A recent crackdown on fraudulent VAT rebate application has made rebates completely unavailable in some areas of Guangdong and Fujian provinces.

China's accession to the WTO is likely to accelerate the phase out of its two-tier tax system for domestic and foreign enterprises. Domestic enterprises have long resented rebates and other tax benefits enjoyed by foreign invested firms. The move towards national treatment will mean the gradual elimination of special tax breaks enjoyed by many foreign investors. In addition, increasingly sophisticated collection methods are reducing loopholes for all market participants. For example, the authorities prohibited the granting of preferential treatment on business tax collection to newly established foreign-owned or invested financial enterprises as of May 1, 2005. (Pre-existing firms, however, can continue to receive preferential treatment until such time as the tax benefit was originally slated to terminate.)

Tariff rates significantly lower than the published MFN rate may be applied in the case of goods that the Chinese Government has identified as necessary to the development of a key industry. This has been particularly true of high technology items. These products benefit from a government policy to encourage investment in high technology manufacturing by domestic and foreign firms. Foreign investment firms that produce certain types of high technology goods, or that are export-oriented, do not have to pay duty on imported equipment which is not manufactured in China and which is for the enterprise's own use. China's Customs Administration has also occasionally announced preferential tariff rates for items that benefit other key economic sectors, in particular the automobile industry.

Customs Valuation: According to Chinese Customs regulations, the dutiable value of an imported good is its CIF price, which includes the normal transaction price of the good, plus the cost of packing, freight, insurance, and seller's commission. In August 1998, the Customs Administration launched an ambitious program to standardize enforcement of customs regulations throughout China as part of a larger campaign to combat smuggling. The program has reduced some of the flexibility of local customs officials to "negotiate" duties. However, customs officials still have wide discretion concerning the category in which an import is placed.

TRADE BARRIERS

The Bilateral Agreement on China's WTO Accession is only the latest of fifteen trade agreements negotiated between the United States and China since 1979. These agreements cover everything from civil aviation and satellite exports to agriculture and intellectual property rights protection. Each of these agreements has played a role in China's gradual process of trade liberalization, and created new opportunities for U.S. exporters.

The Chinese government has recognized for a number of years that economic reform and market opening are cornerstones of sustainable economic growth. Nonetheless, these reforms have been difficult and often painful for certain constituencies, particularly in the aging industrial sector and heavily protected agricultural sector. Thus, while China today has a vastly more open and competitive economy than 15 years ago, there are still many significant barriers in place. Some of the current trade barriers that U.S. firms face are:

High tariffs: For example, some motor vehicles face tariffs of over 80%. U.S. industry points out that tariff rates for sectors in which China is trying to build international competitiveness remain especially high. Under the bilateral WTO agreement, once China accedes to the WTO its industrial tariffs will fall from an overall average of about 15% to an average of 9.4 % several years after accession. The motor vehicle tariffs will eventually fall to 25%. Tariffs for U.S. priority agriculture products will quickly fall from an average 31.5% to 14.4%. If China signs the Information Technology Agreement (ITA), which should occur upon China's WTO accession, tariffs on all ITA goods - such as semiconductors and computer hardware - would be eliminated by January 1, 2005. Until accession takes place, however, tariffs will continue to act as an effective import barrier.

Import Quotas: WTO rules bar quotas and other quantitative restrictions. China has been gradually eliminating them and will continue this process after accession over a several year phase-in period. Specifically, the bilateral agreement with the United States requires China to eliminate existing quotas for the top U.S. priority products upon accession and phase out remaining quotas, generally by two years but no later than five years after accession. At present, however, quotas limit over 40 categories of imports, including automobiles, grains, edible oils, and certain textile products. Monopoly importers, such as those that exist for theatrical film imports, are able to establish de facto quotas.

Tariff-Rate Quotas: In 1996, China introduced tariff rate quotas (TRQ) on imports of wheat, corn, rice, soybeans, cotton, barley, and vegetable oils. The regulations governing TRQ administration have not been made public. Out-of-quota rates are currently as high as 121.6%. In bilateral WTO negotiations, the United States sought and won commitments to increase quota levels and transparency in administration.

Once it accedes to the WTO, China will establish and gradually increase large tariff-rate quotas for wheat, corn, rice, cotton, and soybean oil, with low in-quota duties ranging from 1- 10%. A portion of each TRQ will be reserved for importation through entities other than state trading entities. To ensure full use of the TRQs, China agreed to specific rules for administration of the TRQs, including increased transparency and reallocation to importers of any unused quota.

Import Licensing: Since the early 1990s, China has eliminated many import license requirements, a process that is likely to continue as China prepares for WTO accession. However, many products subject to import quotas also require import licenses, including some wool, grains, oilseeds and oilseed products, cotton, iron and steel products, commercial aircraft, passenger vehicles, fertilizer, hauling trucks, and rubber products. MOFTEC administers the licensing system, but has given primary authority for approval and import of some agricultural items to the General Administration of the PRC for Quality Supervision, Inspection, and Quarantine (AQSIQ). Import licenses are not easy to obtain. The applicant must prove that the import is "necessary" and that there is sufficient foreign exchange available to pay for the transaction.

Administrative Controls: Certain designated commodities must go through an automatic registration process and secure a "Certificate of Registration for the Import of Special Commodities" prior to importation. The certificate is valid for six months.

Transparency: It is increasingly easy to find information about economic and trade regulations in the print and electronic media. The 1992 U.S.-China bilateral market access MOU committed China to publishing all relevant laws, rules, regulations, administrative guidance and policies governing foreign trade that are not currently published. In conjunction with this commitment, China designated the MOFTEC Gazette (Wengao) as the official register for publication of all laws and regulations relating to international trade. Most government ministries have taken to publishing digests of their regulations, both in hardcopy and on their websites. The State Council (www.cei.gov.cn) and MOFTEC (www.moftec.gov.cn) websites are good first sources of information on Chinese foreign trade law. Economic newspapers now routinely carry the text of government policies and regulations. In addition, a number of commercial entities now offer databases and translations of many regulations.

However, despite this progress transparency is still a problem. Chinese officials routinely implement policies based on "guidance" or "opinions" not available to foreign firms and they have not always been willing to consult with Chinese and foreign industry representatives before new regulations are implemented. It can be extremely difficult to obtain copies of draft regulations, even when they have a direct effect on foreign investment. Furthermore, many decisions are left to the discretion of the implementing bureaucrats, who can make decisions without resorting to public comment or open procedures.

Legal Framework: Laws and regulations in China tend to be far more general than in most OECD countries. This vagueness allows Chinese courts and officials to apply them flexibly, which results in inconsistencies. Companies have difficulty determining precisely whether or not their activities contravene a particular regulation. Agencies at all levels of government have rulemaking authority, resulting in regulations that are frequently contradictory. Finally, while there seems to be no shortage of rules and regulations, there are few procedures in place to appeal regulatory decisions.

Trading Rights: The Chinese government has moved to dismantle the near monopoly on import-export rights previously enjoyed by a few state-owned firms. Liberalization of the trading system was given major impetus in early 1999 when MOFTEC announced new guidelines allowing a wide variety of Chinese firms to register to conduct foreign trade. The guidelines allow, for the first time, both manufacturing and "non-production" firms to register for trading privileges. These guidelines were further loosened in 2005. Some goods such as grains, cotton, vegetable oils, petroleum and related products are imported principally through state trading enterprises. Firms with trading rights must undergo an annual qualifications test and certification process. Wholly owned foreign enterprises and individuals are still not permitted to directly engage in import activities, except to bring in material and equipment necessary for production.

As part of its bilateral WTO accession agreement, China committed to phase out many restrictions on trading rights. To meet these commitments, MOFTEC is working on guidelines to allow foreign companies, subject to certain restrictions, to engage directly in trade.

Local Agents: The ability of foreign firms to distribute directly their products in China is subject to strict limitations. In general, foreign firms are only allowed to sell products that they manufacture in China and must go through local agents to distribute imported goods. China has agreed to gradually eliminate distribution restrictions as part of its bid to join the WTO.

Import Substitution Policies: China committed to eliminate all import substitution policies and regulations as one of the conditions of the 1992 market access MOU, but periodically continues to issues such regulations. Recent examples-in the fields of generic medicines, telecom equipment, pharmaceutical pricing, power generation, and the automotive industry-have been the result of informal directives that have not been publicly announced.

Anti-Competitive Practices: China continues to struggle with economic inefficiencies and investment disincentives created by local protectionism, predatory pricing, preservation of industry-wide monopolies, and monopolistic practices designed to protect the state-owned sector. In some cases, industrial conglomerates operating as monopolies or near monopolies (such as China Telecom) have been authorized to fix prices, allocate contracts, and in other ways restrict competition among domestic and foreign suppliers. There are several existing competition laws, and China is drafting a new anti-monopoly law. However, existing laws are ineffective due to poor national coordination and inconsistent local and provincial enforcement.

Anti-Dumping Regulations: China is beginning to use safeguard and anti-dumping measures to control surges in imports of certain products. As trade barriers fall, China's beleaguered state-owned enterprises increasingly are interested in using anti-dumping measures to protect domestic markets. Since China first promulgated Anti-dumping and Anti-subsidy Regulations in 1997, China has imposed anti-dumping duties to control surges in imports of eight products. Without exception, the Chinese complainants in these cases have been large state-run firms, employing large numbers of workers, suddenly facing pressure from both domestic reform and imports. Foreign companies involved in the investigations have complained that pricing methodologies used in making the determination were flawed and that the Chinese investigators relied excessively on information provided by the Chinese petitioners. Indeed, China's anti-dumping procedures (for instance, China's methods of calculating prices and injury) appear incompatible with some aspects of the WTO Anti-dumping Agreement. Likewise, China's anti-dumping regime lacks the transparency called for by WTO rules. Trade officials responsible for investigating dumping allegations have, however, been working to increase transparency and address other technical issues.

Services barriers: China's service sector has been one of the most heavily regulated parts of the national economy - and one of the most protected. The service liberalizations included in the bilateral WTO agreement will improve dramatically foreign access to this sector. The Chinese economy itself will benefit from the increased scope of services, professionalism and technologies that foreign investment in services will bring. There will be substantial efficiency gains to the domestic economy as well from increased foreign participation in financial, insurance, telecommunications, distribution and professional services, after sales service and repair businesses.

At present, however, foreign services providers are largely restricted to operations under the terms of selective "experimental" licenses. The strict operational limits on entry, and restrictions on the geographic scope of activities, severely limit the growth and profitability of these operations.

IMPORT DOCUMENTATION

Normally, the Chinese importer (agent, distributor or joint-venture partner) handles documentation requirements. Necessary documents include the bill of landing, invoice, shipping list, sales contract, an import quota certificate for general commodities (where applicable), import license (where applicable), inspection certificate issued by the General Administration of the PRC for Quality Supervision, Inspection, and Quarantine (AQSIQ) or its local bureau (where applicable), insurance policy, and customs declaration form.

U.S. EXPORT CONTROLS

The Tiananmen Sanctions of 1990 are still in effect and sharply curtail U.S. exporter opportunities to sell crime control equipment to China's police agencies and defense electronics equipment to the Chinese military.

The United States Government's Enhanced Proliferation Control Initiative (EPCI), requires the U.S. Department of Commerce and exporters to closely scrutinize end-users of U.S. exports of all kinds. This regulation requires a Validated License application if the exporter has "reason to know" that the end-users might be involved in missile, nuclear or chemical weapons proliferation. Periodically both the State Dept. and USDOC identify sensitive end-users and add them to the USDOC Entity List. For such identified firms, U.S. exports and U.S. origin re-exports require an individual validated license for virtually all shipments to these entities. The most recent addition of a Chinese firm to the Entity List occurred on June 14, 2005. The Entity List can be viewed at the USDOC Bureau of Export Administration website at www.bxa.doc.gov.

A law passed by Congress in late 1997 requires that the U.S. Government do post shipment verifications (PSV) on all High Performance Computers (HPC) shipped to one of 50 countries including China. An HPC shipped to China after March 20, 2005 is defined as any computer over 85,000 MTOPS (million theoretical operations per second) of performance. There is a USDOC requirement that a MOFTEC issued end-user certificate (EUC) must be obtained by the exporter before the computer is shipped to China. Ordinarily the computer importer or re-seller in China applies for this document and passes it to the exporter. For information on this regulation see the BXA HPC web page at www.bxa.doc.gov/HPC.

USDOC Dual-Use Export Applications: A USDOC dual-use export license application that does not present to the USDOC reviewers serious Chinese end-user concerns is usually approved by the USDOC in about one week. In the past year less than ten USDOC export license applications required a Pre-License Check (PLC). In the case of a PLC requirement, the Department of Commerce requests MOFTEC's permission for an FCS officer from the Embassy to visit the site of an end-user to determine the bona fides of the end-user for the actual end-use of the product. This must be done before Commerce will act further on the export license application. The time required to complete the entire process of a PLC may be two to three months. If in the end no pre-license visit is permitted by the Chinese Government, an export license may not be issued.

For more information on U.S. dual-use export controls, exporters should view the BXA website at www.bxa.doc.gov or contact:

BXA Exporter Services Division
Washington, D.C. Tel: 202-482-4811 Fax: 202-482-3322
Newport Beach, CA Tel: 714-660-0144 Fax: 714-660-9347
Santa Clara, CA Tel: 408-748-7450 Fax: 408-748-7470

U.S. Embassy-Beijing, Commercial Section
Mark Bayuk BXA Officer Tel: 8610-8529-6655 Fax: 8610-8529-6558

State Dept. Defense Trade and Munitions License Applications. In mid 1999, satellite and related technology licensing authority was transferred from the Department of Commerce to the Department of State. For information on State Department export licensing procedures see the relevant State Dept website of the Office of Defense Trade Controls at http://www.pmdtc.org. A point of contact for State Department Licensing business advocacy matters at the State Dept is David Nobles, Tel. 202-647-1817. In the U.S. Embassy in Beijing, the point of contact for State Dept. Licensing matters is the Economic Section, Tel: 86-10-6532-3431, Fax 86-10-6532-6422.

CHINESE EXPORT CONTROLS

Prohibited Exports: China maintains export bans and restrictive licensing procedures on certain items. Products banned from export include musk, copper, platinum, specified chemical compounds, and products whose export is banned under international treaties. Products subject to strict licensing controls include dual-use chemicals, chemical precursors, heavy water, and exports of fish, fresh vegetables and fruits to Hong Kong and Macao. Foreign-invested enterprises are restricted to exporting out of China only the products they manufacture.

The export licensing system is administered by MOFTEC and designated local offices. An export tendering system for a limited but growing number of products has also been introduced. Most licenses are valid for a single use within three months after issuance. For certain items, including 26 categories of agricultural and petroleum products, licenses are granted for six months with multiple use up to 12 times.

Other items that may not leave China include all items that are prohibited from being imported. (See next paragraph) In addition, manuscripts, printed matter, magnetic media, photographs, films or other articles, which involve state secrets; valuable cultural relics; and endangered animals and plants may not be exported.

On June 10, 1998 China promulgated Regulations on the Administration of the export of dual-use(military and civil) Nuclear Facilities and related technologies of the People's Republic of China. The export licenses required under these regulations are issued by MOFTEC.

Prohibited Imports: The following items are prohibited from entering China: counterfeit currencies and counterfeit negotiable securities; printed matter, magnetic media, films, or photographs which are deemed to be detrimental to the political, economic, cultural and moral interests of China; lethal poisons; illicit drugs; disease-carrying animals and plants; foods, medicines, and other articles coming from disease-stricken areas; old/used garments; and RMB. Food items containing certain food colorings and additives deemed harmful to human health by the Ministry of Health are also barred entry.

INSPECTION STANDARDS

Import Commodity Inspection: Chinese law provides that all goods included on a published Inspection List, or subject to inspection pursuant to other laws and regulations, or subject to the terms of the foreign trade contract, must be inspected prior to importation, sale, or use in China. In addition, safety license and other regulations also apply to importation of medicines, foodstuffs, animal and plant products, and mechanical and electronic products.

Chinese buyers or their purchase agents must register for inspection at the port of arrival. The scope of inspection undertaken by local commodity-inspection authorities entails product quality, technical specifications, quantity, weight, packaging, and safety requirements. The standard of inspection is based upon compulsory Chinese national standards, domestic trade standards or, in their absence, the standards stipulated in the purchase or sale contract.

To meet the arrival inspection requirements, it is advisable that Chinese quality certification be obtained from Chinese authorities prior to shipment of goods to China. The quality and safety certification process appears to require extensive investigation and may be time-consuming. If your products are required to have this certification, contact the State General Administration for Quality Supervision and Inspection and Quarantine (AQSIQ) at 15 Fangcaodi Xijie, Chaoyang District, Beijing 100020 China; Tel: (86-10) 6599-4328 or fax: (86-10) 6599-4306. AQSIQ is a new Ministerial level entity whose creation was announced on April 17, 2005. AQSIQ is the result of a merger of the former State Administration for Entry and Exit Quarantine and Inspection (SAIQ) and the China State Bureau of Quality and Technical Supervision (CSBTS). AQSIQ's new structure is expected to be published by AQSIQ sometime in early August 2005. AQSIQ has a website at www.ciq.gov.cn. The website gives a wealth of information on China's import safety certification news, regulations, procedures, policies including reference to WTO accession, and a SAIQ organization chart. This is a valuable source of information and new this year the information is now available in English. As of July 10, 2005 the information on the new AQSIQ merger and organization chart has not yet been added to the website.

The National Institute of Standards (NIST) did a workshop on Chinese standards in Beijing March 10-12, 1999. The summary of the workshop results can be viewed at the following NIST website; http://ts.nist.gov/ts/htdocs/210/216/chinafile/brochure.htm.

A point-of-contact in the USDOC on standards is at the National Institute of Standards and Technology's Global Standards Program, (Mary H. Saunders, Director), 100 Bureau Drive, MS 2100, Gaithersburg, Maryland 20899-2100, Tel: 301-975-6094, Fax: 301-975-4715, e-Mail: gsp@nist.govm, website http://www.ts.nist.gov/gsp. The point-of-contact at USFCS-Beijing is Mark Bayuk at Tel: 86-10-8529-6655 or Fax: 86-10-8529-6558.

Security Software Certification: Hardware and software used for data security or encryption require special security software certification before they can be sold in China. This is separate from the AQSIQ quality assurance procedures. USFCS has an International Marketing Insight (IMI) on this matter published in June 1999 under the title "Security Software Certification."

The office that does this certification is the:
China National Information Security Testing Evaluation and Certification Center (CNISTEC).
No. 36 Xinjiang Gongmen
Hai Dian District, Beijing 100091
Tel: 86-10-6879-6484 Fax: 86-10-6288-0411

Quarantine Inspection: A 1992 quarantine law provides the legal basis for the quarantine inspection of animals, plants and their products, as well as the containers and packaging materials used for transporting these items. The law also establishes the Chinese Animal and Plant Quarantine Administration (CAPQ), since folded into the General Administration for Quality Supervision and Inspection and Quarantine (AQSIQ), which is a Ministerial Level agency created April 17, 2005, which reports to the State Council. AQSIQ has the responsibility to carry out import and export inspections.

The importer must submit an application in advance and the products must undergo the required inspections upon arrival in China. Contracts must specify the requirements for inspection under China's law, as well as indicate the necessary quarantine certificates to be issued by the appropriate agency in the exporting country. Catalogues of the Class A and B infectious or parasitic diseases of animals and the catalogues of the diseases, pests and weeds dangerous to plants are determined and announced by the AQSIQ. The U.S. Department of Agriculture maintains an office of the Animal and Plant Health Inspection Service (APHIS) in Beijing. The office is able to answer questions about Chinese quarantine laws and is the equivalent of AQSIQ. Contact Dale Maki, Tel: 86-10-6505-4575, Fax: 86-10-6505-4574. The APHIS website is http://www.aphis.usda.gov.

LABELING AND MARKING REQUIREMENTS

Under Chinese law governing safety and product-quality standards, certain imported commodities must be inspected and certified to be in compliance with compulsory national, domestic trade or contractually stipulated standards (see Section I). Once a quality certificate for a product is issued, a safety label can be affixed.

All products sold in China must be marked - in the Chinese language - with the relevant information. The National Health and Quarantine Administration require imported (but not domestic) food items such as candy, wine, nuts, canned food and cheese to be affixed with a laser sticker evidencing the product's safety. Importers are charged five to seven cents per sticker, and the stickers must be affixed under State Administration.

Food Labeling Law: On April 1, 2000, a new national Chinese regulation announced on February 15, 2000, was put into effect for the implementation of food label standards. The law supersedes both the Regulation on Management of Import-Export Food Labeling, announced on May 24, 1994, and the Regulation on Management of Labeling Inspection Attached to Import and Export Food, announced on April 21, 1994. This Chinese law requires that all packaged food products (except bulk) must have Chinese labels clearly stating the type of food, brand name, trademark, manufacturer's name and address, country of origin, ingredients, date of production and sell-by date. This law applies to imported as well as locally packaged products. English-language versions of the new regulations and other rules about food additives, such as Food Laws, Labeling Requirements, Food Additives Regulations, Pesticides and other Contaminants, Organic "Green" Food Standards, and Copyright/Trademark, will be obtained in the Food & Agricultural Import Regulations & Standards Report (FAIRS). This report can be accessed by going to http://www.fas.usda.gov, or contact Audrey Talley, USDA/Foreign Agricultural Service, Tel: (202) 720-9408; fax: (202) 690-0677.

SPECIAL IMPORT PROVISIONS

Firms seeking the following exemptions should consult with Customs authorities for information on the procedures and to obtain copies of appropriate forms.

Representative Offices: Resident offices must submit a written application to Customs if they intend to import any personal effects or vehicles. Approval by Customs waives any relevant import license requirements and allows the office to import the equipment in reasonable amounts for office-use only.

Foreign-Invested Enterprises (FIEs): China permits four types of FIEs - equity joint ventures (EJVs), cooperative (contractual) joint ventures (CJVs), wholly foreign-owned enterprises (WFOEs), and foreign-invested joint stock companies. A complicated set of rules exempts selected FIEs from some Customs duties and VAT. Companies should consult the relevant regulations.

Processing Materials and Parts: Raw materials, components, spare parts, auxiliary materials, and packaging materials imported by FIEs for the production of goods which will be exported are exempt from customs duty and VAT. The materials and components must be processed into products and exported within one year from the date of importation. Bonded warehouses may be established within the FIE and are subject to supervision by Customs.

Warehouses: Goods that are allowed to be stored at a bonded warehouse, for up to one or two years, are limited to: materials and components to be used for domestic processing subject to re-exportation; goods imported under special Customs approval on terms of suspending the payment of import duties and VAT; goods in transit; spare parts for free maintenance of foreign products within the period of warranty.

At the end of the two-year period, the goods must be imported for processing and re-exported, licensed for import, or disposed of by Customs. Customs duties and VAT may be assessed depending upon the degree of processing done in China. Goods imported under normal import contracts are not allowed to be stored in bonded warehouses.

For more information on agricultural trade policy, go to http://www.fas.usda.gov to access the latest China Annual Trade Policy Report.

PROHIBITED AND RESTRICTED IMPORTS

The following items are prohibited from entering China: arms, ammunition, and explosives of all kinds; counterfeit currencies and counterfeit negotiable securities; printed matter, magnetic media, films, or photographs which are deemed to be detrimental to the political, economic, cultural and moral interests of China; lethal poisons; illicit drugs; disease-carrying animals and plants; foods, medicines, and other articles coming from disease-stricken areas; old/used garments; and RMB. Food items containing certain food colorings and additives deemed harmful to human health by the Ministry of Health are also barred entry.

In addition, rules went into effect in June 1999, which further restrict or prohibit the importation of certain commodities related to the processing trade. Jointly issued by MOFTEC and the State Economic and Trade Commission, the "Catalogue of Commodities Which are Restricted or Prohibited from Importing for Use in the Processing Trade" is designed to shift the direction of china's processing trade toward handling commodities with higher technological content and greater value-added potential.

The catalogue identifies the following "prohibited commodities": used garments; used publications with licentious content; radioactive or harmful industrial waste; junk cars, used automobiles or components; seeds, seedlings, fertilizers, feed, additives, or antibiotics used in the cultivation or breeding of any export commodity. The catalogue lists seven general types of "restricted commodities": raw materials for plastics, polyester sections, raw materials for chemical fibers, cotton, cotton yarn, cotton cloth, and some steel products. U.S. firms should contact the China General Administration of Customs for guidance regarding the import of any of these types of products.

On November 1, China's State Administration for Entry-Exit Inspection and Quarantine (SAEEIQ), the General Administration of Customs, and the Ministry of Foreign Trade and Economic Cooperation (MOFTEC) jointly issued a circular announcing new requirements for wood packaging materials used to ship goods to China from the United States and Japan. The new requirements apply to all shipments departing from the US or Japan beginning January 1, 2000, and target the elimination of pinewood nematodes, softwood pests that can destroy trees. Some 25-30% of US exports to China could be affected. The new requirements also call for a certification from Animal and Plant Quarantine Service (APHIS) that conifer softwood packaging has been heat-treated, or a label that the shipment contains non-conifer wood packaging, or non-wood packaging.

CUSTOMS CONTACT INFORMATION

Beijing:
General Administration of Customs
Foreign Affairs Division
6 Jianguomenwai DaJie
Tel: 86-10-6519-5243 or 6519-5399
Fax: 86-10-6519-5394
General Administration of Customs Website: http: // www.customs.gov.cn

Shanghai Customs Website:http://www.shcus.gov.cn/apec/index.jsp
Tianjin Customs Website: http://tjc.online.tj.cn/
Guangzhou Customs Website: http://haiguan.gzfeihua.com/customs.htm

TRADE AND PROJECT FINANCING

BANKING SYSTEM

China's banking system has undergone significant changes in the last two decades: banks are now functioning more like banks than before. Nevertheless, China's banking industry has remained in the government's hands even though banks have gained more autonomy. Foreign participation in China's banking industry is severely restricted. China's expected accession to WTO will lead to a significant opening of this industry to foreign participation.

Central Bank: At the top of the system is China's central bank, the People's Bank of China (PBOC), which has been charged with managing the money supply and credit, and supervising the banking system. PBOC, together with the State Administration of Foreign Exchange (SAFE), set foreign-exchange policies.

The PBOC supervises the banking sector's payment, clearing and settlement systems, and audits the operations and balance sheets of all financial institutions in China, as well as implements the regulations regarding the operation of the Commercial banks.

According to the 1995 Central Bank law, PBOC has full autonomy in applying the monetary instruments, including setting interest rate for commercial banks and trading in government bonds. The State Council maintains oversight of PBOC policies.

Commercial Banks: In 1995, the government introduced the Commercial Bank Law to commercialize the operations of the four state-owned banks, the Bank of China (BOC), the China Construction Bank (CCB), the Agricultural Bank of China (ABC), and the Industrial and Commercial Bank of China (ICBC).

The Bank of China (BOC) specializes in foreign-exchange transactions and trade finance. It is estimated that BOC holds a 59% share of China's trade-finance business. The China Construction Bank (CCB) provides financing to infrastructure projects and urban housing development. The Agriculture Bank of China (ABC) specializes in providing financing to China's agricultural sector and offers wholesale and retail banking services to farmers, township and village enterprises (TVEs) and other rural institutions. The Industrial & Commerce Bank of China (ICBC), the largest bank in China, is the major supplier of funds to China's urban areas and manufacturing sector.

Policy Banks: Three new "policy" banks-the Agricultural Development Bank of China (ADBC), China Development Bank (CDB), and the Export-Import Bank of China (Chexim) - were established in 1994 to take over the government-directed spending functions of the four state-owned commercial banks. These banks are responsible for financing economic and trade development and state-invested projects.

CDB specializes in infrastructure financing; ADBC provides funds for agricultural development projects in rural areas; and Chexim specializes in trade financing.

Second Tier Commercial Banks: In addition to the big four state-owned commercial banks, there are smaller commercial banks. The largest ones in this group include the Bank of Communication, China Everbright Bank, CITIC Industrial Bank, Shanghai Pudong development bank, Shenzhen Development Bank, Guangdong Development Bank, Minsheng Bank and Hua Xia Bank. The second tier banks are generally healthier in terms of asset quality and profitability and have much lower non-performing loan ratios than the big four.

Trust and Investment Corporations: In the midst of the reforms of the 1980s, the government established some new investment banks that engaged in various forms of merchant and investment banking activities. Many of the 240 or so international trust and investment corporations (ITICs) established by government agencies and provincial authorities, however, experienced severe liquidity problems after the bankruptcy of the Guangdong International Trust and Investment Corporation (GITIC) in late 1998. The largest surviving ITIC is China International Trust and Investment Corporation (CITIC), which has a banking subsidiary known as CITIC Industrial Bank.

Years of government-directed lending has presented these banks with large amounts of non-performing loans. According to Chinese government, non-performing loans account for 25% to 30% of total lending of China's four big banks. Nonetheless, this ratio comes after RMB1.4 trillion ($157.3 billion) of non-performing assets have been transferred from the banks to the asset management companies (AMC), which were established in 1999 to take over non-performing loans for the Big Four. The AMCs plan to repackage the non-performing loans into viable assets and sell them off to the investors.

PBOC has encouraged banks to diversify their portfolios by increasing their services to the private sector and individuals. In July 2000, a personal credit rating system was launched in Shanghai to be used to assess consumer credit risk and set ratings standards. This is an important move in developing China's consumer credit industry, and increase bank loans to individuals.

Recently, the central government has allowed several small banks to raise capital through bonds or stock issues. Followed the listing of Shenzhen Development bank and Pudong Development Bank, China Minsheng Bank, the only private bank in China, was listed on the Shanghai (A-Share) Stock Exchange in December 2000. More Chinese banks are expected to list in the next three years in order to raise capital.

The reform of the banking system has been accompanied by PBOC's decision to decontrol interest rates. The PBOC announced in August 2000 that it planned to liberalize the interest rates in about three years.

As a first step, the PBOC liberalized the interest rates for foreign currency loans and large deposits (US$3 million and over) in September 2000. Next on the liberalization schedule are the interest rates for certificates of deposits and other money market instruments. There after, the PBOC will liberalize the interest rates for large, fixed term deposits at urban banks. However, the full liberalization of interest rates on other deposit accounts—including checking and saving accounts—is expected to take much longer. On the lending side, market-determined interest rates on loans will first be introduced in the rural areas and then followed by rate liberalization in the cities.

FOREIGN-EXCHANGE CONTROLS

The PBOC and SAFE regulate the flow of foreign exchange in and out of the country, and set exchange rates through a "managed float" system. To better control this flow, almost all Chinese enterprises and agencies are required to turn over their foreign currency earnings to the banks in exchange for renminbi. (Large exporters were allowed to retain up to 15% of their earnings beginning in late 1997.) When foreign exchange is required for import and other authorized transactions, they then apply to designated banks that are members of the interbank foreign-exchange market.

Foreign-invested enterprises (FIEs) are permitted to keep foreign exchange in foreign exchange accounts at commercial banks. The Chinese government has eliminated the foreign-exchange swap centers on which FIEs used to trade among themselves, and all FIEs have been integrated into the formal banking system.

Since 1995 China has required that FIEs submit an annual report on their foreign-currency transactions, known as the Foreign-Exchange Examination Report. This report must be prepared by a certified public accountant registered in China and approved by SAFE and is necessary to qualify for foreign-exchange privileges. The purpose of the report is to ensure that FIEs' foreign-exchange earnings from exports are sufficient to meet their own requirements as well as any obligation to repatriate profits. Once the report is approved, firms receive a stamped Foreign Exchange Registration Certificate that enables them to obtain foreign exchange. China's original goal of achieving a fully convertible currency by the year 2000 has been pushed back because of the Asian financial crisis.

On July 1, 1996, China began to allow all FIEs in China to buy and sell foreign currency and exchange RMB in authorized banks for trade and services, debt payment and profit repatriation. The PBOC has lifted limits on exchanging and remitting currency for non-trade purposes and raised the ceilings for the amount of foreign exchange for private use. In mid-1998, however, SAFE cracked down on many of the loopholes used to get around the controls on capital account transactions. Many FIEs complained that delays occurred when SAFE screened their documentation more closely. SAFE has streamlined its system, but the requirement for proof that all relevant local taxes have been paid is a burden for many offshore service providers.

Foreign banks, their branches and foreign joint-venture banks are authorized to buy or sell foreign exchange from or to foreign-funded ventures. Foreign-funded banks or branches are not allowed to accept local currency deposits or to make RMB loans except if they have been specially licensed in the Pudong district of Shanghai and in Shenzhen, near Guangdong. Elsewhere, foreign banks and their branches are prohibited from accepting RMB deposits (liabilities) but may establish RMB accounts to convert currencies for their joint venture and foreign customers. China has pledged to expand the scope of RMB business gradually and to eliminate all geographical restrictions within five years of entering the World Trade Organization (WTO).

GENERAL FINANCING AVAILABILITY

The sources of financing available for U.S. exporters and investors are:

Export Credits: The U.S. Export-Import Bank, an independent agency of the U.S. government, seeks to increase the competitive position of U.S.-based exporters in overseas markets. By providing export insurance, loan guarantees, direct loans and other types of financing support EX-IM Bank supports the sales of U.S. exports and thereby creates U.S. jobs. EX-IM Bank currently has master credit agreements with both Bank of China and China Development Bank, but can also work with other Chinese banks, including China Construction Bank, Industrial and

Commercial Bank of China, Agricultural Bank of China and Bank of Communications. Private sector importers are eligible for support as long as they meet EX-IM Bank credit standards. The terms and conditions of standard financing are governed by the OECD Arrangement on export credits. Direct lending rates are set monthly and are called Commercial Interest Reference Rates (CIRRs).

Chinese entities actively seek low-interest, long-term loans, and European and Japanese export credit agencies have aggressively sought to accommodate this appetite. Soft loans or concessionary financing are designed to support a country's exporters and are usually offered under annual government-to-government protocols not tied to particular projects. U.S. firms, otherwise competitive on price and quality, sometimes lose contracts because they are unable to compete with such loans. Ex-Im Bank will, under certain circumstances, consider matching the specific financing terms of a competing government offer.

For more information concerning EX-IM Bank programs and application procedures contact EX-IM Bank in Washington, DC at (800) 565-EXIM or (202) 565-3545. In China, contact the EX-IM Bank Representative, Mr. Douglas C. Lee, at the Commerce Department's Foreign Commercial Service Beijing office - Tel: (8610) 8529-6655, Fax: (8610) 8529-6558. Fee calculations and applications can be found on-line at the website www.exim.gov.

Direct grants: U.S. Trade & Development Agency funds feasibility studies, orientation visits, specialized training grants, business workshops and technical assistance worldwide. TDA is active in more than 60 countries and has recently opened its programs in China after a 12-year break. In order to be eligible for assistance, projects must have a procurement process open to U.S. firms, represent an opportunity for sales of U.S. goods and services and be a development priority of the country where the project is located. Contact Mr. Geoff Jackson, Regional Director for Asia/Pacific, at TDA's Arlington, VA office. Tel: (703) 875-4357, Fax: (703) 875-4009. Website: www.tda.gov

Multilateral Agencies: The World Bank, based in Washington, D.C., maintains a large loan program in China. The World Bank's purpose is to help borrowers reduce poverty and improve living standards through sustainable growth and investment. China represents the World Bank's second largest commitment worldwide. The Bank's program policies in China continue to shift away from key infrastructure projects in transportation and energy toward environmental and agriculture support. The World Bank publishes bidding opportunities in the United Nations publication "Development Business." This is available by subscription from United Nations, P.O. Box 5850, Grand Central Station New York, New York 10163-5850.

The World Bank conducts procurement by the rules of international competitive bidding through Chinese tendering organizations; nonetheless, successful bidding requires close coordination with the Chinese government entity responsible for developing a project at the consulting stage, when specifications are being established. The World Bank has a local office in China Tel: (8610) 6554-3361 Mr. Yukon Huang, Country Director. Website: www.worldbank.org.

As a member of the World Bank, The International Finance Corporation has become increasingly active in China. It is mandated to assist joint venture and share holding companies with substantial non-state ownership to raise capital in the international markets. The IFC takes equity positions in these companies. The IFC's core business is "project finance," and it currently has over $1.2 billion invested in "project finance" undertakings in China. The projects have anticipated cash flows that can cover repayments to lenders and dividends to shareholders. They do not enjoy a government guarantee. The IFC can be contacted through its Washington, D.C. Headquarters at (202) 473-0631 or Ms. Karin Finkelfton at the Beijing office, Tel: (8610) 6554-4191, Fax: (8610) 6554-4192. Website: www.ifc.org

The Asian Development Bank (ADB): China continues to be one of ADB's largest borrowers.

Loans are largely for infrastructure and environmental projects. Once a project is initially approved by the ADB and the Chinese government, it is included in a monthly publication called "ADB Business Opportunities" which is available by subscription from the Publications Unit, Information Office, ADB, P.O. Box 789, Manila, Philippines, Fax: (632) 632-5122 or 632-5841. The Commerce Department has established a Multilateral Development Bank Operations Office (Fax: (202) 273-0927) which publishes information to assist companies in winning such contracts. The ADB Resident Mission in China is located in Beijing. Contact Bruce Murray, Resident Representative, or David Sobel, Country Officer at Tel: (8610) 6642-6601, Fax: (8610) 6642-6606. Website: www.adb.org.

TERMS OF PAYMENT

In China's liberalized economic regime, there are many ways to finance imports. The most commonplace are letter of credits and documentary collections. Under these methods, foreign exchange is allocated by the central government for an approved import.

Letters of credit: Although the Bank of China dominates China's trade-finance business, most Chinese commercial banks have the authority to issue letters of credit for imports. These include China Construction Bank, Industrial and Commercial Bank of China, Agricultural Bank of China and CITIC Industrial Bank. Foreign banks with branch or representative offices in China (see Appendix D) can also issue letters of credit.

There are a few peculiarities about letters of credit issued by Chinese banks. First, from time to time local Chinese courts have issued injunctions that bar Chinese banks from clearing letters of credit whose underlying documentation has been challenged. The central government has issued guidance against this practice, which is gradually disappearing. Second, China is not a member of the International Chamber of Commerce and, therefore, is not subject to the Unified Customs and Practices (UCP) 400 code regarding international trade payments. In Chinese practice, terms and conditions are generally negotiable and set on a transaction-by-transaction basis in the form of a "silent" confirmation. Banks can generally be found to take this small risk.

Documentary Collections: This method of payment is similar to a letter of credit, but less formal and more flexible. Just as with letters of credit, the exporter submits a full set of trade documents for payment collection to the bank designated in the contract. The Chinese bank will send the documents to the home office, which examines them and, in some cases, passes them to the buyer for further examination. Payment is made after the documents have met the approval of all parties. This method of payment provides rather thin coverage against default. It can be considerably less expensive than a letter of credit, but should be used with caution. It is the responsibility of the exporter to determine the specific instructions to be used in the collection letter.

Other methods:

Bank or Enterprise Loans: Many Chinese companies have relationships with local banks or other enterprises that will loan funds for the purchase imports.

Foreign Supplier Loan: The supplier helps to finance, on behalf of the Chinese buyer, the purchase of its equipment.

Proceeds sharing/cooperative joint venture: Some suppliers will enter into a cooperative joint venture to ensure the sale and financing of their equipment.

INSURANCE

Insurance: Congress suspended the China operations of the Overseas Private Investment Corporation (OPIC) in 1989 (see section VII M. above). The U.S. Ex-Im Bank has programs that provide guarantees and export credit insurance covering U.S. content. Some private companies, such as American International Group and Home Life, also offer export credit insurance policies for China. AIG Beijing office Tel: (8610) 6597-8889, Fax: (8610) 6597-8878. Home Life Beijing office Tel: (8610) 6552-0608, Fax: (8610) 6552-1883

PROJECT FINANCING

Chinese officials have for years experimented with limited- recourse project financing schemes. Long awaited Build-Operate-Transfer (BOT) laws have been delayed, however, and the overall private finance climate has cooled during the past few years. The U.S. Ex-Im Bank is seeking to implement a limited-recourse, project-financing program in China. Such a project is one in which anticipated cash flows can cover debt service repayment to lenders and payment of dividends to shareholders, and is without government guarantees. Loans under this program will be available to companies operating investment projects that require imports from the U.S. Project financing is also available from the U.S. Export-Import Bank and various multilateral financial institutions as described in Section C above.

CHINA CUSTOMS: BASIC INFORMATION

1. CUSTOMS REGULATIONS			
1.1 Temporary Import			
Applicable:	yes		
Validity of period:	3 months		
Extensions possible:	yes	Duration of each period:	3 month
		Number of extensions:	one
1.2 Temporary Import Bond			
Bond provided by the on-site forwarder:	yes		
Bank guarantee provided by:	-		
Cash deposit provided by:	-		
Others:	-		
Temporary import bond calculation:	-		
Duty and VAT deposit:	-		
1.3 ATA Carnet			
Accepted:	yes		
Restrictions if any:	-		
Letter of power in favour of the clearing agent required:	yes		
1.4 Customs Clearance Time (standard dry cargo)			
Sea cargo LCL:	3-4 days		
Sea cargo FCL:	3-4 days		
Air cargo:	2-3 days		
1.5 Duties and Taxes			
Clearing facilities for:	Duties / VAT / CIT:		
Samples / Giveaways	Depending on quantity and value		
Brochures / Leaflets	Depending on quantity and value		
VAT / GST	17%		
Other local taxes	-		
1.6 Documentation required			
Language:	English + Chinese		
Currency:	US Dollar		
Dimensions:	length X width X height in cm		
Documents to be sent in advance by fax:	yes, original + 3 copies		
Bank guarantee:	-		
1.7 Prohibited Exhibits			
Absolutely prohibited:	weapons		
Restricted exhibits:	-		
2 CONSIGNATION / DEADLINES			

2.1 Consignation			
Consignee:		Name of local forwarder	
Notify:		Name of Exhibition, hall/booth number	
2.2 Deadlines for Documents			
Number of days prior to goods' arrival POD	Sea cargo:	5 days	
	Air cargo:	1 days	
2.3 Deadlines for Shipments			
Number of days from arrival airport/seaport; prior opening date of show	Sea cargo LCL:	15 days	
	Sea cargo FCL:	10 days	
	Air cargo:	7 days	
3 GENERAL INFORMATION			
3.1 Main Exhibition Sites and On-Site Facilities			
Name of Exhibition Site:		Customs office:	Permanent handling:
Beijing		yes	yes
Shanghai		yes	yes
Guangzhou		yes	yes
3.2 Normal Business Hours			
Monday - Friday		Saturday	Sunday
8:30am - 5:00pm		-	-
3.3 Main Holidays			
Spring Festival (normally in February) / Labours Day (normally May 1-7) / National Day (normally Oct. 1-7)			
3.4 Payment Facilities			
Currency:	Renminbi (RMB)	Terms of payment:	Cash/ Banktransfer
4 SPECIAL REQUIREMENTS			
4.1 Fumigation			
Depends			
4.2 Certificates			
Depends			
4.3 Censorship			
yes			

Import and export activities in China are subject to a relatively heavy regulatory environment. Controls over imports are exercised mainly through tariffs, licenses, quotas, commodity inspection, registration requirements and quarantine rules.

Since China entered the World Trade Organization (WTO) in late 2001, efforts have been made by the Chinese authorities to reduce or eliminate barriers to cross-border trade. Licences and quotas will be largely abolished by 2005. The number of product categories requiring import licenses has already been greatly reduced. Tariff rates have been reduced, and will fall further over time based on an agreed schedule and timetable. In addition, China has adopted the WTO Valuation Agreement which precludes China (at least in theory) from their previous practice of setting minimum or reference values as a means to determine customs value.

As part of modernizing its customs in line with international standards, China is beginning to adopt post-importation compliance reviews, complimented by very aggressive audits and investigations.

The General Administration of Customs (GAC) is responsible for enforcing customs and related laws, and for collecting customs duties and other import-related taxes.

Services Offered

We deliver a combination of skills, expertise and services to reduce your import costs, help you manage risks more effectively and increase your speed to market with certainty.

- Customs valuation and tariff classification
- Bonded warehouses and special zones
- Customs compliance "health checks"
- Audit & investigation management
- In-house customs training and awareness
- Supply chain security validation
- Customs broker management
- Import/export processing including capital equipment
- Importing used electrical/mechanical equipment
- First sale for export

China Customs is a State agency that supervises and manages all arrivals to and departures from the Customs territory of the People's Republic of China.It is organized around a tripartite structure:General Administration of Customs(including subordinated units:Guangdong Sub-Customs Administration,Supervising Office of General Administration of Customs in Tianjin,Supervising Office of General Administration of Customs in Shanghai); 41 regional Customs houses, 313 Customs houses.

Additionally, China Customs hosts 2 Customs schools situated in Shanghai and Qinhuangdao.It also has well-established overseas offices in Brussels,Moscow,Washington,etc.With over 48,000 working staff,China Customs maintains efficient Customs control at 247 ports of entry.

China Customs operates the vertical management policy.The General Administration of Customs(GAC) is the highest supervision unit of China Customs,which is itself the full-ministerial-level government agency affiliated directly with the State Council and which manages Customs facilities nation-wide.GAC comprises 15 departments, 6 subordinated institutions,4 social institutions,1 accredited unit and 3 overseas offices.The incumbent Minister is Mr.Mou Xinsheng.
China Customs is implementing its working guideline of"exercising law-based administration,safeguarding the national gateway,serving the national economic interests and promoting social development"and undertaking its principles of "politically staunch, professionally capable and reliable"to meet the management requirements.

China Customs is empowered with the following mandates:

To Control inward and outward means of transportation,goods,personal articles,mails and parcels,etc; To collect Customs duties and taxes; To combat smuggling; To compile Customs Statistics; To transact other Customs affairs.

In China, Customs is responsible for the collection, processing, compilation and dissemination of the country's external merchandise trade statistics - known as Customs statistics. Customs is mandated to do so by the Customs Law of the People's Republic of China which stipulates that compiling Customs statistics is one the four basic functions of China Customs (along with goods control, duty and excise collection and anti-smuggling).

ORGANIZATIONAL STRUCTURE

The Statistical Department (SD) is an executive unit within CGA responsible for drafting regulations and procedures of external trade statistics; organizing nation-wide trade statistical operations; processing compiling and disseminating China's trade statistics; conducting trade analyses. There are five divisions in the SD: General office, Methodology and data verification; Customs data management, Trade analysis; Customs enforcement assessment.

At each of 41 customs districts throughout the country is established a statistical office responsible for trade data collection, verification, processing and transfer to CGA. Currently, there are around 1000 officials working upon trade statistics within China Customs.

Compilation Method

Since 1 January 1980 CGA has adopted the concepts and definitions recommended by the United Nations for use in international trade statistics contained in the IMTS.

CUSTOMS REGULATORY SYSTEM

The General Administration of Customs is responsible for customs operations and for ensuring customs laws and regulations are administered throughout the country. Customs personnel are under a statutory duty to enforce the law in an impartial and diligent manner. This responsibility extends to:

- Monitoring and controlling merchandise which passes through the customs territory of China
- Assessing and collecting any applicable duties, taxes and fees on imported merchandise
- Investigating and preventing smuggling into the country
- Compiling trade statistics
- Enforce and carrying out customs laws and regulations

Generally, the consignee of imported goods is required to make an accurate declaration at the time of importation. Imported goods must be declared to Customs within fourteen days of the arrival of the means of transport. If the consignee fails to make declaration within the required time period, a fee may be assessed.

Valuation of Goods, Assessment and Payment of Duties

The clearance and release of import and export goods will not be granted before applicable duties and fees are paid in full, unless Customs grants a special authorization for release. Customs duties are levied in accordance with the established import or export tariff rates and as may have been reduced pursuant to WTO tariff reduction commitments. Tariffs are generally assessed on an *ad valor* basis. The consignee of imported goods is legally responsible for payment of customs duties and fees.

Generally, payment of import duties and import value added tax must be made within fifteen days from the issuance of a duty memo by Customs. Failure to meet this time limit will result in the assessment of a penalty. When the delay exceeds three months, the administration may issue a demand for payment or may proceed with forfeiture and auction of the goods.

Post-WTO China has committed to abide by the Customs Valuation Agreement which prioritizes the five methods to determine Customs value of imported goods. Pursuant to China's Customs Valuation Measures, Chinese law provides that Customs shall examine and determine the dutiable value of import goods based on the transaction price, defined as the price actually paid or payable by the buyer for purchasing the goods, subject to any adjustments for fees, costs or royalties. The transaction price must include the freight, relevant expenses, and insurance incurred before the unloading of the goods at the port of discharge inside China.

Customs still uses reference price lists to determine dutiable value without regard to true transaction value. In negotiations for China's accession to the WTO, WTO members expressed concern regarding the practice of using minimum or reference prices for certain goods, which would be inconsistent with the Customs Valuation Agreement. China agreed to cease the practice of using minimum or reference prices, although the practice still exists.

When determining the dutiable value of import goods, Chinese law requires the addition of various expenses or costs including:

- Commissions
- Expenses for containers that are an integral part of the goods
- Packing materials and packing services
- Assists costs
- Royalties payable by the buyer to the seller which are related to the goods and constitute a condition of sale of the goods.

For these expenses or values, the consignee shall provide objective and quantified data and information.

The consignee of the imported goods must truthfully declare the transaction price of the import and export goods, and provide documentation, written materials and electronic data necessary to demonstrate the validity of the declared value. Upon request from Customs, the consignee of imported goods must provide supplemental information to substantiate the relationship and transaction activities between the buyer and the seller and other materials in relation to the declared value.

If Customs questions the accuracy of the declared value, Customs must inform the consignor and consignee in writing of the reasons for its concerns and may request further clarification. If, within fifteen days of the service of written notice, the consignor and consignee fail to provide supplemental information, or, after verifying the provided materials, Customs still questions the accuracy of the declared value, it may reject the declared value and assess a dutiable value.

The parties to an import transaction may submit a written application to Customs for the issuance of an advanced ruling on the method for determining the dutiable value of their goods. If Customs must postpone a determination of valuation, the goods may still clear customs subject to the posting of security to cover the duty. However, Customs must complete the valuation assessment process within ninety days after posting of the security.

If Customs suspects that a special relationship between the buyer and seller impacts the transaction value of imported goods, it must provide notice to the parties and may request addition information which indicates that any special relationship does not affect the declared transaction value.

TARIFF CLASSIFICATION

China is a contracting party to the International Convention on the Harmonized Commodity Description and Coding System and observes the Harmonized Tariff Schedule (HTS) for its tariff organization, nomenclature, interpretive rules and numbering system. If an importer is unsure of the classification of its goods, it may informally consult with Customs on classification issues prior to importation. Any information received from Customs is advisory and non-binding.

RULES OF ORIGIN

To determine rates of duty, Customs adopted regulations that outline the rules of origin. The country of origin is defined as the country where the goods are "wholly obtained or produced." Goods that are produced in more than one country originate in the country where they underwent the "last, substantial, economically justified processing," which means that they encountered a tariff shift or a value of thirty percent or more was added to the final product. The importer, upon request from Customs officials, may be required to provide a certificate of the origin issued by a foreign competent authority.

RESTRICTED MERCHANDISE

While not prohibited from entry, certain types of products are subject to inspection, import licensing and approval such as pharmaceutical products and medical devices, used mechanical and electrical equipment, food products and audiovisual products.

Enforcement of Customs Laws

Customs has a number of administrative tools to enforce customs laws and regulations including monetary penalties, detention, exclusion, confiscation and forfeiture. Customs may also refer a matter for criminal prosecution.

Smuggling exposes an importer or other responsible party to both administrative and criminal penalties. China Customs broadly defines smuggling to include:

- Importation of restricted/ prohibited goods
- False declaration of restricted/prohibited goods

- Undervaluation of goods by providing false declarations
- Unauthorized sale of goods in a bonded zone
- Unauthorized sale of goods imported under duty free programs

A party that knowingly purchases or transports smuggled goods is subject to the same administrative and criminal penalties as the party liable for the actual smuggling.

A party that engages in smuggling activities is subject to a monetary fine of RMB 50,000 (US$6,067), confiscation of goods, and in situations involving undervaluation, a monetary penalty up to the value of the goods or three times the duty evaded. If smuggled goods or articles cannot be confiscated, a sum equal to the value of the item may be recovered.

If an act of smuggling is committed by two or more persons, Customs may issue penalties individually in accordance with the seriousness of each case and in accordance with each person's level of culpability. If an individual has knowledge of an act of smuggling and fails to report the matter, illegal gains will be confiscated and a fine of up to two times the amount of those gains may be imposed.

Customs has the authority to pursue administrative sanctions for activities that do not constitute smuggling including:

- Unintentional undervaluation of dutiable value of imports
- Failure/ refusal to properly mark imported merchandise with the country of origin
- Misclassification of merchandise
- Inadequate records and documentation to substantiate a customs transaction
- Importation/exportation of prohibited or restricted merchandise which is declared

For violations of the law that do not fall within the definition of smuggling, Customs may impose a monetary penalty ranging from RMB 5000 (US$605) up to the value of the imported goods.

If a violation of customs supervisory or control provisions is not discovered until at least three years after the violation occurred, the party concerned is exempt from a penalty. Customs may detain goods or means of transport for any suspected violation of the law. In certain situations, Customs may release the items and demand a security deposit or collateral in the same amount of value as the impounded items. Since customs bonds are not recognized in China, Customs usually requires cash as a security deposit.

A foreigner who fails to pay duties or a penalty imposed by Customs must post security or other form of collateral equivalent to the amount due. If customs officials have reasons to believe that the funds are the result of a violation of customs laws and regulations, they may confiscate a foreigner's bank account.

Customs must issue a written penalty notice to the interested party for any act of smuggling or other violation of customs laws and regulations. If an interested party disagrees with a penalty decision of Customs, the party may file an application for review with a higher level of Customs within thirty days of receipt of the penalty notice. A decision on a review application must be made within ninety days. An interested party may appeal an administrative review decision by filing a complaint with the intermediate level People's Court within thirty days of receiving the decision. In addition to an appeal of an administrative review, an interested party may also file an action directly with the People's Court for review of an original penalty notice. A party that elects the remedy of judicial review is not permitted to file an application for administrative review with

Customs. The court process is a less than perfect forum for resolving disputes, although the quality of the courts is improving.

Customs can pursue criminal prosecution for:

- Significant undervaluation
- Intentionally failing to declare the importation or exportation of prohibited or restricted merchandise
- Falsifying records and documents used to substantiate a Customs transactions

Criminal penalties under customs laws and criminal laws include capital punishment, imprisonment, detention, confiscation and fines.

If underpayment of duty is a result of a violation of customs laws and regulations, the limitations period for collection is three years from the date of importation. For actions that are considered criminal violations, there is no statute of limitations.

CUSTOMS AUDITS AND INSPECTIONS

Customs may demand production of various documents including customs declaration documents, accounting books, financial statements, accounting vouchers, computer records, and other relevant data that has a direct relationship to the import/export activities of the company in question. The administration also may demand documentation supporting a customs transaction within three years of the importation date. Customs is only required to give an enterprise three days written notice before conducting an inspection of the production facilities, and to question employees and managers on customs transactions.

CUSTOMS COMPLIANCE STRATEGIES

Given the complexity of Chinese customs laws and their inconsistent application, it is important for companies importing into China to establish a customs compliance system and to monitor customs practices. Importers should adopt a China-tailored customs compliance program based on the US customs reasonable care standard, that is, company policy requires customs transactions to be handled with reasonable care, to comply with both the law and practice, and to be fully substantiated by supporting documentation. Documentation should be maintained to reflect the basis for decisions concerning valuation and classification, and legal opinions obtained concerning to these issues. An overall compliance strategy should also include an internal or neutral third-party audit of customs practices to determine if practices are inconsistent with current requirements.

Employees and managers in China should be trained in China's customs laws, regulations and practices, and on company compliance policies. Since the "Chinese way" of addressing customs issues may be inconsistent with China's written laws and WTO obligations, employees should be trained to exercise caution in dealing with customs transactions. For example, corruption by underpaid customs officials is rampant and while engaging in corrupt practices may be the "Chinese way," such practices violate China's own written laws. In addition, communications with Customs should be delegated to trained and loyal employees. Problem investigations oftentimes are triggered by disgruntled employees over practices that they created. Hence, companies should not rely upon local employees to manage customs compliance practices in a country with a transitioning legal system.

Given that the practices of customs officials at the local level may be at odds with China's WTO obligations or national laws, importers should closely monitor the practices of customs officials at the local level and raise any non-compliance issues at the national level, despite spotty national compliance enforcement. Similarly, it is important that importers raise any non-compliance issues with the US Embassy personnel that actively monitor China's WTO compliance record (specifically the Trade Facilitation Office). A compliance strategy should also include full cooperation with Customs. If in doubt, careful discussions with local and national authorities will help improve an importer's relationship with Customs and better gauge how Customs will react to certain issues.

With mounting pressure on the customs administration to collect revenue to compensate for post-WTO tariff shortfalls, importers must make customs compliance a priority, or risk losing a competitive edge in one of the world's burgeoning markets.

CHINESE CUSTOMS REGULATIONS PROHIBITIONS

Chinese border crossings are generally very easy. All visitors entering China must fill out customs declaration forms upon arrival. The departure copy will be stapled in your passport and must be submitted as you exit China. Reasonable amounts of money (currently up to $5,000 US), alcohol and cigarettes, cameras, and tape-recorders can be brought into China. Certain valuable items, such as amateur video and camera equipment, computers, and gold, must be declared on the form.

NOTE: Tourists may bring 8mm, 1/2 inch VHS, or small-format digital video camcorders by declaring the equipment upon entry-provided that the tapes produced in China are not intended for commercial use. But professional video or audio recording equipment requires special authorization. Importing arms and ammunition, narcotic drugs, and printed or video material "detrimental to China's politics, economy, culture, or ethics" is forbidden.

1. CUSTOMS CLEARANCE

According to related laws and regulations, the luggage of inbound and outbound passengers must be under customs supervision and control. Passengers should make factually declaration to the customs on the actual information on the luggage they carry into or out of the territory.

2. RESTRICTED INBOUND AND OUTBOUND ITEMS

Passenger's Personal Articles
Each passenger is allowed to carry a camera, a portable tape recorder, a small movie camera, a portable video camera, and a portable word processor. If exceeding the scope, he or she should make declaration to the customs. Passengers should bring what they have brought with them back on their departure with the permission of the customs.

Gold, Silver, and Articles Made of These Metals
Passengers with gold, silver, and articles made of these metals, each exceeding 50 grams, should make declaration to the customs, and should carry out. Gold, silver, and their products (including new arts and crafts articles, such as inlays and containers) bought from fixed shops shall be released by the customs after examination of the Special Receipts issued by the People's Bank of China.

Foreign Currencies
There is no limitation for the amount of foreign currencies, traveler's check to carry into China.

Inbound passengers who are residents of China carrying more than US$2,000 or non-resident passengers with more than US$5,000 or an equivalent amount in other foreign currencies should make a declaration to the customs.

Renminbi (RMB)
The limit of Renminbi for inbound and outbound passengers is 6,000 yuan. Inbound and outbound passengers with more than 6,000 yuan will not allowed to enter or leave the territory.

Cultural Relics (including works of died famous contemporary calligraphers and painters)
If inbound passengers with cultural relics want to carry the relics out of the territory, they should make a clear declaration to the customs. Passengers could carry out the relics bought in China with the appraisal by the Chinese administrative departments for cultural relics. When cultural relics leave the territory, the customs shall release them after examination against the export permit from these departments and the appraisal marks stamped on the relics.Passengers trying to carry cultural relics out of the territory without declaring them to the customs may face criminal charge.

3. ARTICLES PROHIBITED FROM ENTRY AND EXIT

Articles Not Allowed into China
◇Various weapons, imitation weapons, ammunition, and explosives;
◇Counterfeit money and forged securities;
◇Printed matter, negatives, re- cords, films, audio and video recordings, laser optical video-discs, computer storage media and other articles containing materials deemed harmful to China politically, economically, culturally, or ethically;
◇Deadly poisons, Opium, morphine, heroin, marijuana, and other narcotics;
◇Dangerous bacteria, harmful insects, and other harmful animals, plants, and their products;
◇Food, drugs, and other articles from epidemic-stricken areas if such articles may be harmful to human beings and animals.

Articles that may not be taken out of China
◇All articles mentioned above as prohibited for entry
◇Manuscripts, printed matter, negatives, photos, records, films, audio and video recordings, laser optical video disc, computer storage medium and similar articles if they contain state secrets;
◇Cultural relics and relics not permitted to exit;
◇Endangered and protected animals and plants (including specimens), their seeds and breeding materials.

CUSTOMS REGULATIONS

Items such as watches, radios, cameras, and calculators imported duty free for personal use may not be transferred or sold to others. Gifts and articles carried on behalf of others must be declared to the customs inspector and are subject to duty.
Chinese customs regulations prohibit the import or export of the following items:

(a) arms, ammunition, and explosives;
(b) radio transmitter-receivers and principal parts;
(c) Chinese currency (renminbi);
(d) books, films, records, tapes, etc. which are “detrimental to China's politics, economy, culture, and ethics” (e.g. pornographic or religious content)
(e) poisonous drugs and narcotics;
(f) infected animal or plant products; and
(g) infected foodstuffs.

Note: Videotapes may be confiscated by Chinese customs to determine that they do not violate prohibitions noted in item (d), above. Tapes are sometimes held for several months before being returned. (There is no guarantee that they will ever be returned.)

Export of the following items is also prohibited:

(a) valuable cultural relics and rare books relating to Chinese history, culture, and art;
(b) rare animals, rare plants and their seeds; and
(c) precious metals and diamonds and articles made from them.

Antiques and imitations approved for export are marked with a red wax seal.

SUPPLEMENTS

SELECTED BUSINESS AND GOVERNMENT CONTACTS

CHINESE GOVERNMENT CONTACTS

1. A. State Council

General Office of the State Council:
2 Fuyou St., Beijing 100017
Secretary General: Luo Gan
Tel: (86-10) 6309-6998:
Contact: Zheng Youmei, Director-general Office

B. State Commissions

State Commission of Science, Technology, and Industry for
National Defence
1 Aimin Street, West City District, Beijing 100034, China
Minister: Liu Jibin
Tel: (86-10) 6603-4714
Fax: (86-10) 6616-9811
Contact: Feng Hui, Officer of Foreign Affairs Bureau

State Development Planning Commission
38 Yuetannanjie, Xicheng District, Beijing 100824, China
Minister: Zeng Peiyan
Tel: (86-10) 6850-2401/ 6850-2117
Fax: (86-10) 6850-2728
Contact: Yu Guodong, Director of Foreign, American, and Oceanic
Affairs

State Economic and Trade Commission
26 Xuanwumen Xidajie, Beijing 100053, China
Minister: Sheng Huaren
Tel: (86-10) 6304-5328
Fax: (86-10) 6304-5326

State Ethnic Affairs Commission
252 Taipingqiaodajie, Xicheng District, Beijing 100800, China
Minister: Li Dezhu
Tel: (86-10) 6603-2288 X6404
Fax: (86-10) 6602-4925
Contact: Li Xinya, Director of Foreign Affairs Bureau

State Family Planning Commission
14 Zhichunlu, Haidian District, Beijing 100088, China
Minister: Zhang Weiqing
Tel: (86-10) 6205-1848
Fax: (86-10) 6205-1865
Contact: Chong Jing, Director

C. Ministries

Ministry of Agriculture
11 Nongzhanguan Nanli, Beijing 100026, China
Minister: Chen Yaobang
Tel: (86-10) 6419-2452
Fax: (86-10) 6419-2468
Contact: Hu Yanan, Director of American Oceanic Cooperation &
Exchange

Ministry of Civil Affairs
147 Beiheyan Dajie, Beijing 100721, China
Minister: Doji Cering
Tel: (86-10) 6525-5674
Fax: (86-10) 6512-1882/6525-4462
Contact: Cai Mei, Dpty Chief of Liaison Office

Ministry of Communications
11 Jianguomennei Dajie, Beijing 100736, China
Minister: Huang Zhendong
Tel: (86-10) 6529-2249
Fax: (86-10) 6529-2201
Contact: Hu Jinglu, Director of Foreign Affairs Office

Ministry of Construction
Baiwanzhuang, Haidian District, Beijing 100835, China
Minister: Yu Zhengsheng
Tel: (86-10) 6839-3833
Fax: (86-10) 6831-3669
Contact: Shen Jian Guo, Director of Foreign Affairs Department

Ministry of Culture
Jia 83 Dong'anmen Beijie, Beijing 100722, China
Minister: Sun Jiazheng
Tel: (86-10) 6555-2035
Fax: (86-10) 6555-1958
6555-1959
Contact: Sun Weixue, Director of External Cultural Relations

Ministry of Education
37 Damacang Hutong, Xidan, Beijing 100820, China
Minister: Chen Zhili
Tel: (86-10) 6609-3647
Fax: (86-10) 6601-1049
Contact: Zhang Xiao Dong

Ministry of Finance
3 Nansanxiang, Sanlihe, Xicheng District, Beijing 100820, China
Minister: Xiang Huaicheng
Tel: (86-10) 6855-2128

Fax: (86-10) 6851-3428
Contact: Zhu Xian, Director of International Cooperation

Ministry of Foreign Affairs
2 Chaoneidajie, Dongcheng District, Beijing 100701, China
Minister: Tang Jiaxuan
Tel: (86-10) 6596-1114
Fax: (86-10)
Contact: Yang Jiechi, Director of American & Oceanian Department
Ministry of Foreign Trade and Economic Co-operation
2 Dongchang'an Jie, Beijing 100731, China
Minister: Shi Guangsheng
Tel: (86-10) 6519-8804
Fax: (86-10) 6519-8904
Contact: Ma Xiaoye, Dpty Director of American and Oceanic Affairs

Ministry of Health
44 Houhaibeiyan, Xicheng District, Beijing 100725, China
Minister: Zhang Wenkang
Tel: (86-10)
Fax: (86-10) 6401-2369
Contact:

Ministry of Information Industry
13 Xichang'anjie, Beijing 100804, China
Minister: Wu Jichuan
Tel: (86-10) 6603-8848
Fax: (86-10) 6201-6362
Contact:

Ministry of Justice
10 Chaoyangmen Nandajie, Beijing 100020, China
Minister: Gao Changli
Tel: (86-10) 6520-5213
Fax: (86-10) 6520-5316
Contact: Xu Jingfeng, Director of Foreign Affairs Office

Ministry of Labour and Social Security
12 Hepingli Zhongjie, Dongcheng District, Beijing 100716, China
Minister: Zhang Zuoji
Tel: (86-10)
Fax: (86-10) 6421-8350
Contact: Zhang Youyun, Director of Foreign Affairs

Ministry of Land and Resources
64 Funeidajie, Xicheng District, Beijing 100812, China
Minister: Zhou Yongkang
Tel: (86-10) 6616-8302
Fax: (86-10) 6617-5851
Contact: Li Yuwei, (Temp) Director of Foreign Affairs

Ministry of National Defense
20 Jingshanqianjie, Beijing 100009, China
Minister: Chi Haotian
Tel: (86-10)
Fax: (86-10) 6201-8356
Contact: Zhang Liantai, Senior Colonel, Foreign Affairs Bureau

Ministry of Personnel
12 Hepingli Zhongjie, Beijing 100716, China
Minister: Song Defu
Tel: (86-10)
Fax: (86-10) 6421-1417
Contact: Xu Zhenhuan, Director of Foreign Affairs Office

Ministry of Public Security
14 Dongchang'anjie, Beijing 100741, China
Minister: Jia Chunwang
Tel: (86-10) 6520-3329
Fax: (86-10) 6524-1516
Contact: Liu Yie Feng, Director of Foreign Affairs Office

Ministry of Railways
10 Fuxing Lu, Haidian District, Beijing 100844, China
Minister: Fu Zhihuan
Tel: (86-10) 6324-2815
Fax: (86-10) 6324-2150
Contact: Tang Wensheng, Director of Foreign Affairs Dept.
Lu Xusheng, Deputy Division Chief-foreign Affairs
Office

Ministry of Science and Technology
15 Fuxinglu, Xicheng District, Beijing 100038, China
Minister: Zhu Lilan
Tel: (86-10) 6851-5544 X1311
Fax: (86-10) 6851-5004
Contact:

Ministry of State Security
14 Dongchang'anjie, Beijing 100741, China
Minister: Xu Yongyue
Tel: (86-10) 6524-4702
Contact: Li Yintang, Director of Foreign Affairs

Ministry of Supervision
4 Zaojunmiao, Haidian District, Beijing 100081, China
Minister: He Yong
Tel: (86-10) 6225-4149
Contact: Li Zhilun, Director of Foreign Affairs Office

Ministry of Water Resources

2 Baiguanglu 'Ertiao, Xuanwu District, Beijing 100053, China
Minister: Niu Maosheng
Tel: (86-10) 6320-2691
Fax: (86-10) 6354-8037
Contact: Shen Guoyi, Director of Foreign Affairs Office

National Audit Office
1 Beiluyuan, Zhanlanlu, Xicheng District, Beijing 100830, China
Minister: Li Jinhua
Tel: (86-10) 6830-1221
Fax: (86-10) 6833-0958
Contact: Chen Hua, Deputy Director General

People's Bank of China
32 Chengfangjie, Xicheng District, Beijing 100800, China
Governor: Dai Xianglong
Tel: (86-10) 6619-4114/6480-1188
Fax: (86-10) 6601-5346
Contact: Zhang Zhixiang, Director of Int'l Affairs Department

D. Bureaux and Administration Directly under the State Council

Bureau of Government Offices Administration
22 Xi'anmen Dajie, Beijing 100017, China
Director: Jiao Huancheng
Tel: (86-10) 6603-6884
Contact: Lu Shiquang, Director of Foreign Affairs

Civil Aviation Administration of China
155 Dongsi Xidajie, Beijing 100710, China
Director: Chen Guangyi
Tel: (86-10) 6401-2233
Fax: (86-10) 6401-6918
Contact: Lu Ruiling, Director of Foreign Affairs Office

Counsellor's Office under the State Council
11 Qianmen Dongdajie, Beijing 100006, China
Director: Xu Zhijian
Tel: (86-10) 6522-5433
Fax: (86-10) 6513-8170
Contact: Yin Junjie, Director of General Office

General Administration of Customs
6 Jianguomennei Dajie, Beijing 100730, China
Director: Qian Guanlin
Tel: (86-10) 6519-4114
Fax: (86-10) 6512-6020
Contact: Mr. Liu Yulin, Director of Foreign Affairs

National Tourism Administration
Jia 9 Jianguomennei Dajie, Beijing 100740, China
Director: He Guangwei
Tel: (86-10) 6520-1318
Fax: (86-10) 6512-2096
Contact: Li Hanben, Director of Foreign Affairs Office

State Administration for Industry and Commerce
8 Sanlihe Donglu, Xicheng District, Beijing 100820, China
Director: Wang Zhongfu
Tel: (86-10) 6801-0463
Fax: (86-10) 6801-0463
Contact: Hu Muying, Director of Foreign Affairs Office

State Administration of Religious Affairs
22 Xi'anmen Dajie, Beijing 100017, China
Director: Ye Xiaowen
Tel: (86-10) 6601-3565
Fax: (86-10) 6601-3565
Contact: Xu Yanjie

State Administration of Radio, Film, and Television
2 Fuxingmenwai Dajie, Beijing 100866, China
Minister: Tian Congming
Tel: (86-10) 6609-3114
Fax: (86-10) 6609-2437
Contact: Mu Yuanhe, Director of Foreign Affairs Office

State Bureau of Quality and Technical Supervision
4 Zhichunlu, Haidian District, Beijing 100088, China
Director: Li Chuangqing
Tel: (86-10) 6204-6181
Fax: (86-10) 6203-1010
Contact: Liu Xinmin

State Bureau of Taxation
5 Yangfangdian Xilu, Haidian District, Beijing 100038, China
Director: Jin Renqing
Tel: (86-10) 6341-7277
Fax: (86-10) 6341-7203
Contact: Xu Jiatong, Director of Foreign Exchange & Cooperation

State Drug Administration
Jia 38 Beilishilu, Xicheng District, Beijing 100810, China
Director: Zheng Xiaoyu
Tel: (86-10) 6831-3344
Fax: (86-10) 6831-5648
Contact: Huang Jiye, Director of Foreign Affairs Office

State Environmental Protection Administration
115 Xizhimennei Nanxiaojie, Beijing 100035, China
Minister: Xie Zhenhua
Tel: (86-10) 6615-3366

Fax: (86-10) 6605-1762
Contact: Cheng Weixue, Deputy Chief of Foreign Affairs

State Forestry Bureau
18 Hepingli Dongjie, Beijing 100714, China
Director: Wang Zhibao
Tel: (86-10) 6422-9944
Fax: (86-10) 6421-3193
Contact: Yang Yuchou, Director of International Cooperation

State Intellectual Property Office
6 Xituchenglu, Jimenqiao, Haidian District, Beijing 100088, China
Director: Gao Lulin
Tel: (86-10) 6209-3276
Fax: (86-10) 6201-9615
Contact: Qiao Dexi

State Press and Publication Administration
85 Dongsi Nandajie, Beijing 100703, China
Director: Yu Youxian
Tel: (86-10) 6512-4433
Fax: (86-10) 6512-7825
Contact: Shi Feng, Director of Foreign Affairs

State Sport General Administration
9 Tiyuguanlu, Chongwen District, Beijing 100763, China
Minister: Wu Shaozu
Tel: (86-10) 6711-2233 Ext. 2324
Fax: (86-10) 6711-1154
Contact: Wu Shaozu, Deputy Director of Foreign Affairs Office

State Statistical Bureau
75 Yuetannanjie, Sanlihe, Beijing 100826, China
Director: Liu Hong
Tel: (86-10) 6326-6600
Fax: (86-10)
Contact: du Weiqun, Director of Foreign Affairs Office

E. Offices

Foreign Affairs Office
Zhongnanhai, Beijing 100017, China
Director: Liu Huaqiu
Tel: (86-10) 6309-8375
Contact:

Hong Kong and Macao Affairs Office
77 Yuetannanjie, Beijing 100037, China
Director: Liao Hui
Tel: (86-10) 6857-6808
Fax: (86-10) 6857-6639
Contact: Zhang Xiaoyu, Director of Foreign Affairs

Information Office
22 Anyuanbeili, Chaoyang, Beijing 100029, China
Director: Zhao Qizheng
Tel: (86-10) 6491-2924
Contact:

Legislative Affairs Office
9 Wenjinjie, Beijing 100017, China
Director: Yang Jingyu
Tel: (86-10) 6309-4168
Fax: (86-10) 6309-7699
Contact: Xuan Lia, Director of Foreign Affairs

Office of Overseas Chinese Affairs
271 Fuwaidajie, Beijing 100037, China
Director: Guo Dongpo
Tel: (86-10) 6832-9955
Fax: (86-10) 6401-4639
Contact: Mr Tao, Director of Division of American Affairs

Research Office
Zhongnanhai, Beijing 100017, China
Director: Gui Shiyong
Tel: (86-10) 6309-7785
Contact:

State Economic Restructuring Office
22 Xi'anmen Dajie, Beijing 100017, China
Director: Liu Zhongli
Tel: (86-10) 6309-9065
Fax: (86-10) 6309-7362
Contact: Wang Zhichen, Director of Foreign Affairs Department

Taiwan Affairs Office
270a Fuwaidajie, Beijing 100037, China
Director: Chen Yunlin
Tel: (86-10) 6846-5135
Fax: (86-10) 6847-8780
Contact:

F. Institutions

China Meteorological Bureau
46 Baishiqiaolu, Haidian District, Beijing 100081, China
Director: Wen Kegang
Tel: (86-10) 6840-6462
Fax: (86-10) 6831-8070
Contact: Wang Xiaomin, Director of International Affairs

Chinese Securities Regulatory Commission
16 Jinrongdajie, Xicheng District, Beijing 100032, China
Director: Zhou Zhengqing
Tel: (86-10) 6621-1188

Chinese Academy of Engineering
3 Fuxinglu, Haidian District, Beijing 100038,

China
President: Zhu Guangya
Tel: (86-10) 6851-9685

Chinese Academy of Sciences
52 Sanlihe, Xicheng District, Beijing 100864, China
President: Lu Yongxiang
Tel: (86-10) 6859-7289

Chinese Academy of Social Sciences
5 Jianneidajie, Beijing 100732, China
President: Ti Tieying
Tel: (86-10) 6513-7915
Fax: (86-10) 6513-8154

Development Research Centre
22 Xi'anmendajie, Beijing 100017, China
Director: Wang Mengkui
Tel: (86-10) 6309-9568/6309-9162/6601-3381
Fax: (86-10) 6601-3530

National School of Administration
11 Changwajie, Haidian District, Beijing 100081, China
President: Wang Zhongyu
Tel: (86-10) 6892-9337
Fax: (86-10) 6842-7895
Contact: Lu Lingxiang

State Seismological Bureau
63 Fuxing Lu, Haidian District, Beijing 100036, China
Director: Chen Zhangli
Tel: (86-10) 6821-5977

Fax: (86-10) 6821-0995
Ca: 222351 Ssb Cn
Contact: Wang Hongzhen

Xinhua News Agency
57 Xuanwumen Xidajie, Beijing 100803, China
Director: Guo Chaoren
Tel: (86-10) 6307-3767
Fax: (86-10) 6307-3735

BUREAUX SUPERVISED BY COMMISSIONS AND MINISTRIES

State Administration for Inspection of Import and Export
Commodities
Jia 10 Chaowai Dajie, Beijing 100020, China
Director: Tian Runzhi
Tel: (86-10) 6599-4329
Fax: (86-10) 6500-2163
Contact: Qiu Yiliang, Director of Supervision & Control Division

State Administration of Foreign Exchange
18 Fuchenglu, Beijing 100037, China
Director: Wu Xiaoling
Tel: (86-10) 6840-2147
Fax: (86-10) 6840-2147
Contact: Mi Ling

State Administration of Traditional Chinese Medicine
Building 13, Bajiazhuang Dongli, Chaoyang District, Beijing
100026, China
Director: Zhang Wenkang
Tel: (86-10) 6506-3322

State Bureau of Cultural Relics
29 Wusidajie, Shatan, Dongcheng District, Beijing 100009, China
Director: Zhang Wenbin
Tel: (86-10) 6401-5577
Fax: (86-10) 6401-3101
Contact: Wang Limei

State Bureau of Foreign Experts Affairs
Friendship Hotel, Haidian District, Beijing 100086, China
Director: Wan Xueyan
Tel: (86-10) 6842-5528

State Bureau of Surveying & Mapping
9 Sanlihelu, Baiwanzhuang, Beijing 100830, China
Director: Jin Xiangwen
Tel: (86-10) 6834-0873

State Coal Industry Bureau
21 Hepingli Beijie, Beijing 100713, China
Director: Zhang Baoming
Tel: (86-10) 6421-7766
Fax: (86-10) 6423-5838
Contact: Bo Ran, Chief of General Office

State Grain Reserve Bureau
Zijincheng Hotel, 15 Suojiafen, Haidian District, Beijing 100088,
China
Director: Luo Zhiling
Tel: (86-10) 6225-6688

State Internal Trade Bureau
25 Yuetan Beijie, Xicheng District, Beijing 100834, China
Director: Yang Shude
Tel: (86-10) 6839-2000
Fax: (86-10) 6839-1296

State Light Industry Bureau
Yi 22 Fuwaidajie, Beijing 100083, China
Director: Chen Shineng
Tel: (86-10) 6839-6114

State Machine-building Industry Bureau
46 Sanlihelu, Xicheng District, Beijing 100823, China
Director: Shao Qihui
Tel: (86-10) 6859-4966
Fax: (86-10) 6859-5474

State Metallurgical Industry Bureau
46 Dongsi Xidajie, Dongcheng District, Beijing 100711, China
Director: Wang Wanbin
Tel: (86-10) 6513-1921
Fax: (86-10) 6513-0074
Contact: Ru Zhiai

State Oceanography Bureau
1 Fuxingmenwai Dajie, Beijing 100860, China
Director: Zhang Dengyi
Tel: (86-10) 6804-2695
Fax: (86-10) 6803-0799
Contact: Li Jingguang, Director of International Affairs

State Petrochemical Industry Bureau
Building 16, 4 District, Anhuili, Yayuncun, Chaoyang District,
Beijing 100723, China
Director: Li Yongwu
Tel: (86-10) 6491-4455
Fax: (86-10) 6491-5707
Contact: He Fan, Director of Department of International
Cooperation

State Postal Bureau
Jia 8 Beilishilu, Xicheng District, Beijing 100808, China
Director: Liu Liqing
Tel: (86-10) 6831-5837

State Textile Industry Bureau
12 Dongchang'anjie, Beijing 100742, China
Director: du Yuzhou
Tel: (86-10) 6308-1114

State Tobacco Monopoly Bureau
11 Hufanglu, Xuanwu District, Beijing 100052, China
Director: Ni Yijin
Tel: (86-10) 6353-3399

H. Associations & Corporations

All-china Federation of Industry and Commerce
93 Beiheyan Dajie, Beijing 100006
Chairman: Jing Shuping
Tel: (86-10) 6513-6677 Ext. 2233, 2234
Fax: (86-10) 6513-1769
Contact: Shao Weisheng, Director of Liaison Department

China Council for the Promotion of International Trade
1 Fuxingmenwai Street, Beijing 100860
President: Guo Dongpo
Tel: (86-10) 68013344
Fax: (86-10) 68011370
Contact: Ding Zhongze, Director of Liaison Department

China Huaneng Group
Room 901, Huaneng Building, 23a Fuxing Road, Haidian District
Beijing 100036, China
President: Liu Jinlong
Tel: (86-10) 6822-3356
Fax: (86-10) 6822-3349
Contact: Li Guanglin (Manager of International Department)

China International Trust and Investment Corporation
Capital Mansion, 6 Xinyuan Nanlu, Chaoyangqu, Beijing 100004
China
President: Wang Jun
Tel: (86-10) 6466-1195
Fax: (86-10) 6466-8816
Contact: Guo Zepei, Division Chief of Public Relations

China National Automotive Industry Corporation
27b Liuyin Jie, Xichengqu, Beijing 100009, China
President: Cai Shiqing
Tel: (86-10) 6601-1319
Fax: (86-10) 6601-1393
Contact: Li Zichun, Director of Foreign Affairs

China National Nonferrous Metals Industry Corporation
B12 Fuxing Lu, Xicheng, Beijing 100814, China
President: Fei Ziwen
Tel: (86-10) 6801-4423
Fax: (86-10) 6801-4424
Contact: Pen Wenju, Head of Foreign Affairs Department

China National Offshore Oil Corp.
Jingwin Building 2a, Dongsanhuan Beilu, Beijing 100027, China
President: Wang Yan
Tel: (86-10) 6466-2195
Fax: (86-10) 6466-2994
Contact: Li Rongguo, Manager of Foreign Affairs

China National Petroleum Corp.
P.o. Box 766, Liupukang, Beijing 100724, China
President: Wang Tao
Tel: (86-10) 6201-6107, 2094798
Fax: (86-10) 6209-4806
Contact: Li Huaiqi, Director of Foreign Affairs

Department

China National Tobacco Corporation:
11 Hufang Rd., Xuanwu District, Beijing 100052, China
President: Xun Xinghua
Tel: (86-10) 6301-3399-2263
Fax: (86-10) 6301-5330
Contact: Mu Chonglin, Director of Foreign Affairs Department

China North Industries Corp.
7a Yuetan Nanjie, Beijing 100045, China
President: Zhang Junjiu
Tel: (86-10) 6801-3716
Fax: (86-10) 6803-3236
Contact: Yang Zeliang, Manager of Foreign Affairs

China Petro-chemical Corporation
24 Xiaoguan Jie, Andingmenwai, Beijing 100013, China
President: Sheng Huaren
Tel: (86-10) 6421-6731
Fax: (86-10) 6426-6731
Contact: Qiao Yingbin, Head of Foreign Affairs Department

China State Construction Engineering Corporation
9 Sanlihe Rd., Xicheng District, Beijing 100835, China
President: Ma Tingui
Tel: (86-10) 6834-7766
Fax: (86-10) 6831-4326
Contact: Bao Jianguo, Director of Foreign Affairs Department

China State Shipbuilding Corporation
5 Yuetanbeijie, Xicheng District, Beijing 100861, China
President: Wang Rongshang
Tel: (86-10) 6831-8833
Contact: Li Jian, Head of Foreign Affairs Department

Everbright Industrial Corp.
Building 5 Xiyuan Hotel, Haidian District, Beijing 100046, China
President: Qiu Qing
Tel: (86-10) 6857-1226
Fax: (86-10) 6857-1121
Contact: Wang Xiaoren, Director of Foreign Affairs

People's Insurance Company of China
410 Fuchengmen Dajie, Beijing 100034, China
President: Ma Yongwei
Tel: (86-10) 6601-6688 Ext.1109; 6601-1870 (Foreign Affairs Office)
Fax: (86-10) 6601-1870
Contact: Xu Yanqing, Division Chief

2. Chambers of Commerce/Trade Associations

American Chamber of Commerce in Beijing
Rudy Schlais, Chairman
Mike Furst, Executive Director
Room 318, Great Wall Sheraton Hotel
Beijing 100026
Tel: (86-10) 6590-5566, X 2378
Fax: (86-10) 6590-5273

American Soybean Association
Phillip W. Laney, Representative
China World Tower, Room 1323
Beijing 100004
Tel: (86-10) 6505-1830, 6505-1831, 6505-3533
Fax: (86-10) 6505-2201

China Chamber of International Commerce
1 Fuxingmenwai Street
Beijing 100860
Tel: (86-10) 6851-3344
Fax: (86-10) 6851-1370

China Council for the Promotion of International Trade
Guo Dongpo, Chairman
1 Fuxingmenwai Street
Beijing 100860
Tel: (86-10) 6851-2867
Fax: (86-10) 6851-1370, 6851-7153

U.S.-China Business Council
Michele Liedeker, Chief Representative
Citic Building, Room 260
Beijing 100004
Tel: (86-10) 6500-2255, X2664 or 2670
Fax: (86-10) 6512-5854, 6592-0727

U.s. Feed Grains Council
Todd Meyer, Director
China World Tower, Room 1320
Beijing 100004
Tel: (86-10) 6505-1314, 6505-1302
Fax: (86-10) 6505-2320

U.s. Wheat Associates
Zhao Shipu, Director
China World Tower, Room 1318
Beijing 100004
Tel: (86-10) 6505-1278, 6505-3866
Fax: (86-10) 6505-5138

3. Market Research Firms

China International Economic Consultants, Inc.
Yao Jirong

13/f Capital Mansion
6 Xin Yuan Nan Road
P.o. Box 9412
Beijing 100004
Tel: (86-10) 6466-0088, X1315
Fax: (86-10) 6466-2468

Connections Consulting Company of China
Zhao Qi
P. O. Box 1131
4a Zhangzizhong Rd., Dongcheng District
Beijing 100007
Tel: (86-10) 6407-7466
Fax: (86-10) 6401-5321

Consultec
He Xinhao, President
B-12 Guanghua Road, Jianguomenwai, Beijing 100020
Tel: (86-10) 6505-1559 or 6505-1560 or 6505-2255, Ext.1217, 1216
Fax: (86-10) 6505-1571

The Gallup Organization
Guo Xin
225 Chaoyang Men Wai Street
China Air Svc.,
Beijing 100020
Tel: (86-10) 6591-4828
Fax: (86-10) 6591-4824

Mti - Management Technologies International, Inc.
Joe T. Peebles
Room 417, 419 , Xingke Dasha
445 Anshanxi Road, Nankai District
Tianjin 300192
Tel: (86-022)747-6490, 7356
Fax: (86-022)747-6491

Wki - William Kent International, Inc.
Min Zhao, Andrew Tilton
5/f, Catch Bldg.
31 Bei San Huan Zhong Road
Beijing, China 100088
Tel: (86-10) 6236-8021-8027
Fax: (86-10) 6236-8028

BANKS

Chinese:

AGRICULTURE BANK OF CHINA
Chen Jianjie, Director of Foreign Affairs Office
40 Fucheng Road, Yulong Hotel 3/F #3008
Beijing, China 100046
Tel: (86-10) 6841-5588 x23007-23009/2301
Fax: (86-10) 6842-6740

BANK OF CHINA (Headquarters)
Li Aihua, Chief of American & Oceanic Division
410 Fuchengmennei Dajie
Beijing, China 100818
Tel: (86-10) 6601-1829; 601-6688 (SB)
Fax: (86-10)6601-4096

CITIC INDUSTRIAL BANK
Dou Jianzhong, President
Fu Hua Mansion, 8 Chaoyangmenbeidajie, Chaoyang District
Beijing , China 100027
Tel: (86-10) 6554-1895
Fax: (86-10) 6554-2181

COMMUNICATIONS BANK OF CHINA (Headquarters)
18 Xianxia Lu, Shanghai 200335
Tel: (86-21) 6275-1234 Ext. for Int'l Department
Fax: (86-21) 6270-6330

EVERBRIGHT BANK OF CHINA
Zhu Xiaohua, President
Peng Yiping, Office of Foreign Affairs
Everbright Building
No. 6 Fuxingmenwai Dajie
Beijing 100045
Tel: (86-10) 6856-1302;
6856-5577
Fax: (86-10) 6856-1301

EXPORT IMPORT BANK OF CHINA
Zhou Keren, President & Chairman
Zhu Wengen, General manger of Int'l Department
Jinyun Building
A43 Xi Zhimen Bei Dajie
Beijing, China 100044
Tel: (86-10) 6227-8899
Fax: (80-10) 6227-7637

FUJIAN INDUSTRIAL BANK
1 Hualin Huanbaolu
Fuzhou 350003, Fujian
Tel: (86-591) 784-2470
Fax: (86-591) 785-6420

GUANGDONG DEVELOPMENT BANK
Lu Jinchang, Executive VP
83 Nonglinxia Road
Guangfa Mansion,
Guangzhou 510120
Tel: (86-20) 8731-0888
Fax: (86-20)8731-0800

HUAXIA BANK
111 Xidanbeidajie, Xicheng District, Beijing 100032
Ma Xiaohua, General Manager

Ye Huatang, Director of Int'l Business Dept.
Tel: (86-10) 6618-8777
Fax: (86-10) 6618-8333

INDUSTRIAL & COMMERCIAL BANK OF CHINA (Headquarters)
XiLiu Tinghuan, President
Han Ruixiang, Chief Manager of Foreign Affairs
15 Cuiwei Road
Beijing 100036
Tel: (86-10) 6821-7273
Fax: (86-10) 6821-7920

INVESTMENT BANK OF CHINA
Cai Jinniu, Deputy GM of International Department
1 Fuwai Dajie, Sichuan Mansion, Beijing 100037
Tel: (86-10) 6384-9938
6836-4987, 6836-4959 x60
Fax: (86-10) 6836-4959

MERCHANTS BANK
Liu Keqing
5/F., Building AB, No. 3 Huaqiang Beilu
Shenzhen 518031
Guangdong Province
Tel: (86-755) 322-4905
Fax: (86-755) 321-4556

MINSHENG BANK OF CHINA
Jing Shuping (Director)
Scite Tower Torch Hall, 22 Jianguomenwai Street
Beijing 100004
Tel: (86-10) 6857-9314,6522-3226
Fax: (86-10) 6526-9572

CONSTRUCTION BANK OF CHINA (Headquarters)
Zhou Xiaochuan, President
Wan Binjiang, Director of Foreign Affairs Office
25 Jinrong Dajie
Beijing, China 100032
Tel: (86-10) 6397-4488
Fax: (86-10) 6759-8569

SHANGHAI PUDONG DEVELOPMENT BANK
50 Ningbo Road, Shanghai 200002
Tel: (86-21) 6329-6188
Fax: (86-10) 6323-2036

SHENZHEN DEVELOPMENT BANK
178 Shennan Zhong Lu
Shenzhen 518028, Guangdong
Tel: (86-755) 224-7128;
556-2114

STATE DEVELOPMENT BANK
Chen Yuan, President
Li Baoping, Dir. Of Int'l Cooperation Department
29 Fuchengmen Wai Dajie
Beijing, China 100046
Tel: (86-10) 6830-6688
Fax: (86-10) 6833-8580

U.S BANKS

AMERICAN EXPRESS BANK
Beijing Representative Office
Jean Young, Deputy Representative
Room 2313, China World Trade Centre
Beijing 100004
Tel: (86-10) 6505-2838
6505-4626
Fax: (86-10) 6505-4626

Shanghai Representative Office
Lennon Lau, Deputy Representative
Room 1502, Ruijin Building, 205 Mao Ming Nan Road
Shanghai 200002
Tel: (86-21) 6472-7589
Fax: (86-21) 6472-8400

BANK OF AMERICA
Beijing Branch
Ben K. L. Cheng, VP, Branch Manager
Unit 9-16, Level 26
China World Tower,
China World Trade Centre
Beijing 100004
Tel: (86-10) 6505-3545
6505-2609 x16
Fax: (86-10) 6505-3509

Guangzhou Branch
Li Mingwei (Manager)
Bank of America Plaza
Unit 2506-2509, 25/F
No. 555 Renmin Zhong Road
Guangzhou 510180
Tel: (86-20) 8130-0888
Fax: (86-20) 8130-0899

Shanghai Branch
James Cheng-Kuang Chiou, Manager
18th Floor, Soush Tower
Shanghai Securities Exchange Building
528 Pudong Road (South)
Pudong New Are,Shanghai 200520
Tel: (86-21) 6881-8686
Fax: (86-21) 6881-8816

BANK OF BOSTON
Beijing Representative Office
Katherine Sun, Chief Representative
10-D, CITIC Building
19 Jianguomenwai Dajie, Beijing 100004
Tel: (86-10) 6593-1850
Fax: (86-10) 6593-1852

BANK OF THE ORIENT
Xiamen Branch
Ernest Go, Manager
G/F., Overseas Chinese Front Building, Xinhua Road
Xiamen 361006
Tel: (86-592) 202-6565
Fax: (86-592) 202-5614

BANKERS TRUST COMPANY
Beijing Representative Office
Simon Wen, Chief Representative
Suite 125, Ground Floor, Lufthansa Center
50 Liangmaqiao Road, Chaoyang District, Beijing 100016
Tel: (86-10) 6594-2496
Fax: (86-10) 6594-2497

CHASE MANHATTAN BANK, N.A.
Beijing Representative Office
Christian Murck, Chief Representative
Room 509/512, China Science & Technology Exchange Centre
Beijing 100004
Tel: (86-10) 6512-3457
Fax: (86-10) 6512-3693

Tianjin Branch
Juan Van Wassenhove, General Manager
14/F., Tianjin International Building, 75 Nanjing Road Tianjin
300050
Tel: (86-22) 2339-5111
Fax: (86-22) 2339-8111

CHEMICAL BANK
Shanghai Representative Office
700A, 1376 Nanjingxi Road
ShanghaiBusinessCity, Shanghai 200002
Tel: (86-21) 6279-7288
Fax: (86-21) 6279-8101

CITIBANK, N.A.
Beijing Representative Office
William To, Chief Representative
16/F, Tower 1, Beijing Bright China Chang-An Building
No. 7 Jianguomen Nei Ave.
Dong Cheng District
Beijing 100005
Tel: (86-10) 6510-2933
Fax: (86-10) 6510-2932

Guangzhou Representative Office
Dong Shaowen, Manager
Room 1215, Main Building, Guangzhou Int'l Hotel, 339 Huanshi
Donglu, Guangzhou 510098
Tel: (86-20) 8332-1711

Fax: (86-20) 8331-1323
Shanghai Branch
John Breeman, Country Corporate Officer in China
Bell Chong, Manager
20/F Marine Tower
No. 1 Pudong Ave.
Shanghai 200520
Tel: (86-21) 5879-1200
Fax: (86-21) 5879-1132

Shenzhen Branch
Brace Leung, General Manager
37/F., International Financial Building
23 Jianshe Road
Shenzhen 528000
Tel: (86-755) 223-2338 Ext. 92300
Fax: (86-755) 223-1238

Xiamen Representative Office
Timmy Chan, Chief Representative
8/F. Merlihua Hotel Xiamen 361006
Tel: (86-592) 603-1666Ext.818
Fax: (86-592) 602-0615

FAR EAST NATIONAL BANK
Beijing Representative Office
Li Mei, Chief Representative
Room 5005, International Hotel
Beijing 100810
Tel: (86-10) 6512-6688 Ext. 5005
Fax: (86-10) 6512-9972

FIRST NATIONAL BANK OF BOSTON
Shanghai Representative Office
Gu Quanbin, Chief Representative
4/F., Shanghai Union Building, 100 Yan An Road East
Shanghai 200002
Tel: (86-21) 329-0808 ext. 55/57
Fax: (86-21) 320-0244

FIRST NATIONAL BANK OF CHICAGO
Beijing Representative Office
Robert W. Poole, Chief Representative
Room 1605, Citic Building
Beijing 100004
Tel: (86-10) 6500-3281/6500-3514; 6500-2255 x 1640/41/50
Fax: (86-10) 6500-3166

REPUBLIC NATIONAL BANK OF NEW YORK
Beijing Representative Office

Li Baoliang, Chief Representative
Room 2201, Liang Ma Tower, Chao Yang District
Beijing 100004
Tel: (86-10) 6506-6548/6506-6549
Fax: (86-10) 6506-6943

SECURITY PACIFIC NATIONAL BANK
Guangzhou Office
Ms. Chen Wen Shan, Secretary
Suite 1350-51, Garden Hotel Office Tower,
368 Huanshi Dong Road, Guangzhou
Tel: (86-20) 333-8999 ext. 1337-38
Fax: (86-20) 335-0706

CHINA INTERNATIONAL FINANCE CO. LTD.
(SECURITY PACIFIC NATIONAL
BANK JV)
Shoji Moriguchi (General Manager)
33/F., International Trade Center
Renmin Nan Road, Shenzhen, Guangdong, PRC
Tel: (86-755) 225-1510/223-7567
Fax: (86-755) 223-7566

U.S. EMBASSY CONTACTS

U.S. EMBASSY BEIJING
No. 3 Xiu Shui Beijie
Beijing, China 100600
Tel: (86-10) 6532-3831

Mailing Address from U.S.:
U.S. Embassy Beijing
Department of State
Washington, D.C. 20521-7300

AMBASSADOR'S OFFICE
Ambassador James R. Sasser
Tel: (86-10) 6532-3831, x6400
Fax: (86-10) 6532-6422

DCM William McCahill, Jr.
Tel: (86-10) 6532-3831, x6800Fax: (86-10) 6532-6422

DEFENSE ATTACHE OFFICE

Brig. General Karl Eikenberry
Defense Attache
Tel: (86-10) 6532-3831, x6667Fax: (86-10) 6532-2160

ECONOMIC SECTION
Minister-Counselor for Economic
Affairs, Robert Ludan
Tel: (86-10) 6532-3831 x6827
Fax: (86-10) 6532-6422
Deputy, Robert Goldberg
Tel: (86-10) 6532-3831 x6539
Fax: (86-10) 6532-6422

FOREIGN COMMERCIAL SERVICE
Minister-Counselor for Commercial
Affairs, Alan Turley
Tel: (86-10) 6532-6924
Fax: (86-10) 6532-3297
Deputy : William Zarit
Tel: (86-10) 6532-6924 x6107
Fax: (86-10) 6532-3297

FOREIGN AGRICULTURAL SERVICE
Agricultural Affairs Office
Minister-Counselor for Agricultural
Affairs, Suzanne Hale
Tel: (86-10) 6532-3431 x5400
Fax: (86-10) 6532-2962
Shanghai Agricultural Trade Office
Scott Reynolds, Attache
Tel: (86-21) 6279-8622
Fax: (86-21) 6279-8336
Guangzhou Agricultural Trade Office Susan
Theiler, Attache
(from August 1st)
Tel: (86-20) 8667-7553
Fax: (86-20) 8666-0703
Animal and Plant Health Inspection Service
Dale Maki, Attache
Tel: (86-10) 6505-4575
Fax: (86-10) 6505-4574

POLITICAL SECTION
Minister-Counselor for Political
Affairs, James Moriarty
Tel: (86-10) 6532-3831 x6848
Fax: (86-10) 6532-6423
Deputy, Morton Holbrook
Tel: (86-10) 6532-3831 x6040
Fax: (86-10) 6532-6423

VISA SECTION
Minister-Counselor for Consular
Affairs, David Lyon
Tel: (86-10) 6532-3431 x5208
Fax: (86-10) 6532-3178
Non-Im Visas, Dennis Halpin
Tel: (86-10) 6532-3431 x5209
Fax: (86-10) 6532-2483

AMERICAN CITIZEN SERVICES
Consul, Mary Kay Carlson
Tel: (86-10) 6532-3431 x5344
Fax: (86-10) 6532-2483

AMERICAN CONSULATE CHENGDU
No. 4 Lingshiguan Road, Section 4
Renmin Nanlu
Chengdu 610041
Consul General, Cornelius Keur
Tel: (86-28) 555-3119;
558-3520
Commercial Officer,Bob Tansey
Tel: (86-28) 558-3992
Fax: (86-28) 558-3520

AMERICAN CONSULATE GUANGZHOU
No. 1 South Shamian Street
Guangzhou 510133
Consul General,
Edward Mckeon (from July 1st)
Tel: (86-20) 8188-8911
Fax: (86-20) 8186-2341
Principal Commercial Officer,
Ned Quistoff
Tel: (86-20) 8667-4011
Fax: (86-20) 8666-0705

AMERICAN CONSULATE SHANGHAI
1469 Huaihai Zhong Lu
Shanghai 200031
Consul General, Joseph Borich
Tel: (86-21) 6433-6880
Fax: (86-21) 6433-4122
Principal Commercial Officer, Will Center
Tel: (86-21) 6279-7630
Fax: (86-21) 6279-7639

AMERICAN CONSULATE SHENYANG
No. 52, 14th Wei Road
Heping District
Shenyang 110003
Consul General, Eugene Pascua
Tel: (86-24) 2322-1198
Fax: (86-24) 2322-2206
Commercial Officer, Jon Frauefelder
Tel: (86-24) 2322-1198,
ext. 144, 147
Fax: (86-24) 2322-2206

6. Washington-based USG China Contacts

U.S. DEPARTMENT OF COMMERCE
International Trade Administration
Office of China Economic Area
Room 1229
14th & Constitution Avenue
Washington, D.C. 20230
Tel: (202) 482-3583
Fax: (202) 482-1576

Multilateral Development Bank Office
Brenda Ebeling, Director
Tel: (202) 482-3399
Fax: (202) 482-5179

TPCC Trade Information Center
Tel: 800-USA-TRADE

U.S. DEPARTMENT OF STATE
Office of China and Mongolia
Bureau of East Asia & Pacific Affairs
Room 4318, 2201 C Street, N.W.
Washington, D.C. 20520
Tel: (202) 647-6796
Fax: (202) 647-6820

U.S. DEPARTMENT OF AGRICULTURE
International Trade Policy
Asia American Division
Foreign Agricultural Service
Stop 1023
14th and Independence SW
Washington, D.C. 20250-1023
Tel: (202) 720-1289
Fax: (202) 690-1093
Email: deatonl@fas.usda.gov

AgExport Services Division
Foreign Agricultural Service
Ag Box 1052
14th and Independence SW
Washington, D.C. 20250-1080
Tel: (202) 720-6343
Fax: (202) 690-4374
Trade Assistance & Promotion Office
Tel: (202) 720-7420

OFFICE OF U.S. TRADE REPRESENTATIVE
China Desk
600 17th Street, NW
Washington, DC 20506
Tel: (202) 395-5050
Fax: (202) 395-3911

U.S.-BASED MULTIPLIERS

U.S.-CHINA BUSINESS COUNCIL
Robert Kapp, President
1818 N Street, N.W., Suite 500
Washington, D.C. 20036-5559
Tel: (202) 429-0340
Fax: (202) 775-2476

MAJOR BANKS IN CHINA

CHINESE BANKS

AGRICULTURE BANK OF CHINA
Chen Jianjie, Director of Foreign Affairs Office
40 Fucheng Road, Yulong Hotel 3/F #3008
Beijing, China 100046
Tel: (86-10) 6841-5588 x23007-23009/2301
Fax: (86-10) 6842-6740

BANK OF CHINA (Headquarters)
Li Aihua, Chief of American & Oceanic Division
410 Fuchengmennei Dajie
Beijing, China 100818
Tel: (86-10) 6601-1829; 601-6688 (SB)
Fax: (86-10)6601-4096

CITIC INDUSTRIAL BANK
Dou Jianzhong, President
Fu Hua Mansion, 8 Chaoyangmenbeidajie,
Chaoyang District
Beijing , China 100027
Tel: (86-10) 6554-1895
Fax: (86-10) 6554-2181

COMMUNICATIONS BANK OF CHINA
(Headquarters)
18 Xianxia Lu, Shanghai 200335
Tel: (86-21) 6275-1234 Ext. for Int'l Department
Fax: (86-21) 6270-6330

EVERBRIGHT BANK OF CHINA
Zhu Xiaohua, President
Peng Yiping, Office of Foreign Affairs
Everbright Building
No. 6 Fuxingmenwai Dajie
Beijing 100045
Tel: (86-10) 6856-1302;
6856-5577
Fax: (86-10) 6856-1301

EXPORT IMPORT BANK OF CHINA
Zhou Keren, President & Chairman
Zhu Wengen, General manger of Int'l Department
Jinyun Building
A43 Xi Zhimen Bei Dajie
Beijing, China 100044
Tel: (86-10) 6227-8899
Fax: (80-10) 6227-7637

FUJIAN INDUSTRIAL BANK
1 Hualin Huanbaolu
Fuzhou 350003, Fujian
Tel: (86-591) 784-2470
Fax: (86-591) 785-6420

GUANGDONG DEVELOPMENT BANK
Lu Jinchang, Executive VP
83 Nonglinxia Road
Guangfa Mansion,
Guangzhou 510120
Tel: (86-20) 8731-0888
Fax: (86-20)8731-0800

HUAXIA BANK
111 Xidanbeidajie, Xicheng District, Beijing
100032
Ma Xiaohua, General Manager
Ye Huatang, Director of Int'l Business Dept.
Tel: (86-10) 6618-8777
Fax: (86-10) 6618-8333

INDUSTRIAL & COMMERCIAL BANK OF
CHINA (Headquarters)
XiLiu Tinghuan, President
Han Ruixiang, Chief Manager of Foreign Affairs
15 Cuiwei Road
Beijing 100036
Tel: (86-10) 6821-7273
Fax: (86-10) 6821-7920

INVESTMENT BANK OF CHINA
Cai Jinniu, Deputy GM of International
Department
1 Fuwai Dajie, Sichuan Mansion, Beijing 100037
Tel: (86-10) 6384-9938
6836-4987, 6836-4959 x60
Fax: (86-10) 6836-4959

MERCHANTS BANK
Liu Keqing
5/F., Building AB, No. 3 Huaqiang Beilu
Shenzhen 518031
Guangdong Province
Tel: (86-755) 322-4905
Fax: (86-755) 321-4556

MINSHENG BANK OF CHINA
Jing Shuping (Director)
Scite Tower Torch Hall, 22 Jianguomenwai Street
Beijing 100004
Tel: (86-10) 6857-9314,6522-3226
Fax: (86-10) 6526-9572

CONSTRUCTION BANK OF CHINA
(Headquarters)
Zhou Xiaochuan, President
Wan Binjiang, Director of Foreign Affairs Office
25 Jinrong Dajie
Beijing, China 100032
Tel: (86-10) 6397-4488
Fax: (86-10) 6759-8569

SHANGHAI PUDONG DEVELOPMENT BANK
50 Ningbo Road, Shanghai 200002
Tel: (86-21) 6329-6188
Fax: (86-10) 6323-2036

SHENZHEN DEVELOPMENT BANK
178 Shennan Zhong Lu
Shenzhen 518028, Guangdong
Tel: (86-755) 224-7128;
556-2114

STATE DEVELOPMENT BANK
Chen Yuan, President
Li Baoping, Dir. Of Int'l Cooperation Department
29 Fuchengmen Wai Dajie
Beijing, China 100046
Tel: (86-10) 6830-6688
Fax: (86-10) 6833-8580

UNITED STATES BANKS

AMERICAN EXPRESS BANK
Beijing Representative Office
Jean Young, Deputy Representative
Room 2313, China World Trade Centre
Beijing 100004
Tel: (86-10) 6505-2838
6505-4626
Fax: (86-10) 6505-4626

Shanghai Representative Office
Lennon Lau, Deputy Representative
Room 1502, Ruijin Building, 205 Mao Ming Nan Road
Shanghai 200002
Tel: (86-21) 6472-7589
Fax: (86-21) 6472-8400

BANK OF AMERICA
Beijing Branch
Ben K. L. Cheng, VP, Branch Manager
Unit 9-16, Level 26
China World Tower,
China World Trade Centre
Beijing 100004
Tel: (86-10) 6505-3545
6505-2609 x16
Fax: (86-10) 6505-3509

Guangzhou Branch
Li Mingwei (Manager)
Bank of America Plaza
Unit 2506-2509, 25/F
No. 555 Renmin Zhong Road
Guangzhou 510180
Tel: (86-20) 8130-0888
Fax: (86-20) 8130-0899

Shanghai Branch
James Cheng-Kuang Chiou, Manager
18th Floor, Soush Tower
Shanghai Securities Exchange Building
528 Pudong Road (South)
Pudong New Are,Shanghai 200520
Tel: (86-21) 6881-8686
Fax: (86-21) 6881-8816

BANK OF BOSTON
Beijing Representative Office
Katherine Sun, Chief Representative
10-D, CITIC Building
19 Jianguomenwai Dajie, Beijing 100004
Tel: (86-10) 6593-1850
Fax: (86-10) 6593-1852

BANK OF THE ORIENT
Xiamen Branch
Ernest Go, Manager
G/F., Overseas Chinese Front Building, Xinhua Road
Xiamen 361006
Tel: (86-592) 202-6565
Fax: (86-592) 202-5614

BANKERS TRUST COMPANY
Beijing Representative Office
Simon Wen, Chief Representative
Suite 125, Ground Floor, Lufthansa Center
50 Liangmaqiao Road, Chaoyang District, Beijing 100016
Tel: (86-10) 6594-2496
Fax: (86-10) 6594-2497

CHASE MANHATTAN BANK, N.A.
Beijing Representative Office
Christian Murck, Chief Representative
Room 509/512, China Science & Technology Exchange Centre
Beijing 100004
Tel: (86-10) 6512-3457
Fax: (86-10) 6512-3693

Tianjin Branch
Juan Van Wassenhove, General Manager
14/F., Tianjin International Building, 75 Nanjing Road Tianjin
300050
Tel: (86-22) 2339-5111
Fax: (86-22) 2339-8111

CHEMICAL BANK
Shanghai Representative Office
700A, 1376 Nanjingxi Road
ShanghaiBusinessCity, Shanghai 200002
Tel: (86-21) 6279-7288
Fax: (86-21) 6279-8101

CITIBANK, N.A.
Beijing Representative Office
William To, Chief Representative
16/F, Tower 1, Beijing Bright China Chang-An Building
No. 7 Jianguomen Nei Ave.
Dong Cheng District
Beijing 100005
Tel: (86-10) 6510-2933
Fax: (86-10) 6510-2932

Guangzhou Representative Office
Dong Shaowen, Manager
Room 1215, Main Building, Guangzhou Int'l Hotel, 339 Huanshi
Donglu, Guangzhou 510098
Tel: (86-20) 8332-1711

Fax: (86-20) 8331-1323
Shanghai Branch
John Breeman, Country Corporate Officer in China
Bell Chong, Manager
20/F Marine Tower
No. 1 Pudong Ave.
Shanghai 200520
Tel: (86-21) 5879-1200
Fax: (86-21) 5879-1132

Shenzhen Branch
Brace Leung, General Manager
37/F., International Financial Building
23 Jianshe Road
Shenzhen 528000
Tel: (86-755) 223-2338 Ext. 92300
Fax: (86-755) 223-1238

Xiamen Representative Office
Timmy Chan, Chief Representative
8/F. Merlihua Hotel Xiamen 361006
Tel: (86-592) 603-1666Ext.818
Fax: (86-592) 602-0615

FAR EAST NATIONAL BANK
Beijing Representative Office
Li Mei, Chief Representative
Room 5005, International Hotel
Beijing 100810
Tel: (86-10) 6512-6688 Ext. 5005
Fax: (86-10) 6512-9972

FIRST NATIONAL BANK OF BOSTON
Shanghai Representative Office
Gu Quanbin, Chief Representative
4/F., Shanghai Union Building, 100 Yan An Road East
Shanghai 200002
Tel: (86-21) 329-0808 ext. 55/57
Fax: (86-21) 320-0244

FIRST NATIONAL BANK OF CHICAGO
Beijing Representative Office
Robert W. Poole, Chief Representative
Room 1605, Citic Building
Beijing 100004
Tel: (86-10) 6500-3281/6500-3514; 6500-2255 x 1640/41/50
Fax: (86-10) 6500-3166

REPUBLIC NATIONAL BANK OF NEW YORK
Beijing Representative Office
Li Baoliang, Chief Representative
Room 2201, Liang Ma Tower, Chao Yang District
Beijing 100004
Tel: (86-10) 6506-6548/6506-6549
Fax: (86-10) 6506-6943

SECURITY PACIFIC NATIONAL BANK
Guangzhou Office
Ms. Chen Wen Shan, Secretary
Suite 1350-51, Garden Hotel Office Tower,
368 Huanshi Dong Road, Guangzhou
Tel: (86-20) 333-8999 ext. 1337-38
Fax: (86-20) 335-0706

CHINA INTERNATIONAL FINANCE CO. LTD. (SECURITY PACIFIC NATIONAL BANK JV)
Shoji Moriguchi (General Manager)
33/F., International Trade Center
Renmin Nan Road, Shenzhen, Guangdong, PRC
Tel: (86-755) 225-1510/223-7567
Fax: (86-755) 223-7566

SELECTED MARKET AND BUSINESS INTELLIGENCE REPORTS

Finance
China's insurance market

Metals

A Summary of Aluminum Processing Industry in China

Chemical Industry

* Chemicals Industry
* China's Polyvinyl Chloride Industry
* China's Polypropylene Industry
* The China's Polystyrene Resin
* China's Polyethylene Industry
* The Current Situation of the Chinese Methanol Market
* China's ABS Resin Market
* Current Production Situation of Polyvinyl Chloride (PVC) Resin in China and Its Prospects in Ninth Five-Year Plan Period
* China's Chemical Fiber Industry
* Current Situation and Development of China's Glass Fibre Reinforced Plastics and Glass Fibre Industries
* Market Demand and Status Quo of China's Coating
* Raw Material Markets of China's Coating Industry
* China's Production Situation of Polyurethane Coating
* China's Automobile Coating Material
* China's Coating Material Industry
* China's Dye Intermediates
* China's Dye Industry
* China's Building Adhesive Industry
* China's Sewage Treatment Agent

Medicine

* Current Situation and Development Trend of Foreign-invested Medical Enterprises in China

* 9th Five-Year Plan For China's Medical Industry and the Situation of the Industry in 1997

Light Industry

* China's paper-making industry(1)

* China's paper-making industry(2)

Michine Building

* The Status Quo and Market Situation of China's Lift Industry
* Current Situation of China's Hydraulic Pressure Machinery Industry and Its Market
* Current Situation of China's Bearing Industry and Its Market
* Status Quo of and Market For China's Machine Tool Industry
* The Current Situation, Objectives and Market Prediction of China's Mold Industry
* China's Forklift Industry
* The Status Quo, Development Prospect and Market Forecast of the Chinese Engineering Machinery Industry
* Current Situation and Market of Chinese Plastics Machinery Industry
* Chinese Agricultural Machinery Industry and Its Market
* Current Situation and Development Prospects of Chinese Environmental Protection Machinery Industry
* The Status Quo, Development Prospect and Market Forecast of the Chinese Engineering Machinery Industry
* Current Situation and Market of Chinese Packing and Food Machinery Industry

* Chinese Food Machinery Industry and Its Market
* China's Packaging Machinery Industry and Market
* China's Battery Industry: the Current Situation and Development Prospect
* The Current Situatiuon and Market of China's Electrical Power Equipment Industry

* Market Research Report On Small Household Electrical Appliance in China (Content)

Motor Vehicles

* Market Demand and Policy Support of Chinese Bus Industry
* China's 9th Five-Year Plan For the Automotive Industry and the Tentative Ideas For the Development of the Auto-Parts Industry
* Current Situation and Development Trend of China's High-Speed Coach
* Current Situation and Development Trend of China's High-Speed Coach
* China's Sedan Car: the Production and the Market
* A Survey of China's Sedan Market, Industry and Importation
* Prospects For China's Light Vehicle Market in 1998
* Analysis and Forecast of the Mini-Vehicle Market in China
* Chinese Automobile Market Forecast in 1998
* The Situation and Forecast of the Heavy-Duty Truck Market in China
* Forecast of the Market For Large-Tonnage Self-Dumping Vehicles, Bulk Cement Carriers and Concrete Mixers

* Prospects of the Development of Special Municipal Engineering Vehicles

Telecommunications
* Present Situation of China's Telecom Sector and Expectation For the 9th Five Year Plan Period

Energy
* Report On China's Energy Development

Building Materials

* China's new building materials industry
* China's Building Materials Industry Works out Strategical Targets for 1998-2000
* Building Materials Market Report of China(1)
* Building Materials Market Report of China(2)
* Building Ceramics Industry
* The Chinese Cement Industry
* Chinese Sheet Glass Industry
* Chinese Plan For Ninth Five-Year Plan Period and Development Outline For 2010 For Popularisation and Application of Chemical Building Materials
* China's Stone Material Production, Import and Export

OFFICES OF ECONOMIC COUNSELORS (CONSULS) OF THE EMBASSIES (CONSULATES)

AFRICAN COUNTRIES

The Economic and Commercial Counsellor's Office of the Embassy of the people's Republic of China in the Arab	Republic of Egypt Add£º22, BAHGAT ALY STREET, ZAMALEK, CAIRO, EGYPT

Tel£°0020-2-3404316,3417423
Fax£°0020-2-3412094
E-mail: ccechina@soficom.com.eg

The Economic and Commercial Counsellor's Office of the Embassy of the people's Republic of China in the Great Socialist People's Libyan Arab Jamahiriya
Add£°NEAR THE PETROL STATION NO.37,KALKALISH STREET, TIPOLI,LIBYA
P.O.BOX 6310 ANDALUS, TIPOLI
Tel£°00218-21-4831234
Fax£°00218-21-4831225,4831877
Telex£°20392 CHINOM LY

Bureau du Conseiller Economique et Commercial de L'Ambassade de la Republique Populaire de Chine en Republique Tunisienne
Add£°ROUTE DE LA MARSA KMG EL AOUINA2405 CITE TAIEB M'HIRI TUNIS,TUNISIE
Tel£°00216-1-845805
Fax£°00216-1-841996

E-mail: bcec.ambachine@email.ati

Bureau du Conseiller Economique et Commercial de L'Ambassade de la Republique Populaire de Chine en Republique Algerienne Democratique et Populaire
Add£°34,BD,DES MARTYRS,ALGER, ALGERIE
Tel£°00213-2-693189,692362
Fax£°00213-2-692362
Telex£°66193 BCCAC DE

Bureau du Conseiller Economique et Commercial de L'Ambassade de la Republique Populaire de Chine au Royaume du Maroc
Add£°2,RUE MEKKI EL-BITAOURI SOUISSI-RABAT-MAROC
Tel£°00212-7-752718,754940
Fax£°00212-7-756966,755769
Telex£°32745 M

Bureau du Conseiller Economique et Commercial de L'Ambassade de la Republique Populaire de Chine en Republique Islamique de Mauritanie
Add£°P.O.BOX5534
NOUAKCHOTT,MAURITANIE
Tel£°00222-2-51205
Fax£°00222-2-58634

Bureau du Conseiller Economique et Commercial de L'Ambassade de la Republique Populaire de Chine en Republique du Niger
Add£°BOITE POSTALE:10777 NIAMEY REPUBLIQUE DU NIGER
TEl£°00227-752859
Fax£°00227-752861

Bureau du Conseiller Economique et Commercial de L'Ambassade de la Republique Populaire de Chine en Republique du Mali
Add£°B.P.1614, BAMAKO, MALI
Tel£°00223-223823
Fax£°00223-229019
E-mail: bcecmali@speder.toolnet.org

Seccao do Conselheirodo Economico e Comercial da Embaixada da Republica Popular da China na Republica de Cabo Verde
Add£°C.P.NO.8, PRAIA;ACHADA DE SANTO ANTONIO PRAIA REPUBLICA DE CABO VERDE
Tel£°00238-615588
Fax£°00238-614034

Bureau du Conseiller Economique et Commercial de L'Ambassade de la Republique Populaire de Chine en Republique de Guinee
Add£°BUREAU DU CONSEILLER ECONOMIQUE ET COMMERCIAL PRES AMBASSADE DE LA REPUBLIQUE POPULAIRE DE CHINE EN REPUBLIQUE DE GUINEE B.P.714 CONAKRY REPUBLIQUE DE GUINEE
Tel£°(224)464366
Fax£°001-212-4794818

The Economic and Commercial Counsellor's Office of the Embassy of the people's Republic of China in the Republic of Sierra Leone
Add£°P.O.BOX 778 B28, KONG HARMAN ROAD, FREETOWN SIERRA LEONE
Tel£°00232-22-240075(ECONOMIC

SECTION),240490 (COMMERCIAL
SECTION),240086
Fax£º00232-22-240086
E-mail: ecco@sierratel.sl

Bureau du Conseiller Economique et Commercial de L'Ambassade de la Republique Populaire de Chine en Republique de Cote D'Ivoire
Add£º06 B.P. 206 ABIDJAN 06 COTE D'IVOIRE
Tel£º00225-420102
Fax£º00225-426373

The Economic and Commercial Counsellor's Office of the Embassy of the People's Republic of China in the Republic of Ghana
Add£ºP.O.BOX M344 AIRPORT RESIDENTIAL AREA ACCRA, GHANA
Tel£º00233-21-777462,772541
Fax£º00233-21-777462,772541
Telex£º091-2116 EMBCHA GH
E-mail: jshchu@ghana.com

Bureau du Conseiller Economique et Commercial de L'Ambassade de la Republique Populaire de Chine en Republique Togolaise
Add£º11,RUE TEVI-BENISSAN A TOKOIN-LYCEE B.P.4714-LOME-TOGO
Tel£º00228-215470,215243
Fax£º00228-218390,215470
E-mail: sinoecom@cafe.lg

Bureau du Conseiller Economique et Commercial de L'Ambassade de la Republique Populaire de Chine en Republique du Benin
Add£ºROUTE NO.2 DE l'AEROPORT ZONE DES AMBASSADES COTONOU, BENIN;08-0167(or)08-0462 COTONOU,BENIN
Tel£º00229-301909,301097
Fax£º00229-301639

The Economic and Commercial Counsellor's Office of the Embassy of the People's Republic of China in the Federal Republic of Nigeria
Add£º161A, ADEOLA ODEKU STREET, VICTORIA ISLAND, LAGOS, NIGERIA
P.O.BOX 72697 V/I,LAGOS
Tel£º00234-1-2612404,2612414
Fax£º00234-1-2612414

Bureau du Conseiller Economique et Commercial de L'Ambassade de la Republique Populaire de Chine en Republique du Cameroun
Add£ºB.P. 11608 YAOUNDE CAMEROUN AMBASSADE DE CHINE
Tel£º00237-209522,203191
Fax£º00237-210091
Telex£ºAMBACHINE 3321 KN

Office du Bureau du Conseiller Economique et Commercial de L'Ambassade de la Republique Populaire de Chine a Douala
Add£ºB.P.4391-DOUALA, CAMEROUN
Tel£º00237-425437
Fax£º00237-426214

Oficina del Consejero Economico-Comercial de la Embajada de la Republica Popular China en la Republica de Guinea Ecuatorial
Add£ºCALLE DE INDEPENDENCIA 26-B-2 CONSEJERO ECONOMICO-COMERCIAL DE LA EMBAJADA DE LA REPUBLICA POPULAR CHINA EN LA REPUBLICA DE GUINEA ECUATORIAL;P.O.BOX MALABO,NO.44
Tel£º00240-9-3440
Fax£º00240-9-3459

The Economic and Commercial Counsellor's Office of the Embassy of the People's Republic of China in the Republic of Sudan
Add£ºMANSHIA DISTRICT,KHARTOUM,SUDAM
P.O.BOX 1425 KHARTOUM-SUDAN
Tel£º00249-11-272274,224816
Fax£º00249-11-272274
Telex£º22806 CHINCC SD

The Economic and Commercial Counsellor's Office of the Embassy of the People's Republic of China in Ethiopia
Add£ºHIGH 24,KEBELE 13,HOUSE,NO.729 JIMMA ROAD, ADDIS ABABA,ETHIOPIA
P.O.BOX 5643
Tel£º002511-712266
Fax£º002511-710059,713066

Bureau du Conseiller Economique et Commercial de L'Ambassade de la Republique Populaire de Chine en Republique de Djibouti
Add£ºRUE DE NAIROBI,HERON,DJIBOUTI
B.P.4001 DJIBOUTI
Tel£º00253-350575
Fax£º00253-354174
Telex£ºCHINADJI 5926DJ

The Economic and Commercial Counsellor's Office of the Embassy of the People's Republic of China in the Republic of Kenya
Add£ºKENYA;NGONG ROAD,NAIROBI,KENYA
P.O.BOX 48190,47030, NAIROBI
Tel£º00254-2-712120,712434
Fax£º00254-2-713451,711029
E-mail: eccoce@africaonline.co.ke

The Economic and Commercial Counsellor's Office of the Embassy of the People's Republic of China in the Republic of Uganda
Add£ºPLOT 112-114-116,LUTHULI AVE.BUGOLOBI
P.O.BOX 8858 KAMPALA UGANDA
Tel£º00256-41-220572,220578,220570
Fax£º00256-41-220379
E-mail: cnecoug@infocom.co.ug

The Economic and Commercial Counsellor's Office of the Embassy of the People's Republic of China in the United Republic of Tanzania
Add£ºNO.1390, MSASANI PENISULA TANZANIA PLOT NO 3621 MSASANI,ROAD DARES SALAAM(ECONOMIC)
Tel£º00255-51-68198,41288
Fax£º00255-51-66177
Telex£º41036 CHINEMBA

The Economic and Commercial Section of the Consulate General of the People's Republic of China in Zanzibar
Add£ºP.O.BOX 1200 ZANZIBAR,TANZANIA CHINESE CONSULATE IN ZANZIBAR
Tel£º0255-054-30816
Fax£º0255-054-32681

Bureau du Conseiller Economique et Commercial de L'Ambassade de la Republique Populaire de Chine en Republique Rwandaise
Add£ºB.P.519 OU 182, KIGALI, RWANDA
Tel£º00250-84965
Fax£º00250-84965
E-mail: becom@rwandal.com

Bureau du Conseiller Economique et Commercial de L'Ambassade de la Republique Populaire de Chine en Republique du Burundi
Add£ºSUR LA PARCELLE 675 A VUGIZO, BUJUMBURA, BURUNDI
Tel£º00257-224246,222558
Fax£º00257-221962
Telex£º5137 BCCHINE BDI
E-mail: conec@crinf.com

Bureau du Conseiller Economique et Commercial de L'Ambassade de la Republique Populaire de Chine en Democratique de Congo
Add£º466, AV. COLONEL LUKUSA, KINSHASA/GOMBE, D'CONGO
Tel£º00243-12-26210,83076,46507
Fax£º001-212-3769255

Bureau du Conseiller Economique et Commercial de L'Ambassade de la Republique Populaire de Chine en Republique du Congo
Add£ºAVENUE MONSEIGNEUR AUGOUARD, BRAZZAVILLE, CONGO
B.P.2838,BRAZZAVILLE,CONGO
Tel£º00242-830952
Fax£º00242-837702

Bureau du Conseiller Economique et Commercial de L'Ambassade de la Republique Populaire de Chine en Republique Gabonaise
Add£ºB.P.3914 LIBREVILLE GABON
Tel£º00241-732873,738839
Fax£º00241-738645,738887

Seccao do Conselheirodo Economico e Comercial da Embaixada da Republica Popular da China na Republica Popular de Angola
Add£ºCAIXA POSTAL NO.704, RUA FERNAO MENDES PINTO NO.26-28 BAIRRO ALVALADE,LUANDA,ANGOLA
Tel£º002442-322803
Fax£º002442-322803
E-mail: luo.taiheng@netangola.com

The Economic and Commercial Counsellor's Office of the Embassy of the People's Republic of China in the Republic of Zambia
Add£ºUNITED NATIONS AVENUE, LUSAKA,ZAMBIA
P.O.BOX 31205 LUSAKA, ZAMBIA
Tel£º00260-1-253601,262363,264123
Fax£º00260-1-262363,253001
Telex£ºCHINEB ZA41360

Seccao do Conselheirodo Economico e Comercial da Embaixada da Republica Popular da China na Republica de Mocambique
Add£ºAV.DO ZIMBABWE N.1088 MAPUTO,AV.DE KIM IL SUNG N.974 MAPUTO C.P.2545;C.P.1105
Tel£º00258-1-490306,491879
Fax£º00258-1-490306,491879v
E-mail: coocai@teledata.mz

Bureau du Conseiller Economique et Commercial de L'Ambassade de la Republique Populaire de Chine en Republique Federale Islamique des Comores
Add£ºB.P. 442 MORONI COMORES
Tel£º00269-732937
Fax£º00269-732866

The Economic and Commercial Counsellor's Office of the Embassy of the People's Republic of China in the Republic of Seychelles
Add£ºP.O.BOX 680 VICTORIA MAHE-SEYCHELLES
Tel£º00248-266808
Fax£º00248-266866
E-mail: ecchina@seychelles.net

The Economic and Commercial Counsellor's Office of the Embassy of the People's Republic of China in Mauritius
Add£ºHAPPY VALLEY,SAINT CLEMENT STREET,CUREPIPE, MAURITIUS
Tel£º00230-4549113,6755635
Fax£º00230-4540362,6743523
Telex£º4829 CHINCOM IW

The Economic and Commercial Counsellor's Office of the Embassy of the People's Republic of China in the Republic of Zimbabwe
Add£º10,CORK ROAD,AVONDALE,HARARE,ZIMBABWE
P.O.BOX 40£¬HARARE,ZIMBABWE;P.O.BOX1340,HARARE,ZIMBAWE
Tel£º00263-4-735194,730516
Fax£º00263-4-700264,735252
E-mail: eccoprc@samara.co.zw

The Economic and Commercial Counsellor's Office of the Embassy of the People's Republic of China in the Republic of Botswana
Add£º3097 NORTH RING ROAD GABORONE BOTSWANA
P.O.BOX 1031 GABORONE BOTSWANA
Tel£º00267-353270,352209
Fax£º00267-300156

The Economic and Commercial Counsellor's Office of the Embassy of the People's Republic of China in the Republic of Namibia
Add£º66 GEVERS STREET,WINDHOEK,NAMIBIA
P.O.BOX 21350
Tel£º00264-61-222702£¬220210£¬221460
Fax£º00264-61-221325
E-mail: nmbyjsc@iafrica.com.na

The Economic and Commercial Counsellor's Office of the Embassy of the People's Republic of China in Eritrea
Add£ºERITREA ASMARA ZONE 4 ADM.02 STREET NO.702 HAUSE NO.74,P.O.BOX204
Tel£º002911-182273
Fax£º002911-182200

The Economic and Commercial Counsellor's Office of the Embassy of the People's Republic of China in the Kingdom of Lesotho
Add£ºIST FLOOR BLOCK 2,257 OXFORD,ROAD ZUOVO, JOHANNESBURG
Tel£º011-8046311
Fax£º011-788-2428

AMERICAN COUNTRIES

The Economic and Commercial Counsellor's Office of the Embassy of the People's Republic of China in Canada
Add£º511-515 ST. PATRICK STREET 7893511 OTTAWA, ONTARIO, CANADA KIN 5H3 P.O.BOX 8935
Tel£º001-613-7893513
Fax£º001-613-7893515
Telex£º053-3770 CHINAEMBA OTT

The Economic and Commercial Section of the Consulate General of the People's Republic of China in Vancouver
Add£º3380 GRANVILLE STREET, VANCOUVER, B.C.CANADA V6H 3K3
Tel£º001-604-7364021
Fax£º001-604-7364343
Telex£º04-54659
E-mail: ecomms@infoserve.net

The Economic and Commercial Section of the Consulate General of the People's Republic of China in Toronto
Add£º240 ST. GEORGE STREET, TORONTO, ONTARIO, CANADA, M5R 2P4
Tel£º001-416-3246455,3246454
Fax£º001-416-3246468

The Economic and Commercial Section of the Consulate General of the People's Republic of China in Calgary
Add£ºSUTTE 100-1011, 6TH AVE,S.W.CALGARY,AB,CANADA.T2P0W1
Tel£º001-403-264-3322
Fax£º001-403-264-6656

The Economic and Commercial Counsellor's Office of the Embassy of the People's Republic of China in the United States of America
Add£º2133 WISCONSIN AVE.,NW WASHINGTON D.C.,20007,U.S.A
Tel£º001-202-625-3380,3360
Fax£º001-202-337-5864,5845
E-mail: chinacom@erols.com

The Permanent Mission of the People's Republic of China to the United Nations
Add£ºWEST. 66TH STREET NEW YORK, N.Y. 10023
Tel£º001-212-8700300 001-213-7873838
Telex£º424465 PRC 423727
E-mail: zguangyao@aol.com

The Economic and Commercial Section of the Consulate General of the People's Republic of China in San Francisco
Add£º1450 LAGUNA STREET, SAN FRANEISCO, CA94115, U.S.A.
Tel£º001-415-5634858,5634874
Fax£º001-415-5630494
Telex£º497021 CCSF

The Economic and Commercial Section of the Consulate General of the People's Republic of China in New York
Add£º520 12TH AVENUE, NEW YORK, N.Y.10036
Tel£º001-212-212£-3307404,3307427,3307428
Fax£º001-212-5020248

The Economic and Commercial Section of the Consulate General of the People's Republic of China in Los Angeles
Add£º443 Shatto Place, Los Angeles, CA90020, USA
Tel£º(213)807-8016,8017,8026
Fax: (213)380-1961

The Economic and Commercial Section of the Consulate General of the People's Republic of China in Houston
Add£º3417 MONTROSE BOULEVARD,HOUSTON,TEXAS 77006, U.S.A.
Tel£º001-713-5244064,5240780,5240778
Fax£º001-713-5243547
E-mail: moftec@wt.net

The Economic and Commercial Section of the Consulate General of the People's Republic of China in Chicago
Add£º104 WEST ERIE STREET,CHICAGO IL.60610 U.S.A.
Tel£º001-312-8030115
Fax£º001-312-8030114
E-mail: ccgc@ais.net

Oficina del Consejero Economico-Comercial de la Embajada de la Republica Popular China en los Estados Unidos Mexicanos
Add£ºCALLE PLATON NO.317,COL POLANCO MEXICO,D.F.11560 MEXICO,D.F.

Tel£º0052-5-2808592,2802970
Fax£º0052-5-2804647,2821646
Telex£º1763515 OCCHME
E-mail: ccocnmcx@infoabc.com

Oficina del Consejero Economico-Comercial de la Embajada de la Republica Popular China en la Republica de Cuba
Add£ºLA,CALLE 42,NO.313, 5 AVENID MIRAMAR PLAYA,CIUDAD DE LA HABANA,CUBA
Tel£º0053-7-332585
Fax£º0053-7-331021

The Economic and Commercial Counsellor's Office of the Embassy of the People's Republic of China in Jamaica
Add£º8,SEAVIEW AVE, KINGSTON 10, JAMAICA W.I.
Tel£º001-876-9276816
Fax£º001-876-9787780
E-mail: chinaemba@cwjamaica.com

The Economic and Commercial Counsellor's Office of the Embassy of the People's Republic of China in Antigua and Barbuda
Add£ºMCKINNONS WAY,ST.JOHN'S,ANTIGUA,W.I.
P.O.BOX1355
Tel£º001-809-4626414
Fax£º001-809-4620986

The Economic and Commercial Counsellor's Office of the Embassy of the People's Republic of China in Barbados
Add£ºCORAL ISLE APARTMENTS, MAXWELL COAST ROAD, CHRIST CHURCH,BARAADOS, W£®I£®P.O.BOX 34A, CHRIST CHURCH, BARAADOS
Tel£º001-246-4283384
Fax£º001-246-4285860

The Economic and Commercial Counsellor's Office of the Embassy of the People's Republic of China in the Republic of Trinidad and Tobago
Add£º40 ELIZABETH STREET, ST. CLAIL PORT OF SPAIN, TRINIDAD, W.I.
Tel£º001-809-6285556
Fax£º001-809-6288020

Oficina del Consejero Economico-Comercial de la Embajada de la Republica Popular China en la Republica de Colombia
Add£ºCALLE 71 NO.2A-41 SANTAFE DE BOGOTA, COLOMBIA
Tel£º0057-1-2115411
Fax£º0057-1-2178985

Oficina del Consejero Economico-Comercial de la Embajada de la Republica Popular China en la Republica de Venezuela
Add£ºQUINTA LA ORQUIDEA CALLE SAN FRANCISCO DESVIACION SAN PEDRO URB.PRADOS DEL ESTE APARTADO 80520, ZONA POSTAL 1080-A CARACAS VENEZUELA
Tel£º0058-2-9761678,9762896

The Economic and Commercial Counsellor's Office of the Embassy of the People's Republic of China in the Cooperative Republic of Guyana
Add£º52,BRICKDAM, GEORGETOWN,COOPERATIVE REPUBLIC GUYANA.
P.O.BOX.101195
Tel£º00592-2-67428, 592-2-69965
Fax£º00592-2-64308

The Economic and Commercial Counsellor's Office of the Embassy of the People's Republic of China in the Republic of Suriname
Add£º120 PLUTOS TRAAT-SURINAME DISTRICT PARAMARIBO
P.O.BOX8116,PARAMARIBO IN SURINAME
Tel£º00597-450490,451281
Fax£º00597-452560

Oficina del Consejero Economico-Comercial de la Embajada de la Republica Popular China en la Republica del Ecuador
Add£ºAV.ATAHUALPA NO.349 Y AV.AMAZONAS QUITO-ECUADOR
CASILLA 17-110-5143
Tel£º00593-2-444362
Fax£º00593-2-444364
Telex£º0308-22614 ECHINA ED

Oficina del Consejero Economico-Comercial de la Embajada de la Republica

Popular China en la Republica del Peru
Add£ºAV.JAVIER PRADO OESTE 2496,MAGDALENA DEL MAR, LIMA, PERU

P.O.BOX 170140, LIMA 17 PERU
Tel£º0051-14-619536
Fax£º0051-14-619855
E-mail: ofcembch@amnet.com.pe

Escritorio do Conselheiro Economico-Comercial da Embaixada da Republica Popular da China na Republica Federeative do Brasil
Add£ºSHIS QL 8, Conjunto 5, Casa 20, Lago Sul, Brasilia-DF
CEP: 71620-255, Brasilia - DF, Brasil
Tel£º0055-61-2481446/2485205/2480776
Fax£º0055-61-2482139
E-mail: sanab843@bsb.nutecnet.com.br

Secao do Economico-Comercial do Consulado Geral da Republica Popular da China em Sao Paulo
Add£ºRUA ESTADOS UNIDOS,170-JARDIM AMERICA-CEP 01437 SAO PAULO-SP-BRASIL
Tel£º0055-11-2829877,8522663
Fax£º0055-11-30641813
Telex£º1139911 CGRH BR

Secao Economico-Comercial do Consulado Geral da Republica Popular da China em Rio de Janeiro
Add£ºRUA MUNIZ BARRETOTS BOTAFOGO,KIO DE JANEIRD CEP 22251-090 BRASIL
Tel£º0055-21-5514878
Fax£º0055-21-5515736,5514533

Oficina del Consejero Economico-Comercial de la Embajada de la Republica Popular China en la Republica de Bolivia
Add£ºNO.33,CALLE 25 ,CALACOTO ,LA PAZ-BOLIVIAZ
Tel£º00591-2-794567
Fax£º00591-2-797577

Oficina del Consejero Economico-Comercial de la Embajada de la Republica Popular China en la Republica de Chile
Add£ºCASILLA 3417;AV.PEDRO DE VALDIVIA 1032, PROVIDENCIA,SANTIAGO, CHILE
Tel£º0056-2-2239988
Fax£º0056-2-2232465

Oficina del Consejero Economico-Comercial de la Embajada de la Republica Popular China en la Republica Argenina
Add£ºLA PAMPA 3410 BUENOS AIRES ARGENTINA
Tel£º0054-1-5541258,5542613
Fax£º0054-1-5538939
E-mail: ofeccocn@ba.net

Oficina del Consejero Economico-Comercial de la Embajada de la Republica Popular China en la Republica Oriental del Uruguay
Add£ºP.O.BOX 18966; RAMBLE REPUBLICA DEL PERU 727/101
Tel£º00598-2-6043899
Fax£º00598-2-6042637
Telex£º00598-2-23323 CHIEMBA

Oficina de Desarrollo Comercial Chino-Panamena
Add£ºEDIFICIO TORRE COSMOS CAMPO ALEGRE,CALLE MANUEL MARIA ZCAZABELLA VISTA,PANAMA,APARTADO 87-4631 ZONA 7,PANAMA REPULICA DE PANAMA
Tel£º00507-654061,654062
Fax£º00507-2654051,2130265

Oficina de Representacion del Consejo Chino Para el fomento del Comercio Znternacional en Santo Domingo
Add£ºCALLE REPOBLACION FORESTAL NO.7,EDIFICIO DON SAMUDL,LOS MILLONES,APARTADO POSTAL 3513, SANTO DOMINGO,REPUBLICA DOMINICANA
Tel£º00566-2620,7063,8430,567-3480
Fax£º(1-809)566-2620

ASIAN COUNTRIES

The Economic and Commercial Counsellor's Office of the Embassy of the People's Republic of China in Mongolia
Address£ºNO.5£¬FRIENDSHIP STREET,

ULANBATOR, MONGOLIA
Tel: 009716-323940
Fax; 009716-311943

The Economic and Commercial Counsellor's Office of the Embassy of the People's Republic of China in the Democratic People's Republic of Korea
Address: KINMAEULI DONG,MAO LANG BONG DISTRIC PYONGYANG,

DEMOCRATIC PEOPLE'S REPUBLIC OF KOREA
Tel£º00850-2-3813119,3813120
Fax£º00850-2-3813425,3813442

The Economic and Commercial Counsellor's Office of the Embassy of the People's Republic of China in the Republic of Korea
Postal Code£º100-452
Tel£º00822-2537521,2537522,2537523
Fax£º00822-2537524

The Economic and Commercial Section of the Consulate General of the People's Republic of China in Pusan
Tel£º008251-4414890 008251-4414891
Fax£º008251-4414892

The Economic and Commercial Counsellor's Office of the Embassy of the People's Republic of China in Japan
Tel£º0081-3-3440-2011
Fax£º0081-3-3446-8242
E-mail: cecj@ma.kcom.or.jp

Consulate General of the People's Republic of China in Sapporo ,JAPAN
Tel£º0081-11-5635563
Fax£º0081-11-5631818

The Economic and Commercial Section of the Consulate General of the People's Republic of China in Fukuoka
Tel£º0081-92-713-7532
Fax£º0081-92-781-8906

The Economic and Commercial Section of the Consulate General of the People's Republic of China in Osaka
Tel£º0081-6-4459471 0081-6-4459481
Fax£º0081-6-4459476

The Economic and Commercial Counsellor's Office of the Embassy of the People's Republic of China in the Socialist Republic of Vietnam
Add£ºSO NHA 46.52 PHO HOANG DIEU,HANOI,VIETNAM
Tel£º00844-8232845
Fax£º00844-8234286

The Economic and Commercial Section of the Consulate General of the People's Republic of China in Ho Chi Minh City£¬Vietnam
Add£ºSO NHA 39 NGNYEN THI MINH KHAI Q.1
Tel£º00848-8292463
Fax£º00848-8231142 The Economic and Commercial Counsellor's Office of the Embassy of the

People's Republic of China in the People's Democratic Republic of Laos
Add£ºRUELLE VATNAK MUONG SISATTANAK, VIENTIANE, LAOS
Tel£º00856-21-315101 00856-21-315107
Fax£º00856-21-315106

Burean du Conseiller Economique et Commercial de L'ambassade de la Republique Populaire de Chine ru Royrume du Cpmbodge
Add£ºNO.156 BLC MAO TSETUNG POHNOM PEUH, CAMBODIA
Tel£º00855-23-720923
Fax£º00855-23-720924¡¡ The Economic and Commercial Counsellor's Office of the Embassy of

the People's Republic of China in Myanmar
Add£ºNO.53, PYIDAUNGSU YEIKTHA ROAD, YANGON, MYANMAR
Tel£º0095-1-222800 0095-1-221399 0095-1-221398
Fax£º0095-1-220386
Telex£º083-21363 083-21346

The Economic and Commercial Counsellor's Office,Embassy of the People's Republic of China in the Kingdom of Thailand
Add£ºCHINESE EMBASSY IN THAILAND, NO.57,RACHADAPISAKE ROAD,DINDAENG, BANGKOK ,10310 THAILAND

Tel£°0066-2-2457038 0066-2-2472122
0066-2-2474506
Fax£°0066-2-2472123 0066-2-2474506
E-mail: clian@mozart.inst.cn.th

The Economic and Commercial Section of the Consulate General of the People's Republic of China in Songkhla,Thailand
Add£°9 SADAO ROOD,SONGKHLA 9000 THAILAND
Tel£°0066-74-322034 0066-74-325045
Fax£°0066-74-323772
E-mail: clian@mozart.inst.cn.th

The Economic and Commercial Counsellor's Office of the Embassy of the People's Republic of China in Malaysia
Add£°NO.39, JALAN UIU KELANG, 68000 AMPANG,SELANGOR DARUL EHSAN,MALAYSIA
Tel£°0060-3-4513226 ,4513555
Fax£°0060-3-4513233
E-mail: comembmy@tm.net.my

The Economic and Commercial Section of the Consulate General of the People's Republic of China in Kuching,Malaysia
Add£°340 Fortune Garden,Lorong 5,Jalan Stampin Timur, off KuchingBy-pass,93350 Kuching,Sarawak,Malaysia
Tel£°0060-82-461344
Fax£°0060-82-461424
E-mail: zhicun@tm.net.com

The Economic and Commercial Counsellor's Office of the Embassy of the People's Republic of China in the Republic of Singapore
Add£°70-76, DALVEY ROAD, SINGAPORE 1025
Tel£°0065-7343307,7343360
Fax£°0065-7338590
E-mail: jsceprc@mbox4.singnet.com.sg
Telex£°RS36878 CHICRO

The Economic and Commercial Counsellor's Office of the Embassy of the People's Republic of China in the Republic of the Philippines
Add£° NO.10, FLAME TREE ROAD, SOUTH FORBES PARK, MAKATI CITY 1200, METRO MANILA, PHILIPPINES
Tel£°0063-2-8195991 0063-2-8195992
0063-2-8939067
Fax£°0063-2-8184553

The Economic and Commercial Office of Consulate of the People's Republic of China in Cebu
Add£°4 TH FL.EURD PACIFIC BLDG,F.GONZALES COMPOUND, CAMPUTHAW ST.LAHUG CEBU CITY,6000,THE PHILIPPINES
Tel£°006332-2316217 006332-2316218
006332-2316219
Fax£°006332-2315697
Tel(During Holidays)£°006332-2548727
006332-2548728
E-mail: wy-zh@hotmail.com

The Economic and Commercial Counsellor's Office of the Embassy of the People's Republic of China in the Republic of Indonesia
Add£°JL.MEGA KUNINGAN,BARAT10,NO.2,JAKARTA12950£¬ INDONESLA.
Tel£°0062-21-5761047,5761048,5761049,5761050
Fax£°0062-21-5761051
E-mail: cydcww@indosat.net.id/muxinh@indosat.net.id

The Economic and Commercial Office of the Embassy of the People's Republic of China in Negara Brunei Darussalan
Add£° SIMPANG 462£¬LOT38868£¬KG SUNGAI TILONG£¬ JALAN MUARA NEGARA BRUNEI DARUSSALAM
Tel£°00673-2-336077
Fax£°00673-2-335163¡¡

The Economic and Commercial Counsellor's Office of the Embassy of the People's Republic of China in the Kingdom of Nepal
Add£°B.P.10777,Niamey,Niger
Tel£°00227-722101/722126/752859
Fax£°00227-752861/723285¡¡

The Economic and Commercial Counsellor's Office of the Embassy of the People's Republic of China in the People's Republic of Bangladesh
Add£°PLOT,.15, PARK ROAD, BLOCK-I, BARIDHARA,

DHAKA,BANGLADESH
Tel£º00880-2-885272,883313,605728
Fax£º00880-2-883082
Telex£º675602 CECOF BG

The Economic and Commercial Counsellor's Office of the Embassy of the People's Republic of China in the Republic of India
Add£ºNO.50,D-SHANTIPATH CHANAKYAPURI NEW DELHI-110021,INDIA
Tel£º0091-11-4672687
Fax£º0091-11-6111099
Telex£º5166250 SINO IN

The Economic and Commercial Section of the Consulate General of the People's Republic China in Bombay
Add£ºP.O.BOX 189,GPO,Mumdai 400001,India
Tel£º0091-22-4973091
Fax£º0091-22-4963310

The Economic and Commercial Counsellor's Office of the Embassy of the People's Republic of China in the Democratic Socialist Republic of Sri Lanka
Add£º120/3A Tel£º00941-684576-7
Fax£º00941-684578,684579

The Economic and Commercial Counsellor's Office of the Embassy of the People's Republic of China in the Islamic Republic of Pakistan
Add£ºP.O.BOX 2601, HOUSE NO.11, STREET NO.19, F-8/2, ISLAMABAD, PAKISTAN
Tel£º0092-51-252426
Fax£º0092-51-256887
E-mail: ecco@comsats.net.pk

The Economic and Commercial Section of the Consulate General of the People's Republic of China in Karachi,Pakistan
Add£º43-6-B,BLOCK 6,P.E.C.H.S.KARACHI
Tel£º0092-21-4530523,4530526
Fax£º0092-21-4530525

The Economic and Commercial Counsellor's Office of the Embassy of the People's Republic of China in the Islamic Republic of Iran
Add£ºNO.180, FARMANIEH AVE., TEHRAN IRAN
Tel£º0098-21-2292284
Fax£º0098-21-2292283
Telex£º213237 COMO IR

The Economic and Commercial Counsellor's Office of the Embassy of the People's Republic of China in the State of Kuwait
Add£ºMISIIRIF,BLOCK 4,STREET 7,HOUSE NO.4 P.O.BOX 25713 SAFAT,13118 SAFAT,KUWAIT
Tel£º00965-5390239 5396160
Fax£º00965-5390291/5386404

The Economic and Commercial Counsellor's Office of the Embassy of the People's Republic of China in the Kingdom of Saudi Arabia
Add£ºP.O.BOX 99882 RIYADH 11625 SAUDI ARABIA
Tel£º00966-1-4655655 00966-1-4622485
Fax£º00966-1-4629617

The Economic and Commercial Section of the Consulate General of the People's Republic of China in Jeddah
Add£ºAL-ANDULOUS ROAD,ANDULOUS DIST.(2) P.O. BOX 51373 JEDDAH 21543 JEDDAH,KINGDOM OF SAUDI ARABIA
Tel£º00966-2-6605430
Fax£º00966-2-6606546

The Economic and Commercial Section of the Consulate General of the People's Republic of China in the State of Bahrain
Add£ºVILLA 1710,ROAD 7332 373,BILAD ALQADEEM MANAMA, STATE OF BAHRAIN
Add£ºP.O.BOX 5260,MANAMA,BAHRAIN
Tel£º00973-785751
Fax£º00973-785772

The Economic and Commercial Counsellor's Office of the Embassy of the People's Republic of China in the State of Qatar
Add£ºNO.63,AL-SHAM STREET,WEST BAY AREA,DOHA P.O.BOX 17514 DOHA,QATAR
Tel£º00974-835680
Fax£º00974-835184
Telex£º5120 CHINEM DH

The Economic and Commercial Counsellor's Office of the Embassy of the People's Republic of China in the United Arab

Emirates
Add£ºAL FALAH STREET,IOTH LANE,35-1 SECTER P.O.BOX 25455 ABU DHABI-U.A.E.
Tel£º00971-2-765525
Fax£º00971-2-764402¡¡
The Economic and Commercial Section of the Consulate General of the People's Republic of China in Dubai
Add£ºP.O.BOX 9374 DUBAI-U.A.E.
Tel£º00971-4-448032 00971-4-449445
Fax£º00971-4-448099
Telex£º46268 COMOF EM

The Economic and Commercial Counsellor's Office of the Embassy of the People's Republic of China in the Sultanate of Oman
Add£ºSHATI AL-QURUM,WAY3021,HOUSE NO.1784 3315 RUWIS
MASCAT,SULTANATE OF OMAN
Tel£º00968-697804
Fax£º00968-697482

The Economic and Commercial Counsellor's Office of the Embassy of the People's Republic of China in the Republic of Yemem
Add£ºP.O.BOX 10285 AL-ZUBEIRY STREET,SANA A YEMEN REPUBLIC
Tel£º00967-1-275339,275411
Fax£º00967-1-275339,272298

The Economic and Commercial Section of the Consulate General of the People's Republic of China in Aden
Add£ºKHORMAKSAR, ADEN,YEMEN
P.O.BOX 6160 KHORMAKSAY, ADEN, YEMEN
Tel£º00967-2-232630
Fax£º00967-2-231377

The Economic and Commercial Counsellor's Office of the Embassy of the People's Republic of China in the Republic of Iraq
Add£ºP.O.BOX 15097, AL-YARMUK,BAGHDAD,IRAQ
Tel£º00964-1-5567897,5562740
Telex£º2195 CHINCOM IK

The Economic and Commercial Counsellor's Office of the Embassy of the People's Republic of China in the Syrian Arab Republic
Add£ºP.O.BOX 2455,DAMASCUS,SYRIA
Tel£º00963-11-6133008
Fax£º00963-11-6133019
Telex£º(0492)413217 CHINEC SY

The Economic and Commercial Counsellor's Office of the Embassy of the People's Republic of China in the Republic of Lebanon
Add£º72,RUE NICOLAS IBRAHIM SURSOCK,RAMLET ELBAIDA, BEIRUT,LEBANON
P.O.BOX 114-5098, BEIRUT
Tel£º00961-830317 00961-830316
Fax£º00961-1-822492 001-212-4781653
Telex£ºCHINCO 21344 LE

The Economic and Commercial Counsellor's Office of the Embassy of the People's Republic of China in the Hashemite Kingdom of Jordan
Add£ºNO.21,ZAHRAN ST.SOUTHERN UM UTHAINA,AMMAN, JORDAN
423 UM ESSOMAQ&KHELDA,AMMAN,11821,JORDAN
Tel£º00962-6-816194,818195
Fax£º00962-6-827417

The Economic and Commercial Counsellor's Office of the Embassy of the People's Republic of China in the State of Israel
Add£ºNO.94, NAMIR ROAD, TEL-AVIV 62337, ISRAEL
Tel£º00972-3-5444915,5444917
Fax£º00972-3-5444918

The Economic and Commercial Counsellor's Office of the Embassy of the People's Republic of China in the Republic of Cyprus
Add£ºP.O.BOX 7088,NO.17 AGAPINOR STREET,NICOSIA, CYPRUS
Tel£º00357-2-375252
Fax£º00357-2-376699
Telex£º4910 CHINA COF CY

The Economic and Commercial Counsellor's Office of the Embassy of the People's Republic of China in the Republic of Turkey
Add£ºUGUR MUMCU CAD,NO.72,06700 GAZIOS-MAN-PASA,
ANKARA-TURKEY
Tel£º0090-312-4377107
Fax£º0090-312-4466762
Telex£º46387 CHCM TR¡¡
The Economic and Commercial Section of the Consulate General of the People's

Republic of China in Istanbul

THE ECONOMIC AND COMMERCIAL SECTION OF THE CHINESE CONSULATE IN ISTANBUL
MECIDIYEKOY, ORTAKLAR CAD. 14, ISTANBUL,TURKEY
Tel£º0090-212-2666590
Fax£º0090-212-2992632
Telex£º26906 CCGT TR
E-mail: sws@netone.com.tr

Office of P.R.China to the PNA (Plestanian National Authority)
Tel£º00972-7-825068 00972-5-864215
Fax£º00972-7-825058

EUROPEAN COUNTRIES

The Economic and Commercial Counsellor's Office of the Embassy of the People's Republic of China in the Republic of Iceland
Add£ºVIDIMELUR 25,REYKJAVIK,ICELAND
P.O.BOX 7290 REYKJAVIK
Tel£º00354-1-5526322
Fax£º00354-1-5623922

The Economic and Commercial Counsellor's Office of the Embassy of the People's Republic of China in the Kingdom of Denmark
Add£ºREGARDS ALLE 12 2900 HELLERUP COPEN-HAGEN,DENMARK
Tel£º0045-39610081
Fax:0045-39612913
Telex£º0045-19106 CHCOEM DK
E-mail: ecc@post7.tele.dk

The Economic and Commercial Counsellor's Office of the Embassy of the People's Republic of China in the Kingdom of Norway
Add£ºINKOGNITOGATEN 11 0258 OSLO 2 NORWAY
Tel£º0047-22-560270,438666
Fax£º0047-22-447230
E-mail: cnembn@online.no

The Economic and Commercial Counsellor's Office of the Embassy of the People's Republic of China in the Kingdom of Sweden
Add£ºRINGVAGEN 56 181 34 LIDINGO, SWEDEN
Tel£º0046-8-7674083,7679625,7678740
Fax£º0046-8-7318404
Telex£º16490 CHINO S

The Economic and Commercial Counsellor's Office of the Embassy of the People's Republic of China in the Republic of Finland
Add£ºVAHANITYNTIE 4 00570 HELSINKI 57,FINLAND
Tel£º00358-9-6848416,6849641
Fax£º00358-9-6849595
E-mail: fin.shangwu@kolumbus.fi
Telex£º126055 CHINA SF

The Economic and Commercial Counsellor's Office of the Embassy of the People's Republic of China in the Republic of Poland
Add£ºBIURO RADCY HANDLOWO-KEONOMICZNEGO PRZY AMBASADZIE CHINSKIEJ REPUBLIKI LUDOWEJ WPOLSCE
UL.BONIFRATERSKA 1 00203 WARSZWA
Tel£º0048-22-313861,313836
Fax£º0048-22-6354211
E-mail: brhchiem@it.com.pl
Telex£º813589 CHINA PL

The Economic and Commercial Counsellor's Office of the Embassy of the People's Republic of China in the Czech Republic
Add£ºVELVYSLSNECTVI CINSKE LI DOVE REPUBLIKY OBCHODNI ODDELENI PELLEOVA 22 16000 PRAHA 6-BUBENEC
Tel£º0042-2-24311324
Fax£º0042-2-323252¡¡

The Economic and Commercial Counsellor's Office of the Embassy of the People's Republic of China in the Slovak Republic
Add£ºJESENESKEHO 7, 811, 01, BRATISLAVA,SLOVENSKA REPUBLIKA
Tel£º0042-7-322103
Fax£º0042-7-367208¡¡
Kinai Nepkoztarsasag Nagykovetsegenek Gazdasagi es Kereskedelmi Tanacsos Hivatala Add£º1068 BUDAPEST BENCZUR U.17 HUNGARY
Tel£º0036-1-3225242
Fax£º0036-1-3229067
Telex£º22-7733 CHIBE H

Wirtschafts-und Handelsabteilung der Botschaft der Volksrepublik China in der Bundesrepublik Deutschland
Add£ºFRIEDRICH-EBERT-STR.59 53177 BONN

BAD GODESBERG
F.R.GERMANY
Tel£°0049-228-955940
Fax£°0049-228-356781
E-mail: trade-embassy.china@metronet.de

Wirtschafts-und Handelsabteilung der Aussenstelle Berlin der Botschaft der Volksrepublik China in der Bundesepublik Deutschland
Add£°ARNOLD-ZWEIG-STR.5 13189 BERLIN GERMANY
Tel£°0049-30-4723118
Fax£°0049-30-4710230
E-mail: trade-embassy.china@snafu.de

Wirtschafts-und Handelsabteilung der Generalkonsulats der Volksrepublik China in Hamburg
Add£°ELBCHAUSSEE 268 22605. HAMBURG, GERMANY
Tel£°0049-40-82276012,82276016
Fax£°0049-40-8226231
Wirtschafts-und Handelsabteilung der Botschaft der Volksrepublik China in der Republik Osterreich
Add£°A-1030 WIEN, METTERNICHGASSE 4
Tel£°0043-1-7143140
Fax£°0043-1-7130037

The Permanent Mission of the People's Republic of China to the United Nations Industrial Development Organization
Add£°UNTERE DONAUSTRASSE 41, 1020 VIENNA, AUSTRIA
Tel£°00431-2163367,2169380
Fax£°00431-2169389

The Permanent Mission of the People's Republic of China to the United Nations and Other International Organizations in Vienna
Add£°POETZLEINSDORFER STRASSE 42 1180 VIENNA, AUSTRIA
Tel£°0043-0222-471364 0043-0222-478338

Wirtschafts-und Handelsabteilung der Botschaft der Volksrepublik China in der Schweizerischen Eidgenossenschaft
Add£°7,J.V. WIDMANNSTRASSE, 3074 MURI BERN,SCHWEIZ
Tel£°0041-31-9511401,9511402,9511403
Fax£°0041-31-9510575
Telex£°912629 HBCH CH
E-mail: com-off.china-embassy@bluewin.ch

The Permanent Mission of the People's Republic of China to the United Nations Office in Geneva and Other International Organizations in Switzerland
Add£°CHEMIN DE SURVILLE 11 1213 PETIT-LANCY,GENEVA,
SWITZERLAND
Tel£°0041-22-7937013,7933270
Fax£°0041-22-7937014
E-mail: eto.cn@ties.itu.int

The Economic and Commercial Counsellor's Office of the Embassy of the People's Republic of China in the Kingdom of the Netherlands
Add£°GROOT HAESEBROEKSEWEG 2A 2243 EA WASSENAAR, THE NETHERLANDS
Tel£°0031-(0)70-5115559
Fax£°0031-(0)70-5111206
E-mail: coce@xs4all.nl

Bureau du Sonseiller Economique et Commercial de la Mission de la Republique Populaire de China a la Communaute Europeenne
Add£°BOULEVARD GENERAL JACQUES 19 1050 BRUXELLES,BELGIQUE
Tel£°0032-2-6404006,6404210
Fax£°0032-2-6403595
Telex£°23328 AMCHIN B
E-mail: comoffchnmsn@pophost.eunet.be

Bureau du Conseiller Economique et Commercial de L'Ambassade de la Republique Populaire de Chine au Royaume de Belgique
Add£°BOULEVARD GENERAL JACQUES 19 1050 BRUXELLES, BELGIQUE
Tel£°0032-2-6404006,6404210
Fax£°0032-2-6403595
Telex£°23328 AMCHIN B

Bureau du Conseiller Economique et Commercial de L'Ambassade de la Republique Populaire de Chine au Grand-Duche de Luxembourg
Add£°BOULEVARD GENERAL JACQUES 19 1050 BRUXELLES, BELGIQUE
Tel£°0032-6404006,6404210,6404006
Fax£°0032-2-6403595
Telex£°23328 AMCHIN B

The Economic and Commercial Counsellor's Office of the Embassy of the People's Republic of China in the United Kingdom of Great Britain and Northern Ireland
Add£°CLEVELAND COURT, 1-3 LEINSTER GARDENS, LONDON W2
6DP,THE UNITED KINGDOM
Tel£°0044-171-2620253,2623911,7238923
Fax£°0044-171-7062777
Telex£°896440 CLEFSL G
E-mail: public@checo.demon.co.uk

The Economic and Commercial Counsellor's Office of the Embassy of the People's Republic of

China in Ireland
Add£º77,AILESBURY ROAD,DUBLIN4,IRELAND
Tel£º00353-1-2600580
Fax£º00353-1-2696966
Telex£º91834 CODE EI
E-mail: chinacomm@tinet.ie

Bureau du Conseiller Economique et Commercial de L'Ambassade de la Republique Populaire de Chine en Republique Francaise
Add£º21, RUE DE L'AMIRAL D'ESTAING 75016 PARIS FRANCE
Tel£º0033-1-53577000
Fax£º0033-1-47209471
E-mail: shangwu@amb-chine.fr

Oficina del Consejero Economico-Comercial de la Embajada de la Republica Popular China en el reino de Espana
Add£ºARTURO SORIA 142,PISO 2-A 28043 MADRID, ESPANA
Tel£º34-914132776/914135892
Fax£º34-915194675
E-mail: prchina@es.dominios.net

Escritorio do Conselheiro Economico-Comercial da Embaixada da Republica Popular da China na Republica Portuguesa
Add£ºRUA ANTONIO DE SALDANHA,NO 42, 1400, LISBOA, PORTUGAL
Tel£º00351-1-3011947
Fax£º00351-1-3014590

Ufficio del Consigliere Economico e Commerciale Dell'amb-sciata Della Repubblica Popolare Cinese Nella Republica Italiana
Add£º00135 ROMA VIA DELLA CAMILLUCCIA, 613 ITALY
Tel£º0039-6-36308534,36303856
Fax£º0039-6-36308552
Telex£º622162 CINAC I
E-mail: gckli@tin.it/qigaoh@tin.it

Sezione Economica e Commerciale del Consolato Generaie Della Republica Popolare di Cina in Milano
Add£ºVIA PALEOCAPA, 4-2-21 MILANO, ITALIA
Tel£º0039-2-72021905,72021988
Fax£º0039-2-86452219

The Economic and Commercial Counsellor's Office of the Embassy of the People's Republic of China in the Republic of Malta
Add£ºCASA VERDALA, SACRED HEART AVENUE, ST. JULIAN'S, SLM13,MALTA
Tel£º00356-330840
Fax£º00356-310072,344730

The Economic and Commercial Counsellor's Office of the Embassy of the People's Republic of China in the Federal Republic of Yugoslavia
Add£ºVASILIJA GACESE 5,11000 BELGRAD,YUGOSLAVIA
Tel£º0038-111-651630¡¢651638
Fax£º0038-111-650726
Telex£º12492 CNCCO YU

The Economic and Commercial Counsellor's Office of the Embassy of the People's Republic of China in the Republic of Slovenia
Add£ºMALCI BELICEVE 123 1000 LJUBLJANA, REPUBLIC OF SLOVENIA
Tel£º00386-61-272759
Fax£º00386-61-233838

The Economic and Commercial Counsellor's Office of the Embassy of the People's Republic of China in the Republic of Croatia
Add£ºBUKOVACKA 8A£¬ 10000 ZAGREB£¬ CROATIA
Tel£º00385-1-2304546
Fax£º00385-1-2304484
E-mail: e.c.office.chn@zg.tel.br¡¡

The Economic and Commercial Counsellor's Office of the Embassy of the People's Republic of China in the Republic of Macedonia
Add£ºST.OSLO 22-B 91000 SKOPJE REPUBLIC OF MACEDONIA
Tel£º0038991-362680
Fax£º0038991-362803

The Economic and Commercial Counsellor's Office of the Embassy of the People's Republic of China in Romania
Add£ºSOSEAUA NORDULUI NO.2, BUCHAREST, ROMANIA
Tel£º0040-1-2321923
Fax£º0040-1-2307786
Telex£º11324 CHIAB R
E-mail: Embchina@dial.kappa.ro

The Economic and Commercial Counsellor's Office of the Embassy of the People's Republic of China in the Republic of Bulgaria
Add£ºSOFIA 3,9,"PLER DEGELDER"STR,1113,SOFIA,BULGARIA
Tel£º00359-2-724988,9712032
Fax£º00359-2-9712416
E-mail: chinabiz@mb.bia-bg.com

Zyra e Keshlltarit Ekonomiko-Tregtare te Ambasades se Republikes Populiore te Kines ne Republiken e Shqiperise
Add£ºRRUGA SKENDERBEJ NR .57 TIRANE ALBANIA
Tel£º00355-42-32077

Fax£º00355-42-32077
E-mail: cnemec@icc.al.eu.org

The Economic and Commercial Counsellor's
Office of the Embassy of the People's Republic of
China in the Hellenic Republic
Add£ºDIADOCHOU PAVLOU
7,P,PSYCHIKON,154 52 ATHENS, GREECE
Tel£º0030-1-6723281
Fax£º0030-1-6741575
Telex£º226848 CPRC GR
E-mail: eccoprc@otenet.gr

OCEANIAN COUNTRIES

States of Micronesia Add£ºP.O.BOX 1836 KOLONIA, POHNPEI
FEDERATED STATES OF MICRONESIA96941
Tel£º00691-320-5072 Fax£º00691-320-7074

The Economic and Commercial Counsellor's Office of the Embassy of the People's Republic of China in Western Samoa
Add£ºPRIVATE BAG, VAILIMA, APIA, WESTERN SAMOA
Tel£º00685-20802 Fax£º00685-21115
E-mail: encco@samoa.net

BASIC TITLES ON CHINA

IMPORTANT!
All publications are updated annually!
Please contact IBP, Inc. at ibpusa3@gmail.com for the latest ISBNs and additional information

TITLE
China Gaming Industry Investment and Business Guide - Strategic and Practical Information
China A "Spy" Guide - Strategic Information and Developments
China A Spy" Guide"
China Agricultural and Food Products Exporters Directory
China Agricultural Chemicals Producers Directory
China Agricultural Laws and Regulations Handbook
China Air Force Handbook
China Antique & Collection Producers Directory
China Apparel & Accessories Exporters Directory
China Army Weapon Systems Handbook
China Army Weapon Systems Handbook
China Army Weapon Systems Handbook
China Army, National Security and Defense Policy Handbook
China Army, National Security and Defense Policy Handbook
China Art & Crafts Producers Directory
China Athletic & Sports Shoes Producers Directory
China Auto Parts Producers Directory
China Auto Repair Tools Producers Directory
China Banking & Financial Market Handbook
China Banking & Financial Market Handbook
China Business and Investment Opportunities Yearbook
China Business and Investment Opportunities Yearbook
China Business and Investment Opportunities Yearbook Volume 1 Strategic Information and Opportunities
China Business and Investment Opportunities Yearbook Volume 2 Leading Export-Import, Business, Investment Opportunities and Projects
China Business Intelligence Report - Practical Information, Opportunities, Contacts
China Business Intelligence Report - Practical Information, Opportunities, Contacts
China Business Law Handbook - Strategic Information and Basic Laws
China Business Law Handbook - Strategic Information and Basic Laws
China Business Law Handbook - Strategic Information and Basic Laws
China Business Law Handbook - Strategic Information and Basic Laws
China Business Law Handbook Volume 1 Srategic Information and Basic Laws
China Business Law Handbook Volume 2 Investment and Trade Laws Volume 2 Investment and Trade Laws
China Business Success Guide - Basic Practical Information and Contacts
China Canned Food Exporters Directory
China Canned Food Exporters Directory
China Canned Food Exporters Directory
China Car & Track Tires Directory
China Car & Track Tires Directory
China Car & Track Tires Directory
China Car Accessories Producers Directory
China Car Accessories Producers Directory

TITLE
China Car Accessories Producers Directory
China Car Electronics (Audio & Video) Producers Directory
China Car Electronics (Audio & Video) Producers Directory
China Car Electronics (Audio & Video) Producers Directory
China Children's Apparel Producers Directory
China Children's Apparel Producers Directory
China Children's Apparel Producers Directory
China Christmas & Holiday Items Producers Directory
China Christmas & Holiday Items Producers Directory
China Christmas & Holiday Items Producers Directory
China Clock & Watch Producers Directory
China Clock & Watch Producers Directory
China Clock & Watch Producers Directory
China Clothing & Textile Industry Handbook
China Clothing & Textile Industry Handbook
China Company Laws and Regulations Handbook
China Company Laws and Regulations Handbook - Strategic Information and Basic Laws
China Computer Products Exporters Directory
China Computer Products Exporters Directory
China Computer Products Exporters Directory
China Constitution and Citizenship Laws Handbook - Strategic Information and Basic Laws
China Corporate and Promotion Gifts Producers Directory
China Corporate and Promotion Gifts Producers Directory
China Corporate and Promotion Gifts Producers Directory
China Country Study Guide - Strategic Information and Developments
China Country Study Guide - Strategic Information and Developments
China Country Study Guide - Strategic Information and Developments Volume 1 Strategic Information and Developments
China Criminal Laws, Regulations and Procedures Handbook - Strategic Information, Regulations, Procedures
China Customs, Export-Import Regulations, Incentives and Procedures Handbook - Strategic, Practical Information, Regulations
China Customs, Trade Regulations and Procedures Handbook
China Customs, Trade Regulations and Procedures Handbook
China Diplomatic Handbook - Strategic Information and Developments
China Diplomatic Handbook - Strategic Information and Developments
China Down & Winter Apparel Producers Directory
China Down & Winter Apparel Producers Directory
China Down & Winter Apparel Producers Directory
China Drugs, Medical Devices Registration Guide
China Drugs, Medical Devices Registration Guide
China Drugs, Medical Devices Registration Guide
China Ecology & Nature Protection Handbook
China Ecology & Nature Protection Handbook
China Ecology & Nature Protection Laws and Regulation Handbook
China E-Commerce Business and Investment Opportunities Handbook
China E-Commerce Business and Investment Opportunities Handbook
China Economic & Business Representations in Foreign Countries and Trade Contacts Handbook
China Economic & Business Representations in Foreign Countries and Trade Contacts Handbook

TITLE
China Economic & Development Strategy Handbook
China Economic & Development Strategy Handbook
China Education System and Policy Handbook
China Electoral, Political Parties Laws and Regulations Handbook - Strategic Information, Regulations, Procedures
China Energy Policy, Laws and Regulation Handbook
China Energy Policy, Laws and Regulations Handbook
China Energy Policy, Laws and Regulations Handbook
China Energy Policy, Laws and Regulations Handbook - Strategic Information, Policy, Regulations
China Energy Sector Handbook
China Energy Sector Handbook
China Essential Oil, Balsam & Fine Chemicals Producers Directory
China Essential Oil, Balsam & Fine Chemicals Producers Directory
China Essential Oil, Balsam & Fine Chemicals Producers Directory
China Export-Import Trade and Business Directory
China Export-Import Trade and Business Directory
China Fishing and Aquaculture Industry Handbook - Strategic Information, Regulations, Opportunities
China Food Safety Laws and Regulations Handbook
China Footwear Exporters Directory
China Footwear Exporters Directory
China Footwear Exporters Directory
China Foreign Policy and Government Guide
China Foreign Policy and Government Guide
China Fruit & Vegetables Exporters Directory
China Fruit & Vegetables Exporters Directory
China Fruit & Vegetables Exporters Directory
China Gaming Industry Investment and Business Guide - Strategic and Practical Information
China Gloves & Mittens Exporters Directory
China Gloves & Mittens Exporters Directory
China Gloves & Mittens Exporters Directory
China Government and Business Contacts Handbook
China Government and Business Contacts Handbook
China Hat & Cap Producers Directory
China Hat & Cap Producers Directory
China Hat & Cap Producers Directory
China Immigration Laws and Regulations Handbook - Strategic Information and Basic Laws
China Industrial and Business Directory
China Industrial and Business Directory
China Infant Apparel Producers Directory
China Infant Apparel Producers Directory
China Infant Apparel Producers Directory
China Information Strategy, Internet and E-Commerce Development Handbook - Strategic Information, Programs, Regulations
China Insolvency (Bankruptcy) Laws and Regulations Handbook - Strategic Information and Basic Laws
China International Laws and Treaties with Foreign Countries Handbook
China International Laws and Treaties with Foreign Countries Handbook
China Internet and E-Commerce Investment and Business Guide - Strategic and Practical Information: Regulations and Opportunities
China Internet Business and Investment Opportunities Handbook

TITLE
China Internet Business and Investment Opportunities Handbook
China Investment and Business Guide - Strategic and Practical Information
China Investment and Business Guide - Strategic and Practical Information
China Investment and Business Guide - Strategic and Practical Information
China Investment and Business Guide - Strategic and Practical Information
China Investment and Business Guide Volume 2 Business, Investment Opportunities and Incentives
China Investment and Business Profile - Basic Information and Contacts for Succesful investment and Business Activity
China Investment and Trade Laws and Regulations Handbook
China Investment, Trade Strategy and Agreements Handbook - Strategic Information and Basic Agreements
China Jeans Producers Directory
China Jeans Producers Directory
China Jeans Producers Directory
China Justice System and National Police Handbook
China Justice System and National Police Handbook
China Labor Laws and Regulations Handbook - Strategic Information and Basic Laws
China Land Ownership and Agriculture Laws Handbook
China Medical & Pharmaceutical Industry Handbook
China Medical & Pharmaceutical Industry Handbook
China Medical and Pharmaceutical Industry Laws and Regulations Handbook
China Medical and Pharmaceutical Industry Laws and Regulations Handbook
China Medical and Pharmaceutical Industry Laws and Regulations Handbook
China Men's Shoes Producers Directory
China Men's Shoes Producers Directory
China Men's Shoes Producers Directory
China Mineral & Mining Sector Investment and Business Guide - Strategic and Practical Information
China Mineral & Mining Sector Investment and Business Guide - Strategic and Practical Information
China Mineral, Mining Sector Investment and Business Guide - Strategic Information and Regulations
China Mining Laws and Regulations Handbook
China Mobile Telephone Market Business Intelligence Report - Practical Information, Opportunities, Contacts
China Mobile Telephone Market Business Intelligence Report - Practical Information, Opportunities, Contacts
China Motorcycle Parts & Accessories Producers Directory
China Motorcycle Parts & Accessories Producers Directory
China Motorcycle Parts & Accessories Producers Directory
China Nuclear Energy Sector Policy, Laws and Regulations Handbook - Strategic Information, Projects, Regulations
China Oil & Gas Sector Business & Investment Opportunities Yearbook
China Oil & Gas Sector Business & Investment Opportunities Yearbook
China Oil and Gas Exploration Laws and Regulation Handbook
China Organic Chemicals Producers Directory
China Organic Chemicals Producers Directory
China Organic Chemicals Producers Directory
China Paint & Coating Producers Directory
China Paint & Coating Producers Directory
China Paint & Coating Producers Directory
China Pharmaceutical Chemicals Exporters Directory
China Pharmaceutical Chemicals Exporters Directory
China Pharmaceutical Chemicals Exporters Directory

TITLE
China Pharmaceutical Chemicals Producers Directory
China Pharmaceutical Chemicals Producers Directory
China Pharmaceutical Chemicals Producers Directory
China Plastic & Polymer Producers Directory
China Plastic & Polymer Producers Directory
China Plastic & Polymer Producers Directory
China Porcelain Producers Directory
China Porcelain Producers Directory
China Porcelain Producers Directory
China President Handbook
China President Handbook
China Privatization Programs and Regulations Handbook
China Privatization Programs and Regulations Handbook
China Recent Economic and Political Developments Yearbook
China Recent Economic and Political Developments Yearbook
China Recent Economic and Political Developments Yearbook
China Research & Development Policy Handbook
China Research & Development Policy Handbook
China Research & Development Policy Handbook
China Rubber & Rubber Products Producers Directory
China Rubber & Rubber Products Producers Directory
China Rubber & Rubber Products Producers Directory
China Starting Business (Incorporating) in China Guide
China Starting Business (Incorporating) in....Guide
China Sugar & Confection Exporters Directory
China Sugar & Confection Exporters Directory
China Sugar & Confection Exporters Directory
China Tax Guide
China Tax Guide
China Tax Guide Volume 1 Strategic Information and Basic Regulations
China Taxation Laws and Regulations Handbook
China Tea & Tea Leaf Exporters Directory
China Tea & Tea Leaf Exporters Directory
China Tea & Tea Leaf Exporters Directory
China Telecom & Internet Market Business Law Handbook - Strategic Information and Basic Laws
China Telecom & Internet Market Business Law Handbook - Strategic Information and Basic Laws
China Telecom Laws and Regulations Handbook
China Telecommunication Industry Business Opportunities Handbook Vol. 1 Strategic Information and Market Development
China Telecommunication Industry Business Opportunities Handbook Vol. 1 Strategic Information and Market Development
China Telecommunication Industry Business Opportunities Handbook Vol. 3 Important Business and Investment Opportunities
China Telecommunication Industry Business Opportunities Handbook Vol. 3 Important Business and Investment Opportunities
China Trade Exhibitions Handbook
China Trade Exhibitions Handbook
China Transportation Policy and Regulations Handbook
China Underwear Producers Directory
China Underwear Producers Directory

TITLE
China Underwear Producers Directory
China Wedding Dress & Ceremonial Clothing Producers Directory
China Wedding Dress & Ceremonial Clothing Producers Directory
China Wedding Dress & Ceremonial Clothing Producers Directory
China Women's Shoes Producers Directory
China Women's Shoes Producers Directory
China Women's Shoes Producers Directory
China: Doing Business and Investing in ... Guide Volume 1 Strategic, Practical Information, Regulations, Contacts
China: How to Invest, Start and Run Profitable Business in China Guide - Practical Information, Opportunities, Contacts

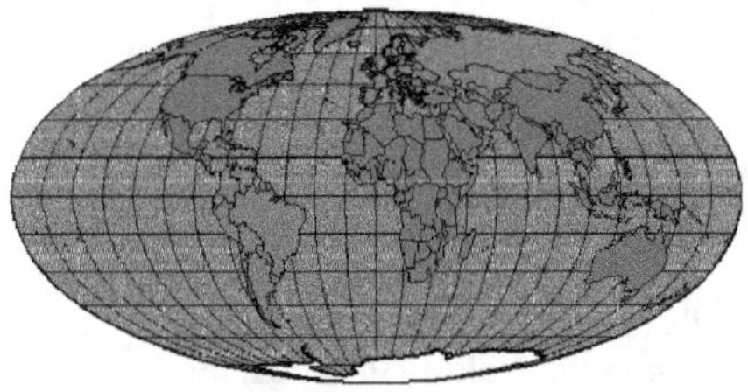

DOING BUSINESS AND INVESTING LIBRARY

World Business Information Catalog, USA: http://www.ibpus.com
Email: ibpusa@comcast.net.

Price: $99.95 Each

TITLE
Abkhazia (Republic of Abkhazia): Doing Business and Investing In...Guide - Practical Informtion, Regulations, Opportunities
Afghanistan: Doing Business and Investing In...Guide - Practical Informtion, Regulations, Opportunities
Aland: Doing Business and Investing In...Guide - Practical Informtion, Regulations, Opportunities
Albania: Doing Business and Investing In...Guide - Practical Informtion, Regulations, Opportunities
Algeria: Doing Business and Investing In...Guide - Practical Informtion, Regulations, Opportunities
Andorra: Doing Business and Investing In...Guide - Practical Informtion, Regulations, Opportunities
Angola: Doing Business and Investing In...Guide - Practical Informtion, Regulations, Opportunities
Anguilla: Doing Business and Investing In...Guide - Practical Informtion, Regulations, Opportunities
Antigua and Barbuda: Doing Business and Investing In...Guide - Practical Informtion, Regulations, Opportunities
Antilles (Netherlands): Doing Business and Investing In...Guide - Practical Informtion, Regulations, Opportunities
Argentina: Doing Business and Investing In...Guide - Practical Informtion, Regulations, Opportunities
Armenia: Doing Business and Investing In...Guide - Practical Informtion, Regulations, Opportunities
Aruba: Doing Business and Investing In...Guide - Practical Informtion, Regulations, Opportunities
Australia: Doing Business and Investing In...Guide - Practical Informtion, Regulations, Opportunities
Austria: Doing Business and Investing In...Guide - Practical Informtion, Regulations, Opportunities
Azerbaijan: Doing Business and Investing In...Guide - Practical Informtion, Regulations, Opportunities
Bahamas: Doing Business and Investing In...Guide - Practical Informtion, Regulations, Opportunities
Bahrain: Doing Business and Investing In...Guide - Practical Informtion, Regulations, Opportunities
Bangladesh: Doing Business and Investing In...Guide - Practical Informtion, Regulations, Opportunities
Barbados: Doing Business and Investing In...Guide - Practical Informtion, Regulations, Opportunities
Belarus: Doing Business and Investing In...Guide - Practical Informtion, Regulations, Opportunities
Belgium: Doing Business and Investing In...Guide - Practical Informtion, Regulations, Opportunities
Belize: Doing Business and Investing In...Guide - Practical Informtion, Regulations, Opportunities
Benin: Doing Business and Investing In...Guide - Practical Informtion, Regulations, Opportunities
Bermuda: Doing Business and Investing In...Guide - Practical Informtion, Regulations, Opportunities
Bhutan: Doing Business and Investing In...Guide - Practical Informtion, Regulations, Opportunities
Bolivia: Doing Business and Investing In...Guide - Practical Informtion, Regulations, Opportunities
Bosnia and Herzegovina: Doing Business and Investing In...Guide - Practical Informtion, Regulations, Opportunities
Botswana: Doing Business and Investing In...Guide - Practical Informtion, Regulations, Opportunities
Brazil: Doing Business and Investing In...Guide - Practical Informtion, Regulations, Opportunities
Brunei: Doing Business and Investing In...Guide - Practical Informtion, Regulations, Opportunities
Bulgaria: Doing Business and Investing In...Guide - Practical Informtion, Regulations, Opportunities
Burkina Faso: Doing Business and Investing In...Guide - Practical Informtion, Regulations, Opportunities
Burundi: Doing Business and Investing In...Guide - Practical Informtion, Regulations, Opportunities
Cambodia: Doing Business and Investing In...Guide - Practical Informtion, Regulations, Opportunities

For additional analytical, business and investment opportunities information,
Please contact Global Investment & Business Center, USA
at (202) 546-2103. Fax: (202) 546-3275. E-mail: rusric@erols.com

TITLE
Cameroon: Doing Business and Investing In...Guide - Practical Informtion, Regulations, Opportunities
Canada: Doing Business and Investing In...Guide - Practical Informtion, Regulations, Opportunities
Cape Verde: Doing Business and Investing In...Guide - Practical Informtion, Regulations, Opportunities
Cayman Islands: Doing Business and Investing In...Guide - Practical Informtion, Regulations, Opportunities
Central African Republic: Doing Business and Investing In...Guide - Practical Informtion, Regulations, Opportunities
Chad: Doing Business and Investing In...Guide - Practical Informtion, Regulations, Opportunities
Chile: Doing Business and Investing In...Guide - Practical Informtion, Regulations, Opportunities
China: Doing Business and Investing In...Guide - Practical Informtion, Regulations, Opportunities
Colombia: Doing Business and Investing In...Guide - Practical Informtion, Regulations, Opportunities
Comoros: Doing Business and Investing In...Guide - Practical Informtion, Regulations, Opportunities
Congo: Doing Business and Investing In...Guide - Practical Informtion, Regulations, Opportunities
Congo, Democratic Republic: Doing Business and Investing In...Guide - Practical Informtion, Regulations, Opportunities
Cook Islands: Doing Business and Investing In...Guide - Practical Informtion, Regulations, Opportunities
Costa Rica: Doing Business and Investing In...Guide - Practical Informtion, Regulations, Opportunities
Cote d'Ivoire: Doing Business and Investing In...Guide - Practical Informtion, Regulations, Opportunities
Croatia: Doing Business and Investing In...Guide - Practical Informtion, Regulations, Opportunities
Cuba: Doing Business and Investing In...Guide - Practical Informtion, Regulations, Opportunities
Cyprus: Doing Business and Investing In...Guide - Practical Informtion, Regulations, Opportunities
Czech Republic: Doing Business and Investing In...Guide - Practical Informtion, Regulations, Opportunities
Denmark: Doing Business and Investing In...Guide - Practical Informtion, Regulations, Opportunities
Djibouti: Doing Business and Investing In...Guide - Practical Informtion, Regulations, Opportunities
Dominica: Doing Business and Investing In...Guide - Practical Informtion, Regulations, Opportunities
Dominican Republic: Doing Business and Investing In...Guide - Practical Informtion, Regulations, Opportunities
Ecuador: Doing Business and Investing In...Guide - Practical Informtion, Regulations, Opportunities
Egypt: Doing Business and Investing In...Guide - Practical Informtion, Regulations, Opportunities
El Salvador: Doing Business and Investing In...Guide - Practical Informtion, Regulations, Opportunities
Equatorial Guinea: Doing Business and Investing In...Guide - Practical Informtion, Regulations, Opportunities
Eritrea: Doing Business and Investing In...Guide - Practical Informtion, Regulations, Opportunities
Estonia: Doing Business and Investing In...Guide - Practical Informtion, Regulations, Opportunities
Ethiopia: Doing Business and Investing In...Guide - Practical Informtion, Regulations, Opportunities
Falkland Islands: Doing Business and Investing In...Guide - Practical Informtion, Regulations, Opportunities
Faroes Islands: Doing Business and Investing In...Guide - Practical Informtion, Regulations, Opportunities
Fiji: Doing Business and Investing In...Guide - Practical Informtion, Regulations, Opportunities
Finland: Doing Business and Investing In...Guide - Practical Informtion, Regulations, Opportunities
France: Doing Business and Investing In...Guide - Practical Informtion, Regulations, Opportunities
Gabon: Doing Business and Investing In...Guide - Practical Informtion, Regulations, Opportunities
Gambia: Doing Business and Investing In...Guide - Practical Informtion, Regulations, Opportunities
Georgia: Doing Business and Investing In...Guide - Practical Informtion, Regulations, Opportunities
Germany: Doing Business and Investing In...Guide - Practical Informtion, Regulations, Opportunities
Ghana: Doing Business and Investing In...Guide - Practical Informtion, Regulations, Opportunities
Gibraltar: Doing Business and Investing In...Guide - Practical Informtion, Regulations, Opportunities
Greece: Doing Business and Investing In...Guide - Practical Informtion, Regulations, Opportunities
Greenland: Doing Business and Investing In...Guide - Practical Informtion, Regulations, Opportunities
Grenada: Doing Business and Investing In...Guide - Practical Informtion, Regulations, Opportunities
Guam: Doing Business and Investing In...Guide - Practical Informtion, Regulations, Opportunities

TITLE
Guatemala: Doing Business and Investing In...Guide - Practical Informtion, Regulations, Opportunities
Guernsey: Doing Business and Investing In...Guide - Practical Informtion, Regulations, Opportunities
Guinea: Doing Business and Investing In...Guide - Practical Informtion, Regulations, Opportunities
Guinea-Bissau: Doing Business and Investing In...Guide - Practical Informtion, Regulations, Opportunities
Guyana: Doing Business and Investing In...Guide - Practical Informtion, Regulations, Opportunities
Haiti: Doing Business and Investing In...Guide - Practical Informtion, Regulations, Opportunities
Honduras: Doing Business and Investing In...Guide - Practical Informtion, Regulations, Opportunities
Hungary: Doing Business and Investing In...Guide - Practical Informtion, Regulations, Opportunities
Iceland: Doing Business and Investing In...Guide - Practical Informtion, Regulations, Opportunities
India: Doing Business and Investing In...Guide - Practical Informtion, Regulations, Opportunities
Indonesia: Doing Business and Investing In...Guide - Practical Informtion, Regulations, Opportunities
Iran: Doing Business and Investing In...Guide - Practical Informtion, Regulations, Opportunities
Iraq: Doing Business and Investing In...Guide - Practical Informtion, Regulations, Opportunities
Ireland: Doing Business and Investing In...Guide - Practical Informtion, Regulations, Opportunities
Israel: Doing Business and Investing In...Guide - Practical Informtion, Regulations, Opportunities
Italy: Doing Business and Investing In...Guide - Practical Informtion, Regulations, Opportunities
Jamaica: Doing Business and Investing In...Guide - Practical Informtion, Regulations, Opportunities
Japan: Doing Business and Investing In...Guide - Practical Informtion, Regulations, Opportunities
Jersey: Doing Business and Investing In...Guide - Practical Informtion, Regulations, Opportunities
Jordan: Doing Business and Investing In...Guide - Practical Informtion, Regulations, Opportunities
Kazakhstan: Doing Business and Investing In...Guide - Practical Informtion, Regulations, Opportunities
Kenya: Doing Business and Investing In...Guide - Practical Informtion, Regulations, Opportunities
Kiribati: Doing Business and Investing In...Guide - Practical Informtion, Regulations, Opportunities
Korea, North: Doing Business and Investing In...Guide - Practical Informtion, Regulations, Opportunities
Korea, South: Doing Business and Investing In...Guide - Practical Informtion, Regulations, Opportunities
Kosovo: Doing Business and Investing In...Guide - Practical Informtion, Regulations, Opportunities
Kurdistan: Doing Business and Investing In...Guide - Practical Informtion, Regulations, Opportunities
Kuwait: Doing Business and Investing In...Guide - Practical Informtion, Regulations, Opportunities
Kyrgyzstan: Doing Business and Investing In...Guide - Practical Informtion, Regulations, Opportunities
Laos: Doing Business and Investing In...Guide - Practical Informtion, Regulations, Opportunities
Latvia: Doing Business and Investing In...Guide - Practical Informtion, Regulations, Opportunities
Lebanon: Doing Business and Investing In...Guide - Practical Informtion, Regulations, Opportunities
Lesotho: Doing Business and Investing In...Guide - Practical Informtion, Regulations, Opportunities
Liberia: Doing Business and Investing In...Guide - Practical Informtion, Regulations, Opportunities
Libya: Doing Business and Investing In...Guide - Practical Informtion, Regulations, Opportunities
Liechtenstein: Doing Business and Investing In...Guide - Practical Informtion, Regulations, Opportunities
Lithuania: Doing Business and Investing In...Guide - Practical Informtion, Regulations, Opportunities
Luxembourg: Doing Business and Investing In...Guide - Practical Informtion, Regulations, Opportunities
Macao: Doing Business and Investing In...Guide - Practical Informtion, Regulations, Opportunities
Macedonia: Doing Business and Investing In...Guide - Practical Informtion, Regulations, Opportunities
Madagascar: Doing Business and Investing In...Guide - Practical Informtion, Regulations, Opportunities
Madeira: Doing Business and Investing In...Guide - Practical Informtion, Regulations, Opportunities
Malawi: Doing Business and Investing In...Guide - Practical Informtion, Regulations, Opportunities
Malaysia: Doing Business and Investing In...Guide - Practical Informtion, Regulations, Opportunities
Maldives: Doing Business and Investing In...Guide - Practical Informtion, Regulations, Opportunities
Mali: Doing Business and Investing In...Guide - Practical Informtion, Regulations, Opportunities

TITLE
Malta: Doing Business and Investing In...Guide - Practical Informtion, Regulations, Opportunities
Man: Doing Business and Investing In...Guide - Practical Informtion, Regulations, Opportunities
Marshall Islands: Doing Business and Investing In...Guide - Practical Informtion, Regulations, Opportunities
Mauritania: Doing Business and Investing In...Guide - Practical Informtion, Regulations, Opportunities
Mauritius: Doing Business and Investing In...Guide - Practical Informtion, Regulations, Opportunities
Mayotte: Doing Business and Investing In...Guide - Practical Informtion, Regulations, Opportunities
Mexico: Doing Business and Investing In...Guide - Practical Informtion, Regulations, Opportunities
Micronesia: Doing Business and Investing In...Guide - Practical Informtion, Regulations, Opportunities
Moldova: Doing Business and Investing In...Guide - Practical Informtion, Regulations, Opportunities
Monaco: Doing Business and Investing In...Guide - Practical Informtion, Regulations, Opportunities
Mongolia: Doing Business and Investing In...Guide - Practical Informtion, Regulations, Opportunities
Montserrat: Doing Business and Investing In...Guide - Practical Informtion, Regulations, Opportunities
Montenegro: Doing Business and Investing In...Guide - Practical Informtion, Regulations, Opportunities
Morocco: Doing Business and Investing In...Guide - Practical Informtion, Regulations, Opportunities
Mozambique: Doing Business and Investing In...Guide - Practical Informtion, Regulations, Opportunities
Myanmar: Doing Business and Investing In...Guide - Practical Informtion, Regulations, Opportunities
Nagorno-Karabakh Republic: Doing Business and Investing In...Guide - Practical Informtion, Regulations, Opportunities
Namibia: Doing Business and Investing In...Guide - Practical Informtion, Regulations, Opportunities
Nauru: Doing Business and Investing In...Guide - Practical Informtion, Regulations, Opportunities
Nepal: Doing Business and Investing In...Guide - Practical Informtion, Regulations, Opportunities
Netherlands: Doing Business and Investing In...Guide - Practical Informtion, Regulations, Opportunities
New Caledonia: Doing Business and Investing In...Guide - Practical Informtion, Regulations, Opportunities
New Zealand: Doing Business and Investing In...Guide - Practical Informtion, Regulations, Opportunities
Nicaragua: Doing Business and Investing In...Guide - Practical Informtion, Regulations, Opportunities
Niger: Doing Business and Investing In...Guide - Practical Informtion, Regulations, Opportunities
Nigeria: Doing Business and Investing In...Guide - Practical Informtion, Regulations, Opportunities
Niue: Doing Business and Investing In...Guide - Practical Informtion, Regulations, Opportunities
Northern Cyprus (Turkish Republic of Northern Cyprus) Doing Business and Investing In...Guide - Practical Informtion, Regulations, Opportunities
Northern Mariana Islands: Doing Business and Investing In...Guide - Practical Informtion, Regulations, Opportunities
Norway: Doing Business and Investing In...Guide - Practical Informtion, Regulations, Opportunities
Oman: Doing Business and Investing In...Guide - Practical Informtion, Regulations, Opportunities
Pakistan: Doing Business and Investing In...Guide - Practical Informtion, Regulations, Opportunities
Palau: Doing Business and Investing In...Guide - Practical Informtion, Regulations, Opportunities
Palestine (West Bank & Gaza): Doing Business and Investing In...Guide - Practical Informtion, Regulations, Opportunities
Panama: Doing Business and Investing In...Guide - Practical Informtion, Regulations, Opportunities
Papua New Guinea: Doing Business and Investing In...Guide - Practical Informtion, Regulations, Opportunities
Paraguay: Doing Business and Investing In...Guide - Practical Informtion, Regulations, Opportunities
Peru: Doing Business and Investing In...Guide - Practical Informtion, Regulations, Opportunities
Philippines: Doing Business and Investing In...Guide - Practical Informtion, Regulations, Opportunities
Pitcairn Islands: Doing Business and Investing In...Guide - Practical Informtion, Regulations, Opportunities
Poland: Doing Business and Investing In...Guide - Practical Informtion, Regulations, Opportunities
Polynesia French: Doing Business and Investing In...Guide - Practical Informtion, Regulations, Opportunities
Portugal: Doing Business and Investing In...Guide - Practical Informtion, Regulations, Opportunities

TITLE
Qatar: Doing Business and Investing In...Guide - Practical Informtion, Regulations, Opportunities
Romania: Doing Business and Investing In...Guide - Practical Informtion, Regulations, Opportunities
Russia: Doing Business and Investing In...Guide - Practical Informtion, Regulations, Opportunities
Rwanda: Doing Business and Investing In...Guide - Practical Informtion, Regulations, Opportunities
Sahrawi Arab Democratic Republic : Doing Business and Investing In...Guide - Practical Informtion, Regulations, Opportunities
Saint Kitts and Nevis: Doing Business and Investing In...Guide - Practical Informtion, Regulations, Opportunities
Saint Lucia: Doing Business and Investing In...Guide - Practical Informtion, Regulations, Opportunities
Saint Vincent and The Grenadines: Doing Business and Investing In...Guide - Practical Informtion, Regulations, Opportunities
Samoa (American): Doing Business and Investing In...Guide - Practical Informtion, Regulations, Opportunities
Samoa (Western): Doing Business and Investing In...Guide - Practical Informtion, Regulations, Opportunities
San Marino: Doing Business and Investing In...Guide - Practical Informtion, Regulations, Opportunities
Sao Tome and Principe: Doing Business and Investing In...Guide - Practical Informtion, Regulations, Opportunities
Saudi Arabia: Doing Business and Investing In...Guide - Practical Informtion, Regulations, Opportunities
Scotland: Doing Business and Investing In...Guide - Practical Informtion, Regulations, Opportunities
Senegal: Doing Business and Investing In...Guide - Practical Informtion, Regulations, Opportunities
Serbia: Doing Business and Investing In...Guide - Practical Informtion, Regulations, Opportunities
Seychelles: Doing Business and Investing In...Guide - Practical Informtion, Regulations, Opportunities
Sierra Leone: Doing Business and Investing In...Guide - Practical Informtion, Regulations, Opportunities
Singapore: Doing Business and Investing In...Guide - Practical Informtion, Regulations, Opportunities
Slovakia: Doing Business and Investing In...Guide - Practical Informtion, Regulations, Opportunities
Slovenia: Doing Business and Investing In...Guide - Practical Informtion, Regulations, Opportunities
Solomon Islands: Doing Business and Investing In...Guide - Practical Informtion, Regulations, Opportunities
Somalia: Doing Business and Investing In...Guide - Practical Informtion, Regulations, Opportunities
South Africa: Doing Business and Investing In...Guide - Practical Informtion, Regulations, Opportunities
Spain: Doing Business and Investing In...Guide - Practical Informtion, Regulations, Opportunities
Sri Lanka: Doing Business and Investing In...Guide - Practical Informtion, Regulations, Opportunities
St. Helena: Doing Business and Investing In...Guide - Practical Informtion, Regulations, Opportunities
St. Pierre & Miquelon: Doing Business and Investing In...Guide - Practical Informtion, Regulations, Opportunities
Sudan (Republic of the Sudan): Doing Business and Investing In...Guide - Practical Informtion, Regulations, Opportunities
Sudan South: Doing Business and Investing In...Guide - Practical Informtion, Regulations, Opportunities
Suriname: Doing Business and Investing In...Guide - Practical Informtion, Regulations, Opportunities
Swaziland: Doing Business and Investing In...Guide - Practical Informtion, Regulations, Opportunities
Sweden: Doing Business and Investing In...Guide - Practical Informtion, Regulations, Opportunities
Switzerland: Doing Business and Investing In...Guide - Practical Informtion, Regulations, Opportunities
Syria: Doing Business and Investing In...Guide - Practical Informtion, Regulations, Opportunities
Taiwan: Doing Business and Investing In...Guide - Practical Informtion, Regulations, Opportunities
Tajikistan: Doing Business and Investing In...Guide - Practical Informtion, Regulations, Opportunities
Tanzania: Doing Business and Investing In...Guide - Practical Informtion, Regulations, Opportunities
Thailand: Doing Business and Investing In...Guide - Practical Informtion, Regulations, Opportunities
Timor Leste (Democratic Republic of Timor-Leste): Doing Business and Investing In...Guide - Practical Informtion, Regulations, Opportunities
Togo: Doing Business and Investing In...Guide - Practical Informtion, Regulations, Opportunities
Tonga: Doing Business and Investing In...Guide - Practical Informtion, Regulations, Opportunities
Trinidad and Tobago: Doing Business and Investing In...Guide - Practical Informtion, Regulations, Opportunities

TITLE
Tunisia: Doing Business and Investing In...Guide - Practical Informtion, Regulations, Opportunities
Turkey: Doing Business and Investing In...Guide - Practical Informtion, Regulations, Opportunities
Turkmenistan: Doing Business and Investing In...Guide - Practical Informtion, Regulations, Opportunities
Turks & Caicos: Doing Business and Investing In...Guide - Practical Informtion, Regulations, Opportunities
Tuvalu: Doing Business and Investing In...Guide - Practical Informtion, Regulations, Opportunities
Uganda: Doing Business and Investing In...Guide - Practical Informtion, Regulations, Opportunities
Ukraine: Doing Business and Investing In...Guide - Practical Informtion, Regulations, Opportunities
United Arab Emirates: Doing Business and Investing In...Guide - Practical Informtion, Regulations, Opportunities
United Kingdom: Doing Business and Investing In...Guide - Practical Informtion, Regulations, Opportunities
United States: Doing Business and Investing In...Guide - Practical Informtion, Regulations, Opportunities
Uruguay: Doing Business and Investing In...Guide - Practical Informtion, Regulations, Opportunities
Uzbekistan: Doing Business and Investing In...Guide - Practical Informtion, Regulations, Opportunities
Vanuatu: Doing Business and Investing In...Guide - Practical Informtion, Regulations, Opportunities
Vatican City (Holy See): Doing Business and Investing In...Guide - Practical Informtion, Regulations, Opportunities
Venezuela: Doing Business and Investing In...Guide - Practical Informtion, Regulations, Opportunities
Vietnam: Doing Business and Investing In...Guide - Practical Informtion, Regulations, Opportunities
Virgin Islands, British: Doing Business and Investing In...Guide - Practical Informtion, Regulations, Opportunities
Wake Atoll: Doing Business and Investing In...Guide - Practical Informtion, Regulations, Opportunities
Wallis & Futuna: Doing Business and Investing In...Guide - Practical Informtion, Regulations, Opportunities
Western Sahara: Doing Business and Investing In...Guide - Practical Informtion, Regulations, Opportunities
Yemen: Doing Business and Investing In...Guide - Practical Informtion, Regulations, Opportunities
Zambia: Doing Business and Investing In...Guide - Practical Informtion, Regulations, Opportunities
Zimbabwe: Doing Business and Investing In...Guide - Practical Informtion, Regulations, Opportunities